Emigrate to New Zealand with peace of mind

We could wish you well in your quest to live in New Zealand. But we would rather make it happen.

When it comes to emigrating, you just don't know what you don't know. Which is why it pays dividends to seek reliable, professional advice from a source sufficiently experienced to provide it. Since 1992, The Emigration Group has successfully helped over 10,000 people make a fresh start in **New Zealand**.

Whatever level of help you need... **Visa application, finding you a Job, or Resettlement help** on arrival (or all three!), we have a service package to suit.

We also offer:

- ☑ Regular Informative Seminars (see website)
- ☑ Free Initial On-Line Eligibility Assessments
- ☑ Exceptional Service (see website testimonials)
- ☑ Affordable Fees & Flexible Payments
- ☑ Licensed Immigration Advisor Expertise

Don't delay. Contact us today.

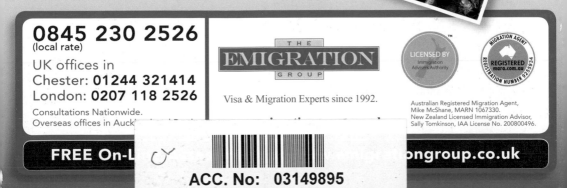

Living & Working in
NEW
ZEALAND

● A Survival Handbook ●

David Hampshire

Survival Books ● Bath ● England

First published 1999
Second Edition 2003
Third Edition 2004
Fourth Edition 2008
Fifth Edition 2010
Sixth Edition 2012

Survival Books Limited
Office 169, 3 Edgar Buildings, George Street, Bath, BA1 2FJ, UK
☎ +44 (0)1935 700060, ✉ info@survivalbooks.net
💻 www.survivalbooks.net

British Library Cataloguing in Publication Data.
A CIP record for this book is available
from the British Library.
ISBN: 978-1-907339-46-2

Printer in Singapore by International Press Softcom Limited

Acknowledgements

M y sincere thanks to all those who contributed to the successful publication of this 6th edition of *Living and Working in New Zealand*, in particular Sally Tomkinson of the Emigration Group (for unravelling the mysteries of the visa system), Peter Read (editing and updating), Alex Browning (proofreading) and Di Bruce-Kidman (DTP and cover design). I would also like to thank the many people who contributed to this and previous editions, including Peter Farmer, John Irvine, Graeme Chesters and the staff at *New Zealand Outlook and New Zealand News UK*, plus everyone else who contributed in any way. Also a big thank-you to Jim Watson for the cartoons and maps.

Last, but not least, special thanks to all the photographers (see page 344) – the unsung heroes – whose beautiful images add colour and bring New Zealand to life.

▲ Warning for 'Ne'er-do-wells'

Let it not be thought that for all persons New Zealand is a suitable home. It is a land of plenty to the colonist who can do such work as the colony requires, or who can employ others to do such work for him. But it is not a suitable home for those who cannot work or employ workers. The mere ability to read and write is not sufficient justification for a voyage to New Zealand.

Above all, let those be warned to stay away who think the colony is a suitable place to repent of evil habits. The ne'er-do-well had better continue to sponge on his relations in Great Britain, than to hope he will find sympathy for his failings and weaknesses in a land of strangers: strangers, moreover, who are quite sufficiently impressed with the active and hard realities of life, and who, being the architects of their own fortunes, have no sympathy to throw away on those who are deficient in self-reliance.

This warning is not altogether uncalled for. It is astonishing how many people are sent to the colonies to relieve their friends of their presence, no heed, apparently, being given to the fact that these countries are not at all deficient in temptations to evil habits, and that those who are inclined to such habits had much better stay away.

Official Handbook of New Zealand, 1875

REVIEWS

Important Note

New Zealand is a diverse country with many faces; numerous ethnic groups, religions and customs; and continuously changing rules and regulations, particularly with regard to immigration, social security, healthcare, education and taxes. I cannot recommend too strongly that you check with an official and reliable source (not always the same) before making any major decisions or taking an irreversible course of action. **However, don't believe everything you're told or read – even, dare I say it – herein!**

Useful addresses, websites and references to other sources of information have been included in all chapters and in **Appendices A** to **C,** in order to help you obtain further information and verify details with official sources. Important points have been emphasised, some of which it would be expensive, or even dangerous, to disregard. **Ignore them at your peril or cost!**

NOTE

Unless specifically stated, the reference to any company, organisation or product in this book doesn't constitute an endorsement or recommendation. None of the businesses, products or individuals recommended in this book have paid to be mentioned (except for the sponsor).

Contents

12. HEALTH — 189

13. INSURANCE — 203

14. FINANCE — 219

15. LEISURE

237

16. SPORTS

255

17. SHOPPING

271

Author's Notes

♦ All times are shown using am (ante meridiem) for before noon and pm (post meridiem) for after noon. Most New Zealanders don't use the 24-hour clock. All times are local, so check the time difference before making international telephone calls (see **Time Difference** on page 299).

♦ All prices are in New Zealand dollars, unless otherwise noted, and should be taken as estimates only (although they were correct at the time of publication).

♦ His/he/him also means her/she/her – please forgive me ladies. This is done to make life easier for both the reader and the author, and isn't intended to be sexist.

♦ Most spelling is, or should be, British (or New Zealand) English and not American English.

♦ Warnings and important points are shown in **bold** type.

♦ The following symbols are used in this book: ☎ (telephone), ▣ (Internet) and ✉ (email).

♦ Lists of **Useful Addresses**, **Further Reading** and **Useful Websites** are contained in **Appendices A**, **B** and **C** respectively.

♦ For those unfamiliar with the metric system of **Weights & Measures**, Imperial conversion tables are shown in **Appendix D**.

♦ A communications map of New Zealand is contained is in **Appendix E** and a map of the regions is inside the back cover.

Taupo Bay, Northland

Introduction

Whether you are already living or working in New Zealand or just thinking about it – this is THE book for you. Forget about those glossy guide books, excellent though they are for tourists; this amazing book was written especially with you in mind and is worth its weight in kiwi fruit. Furthermore, this fully revised 6th edition is printed in colour. *Living and Working in New Zealand* is designed to meet the needs of anyone wishing to know the essentials of New Zealand life – however long your intended stay, you'll find the information contained in this book invaluable.

General information isn't difficult to find in New Zealand; however, reliable and up-to-date information specifically intended for foreigners living and working there isn't so easy to find, least of all in one volume. Our aim in publishing this book is to help fill this void, and provide the accurate, comprehensive and practical information necessary for a relatively trouble-free life. You may have visited New Zealand as a tourist, but living and working there is a different matter altogether. Adjusting to a different environment and culture and making a home in *any* foreign country can be a traumatic and stressful experience – and New Zealand is no exception.

Living and Working in New Zealand is a comprehensive handbook on a wide range of everyday subjects and represents the most up-to-date source of general information available to foreigners in New Zealand. It isn't, however, simply a monologue of dry facts and figures, but a practical and entertaining look at life in New Zealand.

Adjusting to life in a new country is a continuous process, and although this book will help reduce your 'beginner's' phase and minimise the frustrations, it doesn't contain all the answers (most of us don't even know the right questions to ask!). What it will do is help you make informed decisions and calculated judgements, instead of uneducated guesses and costly mistakes. **Most importantly, it will help you save time, trouble and money, and repay your investment many times over.**

Although you may find some of the information a bit daunting, don't be discouraged. Most problems occur only once and fade into insignificance after a short time (as you face the next half a dozen!). Most foreigners in New Zealand would agree that, all things considered, they love living there. A period spent in New Zealand is a wonderful way to enrich your life, broaden your horizons, and with any luck (and some hard work), also please your bank manager. I trust that *Living and Working in New Zealand* will help you avoid the pitfalls of life in NZ and smooth your way to a happy and rewarding future in your new home.

Good luck!

David Hampshire

April 2012

Auckland at night

1.
FINDING A JOB

The major problem facing those wishing to work in New Zealand isn't necessarily finding a job, but rather is meeting the country's stringent immigration requirements, particularly regarding qualifications and English language proficiency (see Chapter 3). Although New Zealand is one of the few countries in the world that's keen to attract migrant workers – many countries positively discourage them – this doesn't mean that it's easy to find a job. New Zealand has a relatively small labour market and there's strong competition for the best paid jobs, although in industries where skilled staff are in short supply it's possible to pick and choose from an abundance of vacancies.

In common with most other developed countries, New Zealand has suffered from the global economic crisis in recent years, which has resulted in a lower demand for migrants and a sharp increase in unemployment, with many companies cutting or freezing staff levels. However, the country still has a steady requirement for professionals, and skilled workers and migrants contribute some £8bn to the economy annually.

If you don't have a job arranged before your arrival, it's essential to have a plan of action; do your homework before your arrival and, if necessary, be prepared to change your plans as you go along.

The Economy

Traditionally, New Zealand's economy was built on a narrow range of primary products, such as wool, meat and dairy products. From around 1920 to 1940, dairy exports comprised some 35 per cent of total exports, and in some years made up almost 45 per cent. However, prices for primary products has declined, and New Zealand lost its preferential trading position with the United Kingdom in 1973 when it joined the European Economic Community. Since 1984, New Zealand's economy has been transformed from an agrarian economy to a more industrialised free market economy,

although the recession in the last few years has highlighted the need for more structural reforms.

Today, New Zealand has a small export-dependent economy. Its small-scale and high-tech manufacturing and service sectors complement a highly efficient agricultural sector (including meat, dairy products, forestry, fruit and vegetables, fish and wool). However, it remains highly dependent on the primary sector with commodities accounting for around half its total exports. Exports of goods and services account for around one third of GDP, while tourism is also an important sector. New Zealand is hugely dependent on international trade, primarily with Australia, the European Union, the United States, China and Japan, which means that its growth prospects are dependent on the economic performance of Asia, Europe and the US.

The free-market reforms of the last few decades have removed most barriers to foreign investment in New Zealand, and the World Bank has praised it for being one of the most business-friendly countries in the world.

Over the past 25 years the New Zealand economy has gone from being one of the most regulated in the Organisation for Economic Cooperation and Development (OECD) to one of the least regulated. After weathering the twin shocks of the Asian economic downturn and severe droughts in 1997-1999, the economy experienced its longest sustained period of growth in three decades between 1999 and 2008, averaging almost 3.3. per cent annually. The economy fell into recession before the start of the global financial crisis and contracted for five consecutive quarters in 2008-09, posting a 1.7 per cent decline in 2009. The country pulled out of recession late in 2009 and achieved 2.1 per cent growth in 2010 and around 2 per cent in 2011. However, the outlook remains uncertain as households, businesses and farmers are attempting to repair over-extended balance sheets in the aftermath of the property boom, and the effects of two damaging earthquakes will also retard recovery.

New Zealand has a relatively large current account deficit, which stood at just over 6 per cent of GDP in 1999 and has since fluctuated between 2.5 and 8.5 per cent (2008), and is a constant source of concern for policymakers. The deficit was $8.7bn (4.3 per cent of GDP) for the year ended September 2011. The reason New Zealand runs persistent current account deficits is that its earnings from agricultural exports and tourism fail to cover the imports of the advanced manufactured goods necessary to sustain the economy.

In recent years, inflation has increased sharply, fanned by higher fuel and food costs; for example, it rose from 1.8 per cent in September 2007 to 5.1 per cent in September 2008 (rising at its fastest rate for 18 years in the second quarter of 2008), well outside the Reserve Bank's target band of between 1 and 3 per cent. However, it started to fall in 2008 and in February 2012 was around 2.5 per cent, which was still higher than had been hoped.

The New Zealand economy is widely considered to be successful, although the generally positive outlook includes a number of challenges. Income levels, which used to be above those of much of Western Europe prior to the '70s, have fallen dramatically in relative terms. In 2011, New Zealand GDP per capita was around US$36,000, although this was boosted by the favourable exchange rate with the US$.

The dynamic growth in the 21st century has boosted real incomes, and broadened and deepened the technological capabilities of the industrial sector. Per capita income has risen for nine consecutive years and reached $31,240 in 2011 (source: *The Economist*) in purchasing power parity terms. However, many at the bottom of the ladder have been left behind and income inequality has increased considerably (along with the cost of living), and a significant portion of the population have quite modest incomes.

EMPLOYMENT PROSPECTS

Although it's more difficult to find a job in 2012 than previously, New Zealand hasn't been as badly affected by the recession as many other countries. The economy is holding up well considering the economic conditions, and is better placed to manage the global downturn than those of many other developed countries.

During the last few decades there has been a major shift in the economy, towards service industries and away from manufacturing. Many manufacturing industries have disappeared altogether (such as car assembly) and many others don't have a bright future. On the other hand, the service sector has expanded rapidly, and up to 75 per cent of the workforce is now involved directly or indirectly in service industries. Job vacancies in the business

and financial services industries increased considerably in the last decade, and it was the fastest growing employment sector in the country prior to the financial crisis.

While some industries have seen a sharp downturn in recent years, notably construction (but see below), retailing and service industries in general, others have been far less affected, including engineering, teaching, biotechnology, healthcare, information technology (IT) and creative fields such as industrial design, fashion and the arts. The sectors where migrant workers are most in demand include the essential services of healthcare and education, plus IT, engineering and biotechnology.

A campaign was started in 2012 to recruit tens of thousands of foreign (particularly British) workers to rebuild the earthquake-stricken city of Christchurch, with New Zealand officials staging jobs' expos in the UK, Canada and South Africa (see 🖳 www.expo-newzealand.com), seeking 30,000 people for the construction, engineering and IT roles needed over the next ten years.

In contrast, the labour market in the banking and finance sector has contracted and has been exacerbated by New Zealand expats returning home from the UK and US. In many fields, employers are enjoying the rare luxury of being able to choose from a wider range of employees. There has also been an increase in casual and contract workers, as employers are increasingly reluctant to take on permanent staff in the current climate.

INZ maintains Essential Skills in Demand Lists (see page 60), which comprise the Long Term Skill Shortage List (LTSSL) and the Immediate Skill Shortage List (ISSL). These detail occupations where there are long-term and immediate shortages of skilled workers. The Department of Labour also publishes a Jobs Online monthly report (🖳 www.dol.govt.nz/publications/jol/report/index.asp).

Many employers have something of a haphazard approach to recruitment and are often reluctant to plan ahead, with the result that they are slow to lay off surplus staff during periods of recession and are equally slow to recruit new employees (and don't pay sufficient attention to improving skills and training) when business picks up. They do, however, appreciate 'old-fashioned' values such as hard work and a willingness to 'muck in' and get things done.

Newcomers should expect to find stiff competition from New Zealanders, particularly as home-grown talent has become much more plentiful in the last few years. The New Zealand workforce is well educated and trained, and highly motivated; the unemployment benefit system helps – you don't get benefits if you don't seek work. You shouldn't expect employers to favour you simply because you've uprooted yourself and your family and travelled halfway round the world (in fact the opposite may be the case). Even well qualified local graduates can no longer expect to walk into a job, as used to be the case, and as many as half of all graduates don't have a job commensurate with their qualifications a year after graduation.

It's important to note that many young (and not so young) people leave the country each year in search of better employment opportunities overseas, mainly in Australia, the UK and the USA (New Zealand has an annual net outflow of around 30,000 workers to Australia). If many New Zealanders cannot find a good job in their own country, it's bound to be more difficult for foreigners.

However, although some people have difficulty finding employment, there are relatively few stories of failure and only a small number of new migrants with good skills fail to find a job; the unemployment rate among skilled migrants is lower than the national average, which itself is relatively low (see below). Most people who are prepared to work hard and adapt to the New Zealand way of doing things often find that they do better in their job or career in New Zealand than they would at home.

Unemployment

In the last decade, New Zealand has enjoyed its lowest level of unemployment since the current recording method began in 1986 and one of the lowest rates in the OECD. Before the economic shocks of the '70s (especially when Britain joined the EEC), actual unemployment was also very low, possibly even lower than today – in 1959, only 21 people were officially unemployed, and the joke went around that the Prime Minister knew the name of every unemployed person!

In 1992, unemployment reached a peak of around 11 per cent, the worst on record in modern times. In the late '90s, however, the economy picked up, and in late 2001 unemployment was around 5 per cent and fell to its lowest ever recorded level (3.4 per cent) in December 2007, when around 70 per cent of the population was employed. Unemployment has almost doubled in the last few years (rising to 6.7 per cent in 2011) and in February 2012 stood at 6.3 per cent (150,000 people), compared with the OECD average of 8.2 per cent. However, employment actually rose in all regions in 2011, with the exception of Canterbury, where unemployment rose sharply in the aftermath of the earthquakes in 2010-11.

If you have a temporary 'work to residence' visa that allows you to apply for residence after two years, and you lose your job, you could lose your right to live in New Zealand (and you may have no right to another job, even if one is available!)

There has been an increase in part-time and contract employment in recent years, although many companies have reduced working hours or salaries rather than making staff redundant.

For the latest unemployment data, see Statistics New Zealand (💻 www.stats.govt.nz).

QUALIFICATIONS

The most important qualification for a job in New Zealand is a good level of spoken and written English. All employers expect their staff to have adequate English, which varies with the type of job you're seeking – the more skilled the position, the better your English must be. When you apply for residence in the Skilled/Business stream (see **Chapter 3**) you need to prove that you have a high standard of English. You must show that you come from an English-speaking background and/or pass a test set by the International English Language Testing System.

With regard to more formal qualifications, it's a condition of employment for most jobs that overseas qualifications must compare with New Zealand's standards and be accepted by local employers. An organisation called The New Zealand Qualifications Authority (NZQA) assesses foreign qualifications to determine whether they meet New Zealand standards. Information and forms are available from Immigration New Zealand or direct from NZQA (PO Box 160, Wellington 6140, ☎ 4-463 3000, 💻 www.nzqa.govt.nz).

Registration

For certain professions and trades (see box) you must be registered with the appropriate New Zealand professional organisation. If applicable, you must have full or provisional registration before lodging an Expression of Interest (EOI) under the Skilled Migration Category (SMC), in order to gain points for qualifications (see page 67).

The registration process includes an assessment of your professional or trade qualifications and leads to membership of the appropriate body, thus permitting you to work in New Zealand. If your trade or profession is one where registration is required, you should contact the relevant body well in advance as you may need to take an examination or

Professions & Trades Requiring Registration

Profession or Trade	Website
Accountants	www.nzica.com
Acupuncturists	www.acupuncture.org.nz
Architects	www.nzrab.org.nz
Barristers & Solicitors	www.nz-lawsoc.org.nz
Chiropractors	www.chiropracticboard.org.nz
Dental Professionals	www.dentalcouncil.org.nz
Dieticians	www.dieticiansboard.org.nz
Doctors	www.mcnz.org.nz
Electrical & Electronics Workers	www.ewrb.govt.nz
Engineers	www.ipenz.org.nz
Financial & Insurance Professionals	www.fpia.org.nz
Medical Laboratory Technologists	www.misboard.org.nz
Medical Radiation Technologists	www.mrtboard.org.nz
Motor Industry Professionals	www.mta.org.nz
Midwives	www.midwiferycouncil.org.nz
Nurses	www.nursingcouncil.org.nz
Librarians	www.lianza.org.nz
Occupational Therapists	www.otboard.org.nz
Optometrists & Opticians	www.optometristsboard.org.nz
Osteopaths	www.osteopathiccouncil.org.nz
Pharmacists	www.psnz.org.nz
Physiotherapists	www.physioboard.org.nz
Plumbers, Gasfitters & Drainlayers	www.pgdb.org.nz
Podiatrists	www.podiatristsboard.org.nz
Psychologists	www.psychologistsboard.org.nz
Real Estate Agents	www.reinz.org.nz
Surveyors	www.surveyors.org.nz
Teachers	www.teacherscouncil.govt.nz
Veterinarians	www.vetcouncil.org.nz

undergo a period of retraining, for which you must pay. In some cases, examinations can be taken in other countries, although they may be held on only one or two days a year. Since January 1996, it has been necessary to obtain registration (where applicable) before applying for permanent residence.

Degrees attained from universities in most Western countries are considered equivalent to those from New Zealand universities, and most school qualifications are recognised by employers and university admissions staff.

Contact Immigration New Zealand (💻 www.immigration.govt.nz) or the New Zealand Qualifications Authority (💻 www.nzqa.govt.nz) for details of the professional organisation representing your profession or trade.

GOVERNMENT EMPLOYMENT SERVICE

The New Zealand government employment service is run by an agency called Work and Income, which is part of the Ministry of Social

Development (MSD). The MSD was established in late 2001 to provide social policy advice to the government and deliver income support and employment services to New Zealanders (which it does to over a million people).

Work and Income has, in government-speak, 'a focus on getting people into employment and gaining independence'. It recommends that job applicants should spend at least 11 hours a week seeking work and should contact Work and Income at least once every two weeks. When people enrol with Work and Income, they're sometimes asked to make a Job Seeker Agreement, which sets out their responsibilities and an agreed plan to help them prepare for work. People caring for a child under 14 aren't required to look for full-time work, but may be asked to seek part-time employment or prepare for future work.

Work and Income runs a Job Bank – updated regularly by employers throughout New Zealand – an online tool which job seekers can access from computers at Work and Income service centres. Work and Income also provides help with job applications, writing CVs and training, and provides useful brochures such as *Getting Work Skills and Experience* and *Need Help to Find Work?*, which can be downloaded from their website.

For information, contact the head office of Work and Income (Level 3, Bowen State Building, Bowen Street, Wellington, ☎ 0800-559 009 or 09-913 0300, 💻 www.workandincome.govt.nz) or a local office which can be found in all major cities and towns (details are provided on their website).

PRIVATE RECRUITMENT AGENCIES

There are many organisations in New Zealand that can help find you a job, broadly divided into recruitment consultants and employment agencies. Recruitment consultants tend to specialise in skilled, professional and executive jobs, while employment agencies handle all kinds of jobs, including unskilled, temporary, casual and contract jobs. You can find local recruitment consultants and employment agencies by consulting the *Yellow Pages* (💻 http://yellow.co.nz), and there's also a list on the Immigration New Zealand website (💻 www.immigration.govt.

nz). Immigration consultants can also arrange an introduction to recruitment agencies.

Some employment agencies cannot help you unless you're physically in New Zealand, although they're usually willing to provide general information about local job prospects over the telephone or you can consult their websites. Once you arrive in New Zealand, agencies will ask to see your visa or migration papers before they will assist you. In the past, agencies were lax about enforcing this requirement (some may still be), but severe penalties for employing illegal immigrants have prompted them to obey the law. If you're working for a temporary employment agency, you're usually employed by the agency rather than the employer for whom you're working.

Both recruitment consultants and employment agencies are engaged by employers to fill vacancies and therefore don't charge you for finding you a job (they're finding an employee for the employer, not vice versa). Other services such as compiling CVs and counselling may be offered, for which you may be charged a fee, therefore check in advance. Some recruitment consultants have offices abroad, and if you plan to use them it pays to make a few simple checks before doing so. For example, the law of your home country may

Recruitment Professionals	
Company	**Website**
Adecco	www.adecco.co.nz
Beyond Recruitment	www.beyondrecruitment.co.nz
Coverstaff International	www.coverstaff.net.nz
Drake	www.drake.co.nz
Enterprise Recruitment	www.enterprise.co.nz
Global Career Link	www.globalcareerlink.com/-25260/new-zealand
Hudson	http://nz.hudson.com
Icon Recruitment	www.iconrcc.co.nz
JobCafé International	www.jobcafe.co.nz
Kelly Services	www.kellyservices.co.nz
Madison	www.madison.co.nz
Manpower	www.manpower.co.nz
Manpower Professional	www.manpowerprofessional.co.nz
Pohlenkean	www.pohlenkean.co.nz
Randstad	www.randstad.co.nz
Ryan Recruitment	www.ryan.co.nz
Taylor & Associates	www.jobfastrack.co.nz
Team Recruitment Ltd.	www.teamrecruitment.co.nz
Ultimate Recruitment	www.ultimaterecruitment.co.nz
Wheeler Campbell	www.wheelercampbell.co.nz

permit them to make a charge for finding you a job or even for simply registering your details. Also check exactly what they will do for you. A recruitment consultant who merely sends your CV to prospective employers is unlikely to find you a job, whereas a consultant with employers on his books in the industry in which you're seeking could prove to be a useful contact.

A number of recruitment companies are listed in the box below and a more comprehensive list is available on the New Zealand Search website (💻 www.nzs.com/business/services/jobs/recruitment-companies). See also the lists under **Internet** on page 28.

TEMPORARY, CASUAL & SEASONAL JOBS

Temporary, casual and seasonal jobs which last for a few days, weeks or months are available throughout the year in New Zealand, particularly during the summer and early autumn when the largest employers, the tourist and farming industries, are at their busiest.

Most nationalities (with the exception of Australians who may work in New Zealand under the 'Closer Economic Relations' agreement without a permit) aren't permitted to work in New Zealand, at least not without wading through a mountain of red tape. There are special working holiday schemes available for young people aged 18-30 from many countries (see **Working Holiday Visas** on page 59), whereby those who qualify are entitled to come to New Zealand and work temporarily for up to 23 months.

Students from the US can spend up to six months working in New Zealand under the 'Work in New Zealand Program' operated by the Council On International Educational Exchange (CIEE, 300 Fore Street, Portland,

ME, 04101, USA, ☎ 1-207-553 4000, 💻 www. ciee.org). Other nationalities can obtain visas for temporary jobs only if there's no New Zealander or other eligible candidate to do a job.

In common with other countries, pay and conditions for casual and temporary jobs are usually poor. You may even be paid less than the minimum wage (see page 34) – although this is illegal – or charges for food and accommodation may effectively reduce your wages below this level, and you may not be entitled to benefits such as holiday pay. Jobs obtained through reputable agencies are likely to be better in this regard than those obtained through small ads or by word of mouth. There are a number of employment agencies that specialise in temporary, casual and contract jobs including Adecco, Coverstaff, Drake, Kelly and Manpower (see list above).

⚠ Caution

If you aren't a permanent migrant or don't have a working holiday visa, it's essential to ensure that you're eligible to work in New Zealand on a casual basis before you arrive.

Tax regulations also make casual work less financially attractive to temporary visitors, as a flat rate deduction is taken from the wages of casual workers by employers to cover income tax and ACC contributions (see page 204). Any extra tax charges or refunds are made after you've filed an income tax return at the end of the tax year, which is easy in theory but difficult if you're no longer in New Zealand. (There are doubts about whether less scrupulous employers pay the tax deducted to the Inland Revenue Department at all!)

If you're seeking a casual or seasonal job, you should be prepared to be persistent and compete with the local casual labour force. Many jobs of this kind are the preserve of Pacific Islanders, particularly Samoans and Pitcairn Islanders, whom the authorities allow to look for work in recognition of the fact that there are precious few job opportunities in the Pacific Islands (most countries have a source of cheap labour and New Zealand is

no exception). These migrants tend to be at the bottom of the jobs heap and are willing to do almost anything for almost any wage. Opportunities for temporary, casual and seasonal jobs include the following:

Business

Some employment agencies (e.g. Drake and Kelly) specialise in temporary and casual job office vacancies, principally in Auckland, Christchurch and Wellington. It's obviously an advantage if you have some experience; if you have a qualification in a profession such as accountancy, banking, finance, insurance or law, you could walk into a well-paid job, as these industries frequently have short-term staff shortages. Hundreds of New Zealand professionals leave the country each year to spend six or 12 months working in Australia or the UK or make the 'obligatory' overseas experience (OE) trip, and qualified replacements are required to fill the vacancies they leave.

Farming

There are thousands of farms of all sizes throughout New Zealand requiring temporary labour, particularly during busy periods such as harvest times or sheep-shearing. Available work ranges from skilled jobs such as cattle herding and sheep shearing to unskilled tasks such as fruit and vegetable picking. The work is likely to be hard and the hours long, but in addition to wages (around $400 per week) you may receive free accommodation and food (all the lamb and kiwi fruit you can eat!).

Good places for fruit picking include Blenheim, the Christchurch area, Gisborne, Kerikeri, Motueka, Nelson, Otago, Tauranga, Te Puke and the Wairu Valley. The soft fruit picking season (apples, grapes, peaches, strawberries and, need I say, kiwi fruit) starts in December and lasts until April or May. There are a number of agents for fruit pickers including Horticulture New Zealand (💻 www. hortnz.co.nz), Pick NZ (☎ 0800-742569, 💻 www.picknz.co.nz), who publish an excellent brochure, Pick a Picker (💻 www.pickapicker. co.nz), Seasonal Work (www.seasonalwork. co.nz), Work in NZ (💻 www.workinnz.co.nz) and Jobs Central (💻 www.jobscentral.co.nz), for jobs in central Otago.

You don't need to go far to find a sheep farm (sheep station) in New Zealand, but the far north-east and south of the North Island, and the Otago and Canterbury regions of the South Island are the main centres for this industry. Vacancies for farm work are sometimes advertised on notice boards in local hostels.

If you think you would enjoy the experience of working on an organic farm (low or no pay, but free accommodation and plenty of organic food), an organisation called Willing Workers On Organic Farms (WWOOF, PO Box 1172, Nelson 7040, ☎ 03-544 9890, 🖳 www.wwoof. co.nz) can arrange placements on around 800 farms throughout the country (a fee is charged for the list of members). You can also contact companies directly, such as the Fonterra Co-operative Group (🖳 www.fonterra.com), New Zealand's largest company and the world's largest exporter of dairy products, and Satara (🖳 www.satara.co.nz), the country's largest kiwifruit and avocado co-operative. A useful publication for temporary job-seekers is the *NZ Dairy Exporter Magazine* (🖳 www.dairymag. co.nz) which advertises farming vacancies.

See also the links below under **The Internet** (Farming).

Hotels & Catering

Hotels, motels, lodges, restaurants and bars usually require barmen and barmaids, chambermaids, handymen, receptionists, chefs and other kitchen staff, and waiters and waitresses throughout the year. Employment agencies usually have vacancies. If you want to go it alone, you can approach hotels and restaurants directly, although it's wise to

telephone and ask about vacancies before travelling to the back of beyond looking for work.

Industry

As in most countries, casual jobs are often available in factories and warehouses, such as cleaning, driving, labouring, portering and security work. Particularly numerous are casual, seasonal and temporary jobs in some of the massive plants that process and pack dairy products, fish, fruit, meat and vegetables. This kind of work is notoriously unreliable, and plants that may be working flat out one week stand idle the next, e.g. when there's a slump in the market or the season is over. Jobs of this kind can be found through employment agencies, in local newspapers or simply by turning up at the factory gate (very early).

There are also a number of employment agencies that specialise in casual and temporary industrial jobs such as Adecco (🖳 www.adecco.co.nz), Manpower (🖳 www. manpower.co.nz), NZ Labour Hire (🖳 www. nzlabourhire.co.nz) and Super Staff (🖳 www. superstaff.co.nz).

Tourism

New Zealand attracts tourists all year round, particularly during the summer (November to March), with the peak over the Christmas and New Year period. Jobs are available in shops, at tourist attractions, and on boats and beaches throughout the country during these periods. For the rest of the year, the tourist industry centres mainly around skiing, when Queenstown in the South Island is the busiest resort.

JOB HUNTING

When looking for a job in New Zealand it's best to leave no stone unturned – the more applications you make, the better your chance of finding something suitable. Contact as many prospective employers as possible, by writing, telephoning or visiting them in person. Positions are often obtained as a result of networking (i.e. through contacts – see below). Naturally it's easier to find a job after you've arrived in New Zealand, although you should start preparing the ground before you arrive by doing research into prospective employers and contacts.

The internet is an invaluable resource when job hunting and includes a vast number of sites including www.job.co.nz, http://myjobspace. co.nz and www.seek.co.nz; plus publications such as the *New Zealand Herald* (🖳 http:// jobs.nzherald.co.nz) and *Trade Me* (🖳 www. trademe.co.nz/trade-me-jobs/index.htm) and government sites, e.g. NZRecruitme (🖳 www. nzrecruitme.co.nz). See **The Internet** on page 27 for more information.

The way you market yourself is important and depends on the type of job you're seeking. For example, the recruitment of executives and senior managers is handled almost exclusively by recruitment consultants. At the other end of the scale, manual jobs requiring no previous experience may be advertised at Work and Income offices, in local newspapers and on notice boards, or may simply be passed around by word of mouth. When job hunting you'll find the resources below useful.

New Zealand Newspapers

Obtain copies of as many New Zealand newspapers as possible, most of which contain job sections. Vacancies are advertised most days, the most popular being Wednesdays and Saturdays. New Zealand's major newspapers are regional rather than national and include *The Dominion Post* (Wellington, employment sections in the Wednesday and Saturday editions, 🖳 www.stuff.co.nz/dominion-post), *The New Zealand Herald* (mainly Auckland news and vacancies with some national coverage, 🖳 www.nzherald.com), *The Otago Daily Times* (Dunedin, 🖳 www.odt.co.nz), *The Press* (Christchurch, 🖳 www.stuff.co.nz/the-press) and the *Waikato Times* (🖳 www.stuff. co.nz/waikato-times).

Most New Zealand newspapers can be accessed online via 🖳 www.world-newspapers.com/new-zealand.html and www. onlinenewspapers.com/nz.htm (listed A-Z by town/city).

Many newspapers also carry a 'Situations Wanted' column, although unless you're exceptionally well qualified or have a skill that's in short supply, you cannot expect much of a response when placing an advertisement of this kind.

Foreign Newspapers

If you're seeking an executive or professional position, you'll find that vacancies are sometimes advertised in the national newspapers of other countries. For example, the UK *Times Higher Education Supplement* and Australia's *Sydney Morning Herald* occasionally carry vacancies for jobs in New Zealand. The fact that employers have gone to the trouble of advertising jobs abroad means that vacancies are proving hard to fill locally, and that they require unusual or exceptional skills and qualifications.

Trade Journals

New Zealand trade journals generally contain job advertisements for qualified and experienced people. The main journals include *NZ Business* magazine (🖳 www. nzbusiness.co.nz), *Education Gazette* (🖳 www.edgazette.govt.nz), *e.nz Magazine* (🖳 www.e.nz-magazine.co.nz), *Management* (🖳 www.management.co.nz) and *Farmnews* (🖳 www.farmnews.co.nz). Opportunities in New Zealand, usually at the executive and professional level, are also advertised in trade journals in other English-speaking countries, mainly Australia, the UK and the US.

For a list of general magazines in New Zealand, see 🖳 www.nzmagazineshop.co.nz. Other trade journals include: advertising and media industry (🖳 www.admedia.co.nz), business to business publications (🖳 www. tplmedia.co.nz), *Business NZ* (🖳 www. businessnz.co.nz), film industry (🖳 www. onfilm.co.nz), *In Wood* (🖳 www.inwoodmag. com), *Mercantile Gazette Marketing* (🖳 www. mgpublications.co.nz), the *National Business Review* (🖳 www.nbr.co.nz) and Nursery World (🖳 www.nursery.net.nz).

Recruitment Consultancies & Employment Agencies

If you're looking for an executive or professional position, you can apply to recruitment consultancies in New Zealand and abroad specialising in the kind of position you're seeking. They will usually be pleased to help and advise you, whether or not you have applied for permission to live in New Zealand. On the other hand, employment agencies can usually help you only if you're already in New Zealand and have been granted permanent residence (or, exceptionally, a working holiday visa).

See also **Private Recruitment Agencies** above and **The Internet** below.

Professional Organisations

If you're a professional it may be worthwhile contacting professional organisations in New Zealand. Although they cannot find you a job, they can often help with advice and provide the names of prospective employers. Se the list under **Registration** on page 20 or contact Immigration New Zealand (🖳 www.immigration.govt.nz) or the New Zealand Qualifications Authority (🖳 www.nzqa.govt.nz).

Government Departments

If you're considering a position or career with a government department or another public body, it's worth contacting the relevant organisation directly. It isn't necessary to be a New Zealand citizen to apply for many official positions, particularly in areas where there's a shortage of skills. The government periodically holds exhibitions abroad, particularly in London, mainly to attract young New Zealand professionals back to their country, but also to attract professionals of other nationalities.

For many years the Ministry of Education has welcomed (in fact, lured and enticed) foreign teachers to fill vacancies in schools in order to combat a serious shortage. Vacancies are advertised through its own recruitment agency, Teach NZ (🖳 www.teachnz.govt.nz), which operates in English-speaking countries worldwide.

The New Zealand police (🖳 www.police.govt.nz) are also suffering a shortage of experienced officers, as several Australian forces have a habit of poaching experienced New Zealand officers with the lure of a 20 to 30 per cent pay rise.

For general information about government jobs in New Zealand, see www.jobs.govt.nz, the gateway to job and career opportunities within state sector organisations.

> **Government Employment Offices**
>
> You can visit Work and Income offices in New Zealand, although jobs on offer are mainly non-professional, skilled, semi-skilled and unskilled.

Unsolicited Job Applications

You can obviously apply to companies directly in New Zealand, whether or not they're advertising vacancies. It's a hit and miss affair, but the advantage is that you aren't competing directly with dozens of other applicants as with an advertised job vacancy. This approach can be particularly successful if you have skills, experience and qualifications that are in short supply in New Zealand or you're able to target companies that specialise in your field of work. Useful addresses can be obtained from trade directories (such as *Kompass New Zealand*, 🖳 www.kompass.co.nz), which are available at major libraries and New Zealand Chambers of Commerce abroad.

Networking

Networking is making and using business and professional contacts. You should make use of contacts in New Zealand and with any New Zealanders you come into contact with abroad, including friends, relatives, colleagues and business contacts. If you're already in New Zealand, seek out expatriate 'hubs' such as clubs, pubs and churches. Generally people who have moved to another country are interested to get to know others in a similar position and are happy to pass on job tips or leads.

THE INTERNET

The internet has rapidly become the number one resource for finding employment, both in New Zealand and elsewhere, and is particularly useful if you're overseas; not only can you get a good idea of the jobs available but you can also register for jobs, lodge your CV and apply for jobs online. Resources include mainstream (High Street) and internet-dedicated employment agencies (temporary, contract and full-time); professional head-hunters; job boards where employers and jobseekers can place ads; companies advertising vacancies on their own websites; and New Zealand government sites.

The main internet job resources include:

♦ Recruitment consultants and employment agencies (see page 27).

♦ Job notice boards, which include 🖳 www.careerjet.co.nz, www.job.co.nz, http://myjobspace.co.nz, www.seek.co.nz and www.trademe.co.nz/jobs. For other job boards, see below.

♦ The government's Work and Income website, 🖳 http://job-bank.workandincome.govt.nz/find-a-job/search.aspx plus other government websites designed to connect employers with skilled migrants (or would-be migrants), such as New Kiwis (🖳 www.newkiwis.co.nz). Career Services (🖳 www.careers.govt.nz) is a comprehensive site with job vacancies, job hunting tips and detailed information about New Zealand industries.

♦ For careers in the public sector, see the New Zealand Government Jobs Online; gateway website (🖳 www.jobs.govt.nz).

A wide selection of company and industry websites are listed on Emigrate magazine's website (🖳 www.emigrate2.co.uk/web_links(1).htm – select New Zealand and Jobs).

General Sites

www.advancedpersonnel.co.nz
www.artisan-recruitment.com
www.capitalrecruitment.co.nz
www.careerjet.co.nz
www.job.co.nz
www.jobcafe.co.nz
http://jobs.nzherald.co.nz
http://myjobspace.co.nz
www.newkiwis.co.nz

www.seek.co.nz
www.trademe.co.nz/trade-me-jobs/index.htm

Accountancy & Finance

www.debbiegraham.co.nz
www.kpmg.co.nz
www.parkerbridge.co.nz
www.phoenixjobs.co.nz
www.randstad.co.nz
www.statusrecruitment.co.nz

Education

www.edgazette.govt.nz/vacancies
www.edperson.co.nz
www.learningmedia.co.nz
www.nzunicareerhub.ac.nz
www.oasis-edu.co.nz
www.teachersonthemove.com
www.teachnz.govt.nz

Engineering & Technical

www.acorva.co.nz
www.asconsultants.co.nz
www.autojobs.co.nz
www.automotiveemployment.co.nz
www.campbellpartners.com
www.careerengineer.co.nz
www.crsrecruit.co.nz
www.ipenz.org.nz
www.lawsonwilliams.co.nz
www.match2.co.nz
www.mcfoodies.co.nz
www.roblawmax.co.nz
www.terrane.co.nz
www.trs.co.nz

Farming

www.agfirst.co.nz
www.atrfegan.com
www.coolstore.co.nz
www.dairymag.co.nz
www.farmnews.co.nz/sitvac.shtml
www.farmonline.co.nz
www.fonterra.com
www.fres.co.nz
www.frenz.co.nz
www.gisbornejobs.co.nz
www.greenstone-recruitment.co.nz
www.maf.govt.nz
www.marvinfarms.co.nz
www.satara.co.nz
www.winejobsonline.com

www.mtr.co.nz
www.radiusnz.co.nz
www.sabrenz.co.nz

Miscellaneous

www.adcorp.co.nz – marketing communications
www.crackerjacks.co.nz – professional contractors
www.domestic.co.nz – domestic service
www.freightwise.co.nz – transport, shipping & freight forwarding
www.hrdirection.co.nz – human resources
www.kiwioznannies.co.nz – nannies
www.marsdeninch.co.nz – advertising
www.nzswrecruit.co.nz – social work
www.police.govt.nz – police services
www.prpeople.co.nz – public relations

CVs & Interviews

Your curriculum vitae (CV) or résumé is of vital importance when looking for employment in New Zealand, particularly when jobs are thin on the ground and applicants are a dime a dozen. Bear in mind that the purpose of your CV is to obtain an interview, not a job, and it must be written with this in mind. This means that it must be individually tailored to each job application (along with your cover letter).

Think of your CV as a advertisement or brochure for your time and skills, and try to see it from a prospective employer's point of view. Would you stand out against the competition (the other candidates) and would the manager want to talk to you about a possible job? Employers may scan a CV for just 30 seconds to decide whether to consider an applicant and may even use an automated scan to short-list candidates. Your CV is your first contact with prospective employers and should be designed to open the door to an interview.

A CV is a 'snapshot' of your education/ qualifications, skills and experience, and must:

♦ be written with the employer's interests in mind

♦ be targeted for a particular job or organisation

♦ be honest without embellishment

Health

www.dentalpersonnel.co.nz
www.doctorjobs.co.nz
www.enzedparamedical.co.nz
www.genevahealth.com
www.healthcareers.org.nz
www.healthrecruitment.com
www.medcall.co.nz
www.medicalstaffing.co.nz
www.medlink.co.nz
www.mercuryrecruit.co.nz
www.moh.govt.nz
www.ncah.com
www.nursingcouncil.org.nz
www.nznursing.co.nz
www.remedyconsultants.co.nz
www.tonix.co.nz

Hospitality & Catering

www.bravogroup.co.nz
www.hospo.com
www.spectrum-international.com

Information Technology (IT)

www.absoluteit.co.nz
www.candle.co.nz
www.dewinter.co.nz
www.itec.co.nz
www.itfutures.co.nz

- provide a clear demonstration of your skills, abilities and achievements
- clearly indicate what you offer the employer
- be professional in appearance
- be word-perfect with no spelling or grammatical mistakes
- be no more than two or three A4 pages in length

If you aren't up to writing a good CV, you can employ a professional CV writer who can turn your humdrum working life into something that Indiana Jones would be proud of. Professional help will also ensure that your CV adheres to a strict code of ethics (so you won't lose your job later for over-embellishing your life story) and some writers guarantee that a CV is in the proper form for the region and industry where you're looking.

Bear in mind that CVs must be in the standard New Zealand format, which isn't the same as in other countries. If your CV isn't in the correct format or doesn't contain the correct information it could be discarded. There are numerous CV writing services available in New Zealand and elsewhere, including www.customcv.co.nz and www.cvworks.co.nz. Government websites such as Work & Income (⌨ www.workandincome.govt.nz) and Careers Information (⌨ www.kiwicareers.govt.nz) also provide information about writing a CV.

In addition to a good CV, employers may require the names of a number (e.g. three) of personal or professional referees, whom they will contact (usually by telephone, so there's no incriminating documentation of any 'candid' remarks).

Job interviews should never be taken lightly in New Zealand, where creating a good impression can make the difference between being on the ladder of success or in the unemployment (or soup kitchen) queue. Some employers rely on phone (e.g. Skype) and video interviews for overseas candidates, although most prefer face-to-face meetings. Those who are prepared to visit New Zealand for interviews are also taken more seriously, depending on the industry and demand.

Dress appropriately, which may entail wearing a suit and tie, even when it isn't required in an office or work environment. The secret is in preparation, so do your homework on prospective employers and try to anticipate every question you may be asked (and then some) and rehearse your answers. Most employers expect you to know something about the company, its products or services, and general reputation in the press – all information you can research in your local library or online. Some employers require prospective employees to complete aptitude and other written tests.

You may be asked to show proof of your immigration status or your eligibility for the appropriate visa, and you may also be required to sign a release authorising a prospective employer to run a credit check (which could be done in your previous country of residence), even for jobs that don't directly involve money or finance. Interviews should always be followed up with a letter, confirming your interest in (and suitability for) the job, and thanking the interviewer for his or her time and interest (it pays to be obsequious when job hunting!).

WORKING WOMEN

New Zealand has a long history of women doing traditionally male jobs, which dates from the pioneering days when women had to run the house, prepare the food, look after the children *and* work on the farm (in some cases

they still do). Consequently, it isn't unusual to find women doing such jobs as truck driving, factory work and 'politicking'. New Zealand women rate highly in international equality of the sexes tables, consistently rating in the top five countries in the world.

Women gained the right to vote in New Zealand in 1893, making it the first country to have full adult suffrage (or voting rights), but women couldn't stand for Parliament until 1919, and it wasn't until 1933 that the first woman Member of Parliament (Elizabeth McCombs) won a seat in the House. The number of female MPs has been steadily rising in recent years and in 2012 women made up around a third of all MPs, and the country has had two female Prime Ministers: Jenny Shipley from 1997 to 1999, and Helen Clark from 1999 until 2008.

Over 45 per cent of women are employed in New Zealand, a relatively high figure that's made possible in part by the country's excellent system of early childhood education (see **Chapter 9**). There's no reason why women shouldn't take jobs in almost any industry, although, as in other countries, women tend towards the caring professions and education. The growth in service industries, always a popular career choice with women, has created additional opportunities. Women have also made good progress in professions such as law and medicine, although few reach the top levels. If you're a professional woman, you may be interested in the online community of professional working women (💻 www.professionelle.co.nz).

For more information about working women in New Zealand, contact the National Advisory Council on the Employment of Women (NACEW, 💻 www.nacew.govt.nz) or the Ministry of Women's Affairs (☎ 04-915 7112, 💻 www.mwa.govt.nz).

All members of the workforce are entitled to equal pay for equal work under the Equal Pay Act 1972, although in practice the average wage tends to be marginally lower for both female and ethnic minority workers. (In June 2010, average weekly wages were $1,063.08 for men and $858.85 for women.) A recent survey by Statistics New Zealand revealed that women's wages were, on average, much lower than men's (some 70 per cent of men's wages), but this is partly because women and ethnic minorities are more likely to do unskilled or semi-skilled work, and because women often work part-time.

Discrimination in the workplace is illegal under the Human Rights Act 1972, which protects employees against discrimination on all grounds that are irrelevant to the performance of the job (women are also entitled to 14 weeks paid parental leave). However, this doesn't extend as far as the home, where male chauvinism is alive and well and the country's reputation as a land of 'rugby, racing and beer' is still largely deserved (although it isn't generally quite as marked as in Australia).

A non-profit organisation, the Equal Employment Opportunities (EEO) Trust, promotes equal opportunities in the workplace and has around 300 member organisations from a wide range of employment sectors. Members are committed to EEO policies and ideas, and employees (of member organisations) generally enjoy greater equality at work. The EEO Trust (PO Box 12929, Penrose, Auckland, ☎ 09-525 3023, 💻 www.eeotrust.org.nz) can provide a list of its members.

SALARY

Salaries in New Zealand are up to 50 per cent lower than those in Europe and North America, and some 25 per cent lower than in Australia. New Zealanders generally work longer hours – although working hours are falling – than their counterparts in most developed countries and have fewer holidays (with the exception of North Americans), and many full-time workers do unpaid overtime. Not surprisingly, the country struggles to hang on to its best workers and has a huge and growing 'brain' drain to Australia. Migrants don't usually come to New Zealand for the money, but for the quality of life and laid-back lifestyle.

It's usually relatively easy to determine the salary you should command in New Zealand, as they are usually quoted in job advertisements. Note, however, that there's a marked difference between salaries in the major cities of Auckland and Wellington and in the rest of the country, where they're often up to 20 to 30 per cent lower. This reflects not only the higher living costs in these cities, but the tendency for jobs in the major cities to carry more responsibility and stress. Auckland is home to a third of the population and GDP is around a third higher than the rest of the country, with a high proportion of jobs in the business, distribution, finance, insurance and property sectors.

Employers can be rather coy when quoting salary figures, using terms such as 'salary to'. For example, 'salary to $55,000' usually means you're highly unlikely to receive $55,000 – the employer is probably thinking in terms of paying $40,000-50,000 and just wants to attract as much interest as possible. The term 'negotiable' is frequently used in job advertisements, e.g. 'salary $65,000 negotiable', which means that you'll need to work hard to convince the employer that you're worth $65,000. However, if you have qualifications or skills that are in short supply, you may be able to negotiate an even higher salary. For example, some years ago the wool industry was thrown into turmoil when shearers began flocking to Australia attracted by higher pay, and the Shearing Contractors' Organisation was forced to raise pay rates by 20 per cent.

A national minimum wage applies in New Zealand, which is currently $13.50 an hour (from 1st April 2012) or $10.80 an hour for those aged under 18 (see **Minimum Wage** below). A survey carried out by Statistics New Zealand a few years ago revealed that some 40,000 adult employees received less than the legal minimum wage but that most (over 1m) earned at least 30 per cent more than the legal minimum wage.

The average hourly wage in September 2010 (the latest published figures at the time

New Zealand Average Hourly Earnings 2010	
Classification	**Average Hourly Earnings**
public sector	$32.61
private sector	$23.72
males	$27.26
females	$23.93
all NZ employees	$25.71

Source: Statistics New Zealand

of writing) was $25.71. Note, however, that few salaries in New Zealand are negotiated on a collective basis, therefore there's often a huge variation in pay in different industries and areas. The average hourly earnings in September 2010 are shown in the table above.

Looking at wages by sector, the highest earners are those in the finance and insurance and IT sectors, in which employees earn twice as much on average as those working in the accommodation, catering and retail sectors. The average hourly earnings by sector are shown in the table opposite.

Executive and professional salaries are lower than in other developed countries such as Australia, France, Germany, Japan, the UK and the US, although a lower cost of living compensates somewhat (although housing costs can be high, particularly in Auckland and Wellington). The average salary for top company bosses is around $250,000. Executive salaries are often subject to much greater annual rises (e.g. 10 to 12 per cent) than average wages, which are usually around just 2 per cent annually. New Zealand companies don't traditionally shower executives with fringe benefits on top of their basic salary package, but may offer certain benefits to lure an outstanding applicant.

Nevertheless, company cars are widespread at executive level, as are health insurance benefits (around 55 per cent) and superannuation/pension schemes (around 60 per cent). Productivity bonuses and profit sharing may also be offered. Relocation costs and contributions towards housing expenses are usually offered only to employees with rare skills (but it's worth asking).

Approximate annual salaries for executives and professionals are shown in the table overleaf. Bear in mind that these are salary ranges. The bottom of the range applies to inexperienced employees working for a small or medium-size employer, while the top of the range approximates the salary of an experienced employee working with a leading employer. It's likely you'll only be offered work in New Zealand if you're already experienced, therefore you certainly shouldn't be expecting a salary at the bottom of any of these ranges.

A free annual Salary Survey & Guide – for both Australia and New Zealand – is produced by Hays Recruitment and available on their website (⌨ www.hays.net.nz/salary). It contains data on the current salaries in well over 1,000 job titles across 16 sectors in 12 locations, with over 1,700 leading Australian and New Zealand employers consulted.

Average Hourly Earnings 2010 (excluding overtime)

Sector	Average Hourly Earnings
Accommodation/cafes/restaurants	$16.20
Retail	$17.18
Arts & recreation services	$21.86
Construction	$23.31
Manufacturing	$23.79
Transport, postal & warehousing	$24.10
Renting, hiring & real estate services	$25.16
Forestry & mining	$25.68
Wholesale trade	$26.45
Healthcare & social services	$27.04
Professional, scientific & technical services	$29.72
Electricity, gas & water	$30.21
Education & training	$30.78
Public administration & safety	$31.48
Information, media & telecommunications	$32.47
Finance & insurance	$35.37

Source: Statistics New Zealand

Annual Salaries in New Zealand	
Profession/Trade	**Average Annual Salary**
Accounting Technician	$45,000-80,000
Auditor	$55,000-100,000+
Bank Manager	$55,000-100,000+
Financial Planner	$35,000-100,000+
Loss Adjustor	$35,000-100,000+
Management Accountant	$40,000-100,000+
Teacher	$40,000-70,000
Educational Psychologist	$40,000-100,000+
Engineer (chem./elect.)	$40,000-100,000+
Environmental Engineer	$40,000-100,000
Road Engineer	$40,000-90,000
Electrical Engineer Tech	$40,000-90,000
Environmental Scientist	$40,000-85,000
Forestry Scientist	$40,000-55,000
Industrial Chemist	$45,000-100,000+
Computer Services Manager	$50,000-150,000+
Systems Analyst	$50,000-100,000+
Computer Helpdesk Operator	$30,000-60,000
Warehouse Manager	$30,000-55,000
Solicitor	$50,000-200,000+
Registered Hospital Nurse	$60,000 basic

Source: Statistics New Zealand

Minimum Wage

There are three minimum wage rates in New Zealand:

♦ The **adult minimum wage** applies to all employees aged 16 and over who aren't new entrants or trainees. This was $13.50 an hour from 1st April 2012 (equal to $108 for an 8-hour day and $540 for a 40-hour week).

♦ The **new entrants minimum wage** applies to employees aged 16 and 17 except for those who have completed 200 hours or three months of employment, whichever is shorter, or who are supervising or training other workers or who are trainees. The new entrants minimum wage is $10.80 an hour (or $86.40 for an 8-hour day and $432 for a 40-hour week).

♦ The **training minimum wage** applies to employees aged 16 and over who are doing recognised industry training involving at least 60 credits a year. The wage is the same as for new entrants (above).

There's no statutory minimum wage for employees who are aged under 16.

By law, employers must pay at least the minimum wage – even when an employee is paid by commission or piece rates. The minimum wage applies to all workers aged 16 years or older, including home workers, casuals, temporary and part-time workers.

Holiday pay must be paid in addition to the minimum wage. If an employee receives 'pay-as-you-go' holiday pay, this must be a separate and identifiable part of their pay. An increase in the minimum wage doesn't affect an employee's other conditions of employment, unless they agree to any changes.

Anyone who's being paid less than the minimum wage should contact the Department of Labour (☎ 0800-209020).

SELF-EMPLOYMENT & STARTING A BUSINESS

The idea of becoming self-employed or starting a business in New Zealand is appealing and often considered by those planning to live there. New Zealanders don't traditionally have a 'wheeler-dealer' personality and there isn't an ingrained enterprise culture. Most people work from nine-to-five for a large company – going it alone, which often involves working up to 12 hours a day, isn't seen as an attractive proposition. However, since the mid-'80s a more adventurous attitude has spread throughout the country, with people starting a wide range of small businesses and around 95 per cent of businesses employ fewer than 20 people (some 90 per cent have fewer than five employees!).

Generally speaking, it isn't wise to start or buy a business in an industry in which you don't have some expertise, particularly if your experience of New Zealand is also limited. Setting up a smallholding or a bungee jumping business may seem like a good idea, but it's rarely as simple as it appears. That said, many experts consider New Zealand to be something of a 'virgin' market for business ideas that are commonplace in the US or Europe. Many business ideas imported from Australia have also successfully taken root in New Zealand.

Professional Advice

Before embarking on a business project in New Zealand, ensure that you take advice regarding the legal and financial aspects from a good lawyer and accountant. Useful guides for anyone going into business in New Zealand are *Start Your Own Business*, available from Work and Income offices or from their website (🖳 www.workandincome.govt.nz) and *Planning for Success* published by BIZ Info (see below). There are many organisations offering information and advice to the self-employed, including the following:

♦ **BIZ Info:** A business information service with comprehensive and useful advice including some *Quick Facts* factsheets and useful publications (🖳 www.bizinfo.co.nz).

♦ **Chambers of Commerce:** There are chambers of commerce in all large towns, such as the Auckland Chamber of Commerce (🖳 www.aucklandchamber. co.nz). Membership is open to all types of businesses and is a particularly effective way to establish new business contacts and find out about local business conditions.

♦ **The Employers and Manufacturers Association:** The EMA (🖳 www.ema.co.nz) is a membership organization that promotes the success of business.

♦ **Home Business:** A comprehensive guide for those planning to run a business from home (🖳 www.homebizbuzz.co.nz).

♦ **Trade Associations:** If you know the type of business you wish to start, you can contact the relevant trade association (🖳 www.nzsearch.co.nz/category. aspx?id=970).

♦ **Trade New Zealand:** An excellent website for investors (🖳 www.tradenz.govt.nz). See also 🖳 www.immigration.govt.nz/migrant/ stream/invest.

There are also over 50 city- and rural-based small business enterprise centres throughout New Zealand, which are community organisations that provide assistance to foster economic and employment development. They specialise in helping small businesses by offering economic development programmes, business development information, business services, business support and employment generation programmes. Most centres provide specialist services for migrants who want to start a business, e.g. see Christchurch Small Business Enterprise Centre (🖳 www.csbec. org.nz).

Government Help

The New Zealand government has established a number of organisations to help people establish, operate, develop and expand a business in New Zealand, including extensive help with exporting.

The Ministry of Economic Development operates several schemes to help and advise those wishing to run their own business (whether starting from scratch or buying an existing business) and also to help small businesses grow. They can help with planning and preparation; the law regarding business names; taxation and other financial regulations; locating premises; marketing; finding staff; and management. For more information contact the Ministry of Economic Development (33 Bowen Street, PO Box 1473, Wellington, ☎ 04-472 0030, 🖳 www.med.govt.nz). The Ministry also publishes *Connectionz*, a quarterly newsletter containing business news and information.

Other government business organisations include the following:

◆ **Business New Zealand** (💻 www.
businessnz.org.nz) – Business NZ is New
Zealand's largest advocacy group for
enterprise.

◆ **Business Government NZ** (💻 www.
business.govt.nz) – brings together free
business resources, tools and information
to help people start, manage and grow
their business.

◆ **Economic Development Association
New Zealand** (EDANZ, 💻 www.edanz.
org.nz) – EDANZ provides a range of
member services, including networking,
conferences, joint projects, access
to information and resources, and
government lobbying.

◆ **Foundation for Research, Science
& Technology** (💻 www.frst.govt.
nz) – government website that assists
companies to invest in innovation for New
Zealand's future.

◆ **New Zealand Trade & Enterprise**
(💻 www.nzte.govt.nz) – the government's
national economic development agency.

◆ **Overseas Investment Office** (155 The
Terrace, PO Box 5501, Wellington 6145,
☎ 4-460 0110 or 0800-665463, 💻 www.
linz.govt.nz/overseas-investment) – the
Overseas Investment Office assesses
applications from foreigners who intend
making substantial investments in New
Zealand, e.g. to obtain residence.

Information about doing business is also
provided on the Immigration New Zealand
website (💻 www.immigration.govt.nz).

Restrictions

There are few restrictions on the kinds of
business that can be started or purchased
by new migrants in New Zealand. Foreign
involvement in telecommunications and
transport used to be heavily restricted, but this
is no longer the case and American investors
raced to snap up New Zealand companies
the minute ownership controls were relaxed.
Restrictions have also been eased in
broadcasting, which was the last bastion to be
protected by law.

Government approval via the Overseas
Investment Commission (💻 www.linz.govt.nz/
overseas-investment) is required in the case

of foreign investments (at least 25 per cent of
a business) when the business or property is
worth over $50m or when the land occupied is
over 5 hectares (12 acres) and/or worth more
than $10m. The main point to bear in mind is
that if your business involves practising a trade
or profession which must be registered in New
Zealand, you must register before you can start
trading (see **Qualifications** on page 20).

☑ SURVIVAL TIP

Finance

You should usually reckon on providing at least
50 per cent of the cost of a business purchase
or start-up. New Zealand banks look more
favourably upon an application for a loan if you
have a substantial lump sum of your own to
invest, not to mention good business experience
and a realistic business plan. As with banks
elsewhere, they also expect security for your
loan, preferably in the form of property in New
Zealand.

Buying an Existing Business

As anywhere, it's much easier to buy a going
concern in New Zealand than to start a new
business; the bureaucracy is considerably
less, as is the risk. It isn't entirely risk-free,
however, and precautions must be taken to
ensure that you don't buy a failing business.
You can find businesses for sale through
local estate and commercial agents, and
through advertisements in local and regional
newspapers. However, it's vital to inspect a
business personally (never rely solely on the
glowing description provided by an agent)
before agreeing to buy it, shop around and
compare it with similar businesses, and obtain
independent advice regarding its value and
prospects.

One of the most important aspects to
consider when buying a business in New
Zealand is its location, particularly if what
appears to be a thriving concern is offered for
a quick sale at a temptingly low price. One
thing to look out for is a situation where a town
centre has been left as a ghost town (or soon

physical, work and business may be mainly seasonal – and there's a lot of competition!

Location

Choosing the location for a business is even more important than choosing the location for a home. Depending on the kind of business, you may need to be in a town or near a housing development, have good access to roads or be close to a tourist resort. Don't forget that future development plans can affect the desirability of the location. Plans for new roads or shopping developments are usually available from the local town council.

will be) by the opening of a new out-of-town shopping mall or the building of a new road which will take potential customers right past your new business – at 100kph! (See also **Location** below.)

Starting a New Business

Most people are far too optimistic about the prospects for a new business, whether in their home country or abroad. Be realistic or even pessimistic when estimating your income, overestimate the costs and underestimate the revenue (then reduce it by another 50 per cent). While hoping for the best, plan for the worst and make sure that you have enough money, not only to set up the business but to keep it going until it's established. Bear in mind that while New Zealand is a virgin market with many new business opportunities waiting to be exploited, it's also a small and relatively conservative market. In the good times, fortunes have certainly been made by shrewd entrepreneurs, but when the economy takes a nose-dive they have been lost just as easily.

While there's always room for another entrepreneur in New Zealand, it makes sense to play it safe and hedge your bets by not choosing anything too risky. Newcomers, in particular, tend to have an idealistic view of starting a business in New Zealand, which is all very well, but try to be practical and consider the possible negative aspects of your proposed 'dream' business. For example, jet-boating, scuba diving and yacht charter businesses, café-bars and smallholdings are all good business ideas, but they involve hard, often

Employees

If you're starting a new kind of business or one that requires specialist skills, you should check that these skills are available in the local workforce. The New Zealand workforce is well educated and trained, but certain sectors have grown so fast in recent years that it's difficult to find skilled and qualified staff in some trades and professions. Even if appropriate staff are available, you may find that they demand sky-high salaries. Make enquiries with Work and Income (🖳 www.workandincome.govt.nz) regarding the availability of labour, as well as with recruitment consultants if you're going to need executives and specialist staff.

The Inland Revenue Department (IRD) publishes two useful booklets, *Employer Obligations* and the *Employer's Guide*, containing information about employers' obligations and how to make tax payments and deductions from employees' wages.

Business Entities

The simplest form of trading entity in New Zealand is an individual trading on his own (sole trader), which involves unlimited liability. There are no accounting, auditing or reporting requirements other than the need to keep accounts for the Inland Revenue Department. You can also form a partnership, which is governed by the Partnership Act 1908, where it's usual to have a formal written agreement between the parties. This doesn't need to be drafted by a lawyer and the rights and responsibilities of each partner are governed by the agreement rather than employment law. A partnership can be either special, where some partners (who cannot be involved in the management of the business) may have limited liability, or general, in which case all partners have unlimited liability.

A limited company or corporation can be established under the Companies Act 1993, which makes no distinction between a public and a private limited company. There's no requirement to appoint a secretary and directors can be held personally liable for the debts of their company if they're found not to have carried out their duties properly. Registration of a company is a relatively simple procedure (costing between around $100 and $200) and involves making an application to the New Zealand Companies Office giving details of the directors, the registered address and the company's constitution (☎ 0508-266 726 or 03-962 2602, 🖳 www.companies. govt.nz). It isn't, however, necessary to have an individual constitution, as the Companies Act serves as a ready-made constitution for companies without their own.

Taxation

The usual financial year for companies in New Zealand runs from 1st April to 31st March. It's possible to adopt an accounting year which doesn't correspond to the financial year, but permission is required from the Commissioner of the IRD. Businesses must prepare and file an income tax return with the IRD and are required to make interim 'provisional' tax payments. The number of instalments you're required to make depends on the way you choose to calculate your provisional tax instalments. If you're registered for Goods and Services Tax (GST), how often you file GST returns also determines how many provisional tax instalments you're required to make.

The amount of provisional tax you need to pay is based on your expected profit for the year or your GST taxable supplies (sales) and depends on the way you choose to calculate your provisional tax instalments. At the end of the year you pay or are refunded the difference

between the amount of provisional tax you've paid and the amount you should have paid, based on your actual profit for the year. For further information, see the Inland Revenue website (🖳 www.ird.govt.nz/business-income-tax).

A sole trader is taxed at the same rates as individuals, while resident companies pay income tax at a rate of 33 per cent on their worldwide taxable income. Employers are also required to make contributions to the Accident Compensation Corporation (ACC) scheme (see **Chapter 13**) and may also be required to pay Fringe Benefit Tax (see page 234 for details).

Goods & Services Tax (GST)

If the turnover (or expected turnover) of your business exceeds $60,000, you must register for GST (see page 230). Note that this figure refers to turnover and not to profit. If your business is registered for GST, you must levy GST (at 15 per cent) on your goods and services, although you can reclaim GST paid on anything you buy for your business and certain other expenses. Registration for GST is made at your local IRD office and once registered you must file a GST return monthly, two-monthly or six-monthly, depending on various factors. There are substantial penalties for not registering for GST or for filing late returns.

Customs

If you're planning to move to New Zealand with the intention of becoming self-employed, buying

an existing business or starting a business and you want to bring specialist tools, equipment, machinery or stock with you, you must prepare an inventory and obtain permission from the Collector of Customs. You may be permitted to bring some tools and business equipment with you free of customs duty; otherwise, you must pay GST at 15 per cent and customs duty on their value. Note that you can bring any household items (which can include those with a combined work and household use) to New Zealand free of GST and duty when you first settle there (see page 230).

For further information contact the Collector of Customs Offices (☎ 0800-428 786, ✉ feedback@customs.govt.nz) or apply to one of the following offices: PO Box 29, Auckland (☎ 09-359 6655), PO Box 14 086, Christchurch (☎ 03-358 0600) or PO Box 2218, Wellington (☎ 04-473 6099).

TRAINEES & WORK EXPERIENCE

New Zealand is a participant in an international trainee programme designed to give young people the opportunity for further education and occupational training, and to enlarge their professional experience and knowledge of other countries. Participating countries include Austria, Belgium, Canada, Denmark, France, Finland, Germany, Ireland, Luxembourg, Netherlands, Norway, Spain, Sweden, Switzerland, the UK and the US.

If you're aged between 18 and 30 (21 to 30 for Americans) and have completed a minimum of two years' vocational training, you may be eligible for a trainee position in New Zealand. The trainee agreement covers many professions but a position must be in the occupation for which you were trained. Positions are usually granted for a year and can sometimes be extended for a further six months. Information about the trainee programme can be obtained from the department of employment in participating countries.

Technical and commercial students who wish to gain experience by working in industry and commerce in New Zealand during their holidays can apply to the International Association for the Exchange of Students for Technical Experience (IAESTE), which has around 85 member countries. A good knowledge of English is essential and applicants must be enrolled at a college or university and be studying agriculture, architecture, engineering, science or a related subject. Your wages should cover your living costs and your employer should insure you against accident and illness. Travel costs must be met by the trainee. Information is available from the IAESTE website (🖳 www.iaeste.org) and in New Zealand from UNITEC Institute of Technology (Private Bag 92025, Victoria Street West, Auckland, ☎ 09-849 4180, 🖳 www. unitec.ac.nz).

Young people who are studying or working in agriculture, horticulture or home management can participate in an exchange programme operated by the International Agricultural Exchange Association (IAEA, 🖳 www. agriventure.com). The IAEA programme is for those aged 18-30 and provides between 6 and 14 months' work experience on a farm in New Zealand. A fee is charged, although participants are paid wages and given 'free' board and lodging. For information, contact the IAEA in your home country or New Zealand (IAEA, P O Box 22, Kaukapakapa 0843, Auckland, ☎ 09-420 5212).

ILLEGAL WORKING

New Zealand developed a reputation as something of a 'soft touch' when it came to illegal working, particularly among immigrants who had been turned away by countries such as Australia, Canada and the US, which have stricter immigration regulations. New Zealand's work regulations and enforcement were lax in comparison and a blind eye was often turned to those working without the necessary visa. Many people who work illegally have been refused a work visa or didn't bother applying at all and simply settled in New Zealand as a permanent visitor.

Asylum seekers have also become a problem. While New Zealand has always been a refuge for victims of oppressive regimes, the number of applicants during the early '90s put a huge strain on the social security budget, when officials struggled to process a never-ending stream of asylum claims and appeals against refusal, which took many months or even years to come to court. Note that it's legal (under certain circumstances) to arrive in New Zealand on a tourist visa, find a job and then apply for residence (most other countries don't allow this).

In the last decade, however, the authorities have become increasingly concerned about the country becoming an immigration 'dustbin' for those refused by other countries, particularly the unskilled from poor Asian countries who have tended to regard the country as a promised land. High unemployment in the early '90s meant that a blind eye could no longer be turned to illegal workers, even those doing unpleasant and poorly paid jobs, which in the past New Zealanders wouldn't entertain.

▲ Caution

In the last decade, new laws have been introduced which provide stiffer penalties for illegal workers (including fast-track deportation) and also fines for employers who employed them. The police and immigration authorities enforce the regulations, mounting periodic 'dawn raids' on companies likely to employ illegal workers, such as fruit farms and large factories.

Despite tougher immigration regulations, many employers still won't ask to see your visa or immigration papers before taking you on. They will, however, usually expect to see your IRD number. This can be obtained from the nearest IRD office by producing your immigration papers and proof of your permanent address in New Zealand, such as a utility bill or driving licence.

LANGUAGE

A good knowledge of English is a pre-requisite for living and working (or even holidaying) in New Zealand. If you cannot speak and write English well, not only will you find it extremely difficult to find a job, but you probably won't qualify for any sort of work visa in the first place. You will, however, be relieved to hear that you won't be required to speak Maori (which was made an official language in 1974) as well. Although New Zealand is officially bilingual and there have even been proposals to replace some English place names with Maori names, only some 4 per cent of the population speak Maori, and English is the language of business and spoken by just about everyone.

New Zealanders aren't generally adept at speaking foreign languages; when your nearest neighbours are hundreds of miles away and even they speak English (of a sort), there's little opportunity to practise French, German or Spanish. Some shrewd New Zealanders with an eye to the future have made great strides in Japanese and other Asian languages, but don't bank on it. If you don't speak English well in New Zealand, you'll be sunk!

New Zealand English is similar to Australian English, with which it shares many slang words and colloquialisms. However, as any New Zealander will tell you, New Zildish is the proper Antipodean version of English and it's the Australians who have corrupted it. The differences often go unnoticed by people from outside the two countries, but New Zildish is more similar to the English spoken in southern England than is Aussie English, and has also been influenced by the Maori language as well as by the pronunciation of the Irish and Scots, who settled in the country in large numbers in the 19th century.

The use of 'proper' English often comes across as rather snobbish or superior in New Zealand, where people at all levels of society use New Zealand's own dialect, even at work. The major distinguishing characteristic of the New Zealand dialect is to shorten words so that they end in 'o', 'y' or 'ie'. For example, 'arvo' for 'afternoon' or 'kindy' for kindergarten. Like accents in any country, a New Zealand accent can vary from slightly difficult to understand to completely unintelligible. Nevertheless, whatever variety of English you speak, if you speak it well, you'll be easily understood. (See also **Language Schools** on page 149.)

The early years of the 21st century have seen New Zealanders of all backgrounds increasingly peppering their speech with Maori words – perhaps a sign that the country is beginning to distance itself from its British heritage and forge its own identity. Until

recently, the only Maori words known to most
white New Zealanders were place names
and terms such as *haka* (the ritual 'dance'
performed by the All Blacks rugby team before
matches) and *kiwi* (the small, hairy fruit). But
words like *kiora* (hello), *mahi* (work), *Pākehā*
(whites) and *whanau* (family) are being used
with increasing frequency, and some popular
English expressions have been given a Maori
flavour with the inclusion of Maori words, for
example, 'he's a couple of *kumera* (sweet
potato) short of a *hangi* (earth oven)'.

2.

EMPLOYMENT
CONDITIONS

Employees in New Zealand generally enjoy good working conditions and terms of employment, which are somewhere between those in the UK or the US, where they're relatively lightly regulated, and those in France or Germany, where they're extensively regulated.

New Zealand industry suffered a large number of trade union disputes and strikes during the '70s and early '80s, but the situation became more conciliatory in the '90s, with employers and employees more willing to discuss and even avoid problems. In the last decade, the annual loss of wages and working days from strikes have been the lowest since figures were first recorded in 1970. Most work stoppages occur in the manufacturing industry, followed by the health and community services.

The cornerstone of modern industrial relations in New Zealand is the Employment Contracts Act 1991, which gave employees the freedom to decide whether they wished to belong to a trade union, and outlawed 'closed shops' (where all employees were required to belong to a union). Most importantly, it gave employees the right to negotiate their terms of employment and raise any problems directly with their employers, rather than comply with collective agreements negotiated by trades unions or other bodies. This has allowed both employers and employees to tailor their working terms and conditions to suit their particular circumstances and therefore avoid unnecessary disputes. As a result, working conditions have improved in many industries, although in others they've become less favourable. For example, many unskilled and part-time workers in service industries feel that their pay and working hours have suffered as a result of the decline in union 'muscle'.

Many companies have taken advantage of the opportunity to negotiate individual agreements, with the result that working hours, holidays, pay and other benefits are no longer standard throughout the country for a particular industry. The Employment Relations Act (October 2000) further consolidated industrial relations and introduced the principle of 'good faith' in negotiations, to which both employers and employees are obliged to adhere.

The National (right wing) government which came to power in November 2008 introduced a 90-day trial period (see below) for new employees, which the unions see as the thin end of the wedge in eroding employee rights and benefits.

Information regarding all aspects of employment relations and conditions can be obtained from the Employment Relations Service at the Department of Labour (☎ 0800-800 863, www.ers.dol.govt.nz), which publishes a number of useful factsheets that can be downloaded from its website.

EQUAL RIGHTS

New Zealand has a relatively good record on equal rights, and the participation rate of women and ethnic minorities in the workplace is favourable when compared with countries with a similar level of economic development. It's also one of the few countries where a woman has been able to reach the highest political office in the land (Prime Minister). As childcare provision is relatively good, substantial numbers of women are able to work full-time, although there are frequent calls for free childcare to be made more widely available to enable more women to work full-time.

All members of the workforce are entitled to equal pay for equal work under the Equal Pay Act 1972. In practice, however, average wages tend to be lower for female and ethnic minority workers. This is often due to the fact that they're more likely to do unskilled or semi-skilled work, or, in the case of women, because they frequently work part-time (see also **Working Women** on page 30).

Discrimination in the workplace is illegal under the Human Rights Act 1972, which protects employees against discrimination on any grounds that are irrelevant to job performance, including age, disability, ethnic group, gender and sexual orientation.

EMPLOYMENT AGREEMENTS

Employees must have a written employment agreement, which can be either an individual or collective agreement. There are certain provisions that must be included in employment agreements by law and also a number of minimum conditions that must be met, irrespective of whether they're included in agreements. Employment law also provides a framework for negotiating additional entitlements.

A standard individual employment agreement may contain the clauses shown in the table opposite.

Under new legislation introduced by the Employment Relations Act, employment agreements must be in writing and oral 'agreements' are illegal. The terms of an agreement can be either collective or individual, i.e. they apply to all employees in the same company (or the same industry) or just to one employee. Collective agreements are less common than they used to be,

Agreement Clauses
1. the parties
2. the position and the duties
3. nature and term of the agreement
4. obligations of the relationship
5. the place of work
6. hours of work
7. wages, salary and allowances
8. holidays and leave entitlements
9. other entitlements/benefits
10. health and safety
11. other employment obligations such as copyright, restraint of trade, parental leave and child care
12. restructuring and redundancy
13. termination of employment
14. resolving employment relationship problems
15. acknowledgement of the agreement
16. declaration

particularly as trade union power and membership have decreased. If you and your employer agree, you can be issued with a collective agreement; alternatively, it's up to you to negotiate an individual agreement with an employer. If you wish, you can appoint a trade union or another person as your agent to negotiate your agreement.

If you're a non-union member and join a company where there's a collective employment agreement in place, your employer must notify you of this and employ you on the terms and conditions of the agreement for the first 30 days of your employment. After 30 days you must decide whether to join the union and accept the collective agreement or negotiate an individual agreement. (Collective agreements are agreements that cover two or more employees who are union members, negotiated between unions and employers.)

An employment agreement must, by law, cover certain areas, e.g. wages and holiday provision. The provisions of the agreement in this regard mustn't be less than the statutory minimum provisions. The agreement must also specify the procedure to be followed in the event of disputes. All agreements must include effective personal grievance and dispute procedures, and, if the agreement is part of a collective agreement, an agreement expiry date.

In addition to an agreement, you should receive a copy of an employer's general rules and regulations regarding working conditions and benefits that are applicable to all (or most) employees, unless stated otherwise in your employment agreement. These usually contain a clause stating the date from which they take effect and to whom they apply.

Trial Period

Since 1st March 2009, employers with fewer than 20 employees (which includes over 95 per cent of all New Zealand companies – some 90 per cent employ five or fewer people) have been able to engage new employees on a trial period of up to 90 days, which must be agreed to by both the employer and the employee and be included in writing in the employment agreement. If an employee agrees to a trial period, it doesn't affect his entitlements to holidays and leave.

If an employment 'relationship problem' arises during the trial period or if the employee is dismissed, the employee and the employer can access mediation services. An employee can be fired at any time during the 90-day period and cannot claim for unjustified dismissal. He may, however, raise a personal grievance on other grounds, such as discrimination or harassment or an unjustified action by the employer that disadvantaged the employee.

For information regarding your rights and the trial period, see 💻 http://fairness.org.nz.

Drug & Alcohol Testing

A number of employers in New Zealand require employees to undergo drug testing, both at the start of their employment and at other times on a random basis. This is legal and, if applicable, is usually stated in your employment agreement. It's common in occupations where you're required to drive or operate heavy machinery. Urine samples are tested for the use of amphetamines, benzodiazepine, cannabis, cocaine, heroin and morphine, and breath tests are also carried out for alcohol. A positive test can lead to instant dismissal.

Salary & Benefits

Your remuneration may be quoted either as an annual salary, payable monthly, or an hourly wage, payable weekly or fortnightly. It's normal to have your salary paid into a bank account by direct credit transfer. If you wish, you're entitled to ask for a cheque (e.g. a cashier's cheque or bank draft), although you aren't entitled to receive cash. Employees don't receive an automatic annual bonus (a so-called '13th month's salary) as in some countries, although some industries operate productivity and performance-related bonus schemes.

For information about salaries and minimum wages in New Zealand, see **Salary** on page 31.

Expenses

Expenses paid by your employer are usually listed in your employment agreement and may include travel costs from your home to your place of work. This is more likely for Auckland and Wellington commuters than residents of other towns, where employers may provide employees with a rail or bus pass or free car parking at or near their place of work. Large employers may provide a subsidised employee restaurant or canteen, whereas

An employer may pay a fixed relocation allowance based on your salary, position and size of family, or he may pay the total cost of removal. The allowance should be sufficient to move the contents of an average house, and you must usually pay any excess costs (such as insurance for valuable items) yourself. If you don't want to bring your furniture to New Zealand or have just a few belongings to ship, it may be possible to obtain a grant towards the purchase of furniture locally up to the limit of your allowance. Check with your employer. When your employer is liable for the total cost, you may be asked to obtain two or three removal estimates. You may be expected to settle the remover's bill and then claim reimbursement, or your employer may instruct a New Zealand remover with agents in your home country to handle the removal and bill the employer directly.

If you change jobs within New Zealand, your new employer may pay your relocation expenses when it's necessary for you to move.

smaller employers may provide employees with luncheon vouchers.

Relocation & Travel Expenses

Travel and relocation expenses depend on what you've agreed with your employer and are usually included in your employment agreement or conditions. Given the expense of moving people and goods to New Zealand, even from Australia let alone from Europe or North America, employers usually pay expenses only for executives or key employees with specialist skills. It's worth asking, however, and even if the entire cost of travel and relocation isn't forthcoming, a prospective employer may be prepared to make a contribution. When New Zealand found itself short of qualified teachers, for example, the Ministry of Education contributed towards the relocation of foreign teachers and New Zealander teachers wishing to return home.

If you're hired from outside New Zealand, your air ticket and other travel costs are usually booked and paid for by your employer or his representative. In addition, you can usually claim any extra travel costs, e.g. transport to and from airports and hotel expenses en route. Employers may contribute towards your relocation costs up to a specified amount, although you may be required to sign an agreement stipulating that if you leave the employer before a certain period, you must repay a percentage of your removal costs.

Working Hours

There aren't standard working hours in New Zealand. Traditionally, the working week has been 40 hours, commencing at 8.30am and finishing at 5pm, Mondays to Fridays, with a half-hour break for lunch. However, since the Employment Contracts Act took effect, employers and employees have been free to set the length of their working week and their start and finish times. The majority of employees still work around 38 or 40 hours over five days a week, although some companies (mainly larger organisations and manufacturing companies) have introduced different working patterns in consultation with their employees. Some large factories, for example, work four ten-hour shifts spread over seven days. Generally, workers in New Zealand expect to have Saturdays and Sundays free, although this is changing as more organisations (particularly service industries) operate at weekends.

On average, New Zealanders work longer hours than their counterparts in some other developed countries, although working hours are falling. The Minimum Wage Act sets out a maximum 40-hour, 5-day working week. Most businesses operate Monday-Friday, 8am-5pm, with a 30-60 minute lunch break. In 2011, the average male employee worked around 37 hours per week, but many employees do voluntary overtime.

New legislation providing paid rest and unpaid meal breaks was introduced on 1st April 2009, and provides for the following:

- ◆ one paid 10-minute rest break if the work period is between two and four hours;

- ◆ one paid 10-minute rest break and one unpaid 30-minute meal break if the work period is between four and six hours;

- ◆ two paid 10-minute rest breaks and one unpaid 30-minute meal break if the work period is between six and eight hours.

Where employees work for periods longer than eight hours, the above provisions automatically reapply for each succeeding work period.

Flexi Work

Many New Zealand employers offer flexible working arrangements in order to attract and retain employees, although they're most common in the public service sector and are more likely to apply to those in administrative, managerial and professional positions.

The Employment Relations (Flexible Working Arrangements) Amendment Act 2007 gave certain employees with caring responsibilities a statutory right to request a variation to their hours of work, days of work or place of work. To be eligible for the 'right to request' an employee must be responsible for the care of a person and have been employed by their employer for six months prior to making the request. When making a request, employees must also explain how the variation will help the employee provide better care for the person concerned. The Act requires employers to consider the request for flexible working arrangements and provides the grounds upon which they can refuse a request.

Flexible work arrangements are becoming important in New Zealand workplaces and can benefit employees, employers, the economy, communities and the environment. They give employees the opportunity to make changes to the hours they work (over a day, a week or a year), the times and days they work, and where they work (where applicable). They also involve how careers are organised, how transitions in and out of work are managed, and how flexible working is managed in the workplace, so that both employees and businesses benefit. Flexible work options are being used by some organisations as part of their travel planning strategies, in order to reduce public transport problems and car trips to and from workplaces.

Overtime

Overtime is traditionally paid at a rate of 'time and a half', although in many industries it has effectively been abolished, as employers have agreed with employees (or have insisted) that they take time off in lieu of overtime.

Holidays & Leave

The law regarding annual holidays (leave/ vacation) and public (national) holidays is outlined below.

Annual Holidays

Under the Holidays Act 2003, employees are entitled to a minimum of four weeks annual holiday after the first year of employment, although there's nothing preventing the parties negotiating better terms. It's the largest area of dispute between employers and employees, and the Department of Labour receives hundreds of complaints each year about breaches of annual holiday entitlement.

From 1st April 2007, all employees have been eligible for a minimum of four weeks annual holiday (it was previously three weeks) after they've completed 12 months employment, and to holiday pay of 8 per cent (previously 6 per cent) of their gross annual salary or wages.

Holiday pay for an employee who's on annual leave must be the greater of their ordinary weekly pay or average weekly earnings, which is calculated as follows:

1. The employer calculates the weekly average of your total gross earnings by dividing your gross earnings (salary, wages, overtime pay, allowances, commission and any previous holiday pay paid) for the whole of the year of employment by 52. This gives your average weekly earnings.

2. Your employer then works out what your ordinary weekly pay is by multiplying your ordinary hourly rate of pay by the number of hours you normally work each week. This gives your ordinary weekly pay.

3. Whichever of the above amounts is the larger is the rate of your weekly holiday pay.

Any leave taken before you've completed 12 months can only be taken as unpaid leave. You're entitled to take two of the four weeks as an unbroken period, but holidays must usually be booked and agreed with your employer at the start of the calendar year. As the peak summer holiday period in New Zealand includes Christmas, you need to plan well in advance to obtain your preferred holiday dates.

Employees who have completed six months employment are also entitled to five days special leave during the following year, which can be used for periods of sickness or for compassionate leave such as attending a funeral. This applies to all employees, including part-time and casual employees.

If your agreement provides for more than four weeks paid holiday a year, you can negotiate with your employer if you wish to receive pay in lieu of the additional holiday. This doesn't, however, apply to any part of the statutory four weeks carried over from previous years; if you have unused holiday, you must take it.

Employers can include holiday pay in ordinary pay – called 'pay as you go' holiday pay – in certain situations where there's a genuine, fixed-term employment agreement for less than 12 months or it's impractical to provide four weeks annual leave because work is too irregular or intermittent.

All holiday pay due to an employee (i.e. total entitlement less any holiday pay already received) must be paid to the employee at the time an employee leaves a job. Employees who work for less than four weeks are entitled to holiday pay of 8 per cent of their total ordinary pay, while employees who work for more than a year are entitled to holiday pay for the completed year plus 8 per cent of total gross earnings for the remaining part year.

Public/National Holidays

New Zealand has 11 statutory annual public holidays on which employees cannot be required to work unless it's stipulated in their employment agreement. In practice, many employees in essential services are required to work on public holidays, for which they're offered additional pay or, more usually, time off in lieu. In some cases, you can take your public holidays on a different day from that on which they occur.

Under the Holidays Act 2003, public holidays over the Christmas (25-26th December) and New Year (1st-2nd January) period come under special regulations. If the holiday falls on a weekend and you don't normally work on the weekend, the holiday is transferred to the following Monday or Tuesday so that you still receive a paid day off. If the holiday falls on a Saturday or Sunday and you usually work on that day, then the holiday remains on the traditional day and you're entitled to that day off with pay.

All other public holidays are celebrated on the day on which they fall. Two public holidays, Waitangi Day and Anzac Day, cannot (by law) be moved and employees cannot be compelled to work on these days. However, when Waitangi Day or Anzac Day fall at the weekend, employees who don't usually work on the weekend have no entitlement to payment for the day.

New Zealand's statutory public holidays are as follows:

Public Holidays	
Date	**Holiday**
1st January	New Year's Day
2nd January	New Year Holiday
6th February	Waitangi Day
Late March/early April	Good Friday
Late March/early April	Easter Monday
25th April	Anzac Day
First Monday in June	Queen's Birthday
Fourth Monday in October	Labour Day
25th December	Christmas Day
26th December	Boxing Day

Each region also has an Anniversary Day, which has the status of an official public holiday in that region.

Pregnancy & Confinement

New Zealand employment legislation provides for an extensive period of parental leave (PPL) for mothers, both before and after the birth of a child. The leave entitlement begins once you've worked for an employer for 12 months and you cannot be dismissed for applying for or taking parental leave. You're eligible for parental leave if you have worked for the same employer for an average of at least 10 hours a week, and at least one hour in every week or 40 hours in every month, in the six or 12 months immediately prior to the baby's expected due date or the date you have assumed the care of a child you intend to adopt. If two spouses/partners assume the care of a child under six years that they intend to jointly adopt, they can nominate which of them is primarily eligible for parental leave.

Parental leave is paid at a maximum of $458.82 per week before tax (from 1st July 2011) for up to 14 weeks, although some mothers (such as the self-employed) don't qualify. However, there's a minimum parental leave payment for the self-employed of $130 per week.

Expectant mothers are entitled to 14 weeks' maternity leave, which can begin up to six weeks before the birth, and are also entitled to ten days special leave during pregnancy for ante-natal care and pregnancy-related illnesses. Fathers (with 12 months eligible service) can take up to two weeks leave around the period of the birth (but aren't entitled to extra time off for pregnancy-related illnesses!). Parents who have worked for an employer for 12 months prior to a birth can take up to 52 weeks (less any PPL taken) job-protected, unpaid, extended leave after a birth, during which the employer is obliged to keep a job open. Extended leave may be shared with your partner.

You can take parental leave multiple times, provided six months elapse between the date you returned to work and the expected date of birth of the subsequent child. You must also meet the eligibility requirements each time.

To encourage more women to return to work after a period of parental leave and help employers retain employees, new employment legislation regarding infant feeding in the workplace became law on 1st April 2009. The new legislation requires employers to provide breaks and facilities for employees who want to breast feed their babies or express milk in the workplace.

For further information, see 🖳 www.ers.dol.govt.nz/parentalleave.

Insurance

Social Security/Insurance

Social security is largely non-contributory in New Zealand, and officially neither employees nor employers make contributions. In practice, however, employees and the self-employed must contribute to the Accident Compensation Corporation (ACC, 🖳 www.acc.co.nz) scheme, which provides compensation in the event of an accident, either at work or elsewhere.

ACC contributions are deducted from salaries, usually via the pay-as-you-earn (PAYE) system, at the rate of $2.04 per $100 of liable earnings up to an earnings limit of $111,669 (2011-2012 – the maximum earnings limit and rate are reviewed annually). For further information see **Chapters 13 & 14**.

It's important to note, however, that receiving any sort of government benefits, which are collectively known as 'government transfers', isn't conditional upon having contributed to the scheme. Unemployment and sickness benefits, for example, are available to all New Zealanders and permanent residents irrespective of their employment history, although there may be other eligibility criteria and means testing.

Health Insurance

Some companies and professional organisations have their own supplementary health insurance schemes that pay for medical expenses, e.g. GP consultation fees, prescription charges and hospital out-patient charges, which aren't covered under the national healthcare system. Some even provide for private medical treatment.

These schemes may be either contributory or non-contributory. In cases where they're non-contributory, they should be considered as part of your salary rather than a 'freebie' from your employer, and the value of the benefits (on which you'll be taxed) depends on the employer's scheme. If the scheme is contributory, it isn't usually obligatory to contribute, although as schemes usually take advantage of bulk insurance rates it's unlikely that you would be able to purchase similar cover for less independently. For more information, see **Chapter 13**.

Health & Safety

No Smoking Rules

Since 10th December 2004, all New Zealand workplaces (including bars, casinos and restaurants) have been smoke-free. As a result, it's common to see groups of furtive-looking people gathering around workplace entrances for the mid-morning or mid-afternoon 'smoko'. No-smoking rules are taken seriously and you may be asked whether you smoke when applying for a job and be discriminated against if you answer 'yes' (although not officially).

New Zealand used to have a poor health and safety record and on average, according to union statistics, some 700 workers were injured and two died at work every week – one of the highest rates in the developed world. Additionally, it's calculated that eight people died each week from work-related ill health and disease. In 2001, there was a high-profile union campaign for a new health and safety law in the workplace, which resulted in health and safety law changes in 2002, primarily the election and training of nearly 20,000 workplace health and safety representatives whose job is to notify employers of any unsafe machinery or work procedures.

Although workplace fatalities initially fell, they rose by 40 per cent in summer 2005-06, half of which were the result of vehicle rollover, crush injuries and falls.

Part-time Job Restrictions

There may be a clause in your employment agreement to the effect that you cannot work part-time or on a freelance basis for a company in the same line of business as your employer. However, there isn't usually a restriction on taking other kinds of part-time work.

Retirement & Pensions

There's no obligatory national retirement age in New Zealand, although the usual retirement age is 65 for both men and women. However, employees may retire earlier or later, and it's illegal for an employer to force an employee to retire because of his or her age. You should, therefore, check your employment agreement to see at what age you'll be expected to retire. It isn't unusual for people to go on working after they reach 65, particularly in family businesses or small companies.

Many employers offer either a contributory or non-contributory pension scheme, which provides you with an additional private pension upon retirement. It isn't obligatory to join, although schemes usually offer a good deal that's difficult to match when buying the same pension independently. See **Chapter 13** for more information.

Union Membership

There are numerous trade unions in New Zealand, most of which are members of the Council of Trade Unions (☎ 0800-186 466, 🖳 http://union.org.nz) which presents (or at least attempts to) a united front to the government on employment issues. Union power and influence has declined considerably in recent decades, particularly since the Employment Contracts Act took away a union's right to negotiate the terms and conditions of employment on behalf of its members. Membership of trade unions is currently around

350,000, compared with a peak of 700,000 in the early '80s. Unions remain strongest in the older industries, such as engineering and manufacturing, but have little influence in the newer service industries.

Employees have a right to choose to join or not join a union, which union to join and whether to resign from a union. It's illegal for anyone to use undue influence to try to make someone join or not join a union, or to resign from a union. Under New Zealand law, trade unions are permitted to organise on any company's premises, although closed shops are banned and unions must be registered with the Department of Labour and be democratic. Trade unions are permitted to negotiate employees' working conditions only when authorised to do so. Employers must recognise unions, but aren't obliged to negotiate or settle with them, although most do so where unions are active. Employers *are*, however, obliged to negotiate and settle with individual employees.

Dismissal, Redundancy & Disputes

The circumstances under which you can be dismissed are specified in your employment agreement and include absenteeism, embezzlement and incompetence. Under the Employment Relations Act of 2000, a new Mediation Service was formed within the Department of Labour consisting of around 40 mediators, who can be contacted by employers and/or employees at any time and will travel to a workplace to mediate *in situ*. In the first six months of operation, mediators dealt with some 2,000 cases and resolved nearly 80 per cent of them successfully.

Problems that cannot be resolved by mediation are referred to the Employment Relations Service (💻 www.ers.dol.govt.nz/problem), whose aim is to resolve disputes in a 'speedy, informal and non-adversarial' way. More serious issues, together with appeals against the decision of the Employment Relations Service, are heard by the Employment Court. Employees generally have no right to redundancy compensation, but this can be negotiated at any time, including after notification of impending redundancy.

In New Zealand you have no right to strike except in a few situations, which include to support bargaining for a collective agreement and at least 40 days after bargaining has started. However, employees who fail to work under the terms agreed with their employer (e.g. by initiating a go-slow or a work-to-rule) can be 'locked out', i.e. prevented from working without formally being dismissed, which is what happens in many industrial disputes in New Zealand.

An employer must have a genuine work-related reason for a redundancy and cannot make you redundant because of concerns about you personally (such as your performance). Your employer cannot decide to make your position redundant until he has consulted with you and your employment agreement should have a process to be followed in redundancy situations. Employers are required to give appropriate notice about any redundancy proposal, be open-minded regarding alternatives to redundancy (such as redeployment), and offer counselling and career advice services.

Generally, you have no right to redundancy compensation unless your employer and you and/or your union have agreed to it. This can be done before or after a redundancy is planned. It's also up to the parties to decide what any redundancy compensation should be. However, in some restructuring situations, employees can ask the Employment Relations Authority to decide what redundancy entitlements they should receive.

CHECKLISTS

When negotiating your terms of employment for a job in New Zealand, the checklists on the following pages will prove useful. The points listed under **General Positions** apply to most jobs, while those listed under **Executive Positions** usually apply to executive and senior managerial appointments only.

General Positions

Salary

◆ Is the salary adequate, taking into account the cost of living? Is it index-linked?

◆ When and how often is the salary reviewed?

◆ Is the total salary (including expenses) paid in New Zealand dollars or in a different currency, with expenses for living in New Zealand?

◆ Does the salary include an annual or end-of-contract bonus?

◆ Is overtime paid or time off given in lieu of extra hours worked?

Relocation Expenses

◆ Are removal expenses or a relocation allowance paid?

◆ Does the allowance include travelling expenses for all family members? Is there a limit and is it adequate?

◆ Are you required to repay the relocation expenses (or a percentage) if you resign before a certain period has elapsed?

◆ Are you required to pay for your relocation in advance? This can run into thousands of dollars for normal house contents.

◆ If employment is for a limited period only, will your relocation costs be paid by the employer when you leave New Zealand?

◆ If you aren't shipping household goods and furniture to New Zealand, is there an allowance for buying furnishings locally?

◆ Do relocation expenses include the legal and agent's fees incurred when moving?

◆ Does the employer use the services of a relocation consultant (see page 81)?

Accommodation

◆ Does the employer pay for a hotel or pay a lodging allowance until you find permanent accommodation?

◆ Is subsidised or free temporary or permanent accommodation provided? If so, is it furnished or unfurnished?

◆ Must you pay for utilities such as electricity, gas and water?

◆ If accommodation isn't provided by the employer, is assistance provided to find suitable accommodation? If so, what sort of assistance?

◆ What does accommodation cost?

◆ Are your expenses paid while you're looking for accommodation?

Working Hours

◆ What are the weekly working hours?

◆ Does the employer operate a flexible working system?

◆ Are you required to clock in and out of work?

◆ Can you choose whether to take time off in lieu of overtime or be paid for it?

Leave Entitlement

◆ What is the annual leave entitlement? Does it increase with length of service?

◆ What are the paid public holidays? Must you take them on the due day or can they be 'moved' to another day, either at your or the employer's request?

◆ Is free air travel to your home country or elsewhere provided for you and your family; if so, how often?

Insurance

◆ Is extra insurance cover provided besides obligatory insurance (see **Chapter 13**)?

◆ Is free life assurance provided?

◆ Is free or subsidised health insurance provided for your family?

◆ For how long is your salary paid if you're sick or have an accident?

Company Pension

◆ Is there a company pension scheme and if so what percentage of your salary must you pay into it?

◆ Are you required or able to pay a lump sum into the pension fund in order to receive a full or higher pension?

◆ Is the pension transferable to another employer?

Employer

◆ What are the employer's or industry's long-term prospects?

◆ Does the employer have a good reputation?

◆ Does the employer have a high staff turnover?

Other Terms

◆ Is a travel allowance (or public transport) paid from your home to your place of work?

◆ Is free or subsidised parking provided at your place of work?

◆ Is a free or subsidised company canteen or restaurant provided? If not, is an allowance paid or are luncheon vouchers provided?

◆ Does the employer provide or pay for professional training or education, either in New Zealand or abroad?

◆ Are free work clothes or overalls provided? Does the employer pay for the cleaning of work clothes?

◆ Does the employer provide any fringe benefits, such as subsidised banking services, low interest loans, inexpensive petrol, employees' shop or product discounts, sports and social facilities, and subsidised tickets to local events?

◆ Do you have a written list of your job responsibilities?

◆ Have your employment conditions been confirmed in writing?

◆ If a dispute arises over your salary or working conditions, under the law of which country will your employment agreement be interpreted?

Executive & Managerial Positions

The following points generally apply to executive and top managerial positions only:

◆ Is private schooling for your children paid for or subsidised? Does your employer pay for a boarding school in New Zealand or abroad?

◆ Is your salary index-linked and protected against devaluation? This is particularly important if you're paid in a foreign currency that fluctuates wildly or could be devalued. Are you paid an overseas allowance for working in New Zealand?

◆ Is there a non-contributory pension fund? Is it transferable and, if so, what are the conditions?

◆ Are the costs incurred by a move to New Zealand reimbursed? For example, the cost of selling your home, employing an agent to let it for you or storing household effects.

◆ Does your employer pay for domestic help or towards the cost of it?

◆ Is a company car provided? With a driver?

◆ Are you entitled to any miscellaneous benefits, such as membership of a social or sports club or company credit cards?

◆ Is there an entertainment allowance?

◆ Is there a clothing allowance? For example, if you arrive in New Zealand in the winter you could find it distinctly chilly, particularly in the south.

Is compensation paid if you're laid off or fired? Standard redundancy or severance payments are usually quite small, but executives often receive a generous 'golden handshake' if they're made redundant, e.g. after a take-over.

3.

VISAS

Before making any plans to live or work in New Zealand, you must ensure that you have a valid passport and the appropriate visa. Nationals of Australia can live and work in New Zealand with no more official documentation than their passport. Most other nationalities must apply for permission to stay in New Zealand, either temporarily or permanently, *before* their arrival. New Zealand makes a distinction between those staying temporarily, who must apply for a visa (with the exception of visa-free visitors), and those wishing to stay permanently, who must apply for residence.

Although New Zealand is a land of immigrants (some 85 per cent of its population are descended from Europeans, most of whom came to the country within the last 150 years), immigration is a contentious issue. Some people wish to increase it (they claim that the South Island could continue to absorb immigrants almost indefinitely) while others wish to cut it sharply (they obviously wish to keep New Zealand's many delights to themselves). This can result in confusing messages being sent to prospective migrants.

In fact, New Zealand currently has a negative balance of migration, i.e. emigration is higher than immigration, and immigrants of the 'right type' are welcomed, indeed encouraged; in the words of the official literature, the country wants people who 'will contribute to New Zealand by bringing valuable skills or qualifications to the country, setting up a business or making a financial investment'. New Zealanders generally feel that there's a need to diversify the country's skills in order to maintain international competitiveness, and one of the ways of doing this is to attract skilled immigrants.

Most people believe that immigration brings significant benefits for the country and stimulates economic growth – migrants bring $billions into New Zealand each year, to say nothing of the wealth they create – and it would be impossible to sustain the economy without the skills, investment and international connections that migrants bring. The major political parties are strongly in favour, but there are a number of 'fringe' parties that are opposed to immigration (particularly from Asia) on economic, social and cultural grounds.

If you plan to migrate to New Zealand, you should 'intend to live there for a long time, be able to adapt to New Zealand's lifestyle, obey New Zealand's laws and be of good character'. In the past, the government took a rather lax approach to immigration, but procedures have become more rigorous in the last decade and illegal immigration and overstaying are taken much more seriously than previously.

Immigration is a complex subject and the rules are constantly changing. You shouldn't base any decisions or actions on the information contained in this book without confirming it with an official and reliable source, such as Immigration New Zealand (see below) or The Emigration Group (see inside the front cover and opposite the back cover). Residence regulations are taken seriously by the authorities and if your application isn't in order it can result in rejection.

The authority responsible for controlling entry to New Zealand is Immigration New Zealand (INZ, 🖳 www.immigration.govt.nz) or *Te Ratonga Manene* in Maori, a service of the Department of Labour.

INZ has had a lot of criticism in recent years and has been dogged by claims of incompetence and even corruption. There have been numerous reports of applications being refused for arbitrary reasons, unacceptable delays in processing, lost passports, endless requests for information and extra fees that seem to make little or no sense. Partly in response to this, the National Party government elected in 2008 replaced the 1987 Act with a new Immigration Act in 2009 (see below).

A list of INZ offices, branches and agencies in New Zealand and worldwide can be found on the INZ website, and New Zealand embassies, consulates and high commissions (see **Appendix A** for a list) also provide information about immigration.

Immigration Act 2009

The Immigration Act 2009 came into effect on the 29th November 2010 and is intended to modernise New Zealand's immigration laws, enhance border security and improve the efficiency of immigration services. However, it doesn't make major changes to the criteria under which people apply to travel to and stay in New Zealand. Key aspects of the new Act include the ability to use biometrics, a new refugee and protection system, a single independent appeals tribunal and a universal visa system.

The new Act uses the single term 'visa' for authority to travel to and stay in New Zealand. The terms 'permit' and 'exemption' are no longer used. The terms 'residence permits', 'residence visas' and 'returning resident's visas' have been replaced by 'resident visas' and 'permanent resident visas'. However, there's no change to the existing categories or criteria for people wishing to settle in New Zealand.

The deportation process has been simplified to better balance efficiency with fairness. The terms 'removal' and 'revocation' are longer used, and instead, the single term 'deportation' is used. People who are deported are prohibited from re-entering New Zealand

for two years, five years or permanently, depending on the seriousness of the offence.

The Immigration Act 2009 introduced 'Interim visas', which took effect from 7th February 2011. They may be granted to maintain a person's lawful status in New Zealand, where someone holds a valid temporary visa and has applied for a further temporary visa. The aim is to benefit visitors, foreign students and workers who wish to extend their stay in New Zealand.

Immigration Advisers

The Immigration Advisers Authority (IAA, 💻 www.iaa.govt.nz) was established in 2007 to promote and protect the interests of those receiving immigration advice and to enhance the reputation of New Zealand as a migration destination. The IAA is responsible for the regulation of the immigration advice industry (although it doesn't provide immigration advice itself) through the introduction of mandatory licensing for immigration advisers, which is designed to protect migrants from unscrupulous operators and provide support for licensed advisers. Since 4th May 2009, it has been mandatory for immigration advisers practising in New Zealand to be licensed and from 4th May 2010 overseas immigration advisers also.

If you use an immigration adviser the fees can be anything from $5,000 to well over $10,000 depending on the complexity of your application, how many people are involved and the services required. For

additional information, contact the New Zealand Association of Migration and Investment (NZAMI, 🖳 www.nzami.org.nz), the professional association for migration advisors.

VISITORS' VISAS

If you plan to visit New Zealand for a short period, e.g. for a holiday, business trip or to evaluate the country before applying for residence, you must apply for a visitor's visa, if applicable. Australian citizens (and those who hold a current Australian permanent residence visa or an Australian resident return visa) don't require a visa to visit New Zealand. Nationals of certain countries (see below) qualify under a 'visa waiver' scheme, which allows them to travel to New Zealand without a visitor's visa and obtain a visa on arrival.

Countries that qualify under the visa waiver scheme include Andorra, Argentina, Austria, Bahrain, Belgium, Brazil, Brunei, Bulgaria, Canada, Chile, Cyprus, Czech Republic, Denmark, Estonia. Finland, France, Germany, Greece, Hong Kong, Hungary, Iceland, Ireland, Israel, Italy, Japan, Korea (South), Kuwait, Latvia, Liechtenstein, Lithuania, Luxembourg, Malaysia, Malta, Mexico, Monaco, the Netherlands, Norway, Oman, Poland, Portugal, Qatar, Romania, San Marino, Saudi Arabia, Singapore, Slovak Republic, Slovenia, South Africa, Spain, Sweden, Switzerland, the United Arab Emirates (UAE), the UK, Uruguay, the USA (except for nationals from American Samoa and Swains Island) and the Vatican City.

> Anyone from a country that doesn't qualify under the 'visa waiver' scheme needs a visitor's visa to travel to New Zealand and won't even be permitted to board a plane without one.

A visitor's visa is usually an endorsement in your passport that allows you to travel to New Zealand, although it may now be issued electronically (see **Electronic Visas** below). A visa may be for a single or multiple journeys, but doesn't necessarily allow you to remain in the country. Those who travel to New Zealand with a visa or visa waiver must complete an arrival card on their outgoing journey, which serves as an application for a visitor visa, which is processed on arrival. A visitor visa allows you to stay for a short period (usually three months, or six months if you're a UK citizen) as a tourist, to see friends or relatives, study, take part in sporting and cultural events, undertake a business trip or undergo medical treatment. It doesn't state on the visa that you may use it to look for a job or visit New Zealand with a view to living there, although many people use it for this purpose (and it's perfectly legitimate).

You must have a valid return ticket, sufficient money to support yourself (usually around $1,000 per month or $400 if staying with friends or relatives) and a passport valid for three months beyond the date you intend to leave New Zealand – and you must intend to stay in New Zealand for no longer than the period of your visa. If you comply with these requirements, you may travel to New Zealand and should be granted a visitor visa on arrival. Visitors may stay for a maximum of nine months (which can be made up of a number of shorter periods) in an 18-month period. Once you've reached the maximum, you're required to remain abroad for nine months before returning to New Zealand as a visitor. Visitor visas can be extended by a further three months on application to the INZ, although this is at their discretion and you're required to be able to support yourself financially without working.

You can be refused a visitor visa if you don't meet the above requirements or are someone to whom section 15 or 16 of the Immigration Act 2009 applies. This includes those who:

◆ have been deported from any country;

◆ are the subject of a New Zealand 'removal order';

◆ have committed a criminal offence which resulted in imprisonment of 12 months or longer;

◆ are believed to have criminal associations or are suspected of constituting a danger to New Zealand's security or public order.

The above restrictions also apply to Australians, who don't need a visa to visit New Zealand.

Visitor's visas can be applied for at INZ offices and New Zealand diplomatic missions. Like Australia, New Zealand operates a system whereby applications for visas in major cities such as London and New York can be cleared almost instantly via an electronic link with the INZ computer in New Zealand (see **Electronic Visas** below).

Fees are usually charged for visas and vary depending on the country where you apply, but are usually $140. They must be paid for in local currency and aren't refundable, even if a visa isn't granted.

Note that as a visitor to New Zealand, you aren't entitled to use publicly funded health services unless you're a resident or a citizen of Australia or a UK national, or hold a residence visa valid for at least two years, e.g. a long-term business visa. Unless you belong to one of these categories, it's strongly recommended that you have comprehensive medical insurance for the duration of your visit (see **Chapter 13**).

Electronic Visas

In recent years New Zealand has introduced electronic visas. These function in exactly the same way as a visa issued in a passport, except that instead of it being a label or stamp in the passport it's a separate printed document, which the applicant keeps with their passport.

When your application is approved, the details are retained electronically in the INZ database, which is used to determine your eligibility to board a flight to come to (or return to) New Zealand. This information is also used to determine your eligibility to enter New Zealand when you arrive there. It's therefore essential that you keep a printed copy of your electronic visa with your passport, and that when you complete an online application you enter your details correctly. The name, date of birth, and passport number in your passport must be the same as those on your application.

SPECIAL VISITOR CATEGORIES

Certain categories of visitors to New Zealand may require special visas or must meet certain conditions when visiting the country. These include the following:

Business Visitors

If you intend to visit New Zealand to discuss and negotiate business deals and plan to stay no longer than three months in a calendar year, you need only a standard visitor's visa (if applicable) and must meet the normal requirements. A visitor visa allows you to undertake business discussions and negotiations, although it doesn't permit you to work in an employed or self-employed capacity.

Conference Delegates

If you're attending a conference in New Zealand, you should check with the organiser to see whether arrangements have been made for conference cards to replace visitors' visas.

Group Visitors

If you're travelling in a group, e.g. as an organised tour or part of an educational exchange, the group may be eligible for a group visa. To qualify, all members of the group must be travelling for the same purpose, have the same travel arrangements and have a leader who's responsible for travel, visa and arrival arrangements.

Medical Treatment

If you're travelling to New Zealand for medical treatment or consultation, you must apply for a visitor's visa and complete a 'Details of Intended Medical Treatment' form (INZ 1009). If this isn't possible (e.g. in an emergency), you should contact the INZ, who may be able to make special arrangements for you. Note that, unless you're a citizen of a country with which New Zealand has reciprocal agreements (e.g. Australia and the UK) or hold a visa valid for two years or more (e.g. a long-term business visa), you aren't entitled to receive publicly-funded medical treatment in New Zealand and must pay the full cost yourself.

Occupational Registration

If you've applied for residence and require New Zealand registration to work in your profession, you may undertake practical or educational training for up to three months with a visitor's visa. If you need more time to obtain your registration, you must apply for either a student or work visa before travelling to New Zealand (see below).

Single Parents

A single parent travelling with a child must provide evidence (e.g. custody or guardianship papers) that the child has the right to leave his country of residence.

TRANSIT VISAS

Those from certain countries wishing to pass through New Zealand on their way to another country (except Australia) require a transit visa. The exceptions are those from a visa-waiver country (see above) and those listed on the INZ website (see 🖳 www.immigration.govt. nz/migrant/stream/visit/transit). All nationals of other countries require a transit visa (fee $130).

This allows you to stay in New Zealand for up to 24 hours, provided you remain within the transit area of the airport. If you wish to stay for longer than 24 hours and/or leave the transit area of the airport, you need a visitor's visa (see above).

WORKING HOLIDAY VISAS

The working holiday scheme allows young people aged 18 to 30 to look for seasonal, temporary and casual employment in New Zealand, particularly in the areas of agriculture, horticulture and viticulture. The working holiday scheme applies to the following countries: Argentina, Belgium, Brazil, Canada, Chile, China, Czech Republic, Denmark, Estonia, Finland, France, Germany, Hong Kong, Ireland, Italy, Japan, Korea, Latvia, Malaysia, Malta, Mexico, the Netherlands, Norway, Peru, Poland, Singapore, Slovenia, Sweden, Taiwan, Thailand, Turkey, the UK, the USA and Uruguay.

Applicants cannot be accompanied by children and must provide evidence of sufficient funds to purchase return travel and meet the conditions of the scheme they apply under; they don't need an offer of employment and can take any casual job on arrival. You must usually apply for the visa (fee $140) from your local New Zealand consulate or high commission before arriving in New Zealand, although applicants from certain countries can apply at an INZ branch in New Zealand. Applicants from Argentina, Chile, China, Taiwan and Uruguay must apply online, while those from Peru must lodge a manual application. All others may apply online or manually. All applicants applying for a 12-month visa in New Zealand require a medical and X-ray certificate, but those applying outside of the country don't (this also usually applies to whose visa is valid for less than six months).

The number of visas available to many countries is restricted and you usually need to apply well in advance, e.g. in autumn of the year before the one in which you plan to work. There are unlimited places available for applicants from Belgium, Canada, Denmark, Finland, France, Germany, Ireland, Italy, Japan, the Netherlands, Norway, Sweden, the UK and the US. For details of each scheme and the number of places available, see 🖳 www.immigration.govt.nz/migrant/stream/work/workingholiday.

The maximum stay is usually 12 months, although those from the UK can stay for up to 23 months. If you apply for a 23-month visa from outside New Zealand, a medical and X-ray certificate is required (but not for a 12-month visa).

Applicants must hold a return ticket or sufficient funds to buy a ticket, and also have a minimum of around $400 per month in available funds to meet their living costs for three months in New Zealand.

Working holiday schemes usually operate on a reciprocal basis, therefore young New Zealanders will benefit from similar schemes when they travel overseas.

See also **Silver Fern Visas** below.

TEMPORARY WORK VISAS

A work visa allows you to travel to New Zealand to undertake a period of temporary work. It isn't usually applicable to those intending to take up residence (see **Residence** below) in the country and applies mostly to contract workers and other short-term employees. Work visas are granted to foreigners only when no suitable New Zealand citizen or resident is available to do a job. Their issue isn't based on a points system and each case is treated on its merits, taking into account the availability of local labour.

The Immediate Skill Shortage List (ISSL) – see below – is used by INZ in relation to temporary work policy. It determines those occupations for which there's a current shortage of skilled workers and helps the Immigration Department to streamline your application for a temporary or short-term work visa.

To obtain a work visa you must have a firm offer of a job in writing and apply to INZ, which can be done from abroad or within New Zealand (if, for example, you arrive as a visitor and then wish to work). The visa fee is between $200 (online) and $230 (depending on where it's issued) and isn't refundable, even if your application is rejected. You'll be issued with a work visa, which applies only to one job for a specified period, usually a maximum of three years (but is often for a much shorter period).

For further information, see the INZ website (www.immigration.govt.nz).

Essential Skills in Demand List

Immigration New Zealand maintains an Essential Skills in Demand List, which comprises the Long Term Skill Shortage List (LTSSL) and the Immediate Skill Shortage List (ISSL). The lists help prospective migrants to determine which visa entry category is most applicable, based on their experience and skills relevant to particular industries and regions. Qualifying for a job on the ISSL or LTSSL enables migrants and their employers to avoid having to prove that there are no New Zealanders available to take the job. You can search the list via the INZ website (www. immigration.govt.nz).

The ISSL is used by Immigration New Zealand to identify those occupations for which there's a current shortage of skilled workers. In contrast, the LTSSL is used for both temporary work policy and residence policy, and is designed to identify occupations for which there's an absolute and ongoing shortage of skilled workers. Migrants entering New Zealand under LTSSL requirements may be eligible for residency under either the Work to Residence (see below) scheme or the Skilled Migrant Category.

The Essential Skills in Demand List is reviewed twice yearly by INZ, which can result in occupations being added or removed from the list, as well as changes to the qualifications or experience required for a particular occupation.

The lists aren't the only options for skilled migrants to enter and work in New Zealand. If your occupation isn't listed, you can still apply for a temporary work visa, although a prospective employer is required to show that they've genuinely searched for suitably qualified and trained resident workers. Alternatively, an employer with approval in principle may be able to conditionally recruit employees from overseas, with approval required prior to the visa application.

Work to Residence

Working temporarily in New Zealand can be used as a step towards gaining residence and settling there permanently after two years. If your talents are in demand or you have exceptional talent in the arts, culture or sports, you can apply to work in New Zealand under the Work to Residence category.

> ⚠ **Caution**
>
> If you have a temporary 'work to residence' visa and you lose your job, you could lose your right to live in New Zealand – and you may have no right to change jobs, even if another one is offered!

There are a number of requirements that you'll need to meet to obtain a visa under the Work to Residence category. As well as meeting the requirements for all applicants, you must meet the requirements of the policy under which you're applying for a Work to Residence visa. Which policy you apply under depends on your occupation and your circumstances. The fee for a Work to Residence visa is $310.

If you have a job offer from a New Zealand employer, the policy that you apply under depends on whether your occupation is on the Long Term Skill Shortage List (LTSSL – see above). If your occupation is on the LTSSL, you may be eligible to apply under the LTSSL work policy for people with skills that are in demand. If you're successful you're issued with a work visa valid for up to 30 months. When you've worked in New Zealand in an occupation on the LTSSL for two years, you can apply for residence.

If you have a job offer from a New Zealand employer but your occupation isn't on the LTSSL, you may be able to apply under the Talent (Accredited Employers) work policy, which is for people who have job offers from employers who are accredited to recruit staff from overseas. There's also a Talent (Arts, Culture and Sports) work policy for those with recognised talents and abilities in the arts, culture or sports fields, who it's deemed will enhance the country's reputation. Finally, you can qualify for a Work to Residence visa under the Long Term Business Visa category (see below), for those who want to establish a business in New Zealand as a step to gaining residence.

Silver Fern Visa

The Silver Fern visa is a new category of 'work to residence' visas introduced on 27th April 2010, which provides 300 visas annually to highly-skilled overseas workers aged between 20 and 35. The purpose of the visa is to broaden the options for young people to make a long-term contribution to New Zealand, and to provide a pathway to permanent residence. The visa is a combination of two policies; the Silver Fern Job Search and Silver Fern Practical Experience.

The Silver Fern Job Search policy allows successful applicants to enter New Zealand for nine months to search for skilled employment. To be eligible you must be outside of New Zealand when applying, be aged between 20 and 35, meet the qualifications' (which must have been obtained in a visa-waiver country – see **Visitors' Visas** on page 57) and language requirements, and have sufficient funds to support yourself during your stay. Once you have found employment, you're permitted to work in New Zealand for up to two years, after which you can apply for permanent residence.

Silver Fern visas have proved very popular – in 2010 the quota was filled in just 30 minutes after the application window opened at 10am! The application process and payment is done online.

For more information, see the INZ website (🖳 www.immigration.govt.nz/migrant/stream/work/silverfern).

Long Term Business Visa

If you wish to move to New Zealand to establish a business, you need to apply for a long term business visa. To be eligible for a long term business visa, there are a number of conditions you need to meet before you arrive, including:

◆ be in good health and of good character;

◆ have a reasonable standard of English;

◆ have a sound business plan;

♦ provide evidence that you have sufficient money, in addition to your investment funds, to support yourself and any partner or children coming with you;

♦ have the right visa for your visit.

If you're accepted, you're granted a work visa that expires after nine months, which is to allow you time to take steps to establish your business. Before the nine months have expired you can apply for a further work visa to extend your stay up to a total of three years. To gain a further visa, you need to show that you're making reasonable progress in setting up your business. This may include:

♦ a certificate of incorporation or other documents that provide evidence of the business' constitution;

♦ audited accounts;

♦ GST records;

♦ other tax records;

♦ documents showing property lease or purchase by the business;

♦ invoices for business equipment and supplies;

♦ other documents such as employment agreements, bank statements, and invoices from phone and power companies.

After two years operating or owning a business in New Zealand, you can apply for residence under the entrepreneur category (see page 67).

Note that a long-term business visa is one of the most expensive, costing $2,800 for most applicants, therefore you need to ensure that you qualify before making an application.

STUDENT VISAS

Those wishing to study in New Zealand on a course longer than three months require a student visa. Like a work visa (see above), this is a temporary visa and applicable only for the course and duration to which it relates. Before applying for a student visa, you must have an offer of a place from a New

Zealand educational institution confirmed in writing. You must also have paid the course fees or have proof that you're able to do so, and have evidence of sufficient funds to support yourself during your course of study.

Sufficient funds usually means at least $1,000 per month (or $400 if your accommodation is already paid for) for short courses and a minimum of $10,000 per year for longer courses. This doesn't mean that you'll be able to live on this sum and you'll almost certainly require more. If you don't have the money yourself, it's acceptable to be sponsored by someone (either in New Zealand or abroad), but you need to provide evidence of sponsorship.

A student visa costs $80 for an online application via an education provider or between $170 and $230, depending on where the application is made.

A student visa allows you to work to supplement your funds only if you have a long-term study course and work for no more than 15 hours per week or during the Christmas period. However, if you can find a suitable job, you can apply for a work visa on the same terms as any other non-resident (see **Temporary Work Visas** above). If a period of work experience is part of your course, then INZ will usually grant a work visa for that purpose.

RESIDENCE

Applying for residence means seeking the right to live and work in New Zealand permanently. Under the Immigration Act 2009, anybody who wishes to immigrate to New Zealand must apply for residence, which entitles you to live, study or work indefinitely in New Zealand. The only foreigners this doesn't apply to are Australian citizens, who need only produce their passports when entering New Zealand, although they're subject to the same good character requirements as other visitors. Applications for residence are assessed by INZ, which must adhere to the government's immigration policy and isn't allowed to 'bend' the rules or make exceptions. If your application is refused, you can appeal to the Independent Residence Appeal Authority. All applicants for residence must provide the information and documentation necessary to meet the current regulations. Most people apply for residence from outside New Zealand, although it's sometimes possible to apply for residence from within the country, provided you're there legally.

A residence visa is usually issued outside New Zealand and allows the holder to travel to New Zealand (if the holder is offshore), an indefinite stay in New Zealand, and multiple re-entry to New Zealand within the validity of the resident visa travel conditions.

The immigration Act 2009 introduced the following residence class visas;

♦ Resident visas – which may be subject to conditions.

♦ Permanent resident visas – which have no conditions.

Residence Visa with Conditions

In most cases, applicants who are approved residence are granted a 'resident visa' with two years of 'travel conditions' that allow the holder to:

♦ Travel to New Zealand (if they are overseas when their visa is granted).

♦ Stay in New Zealand indefinitely.

♦ Re-enter New Zealand before the expiry date of the 'travel conditions'.

A resident visa holder may also be subject to other 'conditions' depending on the residence category they applied under. For example, those approved under the Investor Category are required to invest a certain amount of money in New Zealand and maintain this investment for a certain period. This is referred to as a 'condition on the visa'.

A resident visa holder who wishes to leave New Zealand and return after the expiry date of their travel conditions should obtain one of the following **before** leaving New Zealand:

♦ A 'variation of travel conditions' – this extends the expiry date of the travel conditions, or, if eligible

♦ A 'permanent resident visa' – this allows you to re-enter New Zealand at any time.

If a resident visa holder is **outside** New Zealand when their travel conditions expire, they need to apply for a 'second or subsequent resident visa' if they wish to return to New Zealand as a resident. This is a new type of application that allows their residence status to be reinstated.

Permanent Resident Visa

A permanent resident visa allows the holder to re-enter New Zealand as a permanent resident anytime and isn't subject to any conditions. To obtain a permanent resident visa, a resident visa holder must have:

♦ been a resident in New Zealand for at least two years;

♦ met all the conditions of their resident visa;

♦ met the 'commitment to New Zealand' requirements.

Most people who are eligible are initially granted a resident visa then progress to a permanent resident visa by making another application after they meet the commitment to New Zealand criteria. However, new policy settings enable a small number of residence applicants to progress directly to a permanent resident visa. These are:

♦ foreign national partners of New Zealand citizens (and the partner's dependent children) where:

- a New Zealand citizen who has been living overseas for at least five years, or has been in New Zealand for three months or less after living overseas for at least five years, **and**

- the partnership has been ongoing for at least five years.

♦ people who were granted a temporary work visa under the Talent (Accredited Employers) Work category who have a job with a salary of at least NZ$90,000 gross per annum at the time they apply for residence under the corresponding Residence from Work category, and

♦ refugees and protected people.

Health Requirements

In order to secure residence you must demonstrate that you and any family members coming with you are healthy. This is to safeguard the health of New Zealanders and to avoid placing a burden on the country's health and social services. Your Expression of Interest (EOI, see **Skilled Migrant Category** on page 67) won't be submitted to the pool if:

♦ there's any likelihood that you'll need dialysis treatment;

♦ you have active tuberculosis;

♦ you have required hospital or residential care for a mental disorder or intellectual disability for more than 90 days in the previous two years;

♦ you have a physical incapacity that requires full-time care.

If you're invited to apply for residence, you must have a medical assessment by a doctor and complete medical and chest x-ray certificates (INZ 1007) for each member of your family coming to New Zealand. All certificates must be less than three months old when you

lodge your application. Pregnant women and children under 11 aren't required to submit x-ray certificates unless a special report is required.

In some countries, INZ has a selected panel of doctors and medical institutions which you must use for the medical examination (there's a full list on their website, 🖥 www.immigration. govt.nz). You must meet the costs of any examinations and tests – if you're in New Zealand the costs aren't covered by the health service.

Full details of health requirements are provided in a leaflet *Health Requirements* (INZ 1121).

Character Requirements

You and any family members included in your application must be of good character. Your EOI won't be entered into the pool if you:

♦ have been convicted and sentenced to a prison term of five years or more;

♦ have been convicted and sentenced to a prison term of 12 months or more in the past ten years;

♦ have been deported from New Zealand or any other country;

♦ are believed to have associated with criminal or terrorist groups or are in any way a danger to New Zealand.

If you're invited to apply for residence, you must provide police certificates as evidence of your good character. Certificates are required for everybody aged 17 and over included in the application. Certificates are needed from:

♦ your country of citizenship (unless you can demonstrate that you have never lived there);

♦ any country you have lived in for 12 months or more in the last ten years, whether in one or more visits.

English Language Requirements

New Zealand's two official languages are English and Maori (*Te Reo Maori*). English is the more common language and all prospective residents must have a good level of English before applying or state that they intend to pre-purchase English language training. This requirement isn't just to allow you to find and perform work, but so that you can integrate into New Zealand society. You're exempt if you've been working lawfully in New Zealand for a minimum of 12 months and have used English in your job before lodging a residence application. Acceptable evidence of a good level of English includes the following:

♦ a certificate from the International English Language Testing System (IELTS), which must be no more than two years old at the time of application, showing that you have an 'Overall Band' score of five or more in the IELTS General or Academic Module;

♦ a certificate of completion of primary education and a minimum of three years' secondary education in English;

♦ a certificate showing completion of at least five years' secondary education in English;

♦ evidence that you've previously lived in an English-speaking country (including the duration);

♦ evidence that you've used English in your current or previous employment.

A full list of acceptable evidence is included in the *Guide to Applying for Residence in New Zealand* available from INZ.

Principal applicants may be required to produce an IELTS certificate, even if they've provided evidence of an English-speaking background or circumstances. Principal applicants in the Skilled/Business category who don't meet the minimum standard of English will be refused unless they've been working lawfully in New Zealand for the 12 months prior to the date of application, they meet all other residence requirements and pre-purchase English language tuition (see below). Principal applicants under the business categories, and accompanying family members aged 16 and over who are included in the application, must also meet the specified standard of English or pre-purchase English language tuition.

The amount of English language (ESOL) tuition you need to pre-purchase is determined by your score in the IELTS Test Report Form. ESOL tuition must be pre-purchased from Skill New Zealand (National Office, 3rd Floor, 34-42 Manners Street, PO Box 27-048, Wellington, ☎ 04-801 5588, 💻 www.skillnz.org.nz) and the necessary fee paid to INZ. If your application is approved but you need to purchase ESOL tuition, INZ will advise you of the amount payable. You then have six months to pay the tuition fee, and your residence visa won't be issued until it's paid. Note that failure to pre-purchase ESOL tuition on time may mean that your application is refused.

Fees & Finance

A range of fees are levied by INZ for processing residence applications and registrations, a selection of which is shown

Residence Fees			
Type of Application	**Fee (NZ$)**		
	NZ	**Pacific/ Australia**	**Other**
Skilled Migrant EOI* paper form	$560	$560	$560
Skilled Migrant EOI* online	$440	$440	$440
Investor Category EOI* paper form	$510	$510	$510
Skilled Migrant Residence Visa/Permit	$1,550	$1,350	$2,050
Business Investor Residence Visa/Permit	$3,500	$3,400	$3,400
Family Visa/Permit	$790	$790	$1,350
* EOI = expression of interest			

below (a complete list is provided on the INZ website).

Fees must be paid in the local currency of the country in which your application is lodged. The accepted methods of payment vary from country to country, to reflect local banking systems. Check the INZ website or with your nearest diplomatic office. New Zealand has bilateral fee waiver agreements with certain countries, and citizens of these countries aren't required to pay fees for certain visas. Currently these countries include Austria, Finland, Greece, Iceland, Israel, Italy, Japan, Mexico, the Philippines, Russia, Turkey and the US.

For all categories of residence, all successful applicants and accompanying family members are required to pay a migrant levy. The purpose of the levy is to contribute to the funding of programmes intended to assist the successful settlement of migrants. For example, the levy funds help with costs related to the Language Line telephone interpreting service, the Migrant Employment Assistance service, and the Citizens Advice Bureau Language Link service. The levy also includes a contribution towards English for Speakers of Other Languages (ESOL) tuition for adults and children.

The fee ranges from $155 per successful main applicant and a maximum of $620 for all family members (Pacific Access category), to $310 and $1,240 respectively (various categories, including Family, Family Quota, Skilled Migrant, Business Investor, Entrepreneur, Employees of Relocating Business and Residence from Work).

Income Requirements

If you lodge an adult child or adult sibling residence application and include dependant children in your application, you're required to show that you can meet a minimum income requirement in order to support yourself and your dependants for at least your first four years in New Zealand. During this period, income support (New Zealand social security payments) will be granted only in exceptional circumstances. If a spouse/partner included in your application has an offer of employment in New Zealand, his salary may be included in the assessment of minimum income. In 2009, the minimum income (i.e. total family annual income) ranged from $30,946 for one

dependant child to $47,586 for four or more dependant children.

RESIDENCE CATEGORIES

There are three main categories (known as 'streams') of residence within the INZ programme: the Skilled/Business stream, the Family Sponsored stream and the International/Humanitarian stream, each of which is detailed below. There's also an immigration category for those wishing to retire to New Zealand.

If you have an adult child in New Zealand who's eligible to sponsor you, you can apply for a residence visa through the retirement category; alternatively if you're aged 66 or over and meet the Temporary Retirement Category requirements, you may be eligible for a two-year visa.

Further details can be obtained from New Zealand consulates and embassies, and from INZ, which publishes a useful *Guide to Applying for Residence in New Zealand* which can be downloaded from its website (🖳 www.immigration.govt.nz). The

Emigration Group (⌨ www.emigrationgroup. co.uk) also offer a free 'On-Line Eligibility Assessment.'

Skilled/Business Stream

Skilled Migrant Category

This category is the most popular visa class for permanent residence. In order to be eligible for residence under the Skilled Migrant Category (SMC), your occupation must be listed in Appendix 6 (List of Skilled Occupations) published in the Immigration New Zealand Operations Manual.

The first step to applying under the Skilled Migrant category is to complete an Expression of Interest (EOI) form and lodge it with INZ (PO Box 3705, Wellington, New Zealand, ☎ 0508-558 855 from within New Zealand, 64-9-914 4100 from outside New Zealand, ⌨ www.immigration.govt.nz). However, before

doing this you must have full or provisional recognition with the professional body for your profession or trade, if applicable, without which you won't gain any points for qualifications (see page 20).

In order to enter the pool for consideration, you must score a minimum of 100 points (see list of factors below), be aged under 56 and meet certain health, character and English language requirements (see above). If you don't meet the minimum requirements, it isn't worth applying. You can assess whether you meet them by completing an online EOI. The points score under the EOI is allocated as shown in the table below.

You can qualify for bonus points for various factors, for example being employed in specific industries, being employed outside Auckland (which is intended to encourage people to settle in other parts of the country) and for qualifications gained in New Zealand. Bonus

Points System	
Factors for which you may gain points	**Points**
Skilled employment:	
Current skilled employment in New Zealand for 12 months or more	60
Offer of skilled employment in New Zealand or current skilled employment in New Zealand for less than 12 months	50
Work experience:	
2 years	10
4 years	15
6 years	20
8 years	25
10 years	30
Qualifications:	
Recognised basic qualification (e.g. Bachelors degree, Bachelors degree with honours, diploma or trade qualification)	50
Recognised post-graduate qualification (e.g. Doctorate or a Masters Degree)	55
Close family in New Zealand:	10
Age:	
20-29	30
30-39	25
40-44	20
45-49	10
50-55	5

Bonus Points System

Factors for which you may gain bonus points	Bonus Points
Skilled employment – for employment or offer of employment in:	
An identified future growth area	10
An area of absolute skills shortage	10
A region outside Auckland	10
Spouse/partner employment or offer of employment	20
Work experience (if in New Zealand):	
1 year	5
2 years	10
3 years or more	15
Additional bonus points for work experience in an identified future growth area:	
2 to 5 years	10
6 years or more	15
Additional bonus points for work experience in an area of absolute skills shortage:	
2 to 5 years	10
6 years or more	15
Qualifications:	
1. Two year's full-time study in NZ completing a recognised bachelor degree (level 7) NZ qualification	10
2. One year's full-time study in NZ completing a recognised post-graduate NZ qualification	10
3. Two year's full-time study in NZ completing a recognised post-graduate NZ qualification	15
4. Qualification in an identified future growth area	10
5. Qualification in an area of absolute skills shortage	10
6. Spouse/partner qualifications:	
- recognised level 4-6 qualification	10
- recognised level 7+ qualification	20
7. Close family support in New Zealand	10

points are allocated as shown in the table overleaf.

Expressions of Interest are pooled and ranked by INZ, from highest to lowest points scored. Those who score highest are sent an *Invitation to Apply* for residence. When you apply, you must show evidence of your experience, qualifications, etc., that you claimed on the EOI form, and that you meet the required health, character and English-language requirements detailed previously. If the application is successful, you're granted a residence visa and permit.

Investor Migrant Category

The previous investor category has been replaced by two new 'Migrant Investment' categories. To be granted residence under an Investor Category you need to demonstrate that you could successfully settle in and contribute to New Zealand, by showing that you intend to make the country your main home, and that you can maintain yourself and your family.

The Migrant Investment category is divided into two sub-categories:

♦ Investor Plus

♦ Investor

The category investors apply under will depend on their potential to contribute to New Zealand in financial and human capital, the amount of the investment and the 'activeness' of that investment. Investment must be active or semi-active; having money in a bank account doesn't meet the policy requirements, neither does investment in residential property development. The requirements for each sub-category are as follows

♦ **Investor Plus:** Minimum of $10m invested in New Zealand for three years (no settlement funds); no age, business or language requirements; must spend a minimum of 73 days in New Zealand in each of the last two years of the three-year investment period.

♦ **Investor:** Minimum of $1.5m invested in New Zealand for four years plus $1m of settlement funds (transfer not required); maximum age 65; minimum of three years business experience; English language requirements (see below); must spend a minimum of 146 days in New Zealand in each of the last three years of the four-year investment period.

♦ **Investor category (not Investor Plus) English language requirements:** The principal applicant must have an English-speaking background or an International English Language Testing System (IELTS) test report with an overall band score of three or higher, or be a competent user of English. These language requirements also apply to family members or they must pre-purchase English language (ESOL) tuition.

Applicants under both categories must meet health and character requirements (see above), including their partners and dependant children included in the application.

For more information see the INZ website (🖳 www.immigration.govt.nz).

Entrepreneur Category

The Entrepreneur Category is for migrants who can demonstrate they have been actively participating in their business and contributing to New Zealand's economic development. There are two sub-categories: Entrepreneur and Entrepreneur Plus, which are described in more detail below.

Entrepreneur

If you have successfully established a business in New Zealand, have been 'lawfully working' in your business for at least two years and your business has benefited New Zealand, you may be eligible for residence under the Entrepreneur Category. The first step towards becoming a New Zealand resident under this category is usually to obtain a long-term business visa in order to be able to work in your business.

◆ There's no minimum investment capital requirement, but you must demonstrate that you have sufficient capital to start your business.

◆ You must have business experience relevant to your business proposal.

◆ English language IELTS score of four or higher.

◆ No age requirements.

◆ You business must be of benefit to New Zealand, as indicated in your business plan.

◆ You must have been self-employed in New Zealand in the business for two years.

◆ You must have a minimum of two years residence and a maximum of three years after obtaining approval under Long Term Business Work Instructions

Entrepreneur Plus

Under this category there's no minimum time requirement for which you must have operated your business, and it provides a faster track to residence provided you:

◆ hold a long-term business visa;

◆ have successfully established a business in New Zealand;

◆ have been 'self-employed' in that business;

◆ have invested at least $500,000 in the business, and;

◆ have created a minimum of three new full-time jobs for New Zealand citizens or residents.

Both categories of entrepreneur need to show that their business complies with New Zealand employment and immigration law. Applicants must meet health and character requirements (see above), including their partners and dependant children included in the application.

For more information, see the INZ website (🖳 www.immigration.govt.nz).

Employee of a Relocating Business Category

You can apply for residence if you're a key employee of a business that's relocating to New Zealand. To qualify for this category, however, as well as being a key employee, you must be unable to meet the criteria for approval under any other residence category, and you and any family members accompanying you must have reasonable English language skills.

If your application meets INZ requirements in principle, you're usually invited to apply for a work visa, which allows you to come to New Zealand to make the relocation arrangements. Once you can demonstrate that the business has relocated and meets New

Church of the Good Shepherd, Lake Tekapo, South Island

Zealand's trading requirements, INZ checks with Industry New Zealand (the Government body responsible for helping New Zealand businesses succeed at home and abroad) that it supports the relocation of the business. If it does, you can apply for permanent residence, provided that you can comply with other requirements regarding good health and character (see above).

If you succeed, you're granted a residence visa that initially allows you to stay in New Zealand for two years. You must remain employed in the business for two years after its relocation and the business must meet certain criteria. If you and the business comply, after two years your residence visa becomes permanent.

Family Sponsored Stream

The objectives of the family sponsored stream are to permit New Zealand citizens or residents to be joined by their spouses, partners, parents, siblings or children, and to allow New Zealand citizens or residents to sponsor family members and help them settle. The family stream is therefore available to those who are in a genuine and stable married, de facto or same sex relationship with a New Zealand citizen or resident, or who have immediate family members who are New Zealand citizens or permanent residents.

The family stream is divided into four sub-classes, categories or policies: partnership policy, dependant child policy, parent policy and sibling/adult child policy. Good health and character requirements apply to the family stream, as they do for all other residence streams. The four sub-classes or policies are described below after **Sponsors**.

Sponsors

Sponsors of people coming to New Zealand are responsible for all aspects of maintenance, accommodation and repatriation(or deportation) of the sponsored person.

For temporary entry visas, this broader obligation remains in force for the whole time the sponsored person is in New Zealand. For resident visas, this obligation is in place for a specific period.

Another change allows organisations (companies, charitable trusts and societies) and government agencies to sponsor individuals in some circumstances. These new categories of sponsors are eligible to support visitor visas and also work to-residence and residence-from-work visas under the 'talent' category (arts, culture and sports).

New Zealand citizens or residents sponsoring relatives to settle in New Zealand are required to make a declaration of undertaking under the Oaths and Declarations Act 1957 that they will provide their relatives with any necessary financial support and accommodation for at least the first two years after their arrival. Legal action can be taken to recover costs from sponsors who don't honour their obligations. Sponsors must also:

◆ be aged 18 or over;

◆ be in New Zealand;

◆ be a New Zealand or Australian citizen or the holder of a current residence visa that isn't subject to requirements under section 49(i) of the Immigration Act 2009;

◆ have been a New Zealand or Australian citizen or the holder of a residence visa for at least three years immediately before the date the registration is received by INZ;

◆ have spent a total of 184 days or more in New Zealand in each of the three 12-month segments within the three-year period.

Partnership Policy

To qualify under the Partnership Policy you must:

◆ be currently living together and in a genuine, stable relationship for a minimum of 12 months;

◆ meet New Zealand's partnership requirements, i.e. that you're both aged 18 or over (or, if you're aged between 16 and 18, that you have the support of your parents or guardians), that you met before your residence application and that you aren't relatives;

◆ be in good health and of good character (see above);

◆ be sponsored by your New Zealand partner (who must be eligible to sponsor you).

In order to support your claims you must provide the following;

♦ Evidence that your partnership is genuine and stable. This includes a marriage certificate (if you're married), a civil union certificate (if you're in a civil union), proof of shared residence (e.g. a mortgage or tenancy agreement), proof of shared income or bank accounts, and the birth certificates of any children.

♦ Evidence of your sponsorship (see **Sponsors** above), by attaching to your application a fully completed, signed and witnessed *Sponsorship Form of Residence in New Zealand* (INZ 1178), in which your sponsors declare that they're eligible and attach evidence of their immigration status, e.g. a passport, birth certificate or residence visa.

Dependent Child Policy

To qualify under the dependant child policy, your parents must be living lawfully and permanently in New Zealand, i.e. citizens of New Zealand, resident visa holders or citizens of Australia living in New Zealand. You must:

♦ be aged 17 or younger and single or be aged between 18 and 24, single and have no children of your own;

♦ be either:

– born or adopted before your parents applied for residence and have been declared on your parent's application for residence;

– born after your parents applied for residence;

♦ be adopted by your parents as a result of a New Zealand adoption or an overseas adoption recognised under New Zealand law;

♦ be in good health and of good character (see above);

♦ be totally or substantially dependent on an adult for financial support (whether or not that adult is your parent and whether or not you're living with that adult). If you're aged 16 or younger, you're usually presumed to be financially dependent on an adult. If you're aged between 18 and 24, you may be asked for evidence that you're financially dependent on an adult.

You must supply evidence of your relationship to your parents (e.g. birth certificate or adoption papers) and evidence of your parents' residence status (e.g. a passport or residence permit) and that they're actually living in New Zealand, e.g. a tax return or rates bill.

If a child aged under 16 has a parent living outside New Zealand, the parent in New Zealand must provide evidence that custody or visitation rights of the parent living outside the country wouldn't be breached by the child coming to live in New Zealand.

Parent Policy

To qualify under the Parent Policy you must:

♦ be the parent of an adult child aged 18 or over who's a New Zealand citizen or resident (in some situations grandparents and legal guardians are also considered as parents). If the sponsoring child is aged between 18 and 24, they must provide satisfactory evidence that they can meet the requirements of the sponsorship form.

♦ have the 'centre of gravity' of your family in New Zealand. This means either that you have no dependant children and have an equal or greater number of adult children living legally and permanently in New Zealand than in any single other country, including your home country; or you have dependant children but their number is the same or less than the number of your adult children living legally and permanently in New Zealand.

♦ be in good health and of good character (see above);

♦ be sponsored by your New Zealand child (who must be eligible to sponsor you).

You must supply evidence of your relationship to your sponsor (e.g. a birth certificate or adoption papers), evidence of your relationship to your other children (the same), and evidence of where your other children live, e.g. passports or income tax returns. You must also provide evidence of your sponsorship by attaching to your application a fully completed, signed and witnessed *Sponsorship Form for Residence in New Zealand* (INZ 1024), in which your sponsor confirms that they meet the requirements (see **Sponsors** above) and attaches evidence of their immigration status.

Sibling/Adult Child Policy

To qualify under the Sibling/Adult Child Policy you must:

♦ have no other siblings or parents who are living legally and permanently in the same country in which you're currently living legally and permanently;

♦ be aged 18 or over and not a dependant;

♦ be in good health and of good character (see above);

♦ be sponsored by your adult brother, adult sister or parent in New Zealand (who must be eligible to sponsor you);

♦ provide evidence of your relationship to your sponsor, e.g. birth certificates or evidence of adoption;

♦ prove that your other immediate family members (parents, brothers and sisters) aren't living in your home country, by providing evidence that they're all living legally and permanently in New Zealand or some other country;

♦ have an acceptable offer of employment in New Zealand;

♦ meet a minimum level of income requirement if you have dependant children (between $30,946 and $47,586, depending on the number of children);

♦ provide evidence of your sponsorship by attaching to your application a fully completed, signed and witnessed *Sponsorship Form for Residence in New Zealand* (INZ 1024), in which your sponsor declares that he meets the requirements (see **Sponsors** above) and attaches evidence of his immigration status.

The family member applying for a residence visa must complete an Application for Residence in New Zealand (INZ 1000) form and include a passport and two recent photographs for each person included in the application; birth, medical and police certificates for each person; and evidence of their relationship with their sponsor.

International/Humanitarian Stream

The purpose of this stream is to fulfil New Zealand's obligations 'as a good international citizen'. Included in this stream are United Nations mandated refugees who are approved under the annual refugee quota, and asylum seekers who claim refugee status in New Zealand. Under the government's annual refugee quota programme, New Zealand currently accepts up to 750 refugees each year (the quota is set annually by Cabinet on the advice of the Minister of Immigration and relevant government departments).

The following categories are included under this stream: Refugee Family Quota Category, Pacific Access Category (covering Fiji, Kiribati, Tonga and Tuvalu), Samoan Quota Scheme, Victims of Domestic Violence, and various special policies for specific countries or territories (currently China, the Pitcairn Islands and Sri Lanka).

4.

ARRIVAL

O n arrival in New Zealand your first task will be to negotiate immigration and customs, which fortunately for most people presents no problems. You may find it more convenient to arrive in New Zealand on a weekday rather than on a weekend, when offices and banks are closed. If you arrive in the country by ship, customs and immigration officials may board the vessel to carry out their checks. With the exception of Australians and visitors from countries who qualify under the visa waiver scheme, anyone wishing to enter New Zealand for any reason requires a visa (see Chapter 3 for information).

⚠ Caution

If you need a visa and arrive in New Zealand without one, you'll be refused entry.

There are a number of tasks that should be completed on arrival – described in this chapter – which also contains tips regarding finding local help and information.

IMMIGRATION

When you arrive in New Zealand, your passport and other papers will be inspected by an immigration officer and (provided everything is in order) you'll be given permission to enter and remain for the purpose and the period for which you've applied. It's worth noting that visitors can be refused entry (even with a valid visa) if an immigration officer believes that they could be a threat to public security or health, i.e. a visa doesn't automatically grant right of entry. Visitors arriving from countries that qualify under the visa waiver scheme (see page 57) can apply for a visitor visa on arrival using the form provided on aircraft or ships.

However, bear in mind that you may be required to produce other documents to support your claim for entry, such as a return ticket and/or evidence of funds. New Zealand immigration officials are usually fairly amiable, although certain visitors and young people on working holidays (who rate highly as potential illegal immigrants) may be subject to greater scrutiny.

If you arrive in New Zealand at a location which isn't an authorised customs seaport or airport, you're required to report to an immigration officer within 72 hours of your arrival and must meet the usual visa requirements. The harbour master or airfield staff will tell you where to report. Special arrangements apply to yachts that arrive for the purpose of undertaking essential repairs or to wait out bad weather during the hurricane season (October to April), in which case a visitor visa may be granted for a longer period than usual.

CUSTOMS

New Zealand customs carry out checks at all points of entry into the country to enforce customs regulations, which apply to everyone entering the country, whether residents, visitors or migrants. There are no special concessions,

even for visitors from Australia, despite the 'closer economic agreement' with New Zealand (apparently they're not that close!).

If you travel to New Zealand on a scheduled flight, you'll be given a New Zealand Passenger Arrival Card, which must be completed and handed to customs on arrival. This card includes a declaration stating whether you have any banned, restricted or dutiable goods, i.e. above your duty-free allowance (see below). Most ports of entry operate a red (goods to declare) and a green (nothing to declare) channel system. If you know (or think) you may have goods that should be declared, declare them on arrival. If you don't make a declaration you may be subject to a random check.

Duty-free Allowances

Apart from personal effects (such as clothing), everyone aged over 17 entering the country is allowed certain duty-free allowances which include:

♦ 200 cigarettes *or* 250g of tobacco *or* 50 cigars *or* a combination of these not weighing more than 250g;

♦ 4.5 litres of wine, port, sherry, Champagne (equal to six bottles) or beer (12 cans);

♦ three bottles of spirits or liqueurs up to 1.125litres (if bottles are smaller, the limit is still three bottles);

♦ other goods up to the value of $700 (excluding items for your personal use).

New Zealand law allows you to purchase duty-free goods at a New Zealand airport on arrival, although if you exceed your allowance you can be charged customs duty plus goods and services tax (GST) at 15 per cent. If you're entering the country to take up residence, you can also import your used household effects and a car (see page 163), although it's unlikely you'll have these with you when you arrive at the airport! New Zealanders are entitled to the same allowances when they've been out of the country and living abroad for at least 21 months.

Restricted & Prohibited Goods

In addition to the usual items such as drugs, pornography, guns and explosives (which you cannot import without special permission), New Zealand customs are particularly sensitive about the import of anything with plant or animal origins. No biodegradable products (fruit, vegetables, etc.) can be brought into the country and you must declare all food, plant or animal goods on arrival.

▲ Caution

Breaches of the strict bio-security laws can result in an on-the-spot $200 fine, as well as the prospect of an additional fine of up to $100,000 for an individual ($200,000 for a corporation) and up to five years in prison!

Food, plants, dried flowers, seeds and potpourri mustn't be imported into New Zealand under any circumstances. You can also be fined (although highly unlikely) for importing an apple or kiwi fruit, even if it came from New Zealand in the first place. For information, contact Biosecurity NZ (☎ 9-909 8614, 🖳 www.biosecurity.govt.nz).

There are also special regulations governing the following:

♦ animals or items made from animal feathers, fur, horns, skin, tusks, etc;

♦ equipment used with animals, including riding tackle;

♦ biological specimens;

♦ garden tools, furniture and ornaments;

- lawn mowers, strimmers, etc;
- tents and camping equipment;
- golf clubs;
- vacuum cleaners, brooms and brushes;
- wicker and cane items;
- bicycles;
- walking/gardening boots.

It isn't advisable to import any of the items listed above into New Zealand. If, however, you wish to, you should seek advice from customs and declare them on arrival. Special inspection, cleaning and fumigation procedures are often required, for which you may be charged.

On your arrival card you're asked to declare whether you've been camping or hiking in forest or parkland, or been in contact with animals (other than domestic cats and dogs) in the previous 30 days. You must also list the countries you've visited within the previous 30 days.

Pets and other animals mustn't be imported into New Zealand without prior authorisation from customs. Should you wish to take your pet to New Zealand, you should entrust the job to a specialist pet shipping service. You require a health certificate from a vet in your home country and your pet will need to undergo a period of quarantine after it arrives in New Zealand (limited exemptions apply to pets imported from Australia, Hawaii, Norway, Singapore, Sweden and the UK). The good news is that you won't be charged duty on your pet!

If you bring prescribed medicines with you, you should have a prescription or letter from your GP stating that the medicine is being used under a doctor's direction and is necessary for your physical well being. You should carry medicines in their original containers. You must also declare cash in any currency equal to $10,000 or more.

Information

If you have any doubts about whether anything you wish to import is banned or restricted, you should contact a New Zealand embassy, consulate or high commission, or New Zealand customs (☎ 0800-428 786 or 04-473 6099).

Customs also have a comprehensive website that you can visit for more information (🖳 www.customs.govt.nz) or alternatively you can contact the New Zealand customs office at your point of entry:

Customs Offices

Auckland: PO Box 29, Shortland Street, Auckland 1140 (☎ 09-359 6655).

Auckland International Airport: PO Box 73 003, Auckland Airport, Manuau 2150 (☎ 09-275 9059).

Christchurch: PO Box 14086, Christchurch Airport, Christchurch 8544 (☎ 03-358 0600).

Dunedin: Private Bag 1928, Dunedin 9054 (☎ 03-477 9251).

Invercargill: PO Box 840, Invercargill 9840 (☎ 03-218 7329).

Lyttelton: PO Box 40, Lyttleton 8841 (☎ 03-328 7259).

Napier: PO Box 440, Napier 4140 (☎ 06-835 5799).

Nelson: PO Box 66, Nelson 7040 (☎ 03-548 1484).

New Plymouth: PO Box 136, Taranaki Mail Centre, New Plymouth 4340 (☎ 06-758 5721).

Opua: PO Box 42, Kerikeri 0245 (☎ 029-602 1669).

Tauranga: PO Box 5014, Mount Maunganui, Tauranga 3150 (☎ 07-575 9699).

Wellington: PO Box 2218, Wellington 6140 (☎ 04-473 6099).

Whangarei: PO Box 4155, Kamo, Whangarei 0141 (☎ 029-250 9305).

FINDING HELP

One of the major difficulties facing new arrivals in New Zealand (or any other country) is how and where to find help with day-to-day problems, e.g. finding accommodation, schooling, insurance and so on. This book was written in response to that need. However, in addition to the comprehensive information provided in this book, you'll also require local information. How successful you are at finding help will depend on your employer, the town or area where you live (e.g. residents of cities are better served than those living in rural areas) and your nationality.

There's an abundance of information available in English, but little in other languages. An additional problem is that a lot of information isn't intended for foreigners and their particular needs. Your local community is usually an excellent source of information. You may also find that your friends and colleagues can help, as they can often offer advice based on their own experiences and mistakes. But take care! Although they mean well, you may receive as much misleading and conflicting information as accurate (it won't necessarily be wrong, but may not apply to your particular situation).

As everywhere, it's often not what you know but who you know that can make the difference between success or failure. String-pulling or the use of contacts is invaluable when it comes to breaking through the layers of bureaucracy, where a telephone call on your behalf from a neighbour or colleague can work wonders. Your local town hall, post office, council office, citizens' advice bureau and tourist office may also be able to help. Some companies employ staff to assist new arrivals or contract this job out to a relocation consultant (see page 81), although many employers are oblivious to the problems and difficulties faced by foreign employees and their families.

There are free migrant and newcomers' services in all areas such as the New Zealand Newcomers Network (💻 www.newcomers. co.nz), which offers friendship and support through a wide range of activities and has local branches throughout the country, and the Auckland Regional Migrant Services Charitable Trust (💻 www.arms-mrc.org.nz), a non-profit organisation that supports migrants and refugees to settle successfully in the Auckland Region.

There's a wealth of expatriate organisations in major cities, particularly Auckland and Wellington, where foreigners are well served by English-speaking clubs and organisations. Contacts can also be found through local magazines and newspapers (see page 282), consulates and citizens' advice bureaux. Women living in country areas will find that a good network of support is offered by Country Women's Institutes. Most consulates also provide their nationals with local information, including details of lawyers, interpreters, doctors, dentists and schools.

Embassy Registration

Nationals of some countries are required to register with their local embassy or consulate after taking up residence in New Zealand, and most embassies like to keep a record of their country's citizens who are resident in the country (it helps to justify their existence).

CHECKLISTS

Before Arrival

The following checklist contains a summary of the tasks that should (if possible) be completed before your arrival in New Zealand:

♦ Look for a job, if appropriate. Even if you intend to look for a job after you've arrived, it's wise to do some preliminary research regarding opportunities and prospective employers.

♦ Obtain a visa, if necessary, for yourself and all your family members (see **Chapter 3**). Obviously this **must** be done before arrival in New Zealand.

♦ Visit New Zealand prior to your move to visit prospective employers, compare communities, housing, schools, etc.

♦ Find temporary or permanent accommodation (see **Chapter 5**).

♦ Arrange for shipment of your household and personal effects to New Zealand.

♦ Arrange health and travel insurance for your family (see **Chapter 13**). This is essential if you aren't covered by a private health insurance policy and won't be covered by New Zealand's public healthcare scheme.

♦ Open a bank account in New Zealand and transfer funds (you can open an account with many New Zealand banks from abroad). It's wise to obtain some New Zealand dollars before your arrival, which saves you having to change money immediately on arrival.

♦ Obtain an international driver's licence, if necessary.

♦ Obtain a credit or charge card if you don't have one, which will prove invaluable when travelling and during your first few months in New Zealand, where almost everyone uses 'plastic'.

♦ Don't forget to bring your family's official documents, including bank account and credit card details, birth certificates, divorce papers or death certificate (if a widow or widower), driving licences, educational diplomas, insurance policies, marriage certificate, medical and dental records, professional certificates and job references, receipts for any valuables, school records and student identity cards. You may also need the documents that were required to obtain your residence visa for other purposes, such as to enrol your children at school. It's also worthwhile taking numerous passport-size photographs (students should take at least a dozen for bus and student identity cards, etc.).

After Arrival

The following checklist contains a summary of tasks to be completed after arrival in New Zealand (if not done before):

♦ On arrival at a New Zealand airport, have your visa cancelled and your passport stamped, as applicable.

♦ You may wish to rent a car until you buy one (see page 167) – bear in mind that it's practically impossible to get around in rural areas without a car. Even if you're shipping a car from abroad, it may take some time to arrive and clear customs (see **Car Import** on page 163).

♦ Register with your local embassy or consulate (see box above).

♦ Make courtesy calls on your neighbours within a few days of your arrival. This is particularly important in villages and rural areas if you want to be accepted and become part of the local community.

♦ Do the following in the few days after your arrival:

– Check the availability of local doctors, dentists and hospitals (obtain advice and recommendations from your neighbours).

– Open a bank account at a local bank and give the details to your employer (see page 224).

– Arrange schooling for your children (see **Chapter 9**).

– Obtain an Inland Revenue Department (IRD) number from your local Inland Revenue office.

– Arrange whatever insurance is necessary including health, car and household insurance (see **Chapters 11 and 13**).

♦ Open a bottle of bubbly to celebrate your arrival in New Zealand!

Bluff Hill, Napier, North Island

5.

ACCOMMODATION

I n most areas of New Zealand, finding accommodation to buy or rent isn't difficult. There are, however, a few exceptions. For example, in Auckland, accommodation is relatively expensive – prices are as much as 50 per cent higher than elsewhere – and in short supply (Christchurch also has an acute housing shortage due to the earthquakes).

Property prices rose sharply in New Zealand in the last decade and a booming housing market saw prices double between January 2002 and the end of 2007. In 2008 there was a slump as a result of the credit crunch and recession, during which prices fell throughout the country, although by early 2012 prices had recovered to their 2007 peak (or slightly above) in most regions. Interest rates – which were among the highest in the OECD in 2007-2008 – have been slashed by the central bank and the base rate stood at 2.5 in early 2012, with mortgage rates around 6 per cent. However, there have been many casualties in the construction and property development sector, with new house starts at record lows in recent years.

As in many countries, there has been an increase in apartment living in city centres in recent years, with prices of apartments in some areas comparable with those for houses (although most New Zealanders prefer a house with a garden). Home ownership in New Zealand is around 65 per cent (similar to the UK) and most New Zealanders prefer to purchase their homes rather than rent. In recent years, however, there's been a huge increase in property rentals, particularly in Auckland. A significant number of New Zealanders also own a holiday home (called a 'bach' in the North Island and a 'crib' in the South Island), although it's often quite a modest property.

New Zealanders are mobile and tend to move home much more frequently than people in many other countries, with some 100,000 domestic properties usually changing hands each year (a large number for a country with just over 4m inhabitants). During the last few years there has been a small but marked movement of people from the South to the North Island and from throughout the country to Auckland, which has helped to fuel property shortages and higher prices there.

In the last few years, one of the major problems for those moving to New Zealand has been the high value of the NZ$. Property was a bargain for the British (and others) a few years ago when there was almost $3 to the £GB, but now the exchange rate is around $1.90 to the £GB, meaning property is now 50 per cent more expensive! Some experts advise migrants to rent a home until the exchange rate is more favourable.

The Department of Building and Housing has forecast that New Zealand needs to build 20,000-25,000 housing units a year for the next five years to keep pace with population growth, while the actual building rate is some 15,000 units a year.

RELOCATION COMPANIES

If you've got money to spare or you're fortunate enough to have your move to New Zealand paid for by your employer, you can arrange for a relocation company to handle the details. There are, however, relatively few international relocation consultants dealing with New Zealand and they mainly handle corporate clients who have lots of money to pay their fees. Fees are usually calculated on a daily basis, plus expenses. The main service provided by relocation consultants is finding accommodation (either to rent or purchase) and arranging viewing. Other services include conducting negotiations, drawing up contracts, arranging mortgages, organising surveys and insurance, and handling the move itself. They may also provide reports on local schools, health services, public transport, sports and social facilities, and other amenities and services. Some companies provide an 'advice line' which you can call with queries and problems once you've moved in.

TEMPORARY ACCOMMODATION

On arrival in New Zealand, you'll probably find it necessary to stay in temporary accommodation for a few weeks or months, e.g. before moving into permanent accommodation or while waiting for your furniture and other possessions to arrive. Generally you'll find it easier to move into a hotel, motel or self-catering apartment initially and then look for somewhere more permanent, rather than rushing into renting long-term or purchasing a property which later turns out to be unsuitable, e.g. in the wrong place for work or more expensive than you could have found by shopping around. Finding the right sort of property can take some time and you should allow up to six months between deciding to emigrate and moving into a purchased property, although a move can often be arranged in just a few weeks if you plan to rent a home.

Many hotels, motels and guest houses cater for long-term guests and offer reduced weekly or monthly rates. A motel can be a good choice initially, as many provide a kitchenette and some even have separate living and dining areas and one or two bedrooms. If you're planning to arrive during the winter (May to August), self-catering holiday apartments can be rented quite cheaply, although they're often located in remote areas. There are many online agents listing properties which you then rent directly from the owners, including 💻 www. cottagestays.co.nz and www.holidayhouses.

co.nz. Tourism New Zealand (💻 www. tourism.net.nz/accommodation) also has a comprehensive accommodation guide.

In most large towns and cities, executive and holiday apartments (or apart-hotels) are available, which are self-contained and fully furnished with their own bathrooms and kitchens (albeit small). Satellite TV and internet services may be included. They aren't a cheap option, but are better than staying in a hotel, particularly for families; generally the longer your stay, the lower the daily rate. Note, however, that there may be no room service (cleaning, linen change, etc.), although it may be offered as an (expensive) extra. Apart-hotels and motels don't usually provide restaurants but may offer a breakfast service.

They're cheaper than hotels (e.g. 25 to 50 per cent less than a standard hotel double room), generally have over twice the space and are more convenient. Serviced apartments and apart-hotels can usually be rented on a weekly basis, although some aren't rented for less than a month. The cost varies considerably depending on the location, season and the size of the property, from around $500 per week for a one-bedroom apartment up to $3,000 to $4,000 per month for a two-bedroom luxury apartment. If you're looking for corporate accommodation, there are a number of companies in the major cities, such as Waldorf Apartments in Auckland (💻 www.auckland-apartments.co.nz).

For lists of inexpensive temporary accommodation, obtain a copy of Jasons Motels, Motor Lodges & Apartments (💻 www.jasons. com/guides/new-zealand), which, although mainly intended for tourists, include several establishments that offer long-term discounts, particularly out of season. For further information about hotels, motels, guest houses and hostels, see Chapter 15.

NEW ZEALAND HOMES

Most New Zealanders live in detached homes set on their own plot of land, known as a 'section'. This dates back to the pioneering days when the authorities divided great tracts of land into sections for house building. Each section was a quarter of an acre and the phrase 'quarter-acre paradise' was coined to describe the typical New Zealand home, as well as the country itself. In rural areas there are 'lifestyle blocks' for those who aspire to be lifestyle (hobby) farmers or smallholders – there's even a magazine called *New Zealand Lifestyle Block* (⌨ www.lifestyleblock.co.nz). In country areas, it's common to buy a plot of land with connections to power and water services, and build your own home.

A quarter-acre section (or its metric equivalent, approximately $1,000m^2$) is still the standard plot size in New Zealand, although in urban areas many sections have been subdivided and a second property built in the garden, or in some cases the original house has been demolished and several new properties built in its place. In popular areas, houses are often built 'on top of one another' on tiny plots with small or no gardens and little privacy. At one point, this sub-division threatened to get out of hand, and there are now minimum plot sizes in some areas. In cities and large towns, there's a lot of mixed-density housing – apartments, townhouses and terraced housing – alongside traditional houses, while in wealthy suburbs and rural areas there's a wealth of architect-designed houses in scenic locations with wonderful panoramic views.

Most New Zealand properties are single-storey bungalows (usually called 'houses'), although two-storey houses are becoming more popular. Many two-storey houses have their living room upstairs – to take advantage of the views – and the bedrooms downstairs. If a property is described as a 'villa', don't expect a palace complete with columns, marble floors and a sunken bath worthy of Cleopatra, as they're usually quite modest homes made of wood with a corrugated iron roof (see below). Semi-detached properties, terraced houses (known as townhouses) and apartments aren't as common as detached properties in most of New Zealand. The suburbs of most major cities have large townhouses from the Victorian area, many of which have been lovingly restored, and in recent years new smaller townhouses have been built. Outdoor living is popular and

most houses have decks, patio areas and balconies.

Apartments are largely confined to city centres. Apartment living went out of fashion in the '80s when many people moved out to the suburbs, although it's becoming fashionable again and apartments (many are conversions of old industrial buildings) in the central areas of Auckland and Wellington are highly sought-after. Thankfully, there are few high-rise apartment blocks in New Zealand, which does, however, boast a unique type of housing called a 'unit'. This is a single building containing a number (often four or six) of smaller properties, each with its own plot (part house, part apartment).

New Zealand homes often aren't always built to the same high standards as those common in Europe, and construction methods are similar to those used in Australia and many parts of the US. Brick and stone are less common, except in more expensive properties (and some city suburbs), although cheaper properties may have a single wall in brick or stone to add a touch of 'elegance'. Older properties are built of wooden weather-boards (often Kauri wood) with corrugated iron roofs. As hardwood has become too expensive and environmentally unfriendly, nowadays construction is usually a timber frame with plywood panels sprayed with fibre cement and painted to give the impression of rendered brickwork. Modern roofs tend to be made of textured steel or concrete tiles, rather than corrugated iron.

Although many new arrivals from Europe regard New Zealand home construction as 'flimsy', the materials used are usually adequate for the climate. An advantage of this type of construction is that there's a significant cost saving over brick and stone properties, and repair and maintenance costs are also lower. Note, however, that many older weatherboard – and even modern homes – don't have central heating, double glazing, good insulation or adequate ventilation, and are damp (black mould isn't unusual) and can get very cold in winter. Over a million homes are thought to be inadequately insulated and more than a quarter of all homes could be making their occupants sick, including sinus and mould allergies, asthma, colds, flu, pneumonia and bronchitis (see **Heating & Air-conditioning** on page 103).

New Zealand is officially situated within an earthquake belt (it has been affectionately dubbed the 'shaky isles' or 'quakey isles'), where it's thought that 'flimsier' construction has the benefit of being more flexible in the event of a 'quake, easier to repair, and also less likely to cause serious injury if it comes tumbling down around your ears! However, this tragically wasn't the case in 2010-11 in the Canterbury region – particularly Christchurch – when a number of major 'quakes hit the area causing widespread destruction and loss of life.

The design and layout of New Zealand homes is fairly standard throughout the country. A typical home has a hall, kitchen, living area, dining area (which may be 'open plan' and combined with either the living area or kitchen), bathroom and three bedrooms. Unless you're buying an individual, architect-designed property (rare, except at the top end of the market) the layout of homes is monotonously predictable, although they are functional and quite spacious. New Zealand homes are, on average, a little smaller than American homes, but roomier than average-sized properties in most of Europe.

Most homes, except for the oldest, unrenovated properties, are well equipped. Fitted kitchens with cupboards and built-in appliances are standard, and many newer properties also have a utility or laundry room. Newer properties are also likely to have an en suite bathroom to the principal bedroom as well as a main bathroom (often known as a family bathroom). Bedrooms usually have fitted wardrobes and some homes have walk-in wardrobes. Some modern builders proudly boast that all you need to bring with you when you move in is a lounge suite and a bed! If you find an older property that hasn't been renovated, it will be in stark contrast to a modern home; leaky tin roofs, gaps in the windows and even holes in the weather-boarding are fairly common. It's wise to tread warily if you're offered a house at a tempting price that's described as 'needing TLC', which is usually a euphemism for a dump!

Leaky Home Syndrome

This sounds like a joke, but is far from being one. Leaky home syndrome is the name of the problems affecting some 90,000 houses built in New Zealand in the decade or so prior to 2002, when it first came to light. It particularly affects houses built in the 'Mediterranean style', with flat or sloping roofs with minimal eaves and a white or beige plaster finish, designed to give a hint of Greece or Spain. Unfortunately, many examples of this style of building take in water through the exterior finish known in the building trade as monolithic plaster; however, although it looks like plaster, it's actually a synthetic material which is sprayed on the outside of timber-framed houses.

The leaking monolithic plaster is only the beginning of the problem. After water has penetrated the 'plaster', it soaks into the wooden structure of the house and rots homes from the inside out. The timber in modern houses is untreated, which ties in with New Zealand's 'clean and green image', but is proving to be a disadvantage as a building material because when the wood gets wet, it rots. To make matters worse, buildings affected by leaky home syndrome are a health hazard, as it can cause stachybotrys, a toxic mould that has been linked to serious illness and even death.

Attempts at repairs have mostly been unsuccessful and many homes are beyond repair and outside their ten-year warranty period. Some people have given up waiting for a resolution and simply demolished their leaky homes and re-built. There's even a forum where people can share their experiences related to leaky homes (www.leakyhomeforum.co.nz). The Weathertight Homes Tribunal (www.justice.govt.nz/tribunals/wht) was set up in 2007 to provide a 'speedy', cost-effective and independent adjudication for leaky home claims, although many are still unresolved.

▲ Caution

Needless to say, you should avoid buying or renting a home with a monolithic plaster finish that's prone to leaky home syndrome. If you're in any doubt, have a survey carried out and ensure a property is certified to be free of this problem.

BUYING PROPERTY

Buying a house in New Zealand is usually a sound investment and preferable to renting in the long term. House prices rose 50 per cent in the '90s and doubled between 2002 and 2007 in some areas (notably Auckland). However, after frantic activity in the first half of 2007, the market slowed considerably on the back of interest rate rises and amid fears that houses were over-valued (by up to 50 per cent according to some reports). Although prices fell

in most areas there wasn't, however, a housing crash, largely thanks to the relative shortage of housing (particularly in Auckland), and by 2012 prices were mostly back to their 2007 highs. In recent years, the market has favoured sellers, although in 2012 this looked set to change as more property came to market.

It's important to note that most New Zealanders buy property as a principal home rather than as an investment, and there's less speculative buying than in some countries (such as the UK and US). However, as in many other countries, property is the favoured investment for New Zealanders with cash to spare, although you shouldn't expect to get rich quick when buying a home in New Zealand. It's true that in recent years there have been cases of shrewd entrepreneurs making a killing by snapping up derelict ocean-front properties for renovation or buying townhouses in the 'wrong' districts of Auckland or Wellington, which then became 'yuppified' so that properties rocketed in value. However, these conditions are rare, and you can just as easily lose money as make it by speculating (particularly in the current uncertain property market).

There are a number of websites that provide advice to homebuyers, including the Department of Building and Housing (www.dbh.govt.nz), Quotable Value (www.qv.co.nz/buyingaproperty), New Zealand's largest valuation and property information company, and Terranet (www.terranet.co.nz). In addition to estate agents (see below), property is also advertised for sale on numerous websites, including www.homesell.co.nz, www.nz.open2view.com, www.propertypress.co.nz, www.realestate.co.nz (the official website of the New Zealand real estate industry) and www.trademe.co.nz/trade-me-property.

Estate Agents

When looking for a house to buy, you can visit local estate agents (known as real estate agents in New Zealand) in person, look for a private sale in the small advertisements in local newspapers or online, or tour the area looking for 'For Sale' signs. The easiest option is to visit an estate agent (or a number). There are 'family' estate agents and a number of large national chains, including Barfoot &

Thompson (🖥 www.barfoot.co.nz), Bayleys (🖥 www.bayleys.co.nz), LJ Hooker (🖥 www.ljhooker.co.nz) and Harcourts (🖥 www.harcourts.co.nz). If you wish to see what's available before you arrive in New Zealand, all agents have websites and some offer video 'tours' of properties.

The Real Estate Institute of New Zealand (🖥 www.reinz.org.nz) includes details from a number of agents in different parts of the country on its website. The larger estate agencies also publish property newspapers or magazines advertising properties for sale, available from their branches and many other outlets. For example, Harcourts publish a 'Blue Book' series, which you can download from their website (see above). The *New Zealand Herald* and other daily newspapers have property sections and magazines on a number of days of the week, such as *Herald Homes* on Saturday.

All estate agents in New Zealand must be licensed and registered with the Real Estate Agents Licensing Board (PO Box 1247, Wellington, ☎ 04-520 6949). Don't deal with anyone who isn't registered, because if they cannot meet the standards for registration it's unlikely that they will abide by any other standards either. However, the fact that an agent is licensed shouldn't be taken as a guarantee that he's reputable. It's illegal for an estate agent to mislead you deliberately, but as in other countries, there are lots of tricks of the trade which are perfectly legal, such as exaggerating the desirability of an area or suggesting that other people are clamouring to buy a house that has been on the market for months.

In New Zealand, estate agents' fees are entirely the responsibility of the vendor, and the buyer doesn't pay anything (although the fees are in effect 'built in' to the price of the property). This underlines the fact that the agent is working for the seller, not for you, so you cannot expect him to do you any favours. (In reality, agents are working for themselves, i.e. trying to earn as much money as possible!).

Before visiting an agent you should have an idea of the kind of property you're looking for (e.g. a house or an apartment), the price you can afford to pay and where you wish to live. The agent should then be able to give you a list of properties which fit that description. You should avoid the temptation to look at properties which are outside the areas you've chosen or which cost more than you can afford (agents will always send you details of properties outside your stated price range). If a property you view seems suitable, you'll be pressed to make a decision quickly (see **Purchase Contracts** below). Many agents and owners open homes at weekends for viewing, which is advertised by signs outside properties and announcements in local newspapers. The *Property Press* website contains an open homes directory by city/region (🖥 www.propertypress.co.nz – select 'search/openhomes'), as do most agents' websites.

When you see a property you like, don't hesitate to haggle over the price, which is standard practice, even when the seller or an agent suggests the price is firm or gives the impression that other buyers are keen to snap it up. Usually, an offer of between 5 and 10 per cent below the asking price is 'acceptable', but you can (of course) offer less if you think the price is too high or the vendor is anxious to sell. To get an idea of whether asking prices are realistic, you can check with Quotable Value (🖥 www.qv.co.nz), New Zealand's largest valuation and property information company, which publishes monthly tables of average property prices on a region-by-region basis. Some estate agents also publish regular surveys and reports on the state of the property

Estate Agent Speak	
Term	**Meaning**
B+T	Built from brick with a tiled roof
Bach	A holiday home (North Island)
Back section	A property built behind another with no road frontage
Brs	Bedrooms
Corr	Corrugated iron roof
Crib	A holiday home (South Island)
Dbrs	Double bedrooms
Ens	En suite bathroom
Rumpus room	Playroom
Sleepout	A garden room, similar in concept to a conservatory
TLC	Tender loving care required (estate agent-speak for derelict!)
T/H	Townhouse
Villa	Usually an older house, made of wood with a corrugated iron roof
Whiteware	Domestic appliances – often included in the price of new homes or offered for sale at a separate price in older houses
Section	A plot with a house or to build on
X-lease	Cross lease, i.e. a home built on part of a section (usually half) – see **Conveyance** on page 101
X-leasable	A section which could be divided and partly sold or leased for another property

market and current prices. For information, contact the Real Estate Institute of New Zealand (🖳 www.reinz.org.nz).

When looking at estate agents' details, you'll find a number of obscure terms and incomprehensible abbreviations, which the list above will help you decipher.

Cost

In general, property prices in New Zealand are generally much lower than in Europe (and similar to North America) due to the small population, low cost of land and lower construction costs. There is, however, a huge gulf between Auckland and the rest of the country. Property is much more expensive in Auckland, mainly because most of the best paid jobs are to be found there. It also has one of the best climates in New Zealand, and prices are further increased because a majority of immigrants make Auckland their first choice. The capital, Wellington, is the country's second most expensive property region, with variations less marked throughout the rest of the country.

Apartments are often as expensive as houses and townhouses (or even more so), as they're invariably located in city centres, whereas most houses are in the suburbs or rural areas. When buying a unit in a high-density housing development, bear in mind that ground rents can rise dramatically.

Property prices rose sharply in the decade from 1997 to 2007, with prices doubling between January 2002 and the end of 2007. In 2008 there was a slump (prompted by the credit crunch and recession) and prices fell in most areas, although they have mostly now recovered to 2007 levels (or just above). The average property price in January 2012 was $355,000, although you should bear in mind that average prices are largely influenced by the high prices in New Zealand's major cities of Auckland and Wellington. Advertised prices are usually around 5 to 10 per cent above a property's true market value and substantially above its rateable value (see **Property Taxes** on page 233).

A shortage of housing on the market (exacerbated by the problems of the construction industry) and the large deposits required by lenders have prevented huge price falls in most areas. Prices have held up better in urban areas, with the more remote rural locations (where many properties are bought as second homes) recording the largest falls. In the last few years, prices have been relatively flat in most areas, while the most popular have recorded rises of up to 5 per cent; a far cry from the huge price rises seen prior to 2008.

The average house price by region in February 2011 is shown in the table below.

Frustratingly, many properties for sale have no asking price – not even a price range – and are often shown as 'for sale by negotiation'. Vendors are coy about putting a value on their home, hoping that by not doing so a buyer will pay more than they could ever hope to achieve. If you're interested in a property advertised without a price, ask the listing agent for an indication of the vendors' price expectations and compare the prices achieved for similar properties. If you decide to make an offer, make it conditional on a satisfactory valuation. You can always make a low offer in the hope that the vendor will open negotiations and reveal their expected price.

When calculating your budget, you should also allow for solicitors' fees (see **Conveyance** on page 93) and bear in mind that banks charge a mortgage processing fee equal to 1 per cent of the mortgage amount, and require a deposit on application.

Average House Prices (February 2012)	
City/Area	**Average price**
Auckland	$465,000
Canterbury/Westland	$290,000
Hawke's Bay	$285,000
Manawatu/Wanganui	$238,000
Nelson/Marlborough	$331,000
Northland	$306,500
Otago	$235,500
Central Otago Lakes	$436,000
Southland	$210,000
Taranaki	$285,000
Waikato/BoP/Gisborne	$312,000
Wellington	$408,500
Whole New Zealand	$350,000

source: Real Estate Institute of New Zealand

Buying at Auction

Only a relatively small proportion of domestic properties in New Zealand are offered for sale at public auction, but it's becoming more popular. These are usually properties whose value isn't easily determined, such as unique luxury properties and those requiring major renovation. Properties repossessed from those who've failed to meet their mortgage repayments are also sold at auction (called 'mortgagee sales'). If you have an eye for a bargain or enjoy the thrill of the auction room, you may wish to consider buying a property at auction,.

However, it's absolutely vital to do your homework (due diligence) before buying at auction. In particular, you should ascertain the true market value of the property, arrange your finance, inspect the property thoroughly, check the conditions of purchase and carry out (or instruct your solicitor to do so on your behalf) checks on the property such

as the title, registration, debts and planning developments for the area around the property (see **Conveyance** below). Auction contracts rarely include conditional clauses such as the purchase being subject to a favourable building inspection, which means buying at auction is riskier than a conventional purchase.

You also need to steel your nerves so that you don't get carried away and bid over your budget! If you're interested in an auction property, you could consider making a pre-auction bid of around 20 to 30 per cent less than its market value. Prices fetched at auction are notoriously unreliable, and sellers who are 'jittery' may (legally) agree to a deal before the auction, in which case you could have yourself a bargain. However, bear in mind that an offer is legally binding.

You can engage a buyer's representative to find a house, bid for it at auction and negotiate the sale. Agents may charge as little as a few hundred dollars to bid at an auction or up to 3 per cent of the price if they also conduct searches regarding title, etc. However, this can save you a lot of money, time and trouble.

Most estate agents (see above) list auction properties on their websites.

Buying Off Plan or Without Land

Buying 'off plan' means buying a property that hasn't yet been built, which involves certain risks (as in other countries). The practice is becoming more common in New Zealand, but you should always check the procedure with a solicitor. (See also

---

☑ SURVIVAL TIP

Tips when buying at auction:

- do your research thoroughly – learn the area like the back of your hand;
- be selective – have a number of targets and move on if the price gets too high;
- find the TRUE market value;
- attend open homes to assess the level of interest;
- consider making a pre-auction offer;
- talk to your bank early if you need a mortgage ;
- attend auctions as an observer before bidding;
- stick to your limit – but don't lose a property for the sake of a few thousand;
- be prepared – arrive early – stay calm;
- bid late – wait until a property is 'on the market' (when the reserve has been met);
- don't worry about dummies, i.e. dummy bidding to drive the price up;
- go slow – ignore the recommended bid increase and go up slowly.

Renovation, Restoration & Building
below).

A practice that's rare outside Australia and New Zealand is that of buying a house without land. In some cases, where developers have purchased a quarter-acre plot complete with a house, they will sell the (weatherboard) house separately. All you need to do is find yourself a plot and have your new home delivered to the site and installed there. This method of buying a house is much less common than it used to be, but it's still possible and can be a good way to buy a home cheaply.

The main points to be aware of are not to buy a house until you have somewhere to site it and to make sure that a plot has services (e.g. water and electricity) available. Also confirm the cost of moving the house and reinstalling it, which may exceed the cost of the house itself! The job needs to be done by specialist builders and hauliers who will literally cut the house into two or three sections and move it to your plot.

Information about land is available from Land Information New Zealand (💻 www.linz.govt.nz).

Buying for Investment

Thanks to its relatively low property prices (by international standards), New Zealand property has been an increasingly popular prospect for both domestic and international property investors in recent years. You need to take into account income tax if a property is let and capital gains tax when you sell a second home, and also bear in mind that property isn't always 'as safe as houses' and property investments can be risky over the short to medium term.

If you're a permanent resident of New Zealand, there are no restrictions on the home you can buy. However, if you aren't a permanent resident you may be limited by the Overseas Investment Act 1973 (OIC Act) to buying a home on less than five hectares (12.5 acres) of land. If the land is on, or adjacent to, a sensitive area (e.g. an island or reserve), overseas buyers and those with work visas are sometimes limited to buying less than 0.4 hectares (one acre) of land. Buying apartments, houses and land in urban areas generally isn't affected by the OIC (the government body that oversees foreign investment policies) restrictions. Your solicitor will tell you whether you need to seek agreement from the OIC for a particular purchase. If you do, your solicitor will insert a condition in the contract making the purchase conditional on obtaining OIC consent.

A property investment should be considered over the medium to long term, i.e. a minimum of five and preferably 10 to 15 years, as you need to recoup the purchase costs when you sell.

In general, there are no legal restrictions regarding letting property. It's worth noting, however, that with such a large proportion of the population owning their own holiday homes and a large number of hotels, motels, guest houses and campsites, there isn't a particularly buoyant market for rented property in most parts of New Zealand. The limited demand is largely seasonal (i.e. during the summer in the North Island and the winter in the South Island), therefore you shouldn't expect to make a killing by letting a property (unless it's in a sought-after urban location).

When buying to let, you must ensure that the rent will cover the mortgage (if applicable), running costs and periods when the property isn't let. Bear in mind that rental rates and 'letability' vary according to the region and town, and that an area with high rents and occupancy rates one year may not be so fruitful the next. Gross rental yields (the annual rent as a percentage of a property's value) are from around 5 to 10 per cent a year in most areas and net yields (after expenses have been deducted) 2 to 3 per cent lower. Leasing a house to Housing NZ (🖥 www.hnzc.co.nz), the country's largest landlord, means guaranteed rental returns. Housing NZ owns or manages some 70,000 properties, with leases usually for five (existing properties) or ten years (new construction).

There are many websites for prospective property investors in New Zealand, including the New Zealand Property Investors' Federation (🖥 www.nzpif.org.nz), the Property Council New Zealand (www.propertynz. co.nz), Property Investment Wiki (🖥 http://wiki. propertytalk.com) and the Shape of Money (🖥 www.theshapeofmoney.co.nz/investments/ residential-property). There are also a number of magazines for investors, including *Property Investor* magazine (🖥 www.landlords.co.nz).

Lifestyle Blocks

The term 'lifestyle block' refers to a kind of smallholding – a plot of (often) undeveloped land, usually in the country or on the fringe of city centres, of from one to ten acres. Buyers of lifestyle blocks tend to be independent, rustic types who yearn for a more rural way of life, often referred to as hobby or lifestyle farming. They often build their own home on the plot (or have one built) and may keep horses or ponies or a few farm animals, in addition to growing their own fruit and vegetables. Lifestyle plots are available in many areas and are usually temptingly cheap.

When buying a lifestyle plot, the main points to check are that mains services (electricity, water) are available nearby and that the land is suitable for agricultural purposes, e.g. the quality of the soil, and there's a reliable water supply for irrigation. If you plan to keep animals, good fencing (preferably post and rail) should be included, as the cost of fencing a large plot can be high. You should also check any development plans for the area, as there have been a number of cases where buyers planning a life of seclusion have found some years later that their plot adjoins an industrial park or is divided by a main road.

You should expect to pay around $300,000 for a small lifestyle plot (around 5 acres/2ha) or up to $1m if it's within commuting distance of a city such as Auckland (the practice of working

in Auckland and commuting to a 'farm' in the country has become popular in recent years). More information can be found in the *New Zealand Lifestyle Block* magazine (🖥 www. lifestyleblock.co.nz).

Choosing the Location

As when buying a property in any country, its location is an important factor in determining not only its value but how pleasant a home it will make. The most popular areas of New Zealand are the major cities of Auckland (particularly), Wellington and Christchurch, mainly because the vast majority of people live and work in these cities. Popular regions for retirement and second homes on the North Island include the Coromandel Peninsula, the Bay of Islands, the Bay of Plenty and the Kapati Coast (north of Wellington). In the South Island, the Southern Alps, the Glaciers, Mount Cook, Milford Sound and the northern Marlborough region (e g Blenheim, Nelson and Picton, which are close to the inter-island ferry terminal) are all popular, as is Banks Peninsula south of Christchurch. Some points you may wish to consider are listed below.

> ☑ SURVIVAL TIP
>
> It's important, of course, not to allow the desirability of an area to cloud your judgement, but rather to choose a property in an area that's best suited to your needs.

City or Country

Few places in New Zealand, except for central Auckland and Wellington, have a large city feel. On the other hand, there's a considerable difference between living in a town and living in a rural (and often remote) area. You may like the idea of living in seclusion in the country, but does the idea of travelling many miles to the nearest shop or hardly ever seeing anyone really appeal to you?

Accessibility

Most New Zealanders drive to work, as there are few commuter trains and no underground railways. Therefore, unless you plan to live close to a bus or rail route, you need to check the road links to your place of work. There aren't many multi-lane motorways in New Zealand, so journey times can be longer than you may expect.

Ethnic Areas

As in other countries, people of particular ethnic or social groups tend to prefer to live in the same area. Therefore, you'll find some areas, particularly in the suburbs of Auckland, predominantly occupied by certain ethnic or social groups.

Climate

Broadly speaking, the North Island is milder (the northern tip of the island can feel quite tropical), particularly in summer, while the South Island is chillier and can be quite cold in winter. Rainfall varies only slightly across the country, except that in the South Island it's more likely to fall as snow in winter.

Orientation

New Zealanders tend to place a great deal of importance on the position and orientation of their homes. Properties in positions that catch the sun usually sell at a premium over those in shady spots, because they tend to be not only brighter but also warmer in winter. In Wellington, for example, any property that's sheltered from the wind and isn't forever in the shadows cast by the surrounding hills is likely to be worth significantly more and will also be more pleasant to live in. Also bear in mind that many areas of New Zealand, particularly in the

North Island, are susceptible to flash floods after torrential rain. It's therefore wise to avoid properties situated near rivers and streams (which can quickly become raging torrents after heavy rain) or in hollows.

Schools

The availability of good local schooling is a major preoccupation of parents, and many families have moved house to be close to the best state schools. Even if you don't have children, you'll pay a premium for a property that's within commuting distance of a school with a good reputation. You can, of course, buy a home in an inexpensive area and send your children to a school in a more up-market area, particularly since school catchment areas have been scrapped (previously, state schools had to draw their pupils from the surrounding area). However, the most popular schools are over-subscribed, and school zones have been introduced in many areas (see **Enrolment** on page 138).

Services

It's important to check the local services in an area, particularly if you don't plan to drive. With the expansion of supermarkets, many areas don't have many (or any) local shops and you should also bear in mind that GPs don't usually make house calls in New Zealand. In rural areas, the nearest shop may be half an hour's drive away (or more) and even many city suburbs have been designed with car owners in mind.

Leisure Facilities

Wherever you live in New Zealand, you won't be far from various kinds of leisure facilities, but they may not necessarily be the kind that you enjoy. If you like dining out and cultural activities, you need to be located in a large town or you'll be disappointed by what's available locally. Keen 'yachties' and other water sports enthusiasts will find the slightly warmer waters in the north more to their liking, while the South Island is favoured by skiers and hikers.

Crime

Overall, New Zealand has a low crime rate compared with many other countries, although some inner city suburbs have high rates of burglary, car theft, gang troubles; muggings and even shootings. On the other hand, most rural areas have very little crime, and a car break-in may make headline news.

Conveyance

Transferring the ownership of property (conveyance) is relatively straightforward in New Zealand, as it's easy to establish whether the title to a property is clear. As a result, it isn't mandatory to use a solicitor to do your conveyance, although given the thousand-and-one other things to be done when buying a house, it's unlikely you would want to do it yourself. Conveyance by a solicitor, who's the only professional permitted to charge for conveyance, costs anything between $500 and $2,000, depending on the type and size of a property. The cost may include the land transfer registration fee of around $150 (much less if done online by a solicitor or licensed conveyancer). There's no fixed scale of conveyance charges, as this was abolished in 1984, therefore it's worth shopping around and haggling over the cost.

Once you've instructed a solicitor to act on your behalf in a property purchase, his main task will be to conduct a title search, i.e. to establish that the person selling the property is in fact entitled to sell it. This is usually carried out swiftly (Land Information New Zealand is efficient) and it's rare to discover hidden horrors in New Zealand, such as dozens of relatives laying claim to a property. One peculiarly local concept in property purchase is cross leasing (also known as X-leasing).

This usually applies in a situation where the previous owner of a section has leased part of it for the construction of another home, e.g. the one you're planning to buy. In this case, your ownership of the land is leasehold rather than freehold, usually for the balance of a period such as 100 years, at a nominal rent. To all intents and purposes your title to an X-leased section is as secure as freehold. Your solicitor will explain if there are any particular conditions that you need to be aware of.

You should also ask your solicitor to obtain a Land Information Memorandum (LIM) report from the local council, which includes the title of the land, zoning, boundaries, building consents and flood risks. This useful document (particularly for future reference) can cost anything from $100 to $400, depending on the property and the details included. An application for a LIM must be made in writing to the local council and is usually issued within ten working days. A LIM shouldn't be confused with a PIM – Project Information Memorandum – which is for a proposed project, whereas a LIM provides information about land and buildings that already exist.

Purchase Contracts

The house-buying process in New Zealand is simplicity itself and it's actually possible to buy a home and take possession within a matter of weeks. When you find a house you wish to buy, you need to make a formal offer in writing – most estate agents have a standard form for this purpose. A formal offer has to be made, even if you wish to pay the advertised price. The offer is conditional and conditions may include the approval of finance (e.g. a mortgage), a satisfactory independent valuation, a satisfactory title search or the sale of another home, etc. Unless you've agreed to pay the asking price, there then follows a bargaining process which concludes when both parties have agreed a price for the property.

As soon as you agree the price, you must sign a sales contract, which commits you to go through with the purchase. There are usually exclusions to this commitment (e.g. you aren't obliged to go ahead with the purchase if you find out that a new road is about to be built through the living room), but you cannot back out because you decide that you don't like the house or cannot afford it, without paying compensation. You also cannot subsequently renegotiate the price you've agreed to pay.

⚠ Caution

Many estate agents try to insist that purchasers sign a contract as soon as a sale is agreed, i.e. the day you view the property and indicate that you want to buy it. However, you shouldn't sign a contract before taking legal advice and confirming that the title is clear.

If you feel obliged to sign a contract before the conveyance checks are complete, you should ask your solicitor to insert a clause in the contract to the effect that the contract is null and void if any problems arise. However, there's no legal requirement to sign a contract immediately, provided it's done within a reasonable time, so don't allow yourself to be pressured into signing. It's usually better to pass up a property if, for example, the agent says that another party is keen to sign (which may be a bluff), rather than buy a property that you aren't sure about. The advantage of this system is that the seller cannot accept a higher offer after he has signed a contract with you, although most estate agents will try to push up the price to the highest possible level before pressing the highest bidder to sign a contract.

A deposit of 10 per cent is required when a sales contract is signed. This is usually non-refundable, but most contracts include a clause requiring its return if the title to the property isn't clear or the land is subject to government requisition (compulsory purchase). When buying a property in New Zealand, it's the exception rather than the rule to have a structural survey carried out. The main exception is if you're borrowing over 80 per cent of the value of the property, when the lender usually insists that a survey and valuation is carried out to protect its interests.

Because the time between viewing a property and being required to sign a contract can be short, you should have a mortgage arranged before you start looking. Most banks will give you an 'in principle' decision on a mortgage before you've found a suitable property, and issue a mortgage guarantee certificate. This allows you to make an offer in the knowledge that, assuming the property is in order and your financial circumstances haven't changed, you'll be lent the money to buy the property.

RENOVATION, RESTORATION & BUILDING

Property renovation and restoration is a major pastime in New Zealand, where tens of thousands of people spend their evenings and weekends rebuilding, extending or redecorating their homes (when they've finished rebuilding, extending or redecorating their holiday home, that is!). It may be something you wish to consider – there are plenty of older properties in need of renovation in New Zealand and they're often offered at tempting prices. Planning laws are relaxed in most areas, even in conservation areas, where it isn't unusual to see modern homes sitting alongside traditional Victorian homes (or the facade may be all that remains of a period property).

It isn't particularly expensive to renovate a property in New Zealand, as the basic materials (weather-boarding and corrugated iron) are plentiful and cheap. The major difficulty is likely to be finding somebody who will do the renovation for you, as most New Zealanders are avid 'DIYers' and there's a shortage of people to do odd jobs and small property repairs. On the other hand, if you're keen on DIY yourself, it could be the ideal solution.

Note that a property in need of renovation is sometimes in a serious state of decline, with a rotten wooden frame or weather-boarding and a leaking tin roof. Therefore, even if you intend to do much of the work yourself, you should take advice from a surveyor or builder as to whether a house is worth saving (and at what cost) before committing yourself to a purchase.

Don't believe an agent who says that a property will 'make a charming home with a little work'. Also bear in mind that you're unlikely to make a profit if you decide to sell a property that you've renovated, as it's easy to spend more than you could ever hope to recoup in 'added value'.

yourself and engaging an estate agent to handle the sale for you. If you have an attractive house in a good area and it's in the average price band, you may receive a lot of interest simply by planting a 'For Sale' sign in your garden. If, on the other hand, your property is tucked out of the way or is a highly individual or expensive home, an agent is probably the only realistic choice. You may wish to consider selling at auction (see **Buying at Auction** above), which shortens the selling process to around 40 days.

Estate agents' charges have risen in recent years and are higher than in some other developed countries, which leads many people to try to sell their homes privately, e.g. Trade Me (🖥 www.trademe. co.nz), although many sellers are forced to admit defeat and hand the job over to an agent. If you're selling privately, you can have a registered valuation done by a valuer to establish the market value of your property or it can be done online, which is much cheaper, but it's less accurate without an inspection of your property.

There have been no fixed estate agent fees since the official 'Scale of Real Estate Agents' Commission' was abolished in 1985, and fees can vary between 2 and 5 per cent of the selling price of a property. It's wise to shop around agents and haggle over fees, as an agent who asks only 2 per cent may do just as good (or bad) a job as one who demands 4.5 per cent. It's common practice among New Zealand property sellers to add the agent's commission to the house value before fixing the asking price.

It isn't unusual for a seller to put his property in the hands of several agents (a 'non-exclusive contract'), where the commission goes to the agent who finds the eventual buyer. Take care, however, that your agreement with each agent permits this (it usually does) and that an agent doesn't expect to be paid commission even if he doesn't sell the property. Agents also usually charge a higher percentage for a non-exclusive contract than an exclusive agreement.

Any new building or significant addition to an existing building must comply with town planning regulations. Consent for the work can be obtained from your local council, who will send a building inspector to advise you on what you can and cannot do and monitor the works. If you plan to buy an older building, you should check that it isn't registered with the Historic Places Trust, as extensions and renovations to such properties are strictly controlled. Even many timber buildings which appear to have little or no historical interest are protected in this way, as they're considered part of New Zealand's heritage.

If you decide to build a house or renovate or extend an existing one, you should hire a builder who's a member of the Registered Master Builders Federation (☎ 0800-269 119, 🖥 www.masterbuilder.org.nz), whose members provide a seven-year guarantee. The Certified Builders Association of New Zealand also guarantees that its members are qualified builders (☎ 0800-237 843, 🖥 www. certifiedbuilders.co.nz). Both associations strongly advise customers against paying any builder before work has been completed.

There's a wealth of advice for home improvers available via the internet, including 🖥 www.consumerbuild.org.nz and www. buildyourdream.co.nz.

SELLING PROPERTY

When it comes to selling a home in New Zealand, there's a choice between doing it

RENTED ACCOMMODATION

You may wish to rent a property when you first arrive in New Zealand, in order to give yourself time to look for a home to buy. Many people rent for six months which gives them plenty of time to get to know an area or city and the kinds of property available before buying (after which – hopefully – the exchange rate may also have improved). Property of all sizes and descriptions is available for rent, although only around a third of all property is rented.

However, in recent years there's been an increasing tendency among New Zealand families to rent rather than buy, particularly in Auckland (which accounts for nearly 40 per cent of the rental market), where rented properties can be in short supply. Rented property in cities consists mainly of apartments, although houses are also available. Two-bedroom apartments are the most highly sought-after property in the major towns and cities.

Finding a Rented Property

You can find property for rent through rental agencies, estate agencies, which sometimes handle rentals, and in the small ads in local newspapers. You can also browse rentals online through many sites, including Professionals (🖥 www.professionals.co.nz), RealEstate (🖥 www.realestate.co.nz/rental) and Trade Me (🖥 www.trademe.co.nz), plus many real estate agents' websites.

If you find a rental property advertised in a local newspaper you should arrange to view it straight away, as the best properties are snapped up quickly. You should, however, never rent anything without viewing it first, unless it's just for a few weeks.

New Zealand landlords and agents are notoriously inventive in their descriptions (although legislation has been introduced to try to curb this) and they can make the shabbiest, most tumbledown 'villa' sound like a palace. If you use an agency or estate agent to find a rental property, he will usually charge at least one week's rent as commission.

It's possible to arrange to rent a house or flat before you arrive in New Zealand, and several immigration consultants (and travel agents) can arrange rentals for you. Bear in mind that properties obtained through these sources are often more expensive than those obtained locally. Another drawback of renting from abroad is that it's difficult to picture a property accurately from thousands of miles away (photos are often deceptive) and the location may be less than ideal (although it may look ideal on a map). A good compromise is to stay in a motel or rent a holiday home or corporate apartment for a few weeks, which gives you time to find a long-term rental.

Rental Costs

The main divide in rental costs is between Auckland and Wellington on the one hand, and the rest of the country on the other. In these two cities you pay significantly more to rent a property, particularly in the better areas. There's not a great deal of difference elsewhere and the national average rent of around $250 per week for a two-bedroom house has remained unchanged over the last few years (three-bedroom houses rent for an average of $300 per week). Apart from location, the size and facilities of a property are the main factors affecting the rent.

Typical weekly rental costs for a two-bedroom unfurnished apartment or house range from $225 in the cheaper areas of Dunedin and Rotorua, $250 to $350 in Christchurch, $300 to $500 in Wellington, and between $350 and $600 in central Auckland.

The weekly rent for a three-bedroom house ranges from $275 in Dunedin to between $400 and $650 in central Auckland. Anything with a sea view will cost up to 50 per cent more, particularly in Auckland (there are lots of glorious views in New Zealand, but sea views are the only ones for which landlords charge extra). Basic properties are at a premium in university towns, and rents may be higher than a good quality property elsewhere.

Most landlords prefer to let their properties for at least 12 months at a time and some won't let for less than a year; those who do tend to charge a higher rent, particularly for lets of under six months. If you find a rental property through an estate agent or rental agency, you must usually pay a fee equal to one week's rent.

Tenancy Agreements

When renting property in New Zealand, it's usual to sign a tenancy agreement. The Department of Building and Housing issues a standard agreement for landlords and tenants (🖳 www.dbh.govt.nz/tenancy-forms). If your landlord uses this agreement and you're happy with the details, it isn't usually necessary to have it checked by a solicitor, as the terms and conditions are simple and written in non-legal language.

Most tenancy agreements are on a periodic basis, which means that the tenancy continues indefinitely until either party gives notice. A tenant is required to give 21 days notice to end a tenancy, but a landlord must give 90 days, apart from in exceptional circumstances, such as when he wishes to move into the property himself (in which case he needs to give only 42 days notice). It's also possible to have a tenancy agreement for a fixed period, in which case the tenancy lasts only for the period agreed at the outset, although it can be extended by mutual agreement.

When you take up a tenancy, you must pay a bond to the landlord, which is usually the equivalent of one or two weeks' rent, although legally it can be up to four weeks. The bond isn't held by the landlord but by the Bond Processing Unit of the Tenancy Services Centre (Department of Building and Housing) and the landlord must pay your bond to the Unit within 23 working days of receiving it. At the end of the tenancy, the Bond Processing Unit refunds your bond less the cost of any damage (for which you're responsible under the standard tenancy agreement) and outstanding bills. Rent is usually paid fortnightly or monthly. The landlord must pay rates and home insurance, although your belongings may not be covered under the landlord's policy and you may need to take out separate insurance for these (see page 213).

> ### ☑ SURVIVAL TIP
>
> If you have a dispute with your landlord, the Tenancy Services Centre will advise you on your rights and responsibilities and help resolve the problem (☎ 0800-836 262 between 8am and 5.30pm, Mondays to Fridays for advice, 🖳 www. dbh.govt.nz/tenancy-directory).

The largest causes of disputes in rented property, apart from the tenants' failure to pay the rent on time, are landlords who don't maintain their premises (although they're legally required to), and problems with neighbours (who may also be the same landlord's tenants) in, for example, an apartment block or units.

There's a Tenants Protection Association in most towns and cities, which protects the rights and welfare of tenants.

Inventory

Although you can find furnished and unfurnished rental properties in New Zealand, the majority are unfurnished. However, kitchen appliances such as a stove, refrigerator and washing machine are usually included, and many bedrooms have fitted or walk-in wardrobes, so you'll often find that you don't need a great deal of furniture. Whatever is provided with a house or apartment, it's important to obtain an inventory and check that everything listed in the inventory is actually provided. If appliances are included, check that they work properly and report any faults to the landlord immediately. If you don't, you may find that you're held responsible at the end of the lease. If you rent an unfurnished property and have no furniture, it's possible to rent furniture for $250 to $500 per month for an average size house.

Shared Accommodation

Sharing a house or flat (called flatting) is an answer to high rents, particularly in major towns and cities, and is popular among students and the young. It usually involves sharing the bathroom, dining room, kitchen and living room of a house or apartment, and may even include sharing a bedroom. All bills are usually also shared (in addition to the rent), including electricity, gas and telephone, and in some cases food bills, as well as chores such as cooking and cleaning. Some landlords may include electricity, gas and water in the rent. As always when living with others, there are advantages and disadvantages to shared accommodation, and its success depends on the participants' ability to live together.

If you rent a property with the intention of sharing, you should ensure that it's permitted in your contract. It's possible for all sharers to be joint tenants with one tenancy agreement or individual tenants with individual tenancy agreements, although it's simpler when one person is the tenant and sub-lets to the others. Whatever the arrangement, you should have a single rent book and pay the rent in a lump sum. It's usually the occupants' responsibility to replace flatmates who leave during the tenancy.

The cost of sharing a furnished apartment or house varies considerably according to its size, location and amenities. A rough guide is from $100 to $200 per week. Sharing is particularly common in major cities, where newspapers may contain advertisements for flat-sharers. (Note that the phrase 'broad-minded girl/ guy' in advertisements may be code for 'we are lesbian or homosexual'.) There are also agents in major cities who match sharers with similar interests, and a number of websites that specialise in flat-sharing, including 🖳 www. flatfinder.co.nz, www.goingflatting.co.nz and www.nzflatmates.co.nz.

Public Housing

Public housing isn't the responsibility of the local council in New Zealand, where it's provided by the Housing New Zealand Corporation (🖳 www.hnzc.co.nz), which builds and lets homes, mainly to those on low incomes. The Corporation owns and manages around 70,000 properties and has over 40 offices (called Neighbourhood Units) throughout the country.

☑ SURVIVAL TIP

Housing New Zealand (HNZ) also operates a scheme called 'Welcome Home Loans' for those who can afford the mortgage repayments but don't have a deposit. The banks and building societies offer up to 100 per cent of the house price, while HNZ removes the risk by providing the lenders with mortgage insurance.

MOVING HOUSE

Once you've found a home, permanent or temporary, you can begin to consider the question of moving your belongings to New Zealand. This should be planned well in advance, as it can take anything from six weeks to three months (if you're moving from Europe or North America), depending on the efficiency of your shipping company and allowing for customs clearance. It's usually best to plan to arrive in New Zealand before your possessions, which gives you time to find a home and thus avoid storage costs. It also makes customs clearance easier if you're on the spot when your shipment arrives, which is essential if you haven't engaged someone to do this for you.

Although it's possible to ship every last possession to New Zealand, you should consider whether it's really worth the effort and expense, given that there's little that cannot be purchased locally. It's generally unwise to ship bulky items of furniture and large domestic appliances, which may not even work in New Zealand (see **Electricity** below). On the other hand, it's probably worthwhile taking all your clothes and personal items, together with larger items of great value or anything to which you're particularly attached. If you aren't sure whether something can be replaced in New Zealand, it's best to include it in your shipment.

Shipping the entire contents of a three-bedroom house from Europe or North America to New Zealand costs around GB£7,500/US$12,000, although you can do it for around half these sums if you omit some of the largest items (e.g. beds) and have a groupage (shared) load. Bear in mind that shipping pets (by air) to New Zealand is expensive (see **Pets** on page 296).

Many shipping companies do international removals, although you should use a company that specialises in shipping to New Zealand. Some companies will also pack your belongings in your home country and unpack them in New Zealand, which is naturally more expensive than doing it yourself, but saves a lot of hassle if you can afford it.

It's also important to ensure that your possessions are insured, the cost of which won't usually be included in the removal quote. The cost is likely to be around 2 per cent of their value. If you have anything that's particularly valuable (such as antiques) you should agree an insurance value separately with the insurance company, rather than accept the 'guesstimate' which they usually make based on the likely value of the contents of an average house. Make a complete list of everything to be moved and give a copy to the removal company.

Don't include anything that's illegal or restricted. As well as the usual items (such as most kinds of guns), bear in mind that New Zealand customs are particularly sensitive about the import of anything with plant or animal origins (see **Customs** on page 75). This includes not only live plants and animals, but things such as bulbs, furs, seeds and wicker goods, and even lawn mowers and golf clubs! Although you can sometimes import these, it makes it simpler if you leave them out of your shipment entirely. When packing your possessions, take care not to use any packing which is made from, or includes, plant products (such as straw). If you're travelling from Europe or North America, bear in mind that your shipment must pass through the tropics on its way to New Zealand; packing things in plastic is to be avoided, as it will cause condensation to build up as your belongings sail through 95 per cent humidity, and can lead to mildew.

UTILITIES

Electricity

Two-thirds of New Zealand's electricity is generated by hydro resources, although this cannot be relied upon, with gas-fired and coal-fired power stations making up the other third. The country has four main electricity generators; state-owned Meridian Energy, Genesis and Mighty River Power and privately-owned Contact Energy. The electricity supply in New Zealand is usually reliable, despite the catastrophic and well-publicised cable failures in Auckland in 1998, which left the city centre without full power for several weeks!

The major supply companies are Contact Energy (🖳 www.contactenergy.co.nz), Genesis Power (🖳 www.genesisenergy.co.nz), Mercury Energy (🖳 www.mercury.co.nz), Meridian Energy (🖳 www.meridianenergy.co.nz) and Trustpower (🖳 www.trustpower.co.nz). There are also a number of smaller suppliers. Some companies provide both gas and electricity.

General information about your electricity supply is available from the Electricity Commission (🖳 www.electricitycommission.govt.nz).

Costs

Power prices rose by almost 100 per cent between 2000 and 2011 and there have been alarming price rises in recent years. However, perhaps not unconnected, a Commerce Commission investigation in 2009 calculated that the major electricity generators had overcharged consumers to the tune of some $4bn – an extra $1,000 per household over a six-year period! (The generating companies dispute this.) In January 2012, the typical cost of electricity in Auckland ranged from around $1,900 to $2,200 per year, depending on the supplier.

The energy market in New Zealand is completely privatised, and most major areas have at least two electricity suppliers, therefore you can shop around for the lowest rates. (However, if you live in a remote area, getting electricity extended to a property is prohibitively expensive and you'll need a generator.) To calculate which power company and pricing plan is best for you, you can use the Consumer Power Switch facility (💻 www.powerswitch.org.nz).

Power companies offer a number of plans such as low user, standard user and high user. To determine which is the best plan for you, you need to consider the amount of electricity you use and the metering set-up at your property.

Connection & Payment

To have the electricity supply connected (or the bill transferred to your name when moving into a new home), simply call the local electricity company on the number shown in the telephone directory. Connection charges are around $40, although if the electricity hasn't been disconnected you won't be charged.

You may need to pay a bond, which can be around $250 if you don't meet the company's credit criteria, $100 if you rent a property and no bond if you own it.

You'll be billed every two months (most people pay by direct debit from a bank account) and the typical bill for an average house is around $300 for two months.

Power Rating

The mains electricity supply in New Zealand is 230 volts AC and appliances from countries with a 220V or 240V system (e.g. the UK and Europe) should work fine. However, electrical equipment rated at 110V (for example, from the US) requires a converter or transformer to convert it to 230V, although some electrical appliances (e.g. electric razors and hair dryers) are fitted with a 110/220V switch. Check for the switch, which may be

located inside the casing, and make sure it's switched to 220V *before* connecting it to the power supply. Converters can be used for heating appliances but transformers, which are available from most electrical retailers (and secondhand), are required for motorised appliances. Add the wattage of the devices you intend to connect to a transformer and make sure that its power rating *exceeds* the total.

Generally, all small, high-wattage, electrical appliances such as heaters, kettles, irons and toasters need large transformers. Motors in large appliances, such as cookers, dryers, dishwashers, refrigerators and washing machines need replacing or fitting with a large transformer. In most cases it's simpler to buy new appliances in New Zealand, which are of good quality and reasonably priced. The dimensions of New Zealand cookers, dishwashers, dryers, microwave ovens, refrigerators and washing machines differ from those in some other countries.

If you wish to buy electrical appliances, such as a cooker or refrigerator, you should shop around as prices vary considerably (choose those that have a high energy efficiency rating, which are cheaper to run) – see **Household Goods** on page 280. You shouldn't bring a TV or video recorder from any country other than Australia, as they probably won't work due to the different transmission system in use in New Zealand.

Frequency Rating

The frequency rating is a problem with some electrical equipment, which in certain countries, e.g. the US, is designed to run at 60Hz and not New Zealand's 50Hz. Electrical equipment *without* a motor is generally unaffected by the drop in frequency (except TVs). Equipment with a motor may run with a 20 per cent drop in speed, but automatic washing machines, cookers and electric clocks are unusable in New Zealand if they aren't designed for 50Hz operation. To find out, look at the label on the back of the equipment. If it says 50/60Hz, it should work. If it says 60Hz, you may try it anyway, **but first ensure that the voltage is correct as outlined above.** Bear in mind that the transformers and motors of electrical devices designed to run at 60Hz run hotter at 50Hz, therefore you should ensure that equipment has sufficient space around it for cooling.

Fuses

Most apartments and all houses have their own fuse boxes, which are usually of the circuit-breaker or 'trip' type in modern homes. When a circuit is overloaded, the circuit-breaker trips to the OFF position. When replacing or repairing fuses of any kind, if the same fuse continues to blow or trip, contact an electrician and **never fit a fuse of a higher rating than specified, even as a temporary measure.** When replacing fuses, don't rely on the blown fuse as a guide, as it may have been wrong. If you use an electric lawn mower or power tools outside your home or in your garage, you should have a Residual Current Device (RCD) installed. This can detect current changes of as little as a thousandth of an amp and in the event of a fault (or the cable being cut), switches off the power in around 0.04 seconds.

⚠ Caution

Always make sure that a plug is correctly and securely wired, as bad wiring can be fatal. For maximum safety, electrical appliances should be turned off at the main wall socket when not in use.

Plugs

Unless you've come from Australia, your plugs will require changing or a lot of expensive adapters will be needed. New Zealand (and Australian) plugs have three pins; two diagonally slanting flat pins above one straight (earth) pin, which are unique to these two countries. Plugs

aren't fused. Most appliances purchased new in New Zealand (as in most other countries) are already fitted with plugs. Some electrical appliances are earthed and have a three-core flex – you must *never* use a two-pin plug with a three-core flex.

Bulbs

Electric light bulbs in New Zealand can have either an Edison screw or bayonet fitting. Low-energy light bulbs are widely available, which although more expensive than ordinary bulbs, save money through their longer life and reduced energy consumption. Bulbs for non-standard electrical appliances (i.e. appliances not made for the New Zealand market) such as lamps, refrigerators and sewing machines, may not be available in New Zealand, therefore you should bring some spares with you. Plug adapters for imported lamps and other electrical items can be difficult to find in New Zealand, so you should bring a number of adapters and extension cords with you, which can be fitted with local plugs.

Rewiring

It's illegal in New Zealand for individuals to do anything other than the most basic electrical work in their homes, e.g. rewiring a plug or changing a light bulb. Anything else, such as rewiring or fitting a new socket, must be done by a qualified electrician.

Gas

Natural gas is available in most cities, towns and villages in the North Island – where around 220,000 commercial, industrial and residential customers use natural gas – with the exception of a few remote corners, but not in the South Island. Liquefied Petroleum Gas (LPG) is distributed nationally and is used for heating, hot water and cooking in some 125,000 homes. Natural gas has become one of New Zealand's most important energy sources, although it's a relatively recent development, only dating back to the '70s (it now supplies over a third of the country's energy needs).

Natural gas is available in many parts of the North Island and LPG can be delivered anywhere in the country. To find out whether natural gas is available in your area, contact your local supplier:

◆ **Vector** (🖳 http://vector.co.nz/): Northland, Auckland, Waikato, King Country, Bay of Plenty, Gisborne, Rotorua, Taupo and Otaki to Paraparaumu;

◆ **Powerco** (🖳 www.powerco.co.nz): Wellington region, Taranaki, Hawke's Bay, Manawatu, Wanganui;

◆ **Nova Energy** (🖳 www.novaenergy.co.nz): Wellington region, Hastings, Hawera, Papakura, East Tamaki and Manakau City;

◆ **GasNet** (🖳 www.gasnet.co.nz): Wanganui.

Gas is popular for cooking (it costs less than electricity), although it's less commonly used to provide heating and hot water (gas heaters are, however, becoming more popular). There may be no gas supply in older homes, and modern properties may also be all-electric. If you're looking to rent a property and want to cook by gas, ensure that it already has a gas supply (some houses have an unused gas service pipe).

If you buy a home without a gas supply, you can usually arrange with a local gas company to install a line between your home and a nearby gas main, provided there's one within a reasonable distance, otherwise the cost will be prohibitive. If a home already has a gas supply, simply contact a local gas company to have it reconnected or transferred to your name (there's a connection fee of around $50). A security deposit (e.g. $100) is usually payable if you're renting. You must contact your gas company to obtain a final reading when vacating a property.

In country areas without mains gas, you can buy appliances that operate on bottled gas (some properties are plumbed for bottled gas, i.e. LPG twin-pack cylinders). On payment of a deposit for the bottle and regulator, a local supplier will provide you with gas bottles and replace them when they're empty. Large users can also have a storage tank installed and have gas delivered by tanker. If you need to purchase gas appliances, such as a cooker or heater, you should shop around as prices vary considerably.

Bottle rental for 45kg bottles costs some $130 a year for two bottles (OnGas) – it may vary between the North and South islands – and around $120 for each refill. The price may vary depending on whether you use gas for heating water or only for cooking and gas heating, and where you live (prices are higher in rural areas due to delivery costs). Alternatively, you can buy 9kg gas bottles (around $50) and get a refill at most petrol stations for $25 to $30.

To find your local LPG supplier, contact one of the following: Ongas (🖳 http://ongas.co.nz), Contact (🖳 www.contactenergy.co.nz), Nova Energy (🖳 www.novaenergy.co.nz), Genesis Energy (🖳 www.genesisenergy.co.nz), Elgas (🖳 www.elgas.co.nz) or National Gas (http://nationalgas.co.nz – Palmerston North only).

Gas central heating boilers, water heaters and fires should be checked annually. Ask for a quotation for any work in advance and check the identity of anyone claiming to be a gas company employee (or any kind of 'serviceman') by asking to see an identity card and checking with his office.

⚠ Caution

Bear in mind that gas installations and appliances can leak and cause explosions or kill you while you sleep. If you suspect a gas leak, first check to see if a gas tap has been left on or a pilot light has gone out. If not, there's probably a leak, either in your home or in a nearby gas pipeline. Ring your local gas company immediately and vacate your home as quickly as possible.

Gas leaks are extremely rare and explosions caused by leaks even rarer, although they're often spectacular and therefore widely reported. You can buy an electric-powered gas detector which activates an alarm when a gas leak is detected.

Special controls can be fitted to many appliances to make them easier to use by the disabled and the blind or partially sighted (studded or Braille controls).

General information about your gas supply is available from Gas New Zealand (🖳 www.thebeautyofgas.co.nz).

Water

Although most of New Zealand has an abundant supply of water (see **Climate** on page 287), the country suffers from occasional droughts. The authorities encourage people to conserve water via notice boards, posters and leaflets, and there are restrictions on its use during droughts. In the face of droughts and increasing demand, there have been calls for the mandatory installation of water meters, not least because homes with meters use around 40 per cent less water.

Mains water is available everywhere in New Zealand except in some remote areas, where homes have huge rain-water tanks. The country has one of the highest quality natural water supplies in the world, but it's heavily chlorinated in most towns (e.g. Auckland) but not Christchurch, and although drinkable it often tastes terrible. Better to drink bottled water and also use it for making tea and coffee.

Water is supplied and billed by a local water company, which may be a division of your local council. Usually, you pay an annual water rate, which is set according to the size and value of your property. In most areas, water rates are included in local property taxes (see page 233), but in some areas water is billed separately, e.g. in Auckland some households pay several hundred dollars per year.

In some areas, properties (generally newer homes) have a water meter and you're charged according to your use. Usually, it's cheaper to pay for your water on the rated system, although modest users living in large properties find it cheaper to have a meter fitted. Mains drainage is found throughout New Zealand with the exception of remote rural areas, where properties usually have a septic tank.

HEATING & AIR-CONDITIONING

Although the weather in New Zealand is generally mild in summer, you shouldn't assume that you won't need heating at other times of the year; there are few areas of the country where you won't need effective heating and good insulation (older properties aren't usually well insulated). Only a few areas, such as Northland (the northernmost tip of the North Island), are warm enough to manage without good heating all year round, although you may need air-conditioning.

Most newer homes (and many older homes) have central heating systems consisting of heated water systems or ducted air. These are powered by electricity or gas (mains or bottled) and often double as air-conditioning units in summer (see box). Many homes also have a fireplace, as much for show as for effect. Older properties often have

free-standing electric or gas heaters rather than a central heating system, or a wood burner, which is essentially a stove that heats the room but also provides hot water. Note, however, that although it's attractive, a wood burner requires a good deal of care and attention, and wood is relatively expensive.

Bear in mind that many older weatherboard – and even some modern homes – don't have central heating, double glazing, good insulation or adequate ventilation, and are damp and cold in winter.

Provided a house has double glazing and good insulation, you can install internal heat pumps to provide economical heating in winter and cooling in summer, which are more efficient than other heating systems (for information, see 💻 www.consumer.org.nz/reports/heat-pumps).

Huka Falls, Waikato River, nr Taupo, North Island

6.
POSTAL SERVICES

The New Zealand Post Office (known as NZ Post) is a national institution and one of the world's best postal services – it provides excellent, friendly, reliable and economical domestic and international postal and courier services. NZ Post has a rich and colourful past, similar to the American 'Pony Express'; tales abound of how postmen in bygone days struggled through forests and mountains to ensure that the mail (post) was delivered. Today the postal service remains a mainstay of New Zealand life, particularly for those living in remote regions. The spirit of private enterprise extends to rural postmen (and postwomen!), who aren't NZ Post employees but self-employed people with a concession to deliver mail, and who offer various other delivery and collection services to supplement their income.

In addition to delivering (and collecting) letters and parcels, rural postmen deliver a variety of goods, including bread, milk, newspapers and even livestock. They also offer a haulage service and, in some cases, carry passengers in their trucks and post buses to and from villages and isolated farms. A lot of sorting is still done by hand and postmen need to rely on their geographical and personal knowledge of who lives in their area. Nevertheless, the system is efficient enough and NZ Post manages to deliver even poorly addressed letters on time.

There are over 1,000 post offices throughout the country, known as PostShops, which are operated by NZ Post in major towns and cities. In small towns, PostShops are run by private individuals who also run another business (such as a grocery or dairy – see **Chapter 17**) and are paid either a salary or a commission by NZ Post. Some 70 per cent of PostShops are operated in this way. PostShops offer a friendly, personal service as well as providing a range of other goods and services, such as bill payment (BillPay) and national lottery (Lotto) tickets, and act as a focal point for the local community. Some PostShops also provide banking services via Kiwibank (see page 112);

there's usually a sign indicating the services available. You can find your nearest PostShop via the NZ Post website (🖳 www.nzpost.co.nz – select 'PostShop Locator' from the Useful Tools menu).

Information about NZ Post services is contained in a variety of leaflets available at PostShops, and also via Customer Service (☎ 0800-501 501) or the NZ Post website (🖳 www.nzpost.co.nz), which provides numerous *Step by Step* guides to using the postal service.

New Zealand is one of the few countries in the world that allows private companies to compete with the national (state) postal service, and NZ Post encountered its first serious rival in 1998 when the Australian company Fastway (🖳 www.fastway.co.nz) launched a private postal service, although their market share remains small.

GENERAL INFORMATION

Note the following general information regarding NZ Post services:

♦ As well as at PostShops, stamps can be purchased from many other shops.

- Post boxes are red and some are ornate cast-iron 'monuments' dating back to Victorian times. There are also special post boxes for FastPost (see **Letter Post** below) in major cities and towns.

- When addressing mail, you should always state the name of the nearest large town, as there are several small places with the same name in New Zealand. It isn't necessary to state which island your mail is intended for in your address, unless this is the main way of distinguishing between two towns with the same name. Take care when writing Maori place names, as an extra letter added or dropped accidentally (or bad handwriting) can send your letter speeding off to entirely the wrong place, e.g. Whangara and Whangarei are 600km/370mi apart!

- To avoid mail being lost, you should always use the postcode when addressing mail. There's a useful Postcode Finder on the NZ Post website (⌨ www.nzpost.co.nz – select 'Postcode Finder' from the Useful Tools menu) and information about postcodes is also provided online (⌨ www.nzpost.co.nz – select 'Business Solutions/Addressing for businesses/addressing and envelope standards/About postcodes).

- The address for many isolated properties (usually farms) in New Zealand is often simply the name of the addressee, followed by RD (which stands for rural delivery) and a number (e.g. RD9), and the address of the nearest town. This form of address is adequate to ensure delivery of your mail, as the local postman knows everyone on his route.

- A postman is obliged to deliver your post only as far as the roadside. If you have a long drive you must provide a post box, which is usually fixed to a gate post or fence. There are specifications for post boxes (information is available from PostShops), which must include a flag to indicate whether you have post either for collection or for delivery; you put the flag up to indicate

you have mail to be collected, as will the postman when he delivers mail. In rural areas, the postman collects your letters and parcels for posting when delivering mail.

- Many large post users (i.e. businesses and government departments) have their post delivered to a post office box (also called a private bag) at the main PostShop in the town where they're located. This allows post to be collected from the box several times a day instead of delivered just once. If you're writing to a company with a PO Box or private bag number, always use it even if you know the street address (which is intended for the use of visitors only).

- If you wish to write to a government minister in New Zealand, all you need do is write his name, followed by 'Wellington' on the envelope and it will reach him. You don't even need to affix a stamp when posting a letter in New Zealand.

- When sending post overseas, be sure to mark it clearly with the country of destination, bearing in mind that many places' names are 'imported' from abroad. If you're sending a letter to Canterbury (UK), Canterbury (USA) or Canterbury (Australia), make sure the address makes this clear – if it doesn't, NZ Post will deliver it to Canterbury, New Zealand (where else?).

- Philatelic products are available from NZ Post's Stamps Centre (60 Ridgway Street, Private Bag

3001, Wanganui, 🖳 www.stamps.nzpost. co.nz), which produces a bi-monthly *Focus On Line* magazine.

♦ The last posting dates for Christmas (for delivery by December 24th) for letters and parcels are displayed in PostShops in October.

BUSINESS HOURS

Main PostShops are open from 9am to 5pm, Mondays to Fridays, and some are open on Saturdays (all are closed on Sundays). PostShop opening hours in small towns and villages vary considerably because they're usually privately operated, and opening hours aren't set by NZ Post. Whatever the opening hours of the shop, you won't be able to obtain PostShop services outside the 9am to 5pm period, and in some rural areas shops operate shorter hours or don't open every day.

LETTER POST

There are two categories of domestic letter post in New Zealand; standard post for non-urgent letters, which are usually delivered the next working day within a city and within two to three working days to most other areas, and an express service called FastPost (air mail), which ensures delivery the next working day between major towns and cities. The cost of sending a domestic letter depends on its size and weight, as shown below.

When using FastPost (airmail), you should affix a FastPost sticker to the top left-hand corner of the envelope or use a FastPost envelope (with red and blue markings, as used for air mail in many other countries) and, where possible, post letters in a FastPost post box.

Letters can also be sent by ParcelPost (see below), which includes tracking and envelopes,

and CourierPost (see below) in special 'Ready to Go' bags.

Registered Post

It isn't usually necessary to send mail by registered post unless it's valuable, as you can be fairly confident that ordinary post will be delivered. With registered post you must use a pre-paid plastic envelope available from PostShops in A5 (190x260mm, $9.60) and foolscap (280x380mm, $12.99) sizes, with a maximum weight limit of 1.5kg. Target delivery times (not guaranteed) are overnight for across town and other major towns and cities, and within three working days to rural addresses.

Registered post includes a 'track and trace' service that electronically tracks your letter from pick up to delivery. There's an additional charge of $4.70 for Saturday delivery (not available to rural areas). Delivery cannot be made to a PO Box or private bag address. Compensation is limited to $250 if registered post is lost, damaged or stolen; if additional compensation is required, then you need to send mail by CourierPost (see below).

DOMESTIC PARCELS

ParcelPost is the standard service for sending large parcels (up to 25kg) within New Zealand. There are rates depending on whether a parcel is tracked, its size and weight (actual or volumetric) and the destination. Prices for sample parcels sent by ParcelPost Tracked 'pre-paid zonal tickets' are shown overleaf.

A range of other parcel services are provided, including the standard 'economy' ParcelPost service (one to three day delivery for parcels up to 1.5kn), ParcelPost Fast (an untracked delivery service with a next working day delivery target for small parcels up to 1.5kg), ParcelPost Tracked (a low cost option

Letter Post					
Envelope Size	Dimensions	Thickness	Max. Weight	Standard	FastPost
Medium	130x235mm	6mm	500g	$0.60	$1.20
Large	165x235mm	10mm	500g	$1.20	$1.80
Extra Large	230x325mm	20mm	750g	$1.80	$2.40
Oversize	260x385mm	20mm	1kg	$2.40	$3.00

Prepaid Zonal Tickets			
Sector	**Service Standard**	**Max. Weight**	**Price**
Across town	Next day	Up to 25kg	$ 5.50
Within an island (e.g. Auckland to Wellington)	1 to 2 working days	5kg 5kg 25kg	$ 7.90 $19.50 $31.10
Between islands (e.g. Auckland to Christchurch)	2 to 3 working days	5kg 15kg 25kg	$13.20 $33.20 $53.20

with tracking for domestic parcels up to 25kg – as shown in the table above) and ParcelPost PO Box priority (a fast delivery option for parcels up to 5kg to any New Zealand Post PO Box or private bag, costing between $4 and $7 depending on size).

PostShops offer a wide range of packaging materials and NZ Post publishes a *Parcel Packaging Guide*. It's illegal to send certain items by post, a list of which is available from PostShops.

CourierPost

CourierPost is a NZ Post service for letters and parcels, offering a range of services:

♦ **Same Day Delivery:** Guaranteed same day delivery to most parts of the country, depending on the destination and the time of day it's sent or collected. A timetable of same day destinations is available.

♦ **Overnight Delivery:** Delivery to business addresses by 9am the next working day and to residential addresses the next working day to over 180 major towns and cities.

♦ **Economy Delivery:** Delivery within two to three working days for deliveries between the North and South Islands.

For extra security and peace of mind, the signature of the addressee or the person accepting delivery can be collected for an additional charge. When an item has been delivered you can view the signature online via Track & Trace, which can then be emailed or printed for future reference.

The signature of the addressee can be obtained for an additional $2.50. Compensation for loss or damage is provided up to $1,500 and additional insurance is available up to $50,000. CourierPost can be contacted on ☏ 0800-268 743 or via 🖳 www.courierpost. co.nz. CourierPost no longer offers an international service (see below).

INTERNATIONAL POST

NZ Post offers a number of options for sending international letters and parcels to over 240 destinations: International Air (3-10 working days) and International Economy (10-25 working days) postal services, and International Express (1-5 working days) and International Economy Courier (2-6 working days) courier services. A track & trace option is available for an additional $10.

There are maximum sizes for parcels and rolls/tubes weighing up to 2kg: 900x900x600mm for parcels and 1,040x600mm for rolls and tubes. Parcels weighing over 2kg (up to 30kg) can have a girth of up to 2m and a maximum length on either side of 1.05m.

International Air is a service for letters (maximum weight 200g), small parcels (maximum weight 2kg) and custom parcels (maximum weight 20kg), while International Economy is an inexpensive service for non-urgent mail using the same size and weight bands, and offering the same compensation and insurance as International Air. International Express is a courier service for letters (up to 1kg) and parcels (up to 30kg). Delivery times vary from one to five days depending on the destination. Standard compensation for loss or damage is $2,000 or up to $50,000 with additional compensation cover.

International Economy Courier is a cost effective (30 per cent cheaper than International Express Courier) courier service for sending mail to 25 key destinations worldwide: Australia, Austria, Belgium, Canada, China, Czech Republic, Denmark, Finland, France, Germany, Hong Kong, Ireland, Italy, Japan, Malaysia, Netherlands, Norway, Singapore, South Korea, Spain, Sweden, Switzerland, Taiwan, UK and USA.

In addition to NZ Post, a number of private companies (such as DHL and TNT) also offer fast (but more expensive) courier services to many countries.

International Letters

International letter and document rates are based on their envelope sizes and destination, as shown in the table below.

Letters weighing more than 200g must be sent as parcels.

International Parcels

Pricing is based on weight using continuous weight pricing, which means you pay for the actual weight of parcels in 10g increments. The minimum charge for International Air parcels is 100g. For International Air parcels weighing up to 2kg, you must complete a green customs declaration form (OS008A) listing each item

and its value and attach it to your parcel. For International Air parcels weighing over 2kg or with contents valued at over $250, you need to complete a red consignment note (OS007), listing each item and its value. If a parcel forms part of a commercial transaction, you must attach a copy of the commercial invoice or complete an export invoice (form NCPI025), which can be downloaded from the NZ Post website.

Compensation of up to $250 is paid for loss or damage, plus the reimbursement of postage if lost. If your parcel is valued at over $250 (or $2,000 for International Express and International Economy Courier) up to a maximum of $1,500 (or $5,000 for International Economy Courier and $50,000 for International Express) you can purchase additional insurance, depending on the destination. Insurance costs $10 for up to $1,500 max cover for International Air and International Economy services. For courier services, insurance costs 1.06 per cent of a parcel's value for up to $5,000 cover for International

International Letters					
Size	Dimensions	Thickness	Max. Weight	Australia	Rest of the World
Aerogrammes & Postcards	130x235mm	-	10g	$1.90	$1.90
Medium	130x235mm	10mm	200g	$1.90	$2.40
Large	165x325mm	10mm	200g	$2.40	$2.90
Extra Large	230x325mm	10mm	200g	$2.90	$3.40
Oversize	260x385mm	10mm	200g	$3.60	$5.10

Economy Courier and $50,000 cover for the International Express service. A 'track and trace' facility ($10) is available for parcels over 2kg to selected destinations, including Australia, Japan, the UK and the USA.

DELIVERY & COLLECTION

Post is delivered once a day in New Zealand and delivery times vary from early in the morning to much later in the day, depending on the area. Delivery is from Monday to Friday and there's usually no Saturday delivery. If there's nobody at home when a large or bulky item (or something needing a signature) is delivered, NZ Post won't leave the item, but will leave a card, which you must complete and return, stating when and where you would like the item re-delivered. You can have it delivered to a neighbour or another address (such as your work address) if you prefer.

If you're travelling around New Zealand, post can be sent to you via the *poste restante* service to any major city PostShop, from where you can collect it during normal business hours by presenting proof of identity (such as a passport or driving licence).

If you live in a rural area of New Zealand, you must join the RuralPost Scheme to have your post delivered. To do this you obtain a customer pack from a PostShop and sign a Rural Delivery Service agreement, and are then assigned a Rural Delivery number (e.g. RD3), which is your postal address. You're also required to buy a post box of a specific size and type (information available from PostShops), incorporating a flag to indicate whether you have mail for collection or for delivery. Your RuralPost postman will deliver

and collect post from your mail box as well as sell stamps and a range of other products.

MAIL HOLD & REDIRECTION

NZ Post provides both mail holding and redirection services, both temporary and permanent, and free services for those moving house.

Mail Hold: If you're planning to be away from home temporarily, NZ Post can hold your mail until you return, which means you don't have to rely on friends or family to collect your mail for you. Mail can be held for up to 12 weeks at a time, which includes all letter mail, parcel items weighing up to 3kg as well as Rural Delivery. Rates are from $5.50 for up to one week, plus $5.50 for each additional week (free for senior citizens aged 65+). Three working days' notice is required, and you can apply online or at a PostShop by completing a Mail Hold Request form. Once your hold service expires, your mail will be redelivered to you as normal unless you apply to extend your hold request. For further information, 0800-501 501 or see ⌨ www.nzpost.co.nz/holdmymail.

Mail Redirection: The NZ Post redirection service enables you to redirect your mail almost anywhere in New Zealand or overseas, on a permanent or temporary basis. Three working days' notice is required, and you can lodge a redirection request online or at a PostShop. Complete and sign the 'redirecting your mail' form at your local PostShop or request a redirection form and then take it into your local PostShop. You'll need some form of identification, e.g. a passport, driving licence, HANZ 18+ Card, SuperGold card or community services card. If you're applying to redirect business mail, you'll need a letter stating that you're authorised to act on behalf of the company, which must be printed on the company's letterhead. For further information, ☏ 0800-501 501 or see ⌨ www.nzpost.co.nz/receiving-mail/redirect-mail.

The cost of mail redirection is shown in the table opposite.

Moving House: When moving house permanently you can use the online tools provided by NZ Post on their website (⌨ www.nzpost.co.nz/receiving-mail/change-address) or complete a *Change of Address Request* form

Mail Redirection				
Service Type	**Period (up to and including)**			
	2 Months	**4 Months**	**6 Months**	**12 Months**
Household/Individual				
- Domestic	$25	$35	$50	$90
- International	$80	$110	$150	$200
Senior Citizen 65+:				
- Domestic	free	$15	$30	$70
- International	$80	$110	$150	$200
Business				
- Domestic	$130	$195	$255	$480
- International	$255	$385	$505	$955

available from PostShops. You can use the online 'ChangeMyAddress' facility to save time and effort to inform organisations about your change of address – it's free and easy to use (you need to register to use this facility). NZ Post also provides free, pre-stamped change of address cards. There's also a useful 'Movers Toolkit' containing a movers checklist, packing tips and packing worksheet.

If you going to be away from home for an extended period, it's advisable to have your mail redirected to a relative or friend who can open it and inform you (e.g. by email or phone) of anything of importance requiring your attention (mail can also be scanned and forwarded by email).

MISCELLANEOUS SERVICES

NZ Post provides a range of miscellaneous personal and business services, some of which are listed below:

♦ Bills from over 80 companies and organisations can be paid at PostShops, including energy bills, finance and insurance, government organisations, telecommunications and others.

♦ Buy and sell foreign currency via its Travelex service (☎ 0800-222 490) at PostShops, which also offers a cash passport (for those without an international credit or debit card) and travel insurance.

♦ Offers a large range of stationery and packing supplies which can be purchased from PostShops and online (see 🖥 www.nzpost.co.nz – select 'Products & Services' at the top of the home page).

♦ A range of Business Solutions are provided, including special mail services, addressing, financial services, mail marketing, receiving mail, business accounts and direct marketing. For information, see the NZ Post website (🖥 www.nzpost.co.nz – select 'Business' at the top left of the home page).

NZ Post offers a range of PO box and private bag services for individuals, small businesses and large-volume mail users. For an additional fee you can also arrange a courier pickup and delivery service via CourierPost. For information, see 🖥 www.nzpost.co.nz (select 'Products & Services' > 'Receiving Mail' and 'Applying for a PO Box or Private Bag').

The facility to transfer, send and receive money within New Zealand and abroad. For domestic transactions, money order certificates costing $5 are available for amounts up to $1,000. For the transfer of money to and from abroad, NZ Post uses the services of Western Union and the charge varies depending on the amount sent and the country it's being sent to. The charge is around $85 for sending $1,000 between the UK and New Zealand (it's a very expensive way to send money). Further information is available on 0800-005 253.

The quickest and cheapest way to send money abroad for most people is via Paypal (🖳 www.paypal.com), which can be used to pay anyone provided you have a credit or debit card. Transfers are free when money is transferred from a Paypal balance or a bank account, but there's a 2.9 per cent fee plus US$0.30 when the money comes from a debit or credit card.

KIWIBANK

The post office also provides a comprehensive banking service via Kiwibank (0800-113 355, 🖳 www.kiwibank.co.nz), which handles over 50,000 transactions per day from its network of over 300 PostShops. Among the many advantages of Kiwibank are no monthly account fees or transaction fees (although some service fees apply), no withdrawal fees for electronic and branch withdrawals, and branches that are open at weekends. Kiwibank provides all the usual banking services, including current and savings accounts, personal loans, credit cards, insurance, foreign currency and travellers cheques, and home loans.

7.
TELECOMMUNICATIONS

New Zealand has a relatively low number of telephone lines per 100 people, and mobile phone ownership is also relatively low by international standards. However, New Zealanders have always been enthusiastic telephone users due to the long distances (or at least long travelling times) that separate many communities, and the fact that many New Zealanders are immigrants with family and friends overseas. The telephone system has been extensively modernised in the last decade and all areas are served by modern digital exchanges and some developments already have fibre-optic broadband networks. However, overall, the country's broadband network is limited and the speed generally relatively slow.

The New Zealand telecommunications industry has been extensively deregulated in recent years. The major telecommunications operator is Telecom New Zealand (TCNZ, 🖳 www.telecom.co.nz – New Zealand's largest and most profitable company), known simply as Telecom. It used to be state owned and part of the post office, but was established as a separate company in 1987 and privatised in 1990.

The deregulated environment has allowed Telecom to become more than a telephone company (mobile and fixed line) and it maintains a number of other telecommunications services, including cable networks and internet services. After deregulation, other telecommunications companies such as TelstraClear (🖳 www.telstraclear.co.nz) and WorldxChange (🖳 www.wxc.co.nz) entered the marketplace, although they are small fry compared with Telecom.

INSTALLING A TELEPHONE

Many New Zealand households have traditionally had two or more land lines, although this is less common nowadays with the widespread use of broadband and mobile phones (at least in the major cities). In Auckland and Wellington, you can receive your telephone service via fibre optic cables, which also deliver TV signals. The easiest way to find out whether there's a choice of telephone companies in your area is to ask your neighbours. If a Telecom line and telephone are already installed in your property, you can usually take over the connection, but you aren't obliged to if an alternative is available.

To have a telephone connected, simply call your chosen telephone company. Before connecting your line, Telecom (or another operator) require your name and address, proof of your address (such as a utility bill), details (and proof) of your previous address and your employer, your date of birth, and the address of a relative or friend in New Zealand who you can use as a reference (plus six pints of blood or your first-born as security!). If you've just arrived in New Zealand, your immigration documents should be acceptable as proof of identity; otherwise ask your employer (if you have one) to confirm your identity.

Once your application has been approved, your telephone will be connected within 24 hours if your home has an existing line or within 48 hours if it hasn't, but there are lines nearby. The fee is $63 to reconnect an existing line. If you need a line installed or you live in a remote area, you'll be quoted a price for the labour costs and materials involved (☎ 123 or +64-3-374 0253 from overseas).

You no longer need to rent your telephone line from Telecom and can rent it from any phone company. You can also choose from a wide variety of telephones of all shapes and sizes (plus answering machines and other equipment) at telephone and other shops, with prices starting at around $20.

USING THE TELEPHONE

Using the telephone in New Zealand is simplicity itself. All standard telephone numbers have nine digits and there are just five telephone regions, each with a two-digit regional code:

Telephone Region Codes	
Region	**Code**
South Island	03
Wellington	04
South of North Island	06
Waikato/Bay of Plenty	07
Auckland and Northland	09

The remaining seven digits comprise a three-digit district code and a four-digit subscriber number. When calling a number in another region, you must dial the whole nine-digit number; when calling within a region, you can simply dial the seven-digit number, which you must do even when dialling within the same district. The only drawback to the system is that many people don't quote the regional code in their numbers because they expect callers to know what it is.

In addition to the five regional codes, there are a number of other codes for special numbers. Numbers prefixed with 01 usually connect you to a telephone company service, such as the operator. Mobile telephone numbers are identified by the prefixes 021 or 025. Numbers beginning with 0800 are freephone numbers (although some use 0508), which are common in New Zealand

where many businesses provide an 0800 number for customers.

When you dial a major company (such as a bank or airline), you dial the same number from anywhere in the country, rather than a local number. The telephone system then 'reads' your telephone number to find your location and routes your call, through what's known as a 'value added network', to the office dealing with your location. So, for example, when you dial an 0800 number from Christchurch, you could end up speaking to someone in Christchurch or, equally, to someone in Auckland. Note that 0900 numbers are premium rate numbers (e.g. information lines), where the cost of the call is inflated (typically $3 per minute, but it can be over $10 per minute) to pay for the service. You can block calls to 0900 numbers, free of charge, by contacting Telecom.

If you're unable to get through to a number, dial the operator on 010. If you wish to make a reverse charge (collect) call, dial 010 for domestic calls and 0170 for international calls. For information about Telecom services dial 123.

Telecommunications services for people who are deaf, hearing-impaired, deaf-blind and speech-impaired are provided by NZ Relay (🖳 www.nzrelay.co.nz).

Telephones

All new telephones sold in New Zealand are of the push-button variety, although dial-operated telephones can still be found, mainly in homes (public telephones have buttons). One point to note is that buttons are numbered in reverse order compared with those in most other countries, i.e. the 9 is at the top and the 1 at the bottom.

Dialling Tones

Dialling tones are similar to those in the UK and different from American and other European tones. The ringing tone consists of two short rings followed by a pause, while the engaged (busy) tone consists of alternating beeps of the same length, each at a slightly different pitch.

Contacting Telecom

Telecom provides Service Express (24/7) for queries regarding Telecom services

(☎ 0800-000 000). For information about sales and service dial 123 and to report faults dial 120. Telecom also has numerous e-mail inquiry forms on its website (🖳 www.telecom.co.nz) or you can write to Telecom New Zealand (PO Box 1473, Christchurch).

OPTIONAL SERVICES

Telecom offers a range of optional Smartphone services (a touch-tone telephone is required) which can be ordered individually or as part of a package. (The fees below include GST.) These services are also usually available from other phone companies. Smartphone services include the following, although not all services are available in all areas.

Caller Display

Your telephone displays the number of the person calling you so that you know before you pick up the telephone who's calling (unless they withhold their number!). The caller's number appears on an LCD display, which is either built into a telephone or shown on a separate unit. This allows you to scroll through unanswered calls to see who called. This service isn't available in all areas. Caller

Display costs $4.04 ($2.55 with Anytime, Homeline or a Total Home package).

Note that you can prevent your number being displayed when calling someone with Caller Display by dialling 0197 before the number, which can be used for a single call at any time, free of charge. If you want to permanently withhold your number automatically on all calls, you need to contact Telecom. Note, however, that many people don't answer calls when the number has been withheld.

Call Diversion

Enables you to divert your calls to your mobile phone or to another number when you're away from home. Call Diversion costs $4.04 ($2.55 with Anytime, Homeline or a Total Home package).

FaxAbility

Allows you to have a phone and a fax machine on the same line. A different ringing tone lets you know it's a fax and not a phone call, so you don't interrupt the transmission by answering a fax call. FaxAbility costs $4.04 ($2.55 with Anytime, Homeline or a Total Home package).

Hotline

Hotline is an emergency call service for the sick, the elderly or those living alone. There are two options, Hotline Immediate, which immediately calls a pre-set number when the handset is removed from the phone, and Hotline Delayed, which calls a pre-set number after eight seconds when the handset is removed from the phone and no numbers are dialled. Hotline costs $2.55 per month when calls are billed to a Telecom account and $4.04 per month when billed to another provider.

Call Minder

Call Minder is a telephone message service (much the same as having your own answering machine) which allows callers to leave a message when you aren't at home or your line is busy. The call is automatically answered by the Call Minder service with your personal recorded greeting. You can divert messages to a mobile phone and listen to them from almost any phone in New Zealand. Call Minder costs $10.17 per month ($7.15 with Anytime, Homeline or a Total Home package).

Call Restriction

This service allows you to restrict calls from your telephone to certain numbers, e.g. barring international calls and expensive 0900 calls (see above). To activate and deactivate the restrictions you have an access code and a four-digit PIN. This service is available only in certain areas and costs $4.04 per month ($2.55 with Anytime, Homeline or a Total Home package). You can also block 0900 calls from your home phone (0900 Call Blocking), free of charge.

CallTrack

If you work from home, you can use CallTrack to separate work and personal calls on your phone bill. It's also ideal for apportioning the phone bill if you're living in a flatting (sharing a phone) situation. Call track costs $4.04 a month for up to four CallTrack numbers (or PINS) and $8.08 a month for five to eight CallTrack numbers.

Call Waiting

This lets you know when another caller is trying to contact you (through beeps on the line) when you're already making a call, and allows you to speak to the caller without terminating your current call. Call Waiting costs $4.04 per month ($2.55 with Anytime, Homeline or a Total Home package).

Customerlink

Customerlink automatically directs calls from one landline number to another number of your choice for $23 per month.

Dual Number

Dual Number provides you with two phone numbers on a single line. This allows you to reserve a second phone and number for selected people who need to contact you at any time, to separate private and business calls, or allocate one number to phone calls and the other to faxes. Dual Number costs $2.55 per month when calls are billed to a Telecom account and $4.04 per month when billed to another provider.

Permanent Toll Bar

A Permanent Toll Bar prevents all chargeable calls from being made from your home phone, including charge calls from alternative providers. There's a one-time fee of $50, but there are no on-going charges.

Three-way Call

This enables you to hold a three-way conversation, either within New Zealand or abroad, and costs $2.55 per month when calls are billed to a Telecom account and $4.04 per month when billed to another provider.

CHARGES

New Zealand has a regulatory body which rules on whether telephone charges are fair and reasonable, but otherwise leaves it to 'market forces' (competition) to keep charges competitive. When deregulation was first introduced, Telecom was accused of unfair practices and gross overcharging for the portion of Clear Communication's calls which passed through Telecom exchanges, thus hindering them from offering competitive rates. However, in October 2000 Telecom and Clear (now TelstraClear) signed a public letter agreeing to end all disagreements (perhaps politicians could learn something from this).

Line Rental

Line rental fees vary depending on the 'package' you choose. Telecom's Homeline plan costs $50.23 per month ($41.60 in the Wellington 04 calling region and Christchurch city and most

Telecom Standard Rates

Type of Call	Standard Rates		Anytime Plan	
	Per Minute off-peak	Cap*	Per Minute	Cap*
National Calls	19¢	$3	18¢	$2.50
Home to Telecom mobiles	49¢	$3	39¢	$2.50
Home to other NZ mobiles	55¢	-	48¢	-

* The capped rate applies to each call of up to two hours in duration.

suburbs, and $45.75 in Auckland), which includes unlimited free local calls (the area which qualifies as 'local' is listed in your telephone directory and *doesn't* cover the whole of your regional code area).

You can also rent your phone line from other providers, e.g. TelstraClear (from $46.85 PhoneLine Basic package), and pay just one bill a month to your provider for line rental and calls. With TelstraClear (PhoneLine package from $52.65 per month) the line rental is reduced if your monthly calls spend is over $20, and reduces to zero if you spend over $200 per month.

Telecom Rates

Telecom standard rates and rates for its Anytime plan are shown above – as an example only. **You need to compare the call charges with those of other providers.**

There's an additional monthly charge for Anytime, which varies depending on where you live. The Anytime plan includes your home phone rental as well as discounts on Telecom's standard rates for national, home to New Zealand Telecom mobiles and peak time international calls. The above rates apply 24 hours a day, seven days a week.

Alternative Networks

Although most people rent their telephone line from Telecom, there's no obligation to make all your calls via the Telecom network. Under deregulation, other companies can provide your telephone service even when you have a Telecom line (i.e. pay line rental to Telecom) and if you make a calling plan your main home phone calling plan, it isn't necessary to enter a code before making calls. The cost is charged to your account by the alternative company (usually to a credit or debit card) and doesn't appear on your Telecom bill.

The main alternative network is TelstraClear (☎ 0508-888 800, 🖳 www.telstraclear.co.nz), plus a few smaller players such as Slingshot (☎ 0800-892 000, 🖳 www.slingshot.co.nz), which offer unlimited national calls for $21 per month in New Zealand and Australia, $26 per month for unlimited calls to Australia, Canada, Ireland, UK and the US, and $31 per month for unlimited calls to the top 40 worldwide destinations.

Telstra offers a number of calling plans, including the following:

1. **Talk 24/7** is an all-round calling plan offering both capped calling and competitive per minute rates, 24 hours a day, seven days a week. The national call rate is 25¢ per minute, with a $3 cap for calls of up to two hours (excludes calls to mobiles). Calls to UK and USA landlines are 29¢ per minute, with a two-hour capped rate of $5.75.

2. **Ztalk** is a simple 'no frills' national and international plan with competitive per minute rates, irrespective of when calls are made. Calls to NZ landlines costs 9¢ per minute and calls to NZ mobiles 46¢ per minute. Calls to a UK or US landline cost 9¢ per minute and calls to UK mobiles 41¢ per minute.

3. **Kiwi Yak Paks** are recommended if you make lots of calls to New Zealand landlines, mostly short in duration. Each month you receive a set number of minutes you can use to make national calls, anytime of the day or night, for a fixed charge. You

can sign up for Kiwi 3 (three hours or 180 minutes, $13.24), Kiwi 5 (five hours or 300 minutes, $19.37) or Kiwi 100 (100 hours or 6,000 minutes, $20.39).

4. **Big Back Yard** allows you to make free calls within your local *White Pages* phone book area, which includes the Auckland, Bay of Plenty, Christchurch, Nelson & Bays, Otago, Waikato and Wellington areas. There's a minimum sign-up period of 12-months (with a $99 charge for early termination!).

BILLS

Telecom telephone bills are issued monthly and you have around a week to pay before a reminder is sent. You can pay bills by post, at PostShops and other outlets that are Telecom agencies, by direct debit from a bank account, or via the internet. All telephone bills are itemised, although it's possible to request a non-itemised bill if you wish. You can also decide the level at which itemisation begins, e.g. calls over 50¢, $1 or $5. This is handy if you just want to keep an eye on the more expensive calls and don't want to receive reams of paper listing all your calls (other telephone companies please take note!).

Online Bill is a system whereby you can receive and pay your telephone bill via the internet; to use this system you must register online (💻 www.telecom.co.nz).

INTERNATIONAL CALLS

All international calls from private and public telephones in New Zealand are made via the ISD (International Subscriber Dialling) system. A full list of country codes is shown in the information pages of your telephone directory. To make an international call, dial the international access code of 00, followed by the country code (e.g. 1 for the USA, 44 for the UK), the area code (usually omitting the initial 0) and the party's number. For international operator assistance ☎ 0170.

International telephone calls via Telecom are charged according to the time of day and the part of the world (zone), Australia being in the cheapest zone and the UK in one of the most

expensive. Other companies usually charge a separate rate for each country. It's usually cheaper to use a company other than Telecom to make international calls (see above). If you make a lot of international calls, it's best to sign up to an international calling plan. **You can also make cheap international calls from any phone using a calling card (see below).**

If you're travelling overseas, you can use a pre-paid Telecom Yabba card (💻 www.yabba.co.nz) in over 50 countries worldwide (see website for a list and rates). Sample rates are UK to NZ, $0.15 per minute (landline to mobile $0.40) and USA to NZ, $0.29 per minute (landline to mobile $0.54). Domestic calls cost $0.30 per minute (landline to mobile and vice versa $0.55, mobile to mobile $0.80) – dearer than calls from the UK or USA! See also Calling Cards below.

DIRECTORIES

You're entitled to a free copy of the telephone directory (called the telephone book or *White Pages* in New Zealand) for your local region, which is delivered when your line is connected and annually thereafter. Directories for other regions can be ordered for a nominal fee and charged to your telephone bill. If you live outside the Auckland region, it's wise to order the Auckland book, as most important businesses (e.g. airlines and banks) are located there.

Subscribers are divided into private and business customers and there's also a separate *Yellow Pages* (business) directory for each region (a copy is delivered with your local telephone book). If you don't have a directory handy (or cannot be bothered to look up a number), the number for directory enquiries (known as directory assistance) is 018 for domestic numbers and 0172 for international numbers. The fee is 64¢ and $1.93 respectively from a residential landline.

You can also find business and private telephone numbers via the internet (💻 http://yellow.co.nz).

PAYPHONES

Telecom has a network of around 4,000 payphones located in the streets of towns and villages and at various other locations, including airports, bus stations and PostShops, and they are easily identified by their distinctive yellow and blue livery. All payphones allow local, national and international calls. International calls can also be made via the operator or the Home Direct Service (see **International Calls** above). Most traditional telephone boxes have been replaced by kiosks with push-button telephones. All Telecom payphones accept PhoneCards (see below) and credit cards, but not all accept coins – look for a booth that shows the word 'Coin'. Local calls aren't free from public telephones (as they usually are from private phones) and the minimum charge is around 50¢ per minute.

Some indoor Payphones offer modem access for PC users, which are particularly useful in locations such as airports and hotels, but you need to have your own portable PC to take advantage of this feature. Some external booths are also wi-fi hotspots, whereby laptop or mobile phone users can access wireless high speed internet up to 50m away from payphone booths.

PhoneCard Payphones

Telecom PhoneCards are available from PostShops, petrol stations, supermarkets,

book stores, Telecom Centres and various shops (such as dairies) displaying a Telecom PhoneCard symbol (a green, yellow and blue illustration of a card being inserted into a telephone receiver). Cards are sold in denominations of $5, $10, $20 and $50, and have various designs, usually scenic views of New Zealand (many people collect them and some issues are much sought-after and consequently worth far more than their face value!).

Note that PhoneCards have an expiry date, so don't buy a high value card unless you're sure that you'll use it, as there are no refunds!

The procedure when using a PhoneCard in most public telephones is as follows:

1. Lift the receiver and listen for the dial tone.
2. Insert your PhoneCard into the slot.
3. Wait (while the card is checked).
4. When the remaining credit is displayed, dial the number
5. Hang up when you're finished and **don't forget to remove your card**.

PhoneCard payphones also accept most credit cards (minimum charge $2) – simply insert your card and dial when you have the dialling tone.

Coin Payphones

If you want to make a call using coins, you'll need to find a booth that shows the word 'Coin'. Telephones in blue boxes usually accept 10¢, 20¢ and 50¢ coins. You must lift the receiver and insert at least 50¢ before dialling (the minimum cost of even the shortest local call). In older coin boxes you should insert only small coins (one at a time), because if you speak for less than the time you've paid for, you don't receive any change. In newer boxes (where the amount in reserve is shown on a digital display) you can insert as much money as you like, as completely unused coins are automatically refunded at the end of the call. However, you still won't receive any change from a partly used coin, for example if you insert a $1 coin but make only a 50¢ call.

Making an international call from a coin telephone can be difficult, as you need to insert at least $3 (the minimum charge) in coins. Even if you plan to use the Home Direct

Service (see above), you must insert 20¢ (which isn't refunded) to access the service.

Private Payphones

There are private payphones in bars, hotels, shops and other businesses. They're usually portable units rather than telephone kiosks and operate like any other telephone, except that they don't usually give change therefore you should insert only the amount that you expect a call to cost. The main point to note is that the owner of the telephone can set whatever rates he wishes, which are usually much higher than Telecom's (and he has no obligation to display what the charges are). The same applies to calls from hotels, which charge at least twice as much as normal rates and sometimes much more.

Calling Cards

You can purchase a huge variety of pre-paid calling cards (different from Telecom PhoneCards) in New Zealand, which can be used to make both national and international calls (some cards can also be used to access the internet). Millions are sold annually by gas stations, convenience stores, supermarkets, dairies, delis and numerous other outlets, including online. The cost of international calls with calling cards varies considerably, e.g. from as little as 3.4¢ per minute to the UK, but you also need to check call connection costs. The only drawback is that you need to enter a lot of digits to make calls. Also bear in mind that calls from mobile and public phones with calling cards (and calls to mobile phones from land lines) are MUCH more expensive than calls made from a land line to a land line.

☑ SURVIVAL TIP

The best deal is to buy a 'Good Call' calling card from NZ Post, which is available in denominations of $10, $20 and $30.

Good Call (see 🖳 www.nzpost.co.nz/home/apply-renew-organise/calling-cards/good-call-rates) offers exceptionally low national and international rates, for example $0.0501 per minute for national NZ calls ($0.5009 for calls to mobiles) and just $0.0337 per minute to the UK and USA, and $0.0450 per minute to Australia – and no connection fees. Cards can be used from any landline, but there's a surcharge of 45¢ when calling from a Payphone or mobile phone. Calls to UK mobile phones are $0.4948 per minute but calls to US mobiles are the same rate as for fixed line calls. To use the card you dial the access number (01446) followed by the PIN number found on the back of your card followed by the # (hash). Then follow the voice prompts (15 languages available). To make further calls, simply hold the line when the other person hangs up.

You can also use the card to call New Zealand from 23 countries (see website), including the UK and US. A 'world dial surcharge' ($0.375 per minute from the UK or US) applies, which is in addition to the standard rate per minute (noted above), but it's still good value for money.

MOBILE PHONES

Given the remoteness of many parts of New Zealand, mobile (cellular) phones are popular and there are well over 2m in use. New Zealanders are also textaholics (sending over 600m a month!) and mobile phones and social networking sites like Facebook have revolutionised the way people communicate; Kiwis use their mobiles for everything, from doing the banking and paying for parking, to downloading music and finding and/or dumping partners. Cover is surprisingly good, despite the mountainous terrain in many places, although you may need a satellite phone if you live in a remote area.

The cellular market in New Zealand is largely carved up by Telecom Mobile (CDMA, but switching to GPRS) and Vodafone (GPRS) plus a few smaller players such as Compass Communications (🖳 www.compass.net.nz) and TelstraClear (🖳 www.telstraclear.co.nz). Competition for business is fierce, prices are competitive (although too high) and it's no longer necessary to have a contract (postpaid plan). As the two major players use different technology, with GPRS allowing for greater international roaming, you should choose a network before choosing a phone.

The major companies offer a range of payment plans; Telecom and Vodafone have a bewildering range. Most providers now offer mobile broadband, which is available to some 80 per cent of the population. Calls to and from mobile phones are expensive and vary considerably depending on the payment plan you choose, therefore you should make sure that you choose the one that offers the cheapest calls at the times when you make most calls.

Pre-pay ('pay as you talk') phones are increasingly popular in New Zealand and you can buy phone 'cards' (or maybe just a printed receipt) for $20, $30 and $50 at many outlets, including PostShops and dairies. New Zealand offers a number of options for those who don't wish to sign up to an expensive mobile phone contract, including travellers who wish to make calls overseas from New Zealand and calls to New Zealand from overseas. If you have an overseas GSM mobile phone (which must be unlocked), you can replace the SIM card with a local card and buy pre-paid credits as and when required.

When buying a mobile phone you need to shop until you drop, as prices and services vary considerably, and offers abound. You can compare prices online at 🖳 www.pricespy.co.nz. You can buy a mobile phone from a Telecom or Vodafone shop or from

an mobile phone chain such as Digital Mobile, DS Wireless and First Mobile, who sell only Vodafone products and services, and Leading Edge Communications and Orb Communications, which sell only Telecom products. There are also many small independent stores.

Mobile number portability allows you to keep the same number when changing mobile phones or networks.

INTERNET

The internet is popular in New Zealand, which has among the world's fastest-growing number of broadband users, although the country has a dismal OECD broadband rating. Some developments have fibre-optic broadband networks, although overall the country's broadband network is limited and the speed relatively slow. However, the government is investing $1.5bn to bring high-speed broadband access to over 75 per cent of homes.

There are numerous internet service providers (ISPs), including Compass Communications (🖳 www.compass.net.nz), Orcon (🖳 www.orcon.net.nz), Paradise (🖳 www.paradise.net.nz), Slingshot (🖳 www.slingshot.co.nz), Snap (🖳 www.snap.net.nz), Telecom (🖳 www.telecom.co.nz), TelstraClear (🖳 www.telstraclear.co.nz), Vodafone (🖳 www.vodafone.co.nz), Woosh (🖳 www.woosh.com) and Xnet (🖳 www.xnet.co.nz).

You can compare ISPs at 🖳 http://nz.whatisthis.com/broadband/compare, where you can sort ISPs by price and speed, and at 🖳 http://broadband.t5.co.nz. The monthly magazine *NZ PC World* also regularly publishes a comparison of ISP rates and packages, which can also be viewed online (🖳 www.pcworld.co.nz). The Consumers' Institute also offers an online comparison of ISP rates for the whole of New Zealand (🖳 www.consumer.org.nz/reports/broadband-internet).

Most companies offer dial-up and broadband lines, although the latter aren't available in all areas. Before moving house you may wish to check that broadband is available in an area. You can check via 🖳 www.telecom.co.nz/broadband/getconnected by entering your telephone number (or any local telephone number). Broadband speeds usually vary from 15-25Mbps, with a data allowances of 2-120GB, depending on your package and provider.

Combined internet and telephone (plus TV) packages are common. For example, Telecom offer a Total Home package with an unlimited number of national landline calls (up to two hours each), 10GB of broadband, cheaper home-to-mobile calls within NZ, and lower international calling rates for $99 per month in Auckland, Christchurch and Wellington and $109 elsewhere. TelstraClear offers unlimited dial-up for $16.95 per month, $55.95 for 20GB broadband, up to $135.95 for 120GB (all plus $39.95 line rental fee).

You can find wi-fi hotspots via the internet – see 🖥 www.zenbu.net.nz/zones_map.php and 🖥 http://totalhotspots.com/directory/nz.

Internet Telephony

If you have a broadband internet connection, you can make long-distance and international phone 'calls' for free (or almost-free) to anyone with a broadband connection. Voice over internet protocol (VOIP) is the latest technology which is reshaping the telecoms landscape and may eventually make today's telephone technology (both land lines and mobile networks) obsolete.

All you need is access to a local broadband provider and a headset (costing as little as $15) or a special phone, and you're in business. Calls to other computers anywhere in the world are free, while calls to landlines are charged at a few cents a minute. The downside is that lines are prone to interference and sudden disconnections.

The leading company in this field is Skype (🖥 www.skype.com) with over 50m users, while another major player is VOIP (🖥 www.voip.com). There are also other companies in the market. Some companies and government organisations in New Zealand use Skype and even have links on their websites. If you have an internet enabled mobile phone, you can use Skype to make VOIP calls via your phone, bringing low-cost international calls to your mobile.

FAX & TELEX

Faxes can be sent from a variety of locations in New Zealand, including newsagents, PostShops, stationers and many other businesses, who can also receive them on your behalf. Fax machines (Groups 2/3) imported from abroad may work in New Zealand, but you aren't supposed to connect them unless they're Telecom-approved.

Telex machines aren't widely used any longer in New Zealand, although some major hotels, banks, government offices and large businesses still have them.

EMERGENCY NUMBERS

The emergency number in New Zealand is 111, which can be dialled free from any telephone; you're connected to the emergency operator who then connects you with the police, fire or ambulance service, as required. You don't need any money, even when calling from a payphone, whether it accepts coins, PhoneCards or credit cards. Be ready to tell the emergency operator which service you require and your name. You don't need to give your location, as the telephone from which you're calling automatically 'sends' its identity.

8.
TELEVISION & RADIO

TELEVISION

Television came late to New Zealand and wasn't introduced until 1960, with the establishment of AKTV2 (now TV One) in Auckland. Broadcasting in New Zealand and the ownership of TV and radio stations used to be strictly regulated by the government. However, there has been deregulation since 1991 and a number of new companies (particularly foreign media corporations) have entered the market, making the broadcasting industry somewhat volatile.

New radio and TV companies are constantly starting up or buying existing stations and, just as frequently, closing down. (It doesn't pay to become too attached to a particular programme, as you may find that the next time you sit down in front of 'the box' it has disappeared!). The situation has stabilised in recent years, however, and despite the influx of foreign companies, television programming is still highly regulated by the Broadcasting Standards Authority (🖳 www.bsa.govt.nz); evening programmes receive a classification according to their suitability for younger viewers, e.g. PG (parental guidance).

Many New Zealanders receive their TV service through some sort of multichannel platform, such as Freeview, cable or satellite. If you watch a lot of TV or want to watch sport and films, then you'll find it's essential to subscribe to cable or satellite TV, which provides access to hundreds of channels. Many programmes are broadcast in digital high definition (HD) format, which offers greatly improved picture and sound quality (for which you'll need an HD television) and interactive options.

Stations

Television is popular in New Zealand, where most households have at least one

TV and it's estimated that the vast majority of people watch some television every day. There are seven terrestrial, national free-to-air analogue TV stations in New Zealand: TV One, TV2, TV3, C4, Prime, Trackside and Maori Television, although depending on where you live and your equipment, you may only be able to receive TV One, TV2 and TV3 with a standard aerial. However, a much larger number of stations is available via Freeview (see below) with a Freeview Set Top Box (sometimes called a Decoder) or a TV with a built-in Freeview decoder.

TV stations in New Zealand can broadly be divided into government owned by Television New Zealand, commercial stations, and state and privately-owned regional TV stations (e.g. Triangle TV in Auckland, Canterbury TV in Christchurch, and Channel 9 in Dunedin).

The government owned TVNZ (🖳 http://tvnz.co.nz) stations are listed overleaf.

There are five main commercial stations, listed overleaf.

All stations, even those that are state owned, carry advertising (usually consisting of someone shouting at you – very loudly!), although the amount of revenue channels can raise from advertising is limited.

TV One is TVNZ's major channel and provides a staple diet of news broadcasts, home-produced and imported dramas, and

Public TV Stations	
Station	**Description**
TV One	general entertainment, news, sport
TV2	general entertainment, comedy, reality and drama
TVNZ6	general entertainment for children, families and mature audiences (started service in 2007) available on Freeview and Sky
TVNZ7	24-hour information channel with news, current affairs and documentaries (started service in 2008) available on Freeview and Sky
TVNZ Sport Extra	occasional sport coverage (started service in 2007) available only on Freeview
Parliament TV	live coverage of the New Zealand parliamentary sessions (gripping stuff!)
Trackside	horse and dog racing
Maori Television channel	Maori language
Te Reo channel	Maori language

Commercial TV Stations	
Station	**Description**
TV3	general entertainment, news and sport (TV3 PLUS 1 is a one-hour delayed broadcast of TV3 on Freeview only)
Channel 4	music, reality TV and general entertainment
Prime	general entertainment, news and sport
Triangle-Stratos	public service and access programming in English and other languages (available only in Auckland)
CTV8	Chinese TV (available in Auckland only)

ubiquitous 'lifestyle' programmes. TV One is New Zealand's most popular channel with an audience share of around 40 per cent. TV2 broadcasts children's programmes, drama series and films, and has a market share of some 20 per cent. TV3 targets the 18 to 49 age range and offers mainly home-produced and international series, with some 20 per cent of the audience share, while C4, Prime and Triangle Stratos each have only a few per cent. The balance is made up by pay TV companies such as Sky.

Terrestrial TV is short on the Kiwis' passion – sport – because the major sporting events have been sold to the highest bidder, namely satellite or cable TV, although this has changed to some extent following an agreement between Sky TV and TV3. Otherwise, if you like watching sport, you need to invest in a satellite dish or cable connection to watch the big matches (although you can watch them free at pubs, which show live sport on large-screen TVs – unfortunately the drinks aren't free!).

Prime Television New Zealand is a small national free-to-air TV station, now owned by Sky Television. It airs a mix of programming largely imported from Australia, the UK and the USA, as well as free-to-air rugby (league and union) and cricket matches. Prime's terrestrial signals cover over 90 per cent of the population, although it has 100 per cent national cover via Sky Television's satellite and TelstraClear's cable services, with a paid subscription.

Triangle Television is available in Auckland and is a non-profit trust that runs the public service, non-commercial and Government-owned UHF channel for the Auckland region. It started broadcasting in Auckland on 1st August, 1998 and broadcasts programs in many languages, as it's run as a public station. It's a popular service for ethnic communities in the city who cannot see their own programmes or hear their own languages anywhere else on New Zealand television (apart from the

Chinese, who have had their own TV station – CTV8 – since 2007). It's available on both Sky and TelstraClear.

Digital TV

There are four forms of broadcast digital television in New Zealand: Sky satellite (available nationwide), Freeview satellite (nationwide), Freeview's terrestrial (available in major centres) and TelstraClear cable (available in Wellington and Christchurch). Sky TV launched New Zealand's first nationwide digital TV service in December 1998 and had a monopoly on digital satellite TV until the launch of Freeview's nationwide digital Satellite service in May 2007. High Definition (HD) programming is available via Freeview on terrestrial broadcast only and on SKY TV through the MY SKY HDi decoder. Not all channels are available in High Definition.

Between September 2012 and November 2013 the government will switch off analogue transmissions and TV reception will be from digital transmissions only. The Switch over process will be in four stages as shown below:

Digital Rollout Schedule

1. Hawkes Bay and West Coast: 30th September 2012

2. The rest of the South Island: April 2013

3. Lower North Island: September 2013

4. Upper North Island: November 2013

Freeview

Freeview (🖳 www.freeviewnz.tv) was designed to overcome the poor reception caused by the country's rugged topography and provide New Zealanders with high-quality digital TV and radio. Freeview/HD is a non-profit joint venture launched on 14th April 2008 by a group of free-to-air broadcasters to provide a free-to-air high definition (HD) digital platform on which all free-to-air broadcasters could broadcast their channels (broadcasters decide which channels they will make available on Freeview).

Channels currently available include TV1, TV Two, TV3, Channel 4, Maori Television, TVNZ6, TVNZ7, TV3 Plus 1, CTV8, Te Reo, TV Sports Extra, Triangle-Stratos, Parliament TV,

TV Central and Cue (plus the radio stations, Radio New Zealand National & Concert, Base FM and George FM). Freeview is available via satellite to a dish and via terrestrial UHF transmission to a UHF aerial with a Freeview set top box (sometimes called a decoder) or a TV with a built-in Freeview decoder. The Freeview terrestrial service is available to around 75 per cent of the population and currently serves the areas surrounding Auckland, Christchurch, Dunedin, Hamilton, Napier-Hastings, Palmerston North, Tauranga and Wellington.

A set-top box, a suitable TV tuner card or a digital capable TV, and a UHF aerial or a satellite dish are required to receive Freeview. If you don't have an HD TV, a set top box will convert the digital signal to analogue. Digital Freeview receivers cost from around $79 if you have a satellite dish or $99 if you have a UHF aerial, and are available via the Freeview website (🖳 www.freeviewnz.tv) and from independent retailers such as the Freeviewshop (🖳 www.freeviewshop.co.nz). Once you have purchased a set top box or HD TV, there are no on-going charges, contracts or other expenses.

Programmes

Television in New Zealand doesn't have a particularly good reputation, as most people freely admit. The small population and limited budgets mean that there are relatively few home-produced programmes (around 20 per cent, the lowest percentage in the developed world – a cause for growing concern among certain groups), even fewer good ones, and TV stations prefer to import programmes from other English-speaking nations (mainly Australia, the UK and the USA). Lovers of America's 'Friends' and 'South Park' and the UK's 'Changing Rooms', 'Coronation Street' and 'Eastenders' will be delighted to discover that they're all shown on New Zealand TV. The quality of local documentary programmes is high, and wildlife programmes such as 'Meet The Real Penguins' and 'Mount Cook' have won New Zealand programme makers awards in Asia and Europe.

Viewing figures show that New Zealanders sometimes display better taste regarding TV than their European or North American counterparts. News and documentary programmes often make the top five (rather than soap operas), ranked by audience figures, along with rugby matches (particularly Super 12 games). A TV gardening programme, 'Maggie's Garden Show', once featured in the top rankings, as does the British soap 'Coronation Street'; when TVNZ once announced plans to cut the weekly showings of 'Corrie' from three to two they received a petition of 20,000 signatures in protest! New Zealanders also have their own soaps, of which the most popular is the hospital drama 'Shortland Street', first screened in 1992.

Other popular home-produced programmes include 'Te Tutu', a drama series on TV One, 'Captain's Log', a series about famous voyages around New Zealand, and 'Inside New Zealand', a documentary produced by TV3. Most programmes are broadcast in English, but a small number are broadcast in Maori, including 'Te Karere' (meaning news).

News programmes are presented professionally, although they tend to focus on national rather than international news, and coverage can also be rather superficial, making pay TV's BBC World, CNN and Sky News compulsive viewing for news junkies.

The government-funded organisation, NZ On Air, promotes New Zealand culture and provides funding for home-produced programmes. Home-produced documentaries, drama series and children's programmes account for some 20 per cent of total broadcasting, although in a survey over 60 per cent of New Zealanders claimed they would like to see the proportion substantially increased. This percentage is even higher among the Maori population, whose culture is given top priority by NZ On Air, leading to the founding in 2004 of the state-funded channel, Maori Television, broadcasting partly in Maori. More information about indigenous television can be found on the NZ On Air website (💻 www.nzonair.govt.nz).

New Zealand television stations claim to show the same amount of advertising and other 'promotional messages' as TV stations elsewhere in the English-speaking world – although it sometimes seems like more – and TVNZ has a policy of showing no more than 12 minutes' advertising an hour, an amount they claim is less than in Australia and the US.

Most daily newspapers and many magazines contain TV sections that provide details of programmes on terrestrial, cable and satellite stations. The magazine *TV Guide* ($2.20) has the most extensive listings, including in-depth features on forthcoming films and other programmes, allowing you to plan your viewing (it also happens to be New Zealand's largest-circulating weekly magazine, selling over 200,000 copies). *The Listener* (💻 www.listener.co.nz) is an upmarket magazine of comment and criticism (similar to the now-defunct British publication of the same name), which also contains TV programme listings. There are various online TV guides, including the Free TV Guide (💻 www.freetvguide.co.nz) and TV Now (💻 http://home.nzcity.co.nz/tvnow/tvguide. aspx); TVNZ also provides TV listings on its website (💻 http://tvnz.co.nz/tv-schedule).

An explosion in online piracy has forced New Zealand's free-to-air TV networks to fast-track the screening of top international shows, many of which (such as Heroes, Top Gear, House, Private Practice and Survivor) are illegally downloaded.

LICENCE

There's no annual TV licence fee in New Zealand, which was abolished in 1999. Non-state funding for television and radio programmes on TVNZ comes from NZ On Air and advertising.

PAY TELEVISION CHANNELS

There are two kinds of pay television channels in New Zealand, cable and satellite.

Cable

Cable television has made slow progress in New Zealand and is available only in certain areas, which include Wellington and the Kapiti Coast, Greymouth, Gisborne and several suburbs of Auckland. If you subscribe to cable TV, you can also obtain your telephone and internet service via cable (a phone line is mandatory). Cable TV is the poor relation of pay TV and, despite initial optimistic predictions, isn't very popular. The easiest way to find out whether cable TV is available in your area is to ask your neighbours. The presence of cable 'pillars' (junction boxes) and unsightly, subsiding trenches in the roads and pavements of Auckland and Wellington's smartest suburbs are also a good indication! Cable TV offers exclusive cable channels, as well as terrestrial TV broadcasts and satellite channels such as CNN.

The major cable operator is TelstraClear (🖥 www.telstraclear.co.nz), New Zealand's second-largest telecommunications company with around 400,000 customers (the network was previously know as Saturn TV). Its cable TV service is called 'InHome' and offers a total of around 70 channels (including many Sky TV channels). A basic

package costs $54.90 per month for basic digital TV (including mandatory phone line rental), but it can be considerably more, e.g. $98.62 per month if you add Sky. A separate set top box is required if you wish to receive HD TV and you can also include broadband internet and a mobile phone in your package.

Satellite

Satellite TV is popular in New Zealand, thanks to the country's rugged topography and sparse population outside the cities, where terrestrial TV signals can be poor and cable TV isn't available. It's operated by Sky (🕿 0800 759 999, 🖥 www.skytv.co.nz), the pre-eminent pay TV operator, which offers a wide range of sports, movies, music, on-demand and general content across over 100 channels. The channel line-up includes seven sports channels, six movie channels, seven general entertainment channels, five documentary channels, five news channels, four children's channels, plus various other niche and special interest channels.

You can take out a subscription by contacting Sky and have a dish installed within a few days (if you live in a remote or mountainous area, you may need an extra large dish to receive transmissions). A start-up package to receive Sky TV, including a large dish, receiver/decoder and installation, costs around $300, although Sky have occasional special online offers; for example, in early 2012 Sky were offering free installation plus Sky Sports and The Rugby Channel free for the first month, normally $25.29 and $8.81 respectively (includes the basic package – see below).

Sky viewers pay $45 for the basic package of over 59 channels, to which you can add other packages such as movies and sports,

e.g. Sky Movies ($20.70), Sky Sports ($25.29) and Platinum Sports ($34.10). If you want all channels it will cost you around a whopping $200 per month! Sky Sports' trump card has been to secure exclusive broadcasting rights to many top sporting events in New Zealand, including rugby matches. As sport (especially rugby and particularly the All Blacks) is something which few New Zealanders can live without (literally), it accounts for the impressive following that satellite TV has built up – around 850,000 subscribers in mid-2011.

DVDs

It isn't worth shipping a foreign TV or DVD player to New Zealand, as they're available locally at reasonable prices. Also, a TV made for a foreign market is unlikely to be compatible with New Zealand's transmission system (a PAL variant) and voltage, particularly if it's designed for the American market, although Australian equipment will work. A small TV costs anything from $350 to $550, depending on the size and the manufacturer.

Like flat screen HD TVs, DVD players have become essential items of equipment in New Zealand homes in the last few years.

There are DVD rental stores (non-residents may need to pay a deposit, e.g. $20) in all cities and large towns, usually open seven days a week until late evening. A night's rental of the latest films costs around $8 per night (Blu-ray DVDs cost a bit more) and around $4 or $5 for three or seven days for older films. There may be a reduction if you take out three or more films.

☑ SURVIVAL TIP

One mail-order DVD rental company worth a particular mention is Fatso (💻 www.fatso. co.nz), which has DVD rental plans from $9.95 per month (one DVD at a time and two per month) up to three DVDs at a time and an unlimited number per month for $37.99. It provides a free trial with a pre-paid return service, no late fees and cancellation at anytime.

The cost of DVDs starts at around $10 for the oldest releases, although recent films and major sporting events cost much more. DVD rental is becoming less popular and is increasingly being replaced by pay-per-view films offered by pay TV operators such as Sky and TelstraClear.

RADIO

Radio broadcasting in New Zealand follows the model established for the TV industry and there are state-operated and commercially run stations – see 💻 www.nzradioguide.co.nz for a list of stations. The Radio Bureau (💻 www. trb.co.nz) style themselves the 'Champions of Radio' and provide a wealth of information on their website.

Radio New Zealand (RNZ, 💻 www.radionz. co.nz) operates three national stations; Concert FM and National Radio, which are similar to the BBC's Radio 3 and 4, and the AM Network, which relays Parliamentary proceedings. Radio New Zealand National & Concert (plus Base FM and George FM) are also available in digital on Freeview. RNZ has a good reputation for the quality of its broadcasting, although they're rather staid and have a mainly older (and declining) audience. RNZ stations are entirely state-funded and don't carry advertising. It also operates a network of local radio stations throughout the country, which are partly state-funded and partly funded from advertising. They broadcast mainly rock, pop and easy listening music, local and regional news, and sport.

There's a wealth of national commercial radio stations in New Zealand, mainly broadcasting pop music, and there are also several special interest stations such as Radio Sport (💻 www.radiosport.co.nz), whose commentaries have been widely acclaimed, and religious stations such as Rhema (💻 www. rhema.co.nz). One of the country's top news stations is NewstalkZB (💻 www.newstalkzb. co.nz). MediaWorks (💻 www.mediaworks. co.nz), owners of TV3 and C4, has a network of ten national stations (plus regional stations) – Mai FM, The Edge, George FM, The Rock, More FM, The Breeze, Solid Gold, Radio Live, B Sport and Kiwi FM – broadcasting on 190 frequencies throughout New Zealand.

There's also an abundance of local commercial radio stations, with around 100 FM stations alone, plus others broadcasting on the AM frequency. Radio stations are closely involved with their local communities and play pop or easy listening music and broadcast local news and sport. Because there are so many commercial stations competing for a limited amount of advertising money, stations go to extraordinary lengths to attract listeners.

Most radio stations broadcast in English, although there are a number of state and private radio stations broadcasting in Maori (see Māngai Pāho, 🖥 www.tmp.govt. nz), particularly in regions with large Maori communities such as Auckland (🖥 www. waatea603am.co.nz) and the north-west tip of the North Island. See also Irirangi.net (🖥 www. irirangi.net).

The BBC World Service is re-broadcast on local frequencies in several major cities, including Auckland and Wellington, and can also be received direct (see 🖥 worldservice. co.nz). Details of BBC World Service programmes and frequency information is provided on their website (🖥 www.bbc.co.uk/ worldservice/index.shtml).

You can also receive a wealth of radio stations via the internet, including those listed on the NZ Radio Guide (🖥 www.nzradioguide.co.nz).

Rotorua Museum

9.
EDUCATION

New Zealand has long had an effective and respected educational system, although few aspects of life have gone through more upheaval in the last few decades (see School Reforms below). There have been many critics of the educational reforms over the last 15 years, although most are forced to admit that they've been largely successful.

The New Zealand education system is regarded as one of the best in the world, and, when ranked alongside those from other developed countries, New Zealand students often have superior levels of numeracy and literacy. In the 2009 OECD Programme for International Student Assessment (PISA, 🖥 www.pisa.oecd.org) New Zealand was above average in every category (reading, mathematics and science), ahead of Australia and well ahead of the UK and US. New Zealand is a world leader in 'export education' (see 🖥 www.educationnz.org.nz), i.e. the education of international students, and compares favourably with its major competitors (Australia, Canada, the UK and USA). The International education industry is worth over $2bn and comprises more than 5 per cent of New Zealand's export earnings.

Education is compulsory for children aged between 6 and 16 (the school leaving age was increased from 15 to 16 in the '80s), although most children start school at five. In addition to state and private school education, over 6,000 children are educated at home by parents or tutors (permission is required from the Ministry of Education). Secondary students can also take courses via the Correspondence School (see **Further Education** below) if they aren't offered by their secondary school.

For general information about education in New Zealand, contact the Ministry of Education (Box 1666, Wellington, ☎ 04-463 8000, 🖥 www.minedu.govt.nz). Other useful websites include Te Kete Ipurangi (TKI)/ The Online Learning Centre (🖥 www.tki.org. nz/e/tki), New Zealand's bilingual education portal, and New Zealand Educated (🖥 www. newzealandeducated.com), the government site for overseas students.

STATE OR PRIVATE SCHOOL?

If you're able to choose between state and private education, the following checklist will help you decide:

♦ How long are you planning to stay in New Zealand? If you're uncertain, it's probably better to assume a long stay. Possible integration problems mean that enrolling a child in a New Zealand state school is recommended only for at least a year, particularly if he isn't a native English speaker.

♦ Bear in mind that the area where you choose to live will affect your choice of school(s). For example, it's usually more convenient to send a child to a state school near your home, and if you choose a private day school you must take into account the distance from your home to the school. Note also that some schools are over-subscribed and have a catchment area (see **Enrolment** below).

- Do you know where you're going when you leave New Zealand? This may be an important consideration with regard to a child's language of tuition and system of education in New Zealand. How old is your child and what age will he be when you plan to leave New Zealand? What plans do you have for his future education and in which country?

- What educational level is your child at now and how will he fit into a private school or the New Zealand state school system? The younger he is, the easier it will be to place him in a suitable school.

- How does your child view the thought of studying in New Zealand? If you aren't from an English-speaking country, what language is best from a long-term point of view? Is schooling available in New Zealand in his mother tongue?

- Will your child require your help with his studies, and more importantly, will you be able to help him? If necessary, is special or extra tutoring available?

- What are the school hours? What are the school holiday periods? How will the school holidays and hours influence your family's work and leisure activities?

- Is religion an important factor in your choice of school? Usually only private, church-run schools offer a comprehensive religious education and are run according to their particular religious values.

- Do you want your child to go to a co-educational or a single-sex school? New Zealand state schools are usually co-educational.

- Should you send your child to a boarding school? If so, in which country?

- What are the secondary and further education prospects in New Zealand or another country? Are New Zealand examinations or the examinations set by New Zealand schools recognised in your home country or the country where you plan to live after leaving New Zealand? If applicable, check whether New Zealand (NCEA) examinations are recognised as a university entrance qualification in your home country.

- Does a prospective school have a good academic record? Most schools provide a glowing prospectus, but you should also check the exam pass rate statistics.

- How large are the classes? What is the pupil-teacher ratio?

☑ **SURVIVAL TIP**

Obtain the opinions and advice of others who have been faced with the same decisions and problems as yourself, and collect as much information from as many different sources as possible before making a decision. You may also wish to speak to teachers and the parents of children attending the schools on your shortlist. See also Enrolment below.

Finally, most parents find it pays to discuss alternatives with a child before making a decision. See also **Choosing a Private School** on page 145.

STATE SCHOOLS

The New Zealand state (public) school system educates around 95 per cent of children and is one of the government's largest expenses, consuming around 20 per cent of the national budget. There are state schools throughout New Zealand, where most children attend a day school, although around 10,000 attend state boarding schools. Many of these are children whose homes are in remote areas and for whom boarding school is the only way to receive a full secondary education. However, state boarding schools in cities with reputations for academic excellence also attract local day students. Most state schools are co-educational, including a number of single-sex schools that have opened their doors to the opposite sex in recent years, particularly in the higher grades.

State schools are organised on the comprehensive system and attract students with a wide range of abilities. There's less distinction between 'good' and 'not-so-good' schools compared with many other countries, with schools striving to maintain and improve standards within the terms of their charter. However, as is the case in many other countries, schools in wealthier areas where parents can afford to provide extra finance and support, tend to have much better academic records than schools in poorer areas.

Truancy is a problem in New Zealand, where some 4 per cent (30,000 children) of the 750,000 primary and high school pupils skip school each week. Parents face fines of from $300 to $3,000 for failing to ensure a child goes to school or failing to enrol a child in school.

School Reforms

In the late '80s, New Zealand began a sweeping series of state school reforms. Prior to 1989, primary and secondary state schools were the responsibility of the Ministry of Education via regional or local authority school boards, which managed all schools in their districts. In 1989 the New Zealand Department of Education was dissolved (and replaced by the Ministry of Education) and the governance of local schools was handed over to locally elected boards of trustees, comprising members of staff, politicians, business people and other worthy citizens. Trustees have considerable leeway in how a school is run, but are responsible to the Education Review Office (🖳 www.ero.govt.nz) for their actions and for meeting the standards set by the government. The Education Review Office monitors their progress and reports directly to the Minister of Education.

The reforms set out to achieve their objectives by creating something of a commercial market in the state educational system, with schools being given increased autonomy and the freedom to set their own rules and spend their budgets in a way that most benefited their students. In 1991 there was a radical move to a system of parental choice for schools, which abolished residential attendance zones (catchment areas), except when schools are over-subscribed (see **Enrolment** below), and allowed schools to compete with each other for students.

It's generally accepted that the reforms have been successful for the majority of schools, most of which are either at capacity

or have grown by more than 5 per cent during the '90s, which indicates that most students are getting the kind of education they (or their parents) want. However, it has led to segregation, as some racial and ethnic groups (e.g. Europeans) have been better at using reforms to improve their children's education than others. As a result, schools have become more racially segregated and also more segregated by class, with, not surprisingly, the poorest students ending up in the worst schools (which have become repositories for a disproportionate number of difficult-to-educate students).

Critics of the reforms state that while parental choice is a good thing, the interests of students, educators, administrators, local communities, future employers, and a multitude of others who have legitimate interests in the public schools that serve their communities, have not been best served by the reforms. It's claimed by some that rather than balance interests, market forces have worked to consolidate control within the hands of a narrow set of interests, including very popular schools which now have far more applicants than places.

Curriculum & Facilities

Most state schools follow a balanced curriculum based around the humanities, mathematics, modern languages, practical or vocational skills, and the sciences. The study of the Maori language and culture is compulsory in all schools, although some Polynesian schools focus on this more than others. The majority of schools recognise New Zealand's strengthening links with Polynesian and Asian countries, rather than with Europe. For example, the study of Japanese (and recently Chinese) has been added to the curriculum and often replaces the study of French and German. All state schools have good sports facilities and are usually set amidst extensive sports fields and offer a variety of sports, of which (as would be expected) rugby is the most popular.

Teaching

In general, the standard of teaching is high and teachers have a good reputation among their peers abroad. However, the country suffers from a shortage of qualified teachers and several thousand children in primary education don't have a permanent class teacher. The problem tends to be worse in schools in poorer areas, rural areas and those areas with large Maori communities. To try to solve the problem, the government has set up an organisation called TeachNZ (💻 www.teachnz.govt.nz), offering a package of enhanced pay and benefits to tempt teachers from other countries to come and work in New Zealand, and to encourage expat New Zealand teachers to return home.

Discipline

The standard of discipline is good in most state schools, although some schools in poor or ethnic areas have problems with race relations and gangs. Most schools have strict anti-violence policies where verbal or physical violence isn't tolerated, although the level of enforcement is variable. Bullying is also a problem in some schools. The main threats to discipline in New Zealand schools are alcohol and drugs, which have prompted some schools to introduce drug and alcohol testing for students.

New Zealand Police (💻 www.police.govt.nz/service/yes) operate a Youth Education Service (YES), where police officers work in partnership with teachers in the classroom to promote individual safety and help create safer communities.

Corporal punishment isn't permitted in New Zealand schools in any form (it was banned some years ago), although there have been calls to reintroduce it.

Language

To get the most out of the New Zealand educational system, students must be able to communicate in English. This is a basic requirement imposed by the government and one that's taken into account when prospective migrants apply for residence (see **Chapter 3**). For children whose mother tongue isn't English, most schools (or at least those in areas attracting a significant number of immigrants) provide extra English language tuition. However, the tuition provided varies with the school and may be insufficient for some children.

Many educationalists agree that while children in New Zealand have a similar level of ability in most subjects to children of a similar age in other English-speaking countries, they're generally more advanced in reading and writing than children in Australia, the UK and the USA. In many areas, Maori and other Polynesian children, who receive only minimal Maori tuition at school, attend Maori language 'nests' (known as *Kohanga Reo*), where they learn the Maori language and culture.

Enrolment

Parents are responsible for ensuring that their children are enrolled in the most suitable school. Finding the 'best' school is something that you need to do largely unaided, as there's no central body to allocate your child to the most appropriate or best available school. Indeed, the concept of parental choice is crucial to the new 'market' which now operates in education.

Parents aren't required to enrol their children in their nearest school, as used to be the case, but most children in New Zealand attend the school nearest to their home for the sake of convenience, and in any case, in some areas there's only one primary or secondary school. The above-mentioned ERO booklet suggests that parents take into account the following criteria when choosing a school: The proximity to their home, how safe it is to walk there, and where the child's siblings or friends attend school. It also suggests that parents take into account whether a school operates individual age group or composite classes (where several age groups are taught in the same class by one teacher). Composite classes are found in some rural schools and are generally thought to be detrimental to a child's progress.

If a school has too many children wishing to enrol, the Ministry of Education allows it to operate an enrolment scheme to prevent overcrowding. Under the scheme, each school must have a clearly defined catchment area, known as a 'home zone' or 'zoning', and children who live in the zone have the right to attend the school. If you live outside the catchment area, you must apply for enrolment. There's a priority order to enrolment and children with siblings currently or formerly at the school have priority over others. If after priority has been allocated there are still more applicants than places, a ballot (random draw) is held.

Schools with enrolment systems must advertise in local newspapers the number of places available and the enrolment dates. If you live in the catchment area (zone) of a school with an enrolment scheme and you want to enrol your child, the school is obliged to accept him. If, however, you want to enrol your child in a school with an enrolment scheme and you don't live in its catchment area, you may need to wait until the school organises the next ballot. This has led to parents wishing to get a child accepted at a popular school (i.e. a top-performing school) to move home in order to be within a school's catchment area, which has driven up the cost of homes close to the best schools and restricted the ability of lower socio-economic groups to purchase a house in the zone. For more information about school enrolment zones, see 🖳 http://nzschools.tki.org.nz.

There are many resources for parents faced with choosing a school, including the 'School Directory' feature on the Ministry of Education website (🖳 www.minedu.govt.nz/parents/allages/schoolsearch.aspx), which allows parents to find out incformation about schools, including the subjects taught, student profile, student achievement, contact details and the map location of each school. TKI (🖳 www.tki.org.nz/schools) also allows you to search schools by region and Wikipedia also maintains a list of schools by region (🖳 http://en.wikipedia.org/wiki/list_of_schools_in_new_zealand).

The Education Review Office (ERO, 🖳 www.ero.govt.nz) publishes a booklet entitled *Choosing a School for a Five Year Old*, which is available from their offices (its general principles also apply to choosing a school for older children). The ERO will also supply a list of suitable schools in an area on request and can also provide a report on a particular school.

Visiting schools on your short list and discussing their merits with other parents is recommended before making a decision. You should telephone the schools you're interested in to obtain an information pack or prospectus and to arrange a visit. The ERO recommends that parents take a child's last report from his current school (or last school abroad if you're a new immigrant) and also examples of his work if it's in English, in order to help teachers assess his level of ability as accurately as possible.

Details of schools, universities and polytechnics in New Zealand are contained in a publication called *Excellence: NZ Education Directory* (🖳 www.cervinpublishing.co.nz/

pub_excellence_nz.php) published annually in January, which can be purchased from bookshops or consulted in public libraries.

School Hours & Holidays

Schools are permitted a certain amount of freedom to set their own hours, but these are usually from 8.30 or 9am until 3pm in primary schools (until 3.30 or 4pm in secondary schools), Mondays to Fridays. There's usually an hour's break for lunch and short breaks mid-morning and mid-afternoon. The New Zealand academic year follows the calendar year in common with Australia, but unlike the autumn-to-summer system that operates in most of Europe and North America. This system creates a frantic situation for parents and children alike, as the main school holidays coincide with the Christmas period.

The Ministry of Education stipulates that schools must open for a minimum period each academic year; this varies from year to year, although it's usually around 390 half-days for both primary and secondary schools. There must also be four terms each year and the term dates for state schools throughout the country are set by the Ministry, although schools are allowed some freedom to take half-term breaks and occasional days off. Term dates vary from year to year (see ☐ www.minedu.govt.nz) – those for 2012 are shown below:

School Term Dates	
Term	**Term Dates**
1	between 30th January and 7th February to 5th April
2	23rd April to 29th June
3	16th July to 28th September
4*	15th October to 20th December

* Secondary and composite schools (term 4) end on 14th December.

Costs

Educating children can be an expensive business in any country, no less so in New Zealand. The cost of educating a child in New Zealand is estimated to be around $35,000,

assuming he starts at the age of five and leaves at 16. This can be considered a modest estimate for a child attending a state school where no tuition fees are charged. The cost of a private education, including tuition fees and expenses, is reckoned to be around $250,000 for the same period. This is broadly similar to costs in other developed countries.

State schools aren't permitted to charge fees of any kind, but there are extra expenses associated with educating your children. Many schools suggest that you donate a set amount at the start of each year or term to boost their finances. This is set by individual schools and varies from modest sums in poorer areas (where the majority of families don't pay anything) to larger solicitations in wealthier areas, and is unlikely to be less than $200 annually. Although it's entirely voluntary, parents often feel obliged to pay for fear that they may harm their child's education if they refuse. Donations tend to be spent on essentials rather than 'extras'. If you want your child to take part in any extra-curricular activities, such as specialist sports coaching or music tuition, then you need to allow for the cost.

Schools provide a basic education in these areas, but many parents like their children to pursue extra interests. A year's tuition in a musical instrument can easily cost $1,000. In addition, there are the inevitable (and sometimes expensive) school trips, in which most parents wish their children to participate. Many schools organise residential trips where the entire class spends a week together, for example, studying the environment or participating in adventure sports. The cost of such a trip is likely to be at least $250 and possibly more if special clothing or equipment needs to be purchased or hired.

There are some expenses which are unavoidable even in the 'free' state sector. Schools are entitled to charge for items such as stationery (which includes subject workbooks), for which around $125 per year should be allowed (more for students studying in the higher grades). School textbooks are generally free for primary and secondary school students in the state system. Parents are also expected to buy school uniforms (where worn) and other special clothing

Early Childhood Education

Around 90 per cent of children in New Zealand attend some kind of nursery school before the compulsory school starting age of six, which is known as 'early childhood education'. If you can afford to, you can send your child to a nursery or similar school almost straight from birth and they can attend whatever establishment you choose. The government has a policy of partly funding early childhood education, which means that it subsidises the facilities but doesn't provide all children with free schooling. If you cannot afford to pay, your choice is more restricted and you may need to join a waiting list, with the result that your child may not be able to begin his early childhood education until at least the age of four and possibly not until five.

Early childhood education is provided in various centres, including childcare centres, community playgroups, crèches, kindergartens (known as 'kindys') and play centres. Kindergartens take children from the age of two and usually charge a small fee (around $10 a week), although space is limited. Some kindergartens have huge waiting lists, particularly in Auckland, and it's recommended to register your child as soon as possible (preferably before conception) in order to secure a place. Where private kindergartens are available, they're likely to charge around $800 per term. See 🖳 www.nzkindergarten. org.nz for information.

Play centres, childcare centres and community playgroups are often run by voluntary organisations or groups of parents on a non-profit basis, and are either free or charge a small daily fee to cover expenses. Crèches accept children of any age (from babies upwards) and tend to be more upmarket. They can, however, be quite expensive, although those that are registered and employ qualified staff are state-subsidised.

In Auckland and many other cities there are 'walking school buses' to transport young children safely to school. Each 'bus' walks along a set route, with at least one adult

such as sports kit. The cost of a full, new school uniform can be between $500 and $750 which, depending on how fast a child is growing, may last less than one school year! Parents on a limited budget can buy these items secondhand from local shops.

Class Grading System

In 1998, New Zealand introduced a new system of grading school years, based on a 'year of schooling' system. This is similar to the system that has been used in Australia and the USA for many years, and which is also common in the UK. It measures the number of years a student has spent in the educational system as a whole, rather than the number of years spent in each school, as was previously the case. Students in their first year of compulsory education are classified as 'year one' and when they move on to secondary school for their first year of secondary education, usually at 13, they're classified as 'year nine'. Students who start at a school after the age of six (e.g. new arrivals) are allocated to the same year grade as the majority of children of their age.

Students usually progress to the next grade at the end of each academic year, irrespective of their level of attainment, although a student who has failed to make sufficient progress may be required to repeat the previous year's study, but this is rare. If for some reason your child is absent from the New Zealand educational system for all or most of an academic year, the new system permits them to rejoin the grade they were in when they left.

'driver' (usually one to every eight children), picking children up at designated stops or outside homes and walking them to school. In the afternoons, when the children are coming home from school, the process is reversed.

Primary School

Primary schools educate children aged between five and ten. Your child is required to attend primary school from the age of six, although many schools take children from five, which is a considerable relief for parents who have been paying private kindergarten fees. Indeed, enrolling a child at five is often the only way to ensure that your child attends the school of your choice, as there may be no places remaining for the admission of six-year-olds. If you want your child to attend one of the better primary schools, it's wise to make enquiries well in advance rather than waiting until he's almost six.

Primary school education in New Zealand concentrates on studying spoken and written English (reading, spelling and writing) plus art, health education, maths, music, physical education (PE), sciences and social studies. The standard of primary reading and writing education is particularly high, which some put down to the fact that teaching still relies heavily on 'old fashioned' methods such as learning by rote and having children read aloud to teachers and classroom assistants.

Primary school pupils don't wear uniforms, although some schools produce a school T-shirt or sweatshirt that they sell to raise funds, which pupils wear on a 'voluntary' basis – although try telling your kids that it's voluntary when all their friends wear them!

Intermediate School

Intermediate school caters for children aged 11 and 12 and, as the name implies, serves as a bridge between primary and secondary schools. In some country areas, intermediate school education has traditionally been provided within the local primary school, and it's becoming common in many areas for students to remain at primary school until the age of 12 and then move directly to secondary school, or even for secondary schools to take students at 11. This is thought to be beneficial to children as they suffer only one

upheaval in their schooling, rather than two changes of school within two years. Students at intermediate and secondary schools wear uniforms which parents must pay for.

Intermediate school education in New Zealand concentrates on studying spoken and written languages (reading, spelling and writing) plus art, health education, maths, music, PE, sciences and social studies, as well as more practical skills such as wood and metalwork and domestic science. The main difference from primary school is that subjects are taught by specialist subject teachers in their classrooms, with students rotating between them rather than being taught all lessons by one class teacher.

Secondary School

At secondary school, students study a core curriculum consisting of arts and crafts, English, general science, health, home economics, mathematics, music, PE and social studies. They can also study other optional subjects, e.g. economics, geography, history and languages such as French and German or, increasingly, Chinese and Japanese. Exactly what subjects a student studies is decided in conjunction with parents and teachers. There's also some variation in the range of optional subjects from school to school, with individual schools competing to offer subjects regarded as either beneficial to students' future careers or fashionable, such as information technology and Chinese.

While all secondary schools must offer the core curriculum, there's a tendency for some to specialise in certain areas such as business, sciences or vocational skills. This means that choosing a secondary school requires more thought and planning with regard to a child's future career than previously. Attendance at secondary school is compulsory until the age of 16.

Examinations

Until 2002, New Zealand senior school students took the School Certificate (usually in year 11), Sixth Form Certificate (year 12), and Higher School Certificate and University Entrance, Bursaries and Scholarships (year 13). In 2002, the examination system for senior school students was renamed the National Certificate of Education Achievement (NCEA), which encompasses a wide range of courses and subjects, the main objective being to combine academic and vocational learning and offer students a wider variety of subjects. Each certificate is awarded according to both internal (i.e. school) and external assessments.

There are four levels, as shown below:

Level 1

The NCEA Level 1 replaced the School Certificate in 2002 and is taken by most students after three years at secondary school, at the age of 16. It's awarded after a written examination, an internal assessment, or a combination of the two, and students may study courses in any number of subjects (usually six), depending on their ability and interests. A student's result for each subject (sometimes known as 'standards') is assessed by the following grading (credit) system: 1 (achieved the standard), 2 (achieved the standard with merit) or 3 (achieved the standard with excellence). NCEA Level 1 is equivalent to Australia's School Certificate (SC), the UK's General Certificate of Secondary Education (GCSE) and the level reached by students who graduate from the tenth grade in the USA.

NCEA Level 2

The NCEA Level 2 replaced the Sixth Form Certificate in 2003 and is awarded to students after they've studied a subject at a more advanced level than NCEA Level 1 for one year. Any number of subjects can be studied, which must include English, although it isn't compulsory to take an English exam. Results are graded as for Level 1 (see above). NCEA Level 2 is equivalent to the UK's AS level examination.

NCEA Level 3

The NCEA Level 3 replaced the Higher School Certificate and University Bursaries in 2004, and is awarded to pupils who have studied an advanced course for two years in at least three subjects (chosen by students). There are minimum requirements for literacy and numeracy for university entrance. It's similar in standard to the HSC in Australia, the UK's 'A levels' and the standard required to graduate from the twelfth grade in the USA.

NCEA Level 4

The NCEA Level 4 is for outstanding students, taken as they finish secondary schooling. Students who pass Level 4 may earn, not only a place on their chosen higher education course, but also a scholarship (bursary). Scholarships are awarded in various categories for various amounts, ranging from $1,500 to $15,000. It's estimated that 3 or 4 per cent of students will eventually sit Level 4 (which is around the same percentage sought by the UK's Oxford and Cambridge universities to sit exams for popular courses).

The Ministry of Education produces a series of pamphlets called What's New, outlining the changes in examinations as well as the latest curriculum developments. The pamphlets are available from Learning Media Customer Services, PO Box 3293, Wellington. Information can also be obtained from the New Zealand Qualifications Authority (NZQA, PO Box 160, Wellington 6140, ☎ 04-463 3000, 🖳 www.nzqa. govt.nz).

PRIVATE SCHOOLS

New Zealand has a flourishing private school sector, although it serves only around 5 per cent of pupils. In recent years, a number of state schools have effectively become private schools, as the government now gives greater autonomy to state schools and several have been encouraged to join the commercial market. However, you shouldn't assume that all private schools are excellent or that they offer a better education than state schools, which certainly isn't true.

Private schools range from nursery schools (see **Early Childhood Education** on page 141) to secondary schools, both day and boarding, and from traditional-style schools to those offering 'alternative' education such as Montessori and Rudolf Steiner schools. Private education includes schools sponsored by churches and religious groups (known as parochial schools), educational foundations and private individuals, schools for students with learning or physical disabilities, and for gifted children.

In addition to mainstream parochial (e.g. Catholic) schools, there are also schools for religious and ethnic minorities, for example Muslims, where there's a strict code regarding the segregation of boys and girls. Most private schools are single sex, although some have become co-educational in recent years. There are also private boarding schools, although few accept only boarders and many cater for both day students and boarders.

Most private schools provide a similar curriculum to state schools and set the same examinations, although some offer the International Baccalaureate (IB) examination, an internationally recognised university entrance qualification, which could be an important consideration if you intend to remain in New Zealand for only a few years.

Fees vary considerably according to a variety of factors, including the age of students, the reputation and quality of the school, and its location (schools in major cities are usually the most expensive). Private schools receive some government funding, although most of their budget comes from the fees paid by parents. School fees have risen in recent years and usually range from $5,000 to $15,000 a year, but for high school day students are typically $15,000 a year (up to $21,000) and up to $25,000 a year for boarders. Fees for international students whose parents aren't resident in New Zealand are significantly higher. Some schools offer reduced fees to parents with two or more children attending a school. To the fees must be added another $2,500 to $5,000 per year for books, building levies, computers, excursion charges, special equipment (e.g. for sports), uniforms and various surcharges.

The advantages of private schools are manyfold, not least their excellent academic record, which is generally better than that of state schools. Private schools place the emphasis on traditional teaching, including consideration for others, good manners, hard work, responsibility, and not least, a sense of discipline (values which are sadly lacking in some state schools). They provide a broad-based education (aimed at developing a pupil's character) and generally provide a more varied approach to art, drama, music and sport, and a wider choice of academic subjects than state schools. Many private schools have resolutely embraced new technology and the use of computers and the internet is widespread.

Their aim is dedicated to the development of the child as an individual and the encouragement of his unique talents, rather than teaching on a production-line system (as is often the case in state schools). This is made possible by small classes (an average of around 15 to 20 pupils, or as little as half that of some state schools), which allow teachers to provide pupils with individually tailored lessons and tuition. Private schools are also better equipped to cater for special needs, including gifted children, slow learners or those who suffer from dyslexia, children requiring boarding facilities, and children whose parents wish them to be educated in

the customs of a particular religious belief or language.

You should make applications to private schools as far in advance as possible. The best and most popular schools have a demanding selection procedure and long waiting lists (in some cases many years), and parents register a child for entry 'at birth' for some schools. Obviously, if you've just arrived in New Zealand, you won't be able to apply a long time in advance. However, if possible, start planning long before your arrival in New Zealand. Don't rely on enrolling your child in a particular school and neglect the alternatives, particularly if your preferred school has a rigorous entrance examination. When applying, you're usually requested to send previous school reports, exam results and records. Before enrolling your child in a private school, make sure that you understand the withdrawal conditions in the school contract.

For information about private schools in New Zealand, contact Independent Schools of New Zealand (ISNZ, PO Box 5222, Wellington 6145, ☎ 04-471 2022, 🖥 www.isnz.org.nz). ISNZ is a group of 43 innovative and successful independent schools, some of which were established over 150 years ago and some new, educating over 25,000 students annually. Schools range from pre-school to year 13, and are either co-educational or single sex.

Choosing a Private School

The following checklist will help you choose an appropriate private school in New Zealand:

◆ Does the school have a good reputation? How long has it been established?

◆ Does the school have a good academic record? For example, what percentage of students obtain good examination passes and go on to university? All the best schools provide exam pass-rate statistics.

◆ What does the curriculum include? What examinations are set? Are examinations recognised both in New Zealand and internationally? Do they fit in with your education plans? Ask to see a typical student timetable to check the ratio of academic to non-academic subjects. Check the number of free study periods and whether they're supervised.

◆ How large are the classes and what is the student/teacher ratio? When visiting a school, check that the stated class size tallies with the number of desks/seats in the classrooms.

◆ What are the classrooms like? For example, their cleanliness, furnishings and equipment such as computers, furniture, lighting, size and space. Are there signs of creative teaching, e.g. wall charts, maps, posters and pupils' work on display?

◆ What are the qualification requirements for teachers? What nationalities are the majority of teachers? Ask for a list of the teaching staff and their qualifications.

◆ What is the teacher turnover? A high teacher turnover is a bad sign and may suggest inadequately paid teachers with poor working conditions.

◆ What extras must you pay for? For example, art supplies, computers, clothing, health and accident insurance, lunches, outings, sports equipment, stationery and text books. Most private schools charge parents for absolutely everything.

◆ Which countries do most students come from?

◆ Is religion an important consideration in your choice of school?

◆ What provision is available for children whose mother tongue isn't English?

◆ What standard and kind of accommodation is provided? What is the quality and variety of food provided? What is the dining room like? Does the school have a dietician?

◆ What languages does the school teach as obligatory or optional subjects? Does the school have a language laboratory? (Some private schools focus on French and German, which are of minimal use in New Zealand, whereas state schools tend to

be strict, although corporal punishment is forbidden.

♦ What reports are provided for parents and how often?

♦ Last but not least, unless someone else is paying, what are the fees?

Before making a final choice, it's important to visit the schools on your shortlist during term time and talk to teachers and students (if possible, also speak to former students and their parents). Where possible, check the answers to the above questions in person and don't rely on a school's prospectus or principal to provide the information. If you're unhappy with the answers, look elsewhere.

Finally, having made your choice, keep a check on your child's progress and listen to his complaints. Compare notes with other parents. If something doesn't seem right, try to establish whether a complaint is founded or not; if it is, take action to have the problem resolved. You (or your employer) are paying a lot of money for your child's education and you should ensure that you receive good value. See also **State or Private School?** on page 135.

teach Asian languages which students may find more useful.)

♦ What is the student turnover?

♦ What are the school terms and holiday periods? This is important with regard to scheduling family holidays.

♦ If you're considering a day school, what are the school hours? Is transport provided to and from school?

♦ What are the withdrawal conditions, should you need or wish to remove your child? A term's notice is usual.

♦ What sports instruction and facilities are provided? Where are the sports facilities located?

♦ What are the facilities for art and science subjects, for example, arts and crafts, biology, computer studies, cookery, drama, hobbies, music, photography and science? Ask to see the classrooms, equipment, facilities and some students' projects.

♦ What sort of outings and school trips are organised?

♦ What medical facilities does the school provide, e.g. infirmary, resident doctor or nurse? Is medical and accident insurance included in the fees?

♦ What punishments are applied and for what offences? Private schools are likely to

APPRENTICESHIPS

A system of apprenticeships operates in New Zealand, usually known as industry training, whereby youths undergo a period of training that meets industry standards. Currently, there are some 20,000 young people undertaking industry training throughout the country. There's no rigid format to training, which is offered by large and small employers, but by no means all employers. Some employers provide on-the-job training, whereas others provide training in the workplace and at a polytechnic or other college.

See Modern Apprenticeships (🖥 www.modern-apprenticeships.govt.nz) and World Skills (🖥 www.worldskills.org.nz) for further information.

HIGHER EDUCATION

Higher education and further education (see below) are known as post-compulsory education in New Zealand. Higher education is provided by eight universities, 20 polytechnics and a number of colleges of education specialising in teacher training. Higher education institutions are expected to operate on a 'free market' basis and compete with one another for students. They're funded partly by student fees and partly by government subsidies, which are allocated according to student numbers rather than on the basis of need.

Universities

Universities are the most prestigious educational establishments in New Zealand, of which there are eight: Auckland University of Technology, Lincoln University (near Christchurch), Massey University (at Albany near Auckland, Palmerston North and Wellington), the University of Auckland, the University of Canterbury (in Christchurch), the University of Otago at Dunedin, the University of Waikato (located in Hamilton) and Victoria University (Wellington). The total student body is around 500,000. For further information and links to university websites, see 🖥 www.intstudy.com/study_abroad/nzlist.htm and www.universitiesnz.ac.nz.

All universities offer a wide choice of courses, although each tends to have certain specialties in which it's regarded as a 'centre of excellence'. For example, the University of Otago specialises in dentistry, home science, medicine, pharmacy, physical education (PE) and surveying, while Lincoln University specialises in agriculture and horticulture. The University of Auckland specialises in architecture, art, engineering, medicine, optometry and planning, and the University of Canterbury in engineering, fine art and forestry.

Victoria University is the main institution for public administration and social work, whereas Massey University is noted for agriculture and horticulture, and also produces most of New Zealand's veterinary surgeons. The University of Waikato specialises in arts, computing and mathematics, education, engineering, law, and Maori and Pacific studies, while it would be an insult to the intelligence of readers to explain what Auckland University of Technology concentrates on.

No university is regarded as better or worse than any other, although a degree in a subject from a university that's a centre of excellence in that subject is more highly valued than a degree from a university which isn't.

Auckland is the largest university in terms of student numbers (over 30,000) and offers the widest range of courses. It's also more cosmopolitan, whereas the others, both geographically and intellectually, are more provincial.

Honours degree programmes last for three or four years. Entry requirements depend on the individual course, and some courses, such as medicine, demand nothing less than the best grades. Each university organises its own admissions and most distribute an enrolment pack in the first week of September, with applications required by the end of the first week of December. The university and polytechnic academic year runs from February to November.

Polytechnics

While universities specialise in academic study, polytechnics tend to specialise in applied studies. They don't compete directly with universities, although some subjects (e.g. accountancy) can be studied at both universities and polytechnics. Polytechnics usually offer diploma or certificate courses rather than degrees, and provide mainly short courses or courses for those who are already in work and wish to study part-time.

Accommodation

All universities provide accommodation in halls of residence for a proportion of students, either on campus or nearby, although many students live in shared houses or as boarders in private homes. Given their financial situation (see below), it's much more cost-effective for students to live at home with their parents, although (not surprisingly) relatively few choose to do so.

Student Finances

Higher education in New Zealand isn't free and students must pay tuition fees, which go towards funding their course and to support them during their studies. The fee for the least expensive standard, full-time Bachelor of Arts course for domestic students is around $5,000 per year, while engineering students pay around $6,500 per year, and those taking specialist science and medicine courses substantially more. International students pay from around $22,000 a year for a Bachelor of Arts degree up to over $60,000 for a Bachelor of Medicine course. Basic living expenses (including accommodation and food) are unlikely to be less than $300-400 per week, in addition to the cost of books, entertainment and transport. International students also aren't eligible for student allowances or loans (see below).

Few students are fortunate enough to have parents who can afford to pay all their expenses or are able to find jobs to finance their studies. Students can apply for a Student Allowance, although the income limits are relatively low in New Zealand terms and most students don't qualify. Allowances, which are non-refundable grants to students of limited means, are means tested and the amount granted depends on residential and citizenship qualifications, age, location, marital status, dependent children as well as personal, spousal or parental income. Allowances are reduced progressively as parental income increases and isn't paid once it reaches $82,953.82 for students living at home or $89,936.68 for students living away from home.

The allowance is intended for living expenses, therefore most students receiving an allowance will also need a student loan (see below) to pay their tuition fees. The StudyLink website (see box) contains an allowance calculator. Students can earn up to $201.13 per week before tax (from 1st April 2011) before their student allowance payments are affected.

Universities offer a number of scholarships to promising students, although the number is limited and few students can depend on them to finance their studies (see also 🖳 www.fis. org.nz)

For information about student allowances and loans, contact Study Link (☎ 0800-889 900, 🖳 www.studylink.govt.nz).

Loans

Most students obtain a loan to cover the difference between their Student Allowance (see above) or their parents' contribution, and their tuition fees and living expenses – a gap that's set to increase as universities increase their fees. New Zealand introduced a system of student loans in 1992, which allows students to borrow either part or the total amount of their compulsory fees, up to $1,000 for course-related costs and $169.51 per week (from 1st April 2011 – increased annually in line with inflation/CPI) for living costs. Factors such as age, credit rating, income and parental income don't affect your entitlement to a loan, nor is it necessary to provide security or a guarantee. Loans are restricted to New Zealand citizens and permanent residents.

To qualify for a loan, students must be studying a course that's either funded by the Ministry of Education or recognised as a qualifying course. The latter category refers to courses offered by private organisations rather than state colleges and universities, and these must consist of full or part-time study for at least a year. Students can usually take out a loan for living costs, even if the course they're following isn't Ministry-funded.

Those who receive a student allowance can also apply for a student loan (indeed they usually need to), but aren't entitled to the part of the loan that applies to living costs. For example, if you receive a student allowance of $100 a week after tax, you'll only be able to get a loan of up to $69.51 per week for living costs. You can apply for a student loan via the Study Link website (🖳 www.studylink.govt.nz), for which there's a $60 'establishment' fee.

Student loans must be repaid through deductions from your salary once you're working. Your employer deducts a fixed monthly amount and sends it to the Inland Revenue Department (IRD). The repayment rate is 10 per cent of your income above $19,084 per year (fixed until 31st March 2015), equivalent to $367 per week or $1,590 per month. If you make voluntary repayments of $500 or more in a year to the IR you may qualify for a 10 per cent voluntary repayment bonus. Since 2006, interest on student loans for New Zealand residents has been abolished.

If the financial situation for New Zealand students isn't good, it's much worse for foreign students, who don't qualify for a student loan and are charged much higher fees by universities and colleges. Education New Zealand (PO Box 10-500, Wellington, ☏ 04-472 0788, 🖥 www.educationnz.org.nz) provides information and advice to overseas students wishing to study at higher education institutions in New Zealand.

Postgraduate Studies

All universities provide facilities for postgraduate study, usually only within their specialty subjects. Students who climb this far up the academic ladder are rewarded by much lower tuition fees than for first degree courses. This reflects the contribution that postgraduate studies make towards a university's reputation and prestige. It's also common for New Zealand students to undertake postgraduate studies at foreign universities, usually in Australia, the UK or the USA, particularly when their area of expertise isn't well catered for in New Zealand. Foreign postgraduate students are also welcomed at New Zealand universities, and are offered the same favourable course rates as local students.

FURTHER EDUCATION

It's government policy to encourage New Zealanders to study and learn at all stages of their lives. A keystone of the government's further education programme is the Correspondence School (*Te Kura ā-Tuhi*) in Wellington, which is the largest 'school' in New Zealand, with over 22,000 students. The Correspondence School (see box) was established in the '20s and is something of a New Zealand institution, providing distance education from early childhood level to Year 13. Secondary students can also take courses if they aren't offered by their secondary school, and New Zealand children abroad can follow both primary and secondary school programmes. Courses include correspondence courses for adults wishing to gain qualifications in order to obtain a job or New Zealanders who just want to improve their academic ability, either in New Zealand or overseas.

The school is manned by a team of student advisers and clerks who offer pre-enrolment advice, course counselling and student support. Students receive tuition by means of written courses, via telephone and the internet, and at seminars. There are academic, vocational and general interest courses, including the full range of secondary school subjects, as well as more practical and general interest courses.

For information, contact the Correspondence School (Private Bag 39992, Wellington Mail Centre, Lower Hutt 5045, ☏ 0800-659 988 or 04-473 6841, 🖥 www.correspondence.school.nz).

LANGUAGE SCHOOLS

Obtaining a working knowledge of or becoming fluent in English while living in New Zealand is relatively easy, as you'll be constantly immersed in the English language and will have the maximum opportunity to practise. However, if you wish to speak or write English fluently, you'll probably need to attend a language school or find a private tutor. It's usually necessary to have a recognised qualification in English to be accepted at a college of higher or further education in New Zealand. If you wish to learn another language, you can enrol in a language course at one of the many language schools in New Zealand. Many languages are spoken in New Zealand, therefore there's plenty of opportunity to learn and practise foreign languages with immigrants.

English-language courses at all levels are offered by the Correspondence School (see above) and other distance learning organisations, foreign and international organisations, language schools, local associations and clubs, private colleges, private teachers and universities. Classes range from language courses for complete beginners to special business or cultural courses, and university-level seminars leading to recognised diplomas. There are language schools in cities and large towns throughout New Zealand, many equipped with bookshops, computers, language laboratories, libraries and video studios. To find a language school, see English Schools New Zealand (🖳 www.english-schools.co.nz).

Most language schools offer a variety of classes depending on your current knowledge, how many hours you wish to study per week, how much money you want to spend and how quickly you wish to learn. Full-time, part-time and evening courses are offered by most schools, and many also offer residential courses or accommodation with local families (highly recommended to accelerate learning).

Many language schools offer optional extras such as golf, horse-riding and skiing, in an attempt to lure international students, particularly from Asia. Courses that include accommodation (often half board, consisting of breakfast and an evening meal) are usually good value. Bear in mind that if you need to find your own accommodation, particularly in Wellington or Auckland, it can be difficult and expensive. Language classes generally fall into the following categories:

Most schools offer compact or intensive courses and also provide special courses for businessmen and professionals (among others), and a wide variety of examinations, most of which are recognised internationally. Course fees vary considerably and are usually calculated on a weekly basis. Fees depend on the number of hours' tuition per week, the type of course, and the location and reputation of the school. Expect to pay up to $1,000 per week for an intensive course and around $500 a week for a compact course.

Total immersion or executive courses are provided by some schools and usually consist of private lessons. Fees can run to $4,000 or more per week and not everyone is suited to learning at such a fast rate (or has the financial resources). Whatever language you're learning, you shouldn't expect to become fluent in a short period unless you have a particular flair for languages or already have a good command of a language. Unless you desperately need to learn a language quickly, it's better to arrange your lessons over a long period. Don't commit yourself to a long course of study (particularly an expensive one) before ensuring that it's the correct one. Most schools offer a free introductory lesson and free tests to help you find your appropriate level. Many language schools offer private and small group lessons.

It's important to choose the right course, particularly if you're studying English in order to continue with full-time education in New Zealand and need to reach a minimum standard or gain a particular qualification.

Category	Hours per Week
Compact	10-20
Intensive	20-30
Total immersion	30-40+

Abel Tasman National Park, South Island

10.
PUBLIC TRANSPORT

The population of New Zealand is dispersed over a wide area, which makes it difficult and prohibitively expensive to have a comprehensive public transport system. Public transport in New Zealand is centred around road, rail and air links, plus the essential umbilical ferry link connecting the North and South Islands. Most people find it mandatory to have their own transport, even if they live in downtown Auckland (which is a very large city with no rail service over the Auckland harbour bridge) or Wellington.

Apart from the patchy and intermittent public transport, the roads are relatively uncongested and therefore driving has many advantages over public transport. Even in metropolitan Auckland and Wellington, commuters travelling into the centre often drive (although traffic congestion has encouraged more drivers to switch to public transport).

The SuperGold Card (☎ 0800-254 565, 💻 www.supergold.govt.nz) is a free discount card for seniors and veterans which provides free off-peak travel from 9am and on weekends and public holidays. Contact the local regional council for information about the services in your area. All public transport timetables in New Zealand use the am/pm time system rather than the 24-hour clock.

For general information about public transport, see the Ministry of Transport website (💻 www.transport.govt.nz). Auckland Regional Transport Authority (ARTA, 💻 www.arta. co.nz), New Zealand's only regional transport authority, was established in 2004 to plan, fund and develop a successful transport system for the rapidly growing Auckland region.

DISABLED TRAVELLERS

Like many countries, New Zealand has started to take the needs of disabled travellers seriously only within the last decade or so. Domestic airlines and trains cater fully for disabled travellers, but you should inform them if you need special assistance when booking. Because most taxis are simply converted saloon cars, they aren't much use if you cannot access a standard vehicle, e.g. with a wheelchair. There are, however, wheelchair-accessible taxis in cities, although you need to book them in advance (particularly for the return journey) as their number is limited. There are no special facilities for the disabled on coach and bus services, although discounts on fares are widely available.

Further information can be obtained from the Disability Information Service (Community House, 301 Moray Place, Dunedin, ☎ 03-471 6152 or 0800-693 342, 💻 www.disabilityinfo. co.nz).

TRAINS

New Zealand's rail network is operated by Tranz Scenic, the country's only passenger rail company (💻 www.tranzscenic.co.nz). (Kiwi Rail, 💻 www.kiwirail.co.nz, is the government-owned freight rail service.) The network is limited, mainly because of the mountainous terrain in many parts of the country and, of course, by the fact that lines cannot cross the Cook Straits (unless a bridge or tunnel is built). The service itself is modern and comfortable (part of the Auckland-Wellington line has recently been electrified), but neither frequent nor fast, although stops at small stations on long-distance lines have been eliminated, making journey times shorter. As a result, rail services are widely promoted as a tourist attraction rather than as a commuters' service. In this regard the rail service is excellent, as many lines pass through alpine passes and native forests, and past volcanic peaks, offering spectacular panoramic views. There are the following four main railway routes in New Zealand:

Name	Route
The Overlander	Auckland-Wellington
Capital Connection	Palmerston North-Wellington
TranzCoastal	Christchurch-Picton
TranzAlpine	Christchurch-Greymouth

There are many special offers on fares, for example, ten-trip fares and monthly fares on the Capital Connection route, and flexi-saver, super-saver and combo-saver fares on the TranzAlpine route. If you're a student or disabled, you qualify for a 50 per cent discount off the standard fare, although you need proof of identity and must book in advance. There's only one class of travel whichever service you choose.

Some services provide free refreshments and/or a free lunch, and there are also buffet cars selling more substantial meals and a bar on some trains, which may also provide guided tourist commentaries (whether you're a tourist or not). If you wish to take a bicycle on a train you should check when booking, as they aren't permitted on many services and only limited space is available when they are. Smokers may also have a tough time travelling by train in New Zealand, as smoking isn't permitted on any train, although some journeys are long.

Timetables & Information

You can enquire about services and obtain a copy of timetables from travel agents or Tranz Scenic travel centres (☎ 0800-872 467 or 04-495 0775).

Buying Tickets

The easiest way to book a trip by train is to call Tranz Scenic on ☎ 0800-872 467 and pay by credit card, although you can also book at travel agents (a booking fee is charged) or free at stations. Tranz Scenic also has numerous agents overseas where you can book tickets and you can also book online (🖳 www.tranzscenic.co.nz). If you travel on a train without a ticket (or with an invalid ticket or pass), you must pay the full fare plus a modest surcharge, but you won't be forced to leave the train in the middle of nowhere!

Given the limited rail services in New Zealand, there are no season tickets, although a number of discounted tickets are available on each journey.

Stations

Tranz Scenic stations have few facilities. This is mainly because, in many cases, there's only one arrival or departure a day and hence no demand for bars and buffets, or the range of other services you usually find at major railway stations. There's an enquiry office open from before the first train leaves (or at least 7.30am) until 5.30pm for information and reservations. Taxis and buses don't stop at stations throughout the day, but tend to congregate when a train arrives. This means that you may have to wait in a queue, although you're unlikely to be left stranded as there's usually a connecting bus service timed to meet the last train.

Stations aren't always conveniently situated for city centres; for example Auckland's is on Beach Road, a 15-minute walk from the city centre, and isn't on a regular bus route. Wellington's station is on Waterloo Quay on the edge of the central area near one of the city's bus stations, and is served by the city's commuter railway services and also connected by shuttle bus to the Interislander ferry terminal.

Commuter Railway Services

There are no underground railway (metro) services anywhere in New Zealand, but there are commuter rail networks in Auckland and Wellington.

Auckland's rail network is operated by Maxx (🖳 www.maxx.co.nz), which also operates buses and ferries. There's a relatively new (2003) main railway station in Auckland

(Britomart, 🖥 www.britomart.co.nz), which has been a huge success, but unfortunately insufficient room was allowed for expansion and there are already problems with tunnel and platform capacity. There are just two lines, one to Waitakere in the west and the other to Papkura in the south. Peak-hour services are packed (there are some 7m passenger trips a year) and there's a growing number of passengers, although more trains are being provided. There are plans to buy 35 electric trains (140 carriages), which are expected to go into service between 2011 and 2013.

Maxx offers various kinds of ticket, including single, ten trip, day, monthly and special passes, e.g. day pass, family pass, discovery pass and special event tickets. Day passes include the day rover ($12), family pass ($23, for one adult and up to five children or two adults and four children), the discovery pass ($15) and tickets for bicycles ($1 per trip). There are concessions for children, school students, tertiary students, 65+ (NZ residents only), and the blind and handicapped. Maxx are considering installing turnstiles due to the high number of fare dodgers (around 7 per cent of passengers fail to buy a ticket) – surprisingly operators have no power to fine people on trains or buses. A smartcard integrated ticketed system is planned (to be paid for by a special fuel tax).

Wellington's commuter rail network is operated by Tranz Metro (🖥 www.tranzmetro.co.nz) and the main station has four Tranz Metro lines going to Johnsonville, Melling, Paraparaumu and Wairarapa. There are no commuter rail services in other New Zealand cities.

BUSES & TRAMS

Most towns and cities in New Zealand have a good public bus service and some cities operate double-decker buses, like those in the UK. Bus services have been deregulated and privatised to some extent in recent years, although in many cases the original public bus company is still the largest operator on the majority of routes. Bus stop electronic display signs are used in Auckland and other cities, but they aren't always accurate due to bus drivers not logging in successfully. You usually

Cable Car, Wellington

buy your ticket from the driver as you enter the bus, some of which accept the exact fare only In the major cities you can obtain a travel cash card, such as Go Rider in Auckland, Snapper in Wellington and Metrocard in Christchurch, where you load money onto the card (e.g. $10) and the fare is automatically charged each time you travel (and fares are lower).

One of the drawbacks of the Auckland public bus service (see 🖥 www.maxx.co.nz) is that it ends early, and on Saturdays and Sundays the last services leave at around 5pm. Even during the week in Auckland you won't find a public bus running after 11.30pm (many routes finish much earlier) and some services are suspended altogether at weekends. Auckland bus services include the Link, which runs at ten-minute intervals around the main areas of the city in a loop. NZ Bus (🖥 www.nzbus.co.nz) is the principle bus company in Auckland, with North Star, Metrolink, LINK, GO WEST and Waka Pacific buses (over 650) covering more than 90 routes.

If you plan to live on Auckland's North Shore and commute into the CBD, you'll find it advantageous to live somewhere on the main Northern Busway express bus route into the city. The Northern Busway (🖥 www.busway.co.nz) was opened in 2008 and is New Zealand's first purpose built road dedicated to bus transport. It's part of the public transport network linking North Shore City and the

Tram, Christchurch

Hibiscus Coast with the Auckland CBD. Express services and local bus services link into the Busway through five new stations at Albany, Constellation, Sunnynook, Smales Farm and Akoranga (it may be extended to Orewa).

In Wellington, the bus service is run by Go Wellington (🖥 www.gowellingtonbus.co.nz) – now owned by NZBUS – and has frequent services, including an after-midnight service from the entertainment district to outlying suburbs. Timetables and other information are available on ☎ 0800-801 7000. Christchurch buses are among the best in the country, with cheap and frequent services. A free Shuttle bus runs around the city centre at ten-minute intervals (information is available from Bus Info ☎ 03-366 8855, 🖥 www.metroinfo.org.nz).

One benefit of bus deregulation is that small private companies have been allowed to enter the public transport business, and some operate services late into the evening and at weekends when the major operators have suspended their services. Some services, using minibuses and cars, can be ordered by telephone when required. As several companies now operate in most towns, there's no centralised information office where you can obtain timetable information.

Check your telephone directory for details of where to obtain information about services and a copy of timetables. In larger cities there's more than one bus station serving the different companies and routes. In Wellington, the main stations are at Waterloo Quay and Courtenay Place; while in Auckland, buses use the

Downtown and Midtown terminals (although Midtown is only a series of lay-bys rather than a proper terminal).

Bus Fares

Fares for town bus services are calculated on a zone basis and depend on how many zones you travel through and whether you pay with a cash pass, such as HOP in Auckland and Wellington, which offer discounts.

In Auckland and Wellington, A HOP card (a rechargeable card launched in 2011) costs a non-refundable $10 and can be loaded with up to $300 'e-money'. Using a HOP card, journeys are free on City LINK (normal $0.50), £1.50 on Inner LINK (normal $1,80), with discounts from 10 to 17 per cent on all other fares, depending on the number of fare stages. Bus fares in Christchurch are $2.30 for a single trip with a Metrocard ($3.20 cash) and $4.60 for all day travel.

Most towns and cities offer daily and weekly passes, which work out much cheaper if you plan to do a lot of travelling by bus. The Auckland Discovery Day Pass costs $15 for unlimited rides on buses, ferries and trains. Similar passes are available in other cities. In most cases you cannot begin your journey until 9am on weekdays, although there are no restrictions at weekends.

Trams

Trams operate in several cities in New Zealand, including Wellington, where they're called trolley buses and operate on several routes in the city centre and inner suburbs. The cost is the same as for buses (see above) and the Daytripper pass issued for buses can also be used on trams. Wellington also has a cable car operating between Lambton Quay and the Botanic Gardens in Kelburn. This is a popular tourist attraction, but is also used daily by commuters, as it's an easy way to travel up one of Wellington's steepest hills. Trams operate between 9am and 6pm on a city centre loop in Christchurch, stopping at nine points along the way, and mostly attract tourists, but are handy for commuters and shoppers in the city centre. You can buy a one-hour, half-day or full-day ticket from the conductor on board.

COACHES

New Zealand has a comprehensive and reliable long-distance coach service, which is the main way of travelling long distances for those without a car or who cannot afford (or don't want to) fly. Services are provided by two major companies: InterCity Group (NZ) Limited (operating as InterCity Coachlines, 🖥 www.intercitycoach.co.nz) serves 600 destinations, while Newmans (🖥 www.newmanscoach.co.nz) its main competitor, also serves a large number of destinations. There are also around a dozen smaller companies, such as Northliner Express Coachlines (🖥 www.northliner.co.nz) and Naked Bus (🖥 http://nakedbus.com), which claims to be the cheapest long distance bus operator.

Coach services, even those provided by competing companies, are well co-ordinated so that they connect, not only with other coach services, but also with other modes of transport. So, for example, if you take the train from Auckland to Wellington, the Interislander ferry across the Cook Strait and then a coach to Christchurch, it's possible to plan a route which connects smoothly, allowing enough time to get from one terminus to another. Unlike trains, there are several coach services per day on the major routes such as Auckland to Wellington.

Coaches are modern and provide facilities such as toilets, reclining seats and air-conditioning. On routes popular with tourists, the driver usually provides a commentary on sights and places of interest. On services operating in more remote areas, you may find that half the coach is given over to freight and parcels. Snacks and drinks aren't available on board coaches but they stop regularly for refreshments, although drivers tend to choose the more expensive places (so you may wish to take your own snacks with you). Smoking isn't permitted on coach services.

Bookings

It's usually possible just to turn up and travel by coach, except at busy times such as during summer and public holiday periods. However, if you know when you want to travel, it makes sense to book, as it costs no extra when booking direct. Bookings can be made by telephone or via the internet; the telephone numbers and website addresses of the three main companies are:

♦ **InterCity Coachlines:** ☎ Auckland 09-583 5780, Christchurch 03-365 1113, Dunedin 03-471 7143, Hawkes Bay 06-835 4326, Queenstown 03-442 4922, Rotorua 07-348 0366, Wellington 04-385 0520, 🖥 www.intercitycoach.co.nz.

♦ **Newmans:** ☎ 09-583 5780, 🖥 www.newmanscoach.co.nz.

♦ **Northliner:** ☎ see Intercity Coachlines above, 🖥 www.northliner.co.nz.

♦ **Naked Bus:** ☎ 0900-62533, 🖥 http://nakedbus.com.

> You can also book at InterCity Travel Centres in the major towns or with a travel agent (where you're charged a booking fee).

When booking, take note of exactly where your service operates from, which depends on the coach company and isn't necessarily the same location as the departure point of local city buses. In Wellington, Newmans' services operate from the Interislander ferry terminal, while InterCity services operate from near the railway station. In Auckland, InterCity services depart from Hobson Street, whereas Newmans operate from Quay Street.

Fares

Coaches are often the cheapest way of travelling long distances in New Zealand, although special fares on the trains can be cheaper. For example, the single adult fare from Auckland to Wellington is from around $35 (11-13 hours), from Rotorua to Wellington $29 (around eight hours) and from Picton to Christchurch $31 (around 5 hours 45 minutes). If you're travelling from the North to the South Island or vice versa, it's worth noting that the Interislander ferry fare (see below) isn't included in the coach price and you need to pay separately for the North and South Island legs of your trip (although you can book them together and services are timed to connect).

Special offers are available when travelling at off-peak times, e.g. Super Saver Fares with a reduction of 50 per cent and Saver Fares with a

25 per cent discount. 'Golden Age' passengers (men over 65 and women over 60) qualify for a 25 per cent discount on production of identification.

Children under two travel free if they don't occupy a seat and there are reductions of 33 per cent for children aged between 3 and 12. You can take one large and one medium size suitcase per person on coach services, and excess baggage incurs a small fee. Bicycles can be carried for a flat fee of around $10 per journey, irrespective of the length of the trip (you must remove the pedals and wrap the chain, e.g. in newspaper).

Each of the main coach lines offers a travel pass allowing unlimited travel for a fixed period. For example, Intercity offer a Flexi-Pass (🖥 http://flexipass.intercity.co.nz/pricing) sold in blocks of time, e.g. 20 hours for $155, 40 hours for $305 and 60 hours for $449. Passes can be topped up, like a pre-paid telephone card.

Timetables

You can obtain a copy of coach timetables from InterCity Travel centres (for InterCity Coachlines) in cities and large towns, Visitor Information Network (VIN) centres or by calling the numbers listed under Bookings above.

Backpackers' Buses

An economical way of travelling for young people is backpackers' buses, which operate throughout New Zealand (similar to those in Australia). Backpackers' buses are operated by a number of companies, of which Kiwi Experience and Magic Bus are the best known. Services operate on a pass basis, whereby once you've purchased a ticket you can switch buses and stop off along the route, whether for a few hours or a few days. Sporting and adventure activities are also sometimes offered along the way, such as white-water rafting or kayaking.

Backpackers' buses tend to be cheap and cheerful and are targeted at those aged between 18 and 35. You must pay extra for accommodation, although this is usually low-cost and there's also the option of camping. See the Backpackerbus website (🖥 www.backpackerbus.co.nz) for details of travel passes and trips. Booking is essential in summer.

TAXIS

Taxis are plentiful in most cities and towns in New Zealand, where most people rate their taxi service highly. They are usually ordinary saloon cars (or minibuses) painted in distinctive colours, which vary with the town or city. You can pick one up at a taxi rank or order one by telephone; they cannot be hailed in the street and will pick you up only if they're stopping to drop a passenger (so you had better be quick!).

All taxi fares are metered, with a minimum charge (flagfall) of $3, plus $3 per km – and you pay only the amount showing on the meter and aren't expected to tip (Americans please note!). An extra charge is made for telephone bookings, items of luggage and when travelling during the evening and at weekends, when taxis are most in demand due to the curtailment of bus services. There's also a surcharge for waiting (e.g. $1 per minute) and for journeys to and from airports (around $1).

AIRLINE SERVICES

New Zealand is served by some 25 international airlines, most of which fly to Auckland or Christchurch. New Zealand's main flag carrier is Air New Zealand (☎ 0800-737 000, 🖥 www.airnewzealand.co.nz), which was previously state-owned but is now privatised and widely acclaimed as one of the world's best airlines. In 2001, Air New Zealand (ANZ) came close to bankruptcy when it attempted to buy the remaining 50 per cent of Ansett Australia (it already owned 50 per cent), which went into liquidation in mid-2001. The government, in an attempt to save the airline, announced a $500m rescue package, which effectively makes the government the majority shareholder in the company. (Many New Zealanders believe that the airline shouldn't have been privatised in the first place).

ANZ has a comprehensive route network, with over 470 flights per day to 25 domestic destinations, and flights to destinations in Asia, Australasia, Europe and North America (including two in Mexico). ANZ frequent flyers (www.myairnz.com) can obtain an ePass (containing a chip with a unique identity code) which replaces the standard boarding pass.

ANZ's major domestic competitor is Qantas (🖥 www.qantas.com.au), which serves a large number of destinations. Mount Cook Airlines (based in Christchurch), Air Nelson (Nelson, 🖳 www.airnelson.co.nz) and Eagle Airways (Hamilton, 🖳 www.eagleair.co.nz) are subsidiaries of ANZ and operate scheduled services under the ANZ Link brand.

New Zealanders travel by air as frequently as possible, as it's by far the quickest way to get around the country and the most relaxing, with fares that are among the lowest in the world (see below). Many domestic services provide in-flight bar facilities, which is something of an innovation in New Zealand, where the sale of alcohol is subject to strict licensing hours. Smoking isn't permitted on domestic services, although the health-conscious New Zealanders surprisingly haven't banned that other risk to the well-being of air travellers – airline food!

There are also a number of mini-airlines serving minor destinations, often using aircraft with as few as four seats. Great Barrier Airlines (☎ 0800-900 600, 🖳 www.greatbarrierairlines. co.nz) and Mountain Air (☎ 0800-922 812, 🖳 www.mountainair.co.nz) both operate services to Great Barrier Island (a paradise-like island, likened to Fiji or Tahiti) in the Hauraki Gulf off Auckland. Hiring a plane to take you to a remote area can be a cost-effective alternative to driving, considering the time saving. Pleasure flights in small fixed wing aircraft and helicopters are available from numerous small 'airfields' throughout New Zealand.

Fares

ANZ's services were notoriously expensive until the now-defunct Ansett arrived on the scene, which prompted more competitive pricing. Due to increased competition in recent years, and the recession forcing airlines to cut costs and attract customers, fares are now much lower. However, it's still necessary to shop around and compare prices to obtain the best deal – for example by using Flight Centre (🖳 www.flightcentre.co.nz). The cheapest fares are usually to be found by booking at least seven days ahead.

ANZ Flights are very competitive, particularly domestic flights which include their 'grabaseat' promotion where you can fly one way from $79 (e.g. Auckland to Wellington) or $69 (Auckland/Wellington to Christchurch). Flying within New Zealand is so easy and convenient as to make driving almost obsolete, especially when you can hire a car for less than $30 per day at your destination. Flights to Australia are also good value. ANZ charges no fuel surcharges, which are incorporated into fares.

Airports

New Zealand's main international airport is Auckland, which is connected by direct flights to most major cities in Asia, several cities in the USA and Europe (particularly London), plus several Polynesian destinations. The airports at Wellington and Christchurch also dub themselves as 'international', but offer a much smaller number of international flights, mainly to Australia, although Christchurch serves some other countries, including the UK. Wellington is the country's domestic air hub, as many flights from all points north and south stop there to allow passengers to change planes. There are also airports at Blenheim, Dunedin, Gisborne, Hamilton, Hastings, Hokitika, Invercargill, Kaitaia, Mount Cook, Napier, Nelson, New Plymouth, Palmerston North, Queenstown, Rotorua, Taupo, Tauranga, Te Anau, Wanganui, Whakatane and Whangerei. These serve mainly domestic flights and private planes, and their facilities range from a modest (but modern) terminal building to a motley collection of huts.

Auckland International airport is 21km (13mi) south of the city at Mangere and has three terminals. An AirBus (🖳 www.airbus. co.nz) shuttle connects the airport with the city centre (the ferry terminal) every 15 minutes costing $16 single and $26 return. A taxi downtown is around $80. Auckland has DIY check-in desks where you weigh your own baggage. Surprisingly, the airport doesn't have one decent restaurant – fine dining is a hamburger! Airport information is available on ☎ 09-256 8899 or 🖳 www.auckland-airport. co.nz. Inexpensive airport parking is available at AeroParks (🖳 www. aeroparks.co.nz).

Wellington International Airport is 7km (5mi) south of the city at Rongotai. It has been designated a 'low noise' airport and may be used only by the quietest planes, which, even so, aren't permitted to arrive or depart at night. Wellington's airport is notoriously windy and renowned among pilots as a difficult place to land or take off. As with Auckland, there are three terminals. The bus service to the city runs every half an hour or hour (weekends and public holidays) and costs between $5 (concession) and $8.50, depending on the distance travelled, and takes 30 minutes to central Wellington. Airport information is available on ☎ 04-385 5100 or 🖳 www. wellington-airport.co.nz.

Christchurch International Airport, whose facilities have recently been greatly improved, is 11km (7mi) north of the city centre and is easily reached by bus (fare $7). For information ☎ 03-358 5029 or see 🖳 www.christchurch-airport.co.nz.

A separate departure tax of $25 – which must be paid before you pass through immigration – is levied on passengers departing on international flights from Queenstown, Hamilton, Rotorua and Wellington, but not Auckland, Christchurch and Dunedin, where it's included in the ticket price.

HOLIDAY & VISITORS' PASSES

A variety of travel passes is available for travel within New Zealand. Among the best is the InterCity Travel Pass New Zealand (🖳 http:// travelpass.intercity.co.nz), which offers a range of Intercity coach passes and national passes combining Intercity coach and (Cook Strait) ferry travel, enabling you to travel between the North and the South Islands.

If you wish to travel around New Zealand by train you can buy a 7- or 14-day Scenic Rail Pass (🖳 www.tranzscenic.co.nz). Travel is unlimited and you can choose your own route and stop off wherever you like. The cost of passes (valid until 30th September 2012) is shown below:

Pass	Adult	Child
7-day all services with one ferry journey	$418	$292
14-day all services with one ferry journey	$528	$402
7-day TranzAlpine/TransCoastal services	$307	$215

FERRIES

As a country consisting mainly of two large islands, the North and the South, separated by the Cook Strait, New Zealand is highly dependent on the ferry service between the two. In addition to the Interislander, there are several smaller ferry services linking the two main islands, as well as some serving smaller islands.

There are other ferry services throughout the country, including car ferries. The largest network is operated by Fullers ferries (🖳 www.fullers. co.nz) in Auckland, which operates a number of routes from Auckland ferry terminal to the lower North Shore including Bayswater, Birkenhead and Devonport and to a numbers of islands. You can buy a 10-trip ticket and have it punched each time you travel. On most routes there's an hourly or half-hourly service and there are also excursion trips to the islands, e.g. wine tours of Waiheke Island.

If you're planning to live on an island – such as Waiheke in the Hauraki Gulf – bear in mind that the high cost of ferry fares may be an issue if you commute to work daily to downtown Auckland. If you have a SuperGold card, you can travel free on Fullers' ferries from 9am weekdays and all day weekends and public holidays.

Interislander

The Interislander ferry service (🖳 www. interislander.co.nz) is highly efficient and employs two roll-on roll-off ferries most of the year, the Arahura (the larger) and the Aratere (the newer), both of which carry passengers, vehicles and railway carriages. They sail between Wellington in the North Island and Picton in the South Island, taking three hours ten minutes. The ferry route is 96km (60mi), although the Strait is only 20km (12mi) wide at its narrowest point. Purbeck, a freight vessel, also operates across the Strait, as does a fast ferry, the Linx.

The number of daily sailings varies between summer and winter. In summer (December to April) there are five daily sailings (but only four on Sundays and Mondays), while in winter the service is usually reduced to two or three crossings a day, as one of the vessels is taken out of service for maintenance. Timetables vary only slightly from year to year: Ferries leave Wellington at 2.35am, 8.25 am, 10.25am (peak season only, between 10th November and 30th April), 2.05pm and 6.25pm, and Picton at 6.25am, 10.05am, 1.10pm, 2.25pm (peak season only), 6.05pm and 10.25pm.

Bookings & Fares

It isn't essential to book for the Interislander ferry except at busy times, such as the start of school holidays, although it's cheaper, as discounted tickets can only be purchased in advance. If you turn up without a ticket, you must pay the full fare, even if you're travelling off-peak. Reservations can be made up to six months in advance (☎ 0800-802 802, 🖳 www.interislander.co.nz).

A wide range of fares, offers and conditions apply to ferry travel, which are covered in detail on the website. Children under two travel free and groups of 20 or more may be eligible for a group discount. Interislander offer three fare options (from lowest to highest): Web Saver (non-refundable and can only be booked in NZ or Australia), Saver Charge (50 per cent cancellation fee) and Easy Change (no cancellation fee). A single Easy Change fare cost $75 for an adult and $38 for a child in early 2012. Two adults, two children and a vehicle less than 1.8m in height pay family rates.

Interisland Terminals

Interislander ferries depart from the Interisland terminals in Wellington and Picton, both of which are well signposted. There are terminal buildings at both terminals where tickets can be purchased and where foot passengers can check in their luggage for the journey rather than carry it on board. There are also car parks and car hire facilities, and if you have a hire car or are staying on the other island for a short time only,

it's cheaper to leave your car on one island and hire another when you arrive (see **Car Rental** on page 170). A free bus service (the Interislander Shuttle Bus) runs between Wellington railway station and the Interisland terminal. A bus departs from the Interisland terminal and arrives at the railway station in time to catch the evening train to Auckland. At Picton, shuttle buses operate from the Interisland terminal to the station to meet the arrival and departure of trains, which run directly to Christchurch.

The latest check-in time is 30 minutes before departure for foot passengers and one hour for those with vehicles. Foot passengers may take only two pieces of luggage weighing a maximum of 30kg and no more than 200 'linear' centimetres in size (a combination of the height, width and breadth).

Interislander ferries are well equipped, with a cinema, telephones, several bars, children's nursery and play areas, Visitor Information Network (VIN) centres and a number of eating places, including fast food outlets. There are also fruit machines, something of a novelty in a country where gambling is so tightly controlled. For a supplement, you can also use the club class lounge which provides free drinks and snacks, newspapers and an oasis of peace before boarding the ship (children under 18 aren't permitted!).

Mt Cook

11.

MOTORING

I n the absence of a comprehensive rail system, the road network is the mainstay of public and private transport in New Zealand, extending to 92,207km (57,295mi), of which some 65 per cent are sealed (i.e. tarmac or asphalt). The country has no national motorway (freeway) network and those that exist are short, e.g. in and around cities such as Auckland and Wellington, although more are planned. Most New Zealand roads have just one lane in each direction, but they're invariably well surfaced and maintained, even when they pass through areas with difficult terrain (which is frequently). All roads used to be toll-free, but that changed with new Orewa-Puhoi toll motorway extension north of Auckland.

New Zealand has one of the highest rates of vehicle ownership in the world, at around 700 per 1,000 people, which is second only to the USA. The reason for this devotion to the motor vehicle is that driving is the most convenient way of getting around the country, and many places aren't accessible by public transport or services are infrequent. A car is essential if you live in a rural area, where you'll find getting around difficult without one. Even in Auckland (which covers a vast area) and Wellington, people are loathe to forsake their cars, and although traffic congestion and parking are increasing problems, using public transport is usually even slower.

The travel brochures portray motoring in New Zealand as an idyllic pursuit, where roads are traffic-free most of the time and the scenery breathtaking. This is often true in rural areas, particularly outside the main tourist season, when it's possible to drive for miles without seeing another motorist (or having to crawl behind a caravan). However, it disguises the fact that the country has moderately dangerous roads.

New Zealand road deaths (375 in 2010) are among the highest in the world per capita, alongside Cambodia, Malaysia, Lithuania and Slovenia. Road-fatality figures published in 2010 from 33 countries released by the International Transport Forum (ITF) showed that New Zealand has the seventh-highest ratio of deaths per billion vehicle kilometres travelled and the ninth highest in deaths per capita. Speeding and drunken driving are a huge problem, particularly among young drivers (who can take to the roads at 15!), plus driving while using mobile phones (not yet illegal) or fiddling with radios and CDs, all play a large part in accidents.

For general information about driving in New Zealand, see the New Zealand Transport Agency (🖥 www.nzta.govt.nz) and the Ministry of Transport (🖥 www.transport.govt. nz) websites. The NZ Road Code is available online (🖥 www.nzta.govt.nz/resources/ roadcode) and from NZ Transport Agency agents and bookshops.

CAR IMPORTATION

The long sea crossing from most countries means that it's usually cheaper to buy a car on arrival in New Zealand than to import one. Note also that some vehicles don't comply with New Zealand's registration requirements (see below) and therefore cannot be used in the country, therefore if you own an unusual car (particularly one made from a kit), you should check the regulations in advance.

New Zealand has a competitive used car market and importing your car can often prove uneconomical, especially when you consider the cost of shipping, duty and tax (see below). However, if you have a collector's car or a vehicle to which you're particularly attached (or you're making the comparatively short trip across the Tasman from Australia), you may wish to import a car.

Left-hand Drive Cars

New Zealanders drive on the left, therefore vehicles used there need to be right-hand drive. Consequently there's a restriction on importing and registering left-hand drive cars, such as vehicles from continental Europe and the USA. If you wish to import a left-hand drive car, you should first make enquiries with Land Transport New Zealand (see below). Left-hand drive cars aren't usually allowed to be registered for ordinary daily use unless they're left-hand drive for practical purposes, e.g. plant or agricultural machinery.

Shipping

As there are no regular international ferry services to New Zealand, vehicles must be shipped on cargo vessels. Most International shipping companies can arrange this. It takes at least five weeks to ship a vehicle from Europe and three weeks from the west coast of the USA, although it can take much longer when loading, unloading and customs clearance are included. You're recommended not to pack belongings in your vehicle when it's shipped because of the risk of theft, and many shippers won't accept vehicles for shipment if they contain personal items.

Arrival

The following documents are required to clear a vehicle's arrival in New Zealand:

♦ an invoice receipt showing the total price paid and the date of purchase;

♦ registration papers, e.g. a Certificate of Permanent Export (UK) or a Certificate of Title (USA);

♦ an invoice showing freight and insurance costs to New Zealand;

♦ a bill of lading;

♦ the odometer reading at the time of purchase or export to New Zealand;

♦ the odometer reading at the time of import into New Zealand.

Duty & Tax

If you're coming to New Zealand for the first time to take up residence, you're permitted to import one car, motorcycle or other motor vehicle (other than a motor home – see below) free of customs duty, provided that:

♦ you have legal authority to take up permanent residence in New Zealand (a valid visa is required as proof);

Duty & Tax Calculation

(a) Value for duty of vehicle in GB pounds	£ 8,500.00
(b) Value for duty of vehicle (exchange rate = 0.31*)	$27,419.00
(c) Value for duty after 27.5% depreciation allowed	$19,879.00
(d) Shipping and insurance costs	$ 4,500.00
(e) GST value = (c) + (d)	$24,379.00
Goods and Services Tax payable at 15%	**$ 3,656.85**

* Exchange rate is taken from NZ customs website

♦ you've never previously lived in New Zealand (short stays as a non-resident are excluded);

♦ you've owned and used the vehicle yourself for at least three months before arriving in New Zealand. A purchase invoice or registration document is required as proof.

♦ you're importing the vehicle for your own use and not with the intention of giving it away or selling it (nor may it be used in a business);

♦ you intend to keep and use the vehicle for at least two years. You must give a written undertaking that if you sell it or give it away during this period, you'll pay taxes and charges on its full value.

You may be allowed to import more than one vehicle duty-free, provided the same conditions are met for each. Note that the conditions are strictly applied and there are heavy penalties, including fines and even confiscation of a vehicle for making false or misleading declarations. If you're unable to comply with the conditions or you wish to import a motor home, you must pay customs duty at 17.5 per cent on each vehicle imported. Duty is calculated according to a vehicle's local market value, and not its value in your home country.

The local market value of a vehicle is determined by calculating the purchase price paid or payable overseas by the importer, minus any overseas duties or taxes included in the price that were refunded before the vehicle arrived in New Zealand. There's an allowance for depreciation ranging from 13 per cent for vehicles owned for more than three months (but less than four months) to 75 per cent for vehicles owned for over four years. The net value is the amount on which customs duty is levied. There's a zero rate of duty on private imported vehicles.

The above table shows an example of how customs duty and tax is calculated on a vehicle imported from the UK that has been owned and used overseas by the importer for six months but less than nine months.

You should check what the tax and duty will be in advance, to prevent any unexpected tax demands after a vehicle has arrived in New Zealand. The Collector of Customs publishes a booklet called *Advice on Private Motor Vehicle Imports*, which explains how tax is calculated and how to calculate your tax liability, or you can ask customs to assess the tax due. You can contact the Collector of Customs (☎ 0800-428 786, 🖥 www.customs.govt.nz) or any regional customs office (see page 75).

Testing & Registration

All motor vehicles entering New Zealand must be checked, certified, registered and licensed before they can be used on the road. This process is called entry certification and involves having a vehicle tested at an approved testing station.

Vehicles must be certified by the NZ Transport Agency as complying with New

Zealand legal requirements before they can be registered for use. You must provide documentation proving the vehicle's original compliance with approved standards, which will be checked.

Some vehicles (e.g. kit cars) don't comply with New Zealand registration requirements and therefore cannot be imported. This may also be the case for vehicles whose manufacturers are unable to supply information regarding compliance with approved standards. You're therefore advised to contact the NZTA and obtain the necessary information and documentation before making arrangements to import a vehicle into New Zealand. For more information, see 🖥 www.nzta.govt.nz/vehicle/warrants-certifications/entry.html.

Vehicle Cleaning

All used vehicles entering New Zealand must be inspected and, if necessary, cleaned, before being released by the Ministry of Agriculture and Forestry (MAF) Quarantine Service (🖥 www.maf.govt.nz). This is to ensure that there are no insects, plant material, soil and other contaminants, in line with New Zealand's strict policy of excluding plant and animal pests. If any are found, the vehicle must be cleaned at a MAF-approved decontamination facility.

REGISTRATION

Vehicle registration refers to the initial recording of a vehicle on the Motor Vehicle Register and the issuing of registration plates. It isn't to be confused with the vehicle license fee (see below) which is an annual fee for using a vehicle on public roads. Most vehicles are usually only registered once, after they

have had a safety inspection (see above) to ensure they are safe to be used on the road, although if they've been significantly modified or rebuilt they must be re-registered. The registration fee depends on the type of vehicle and the size of its engine, as show in the table below (from 1st May 2011).

When you register a vehicle for the first time, you receive an alphanumeric registration plate containing up to six characters. Personalised plates are popular in New Zealand.

Since 1998, official NZ plates have contained a silver fern hologram image in order to thwart counterfeiters who make false plates.

Note that the registration fee must be paid annually and isn't a one-time fee.

For more information, see 🖥 www.nzta.govt.nz/vehicle/registration-licensing.

VEHICLE LICENSE FEES

Vehicle licensing is the annual fee to use your vehicle on public roads. You can license your vehicle online at the New Zealand Transport Agency (🖥 www.nzta.govt.nz) or at any NZTA agent (including AA outlets and PostShops).

The license fee varies depending on several factors, including the type of

Registration Fees for Passenger Vehicles		
Fuel & Engine Size	**Registration Fee**	
	6 months	**12 months**
Petrol driven:		
1,301-2,600cc	$290.99	$431.06
2,601-4,000cc	$322.04	$462.11
Non-petrol driven:		
1,301-2,600cc	$355.92	$560.92
2,601-4,000cc	$386.97	$591.97

License Fee for Passenger Vehicles			
Fuel & Engine Size	**Registration Fee**		
	3 months	6 months	12 months
Petrol driven (private)	$77.68	$147.68	$287.75
Non-petrol driven (private)	$110.15	$212.61	$417.61

vehicle, its use and the size of the engine. The fees for private passenger vehicles (from 1st May 2011) are shown in the table above.

When you pay, you receive a label (showing the license's expiry date) which must be displayed behind the windscreen of your vehicle.

For more information, see 🖳 www.nzta. govt.nz/vehicle/registration-licensing.

Road User Charge

If you own a diesel (or electric) car, ute (utility) or van or a vehicle over 3,500kg gross laden weight, you must usually pay a road user charge (RUC). This is a charge over and above the cost of diesel fuel, as other road users pay levies which are included in the price of their fuel at the pump. A distance license is purchased in 1,000km (621mi) units (or multiples of 1,000km). The amount you pay depends on your vehicle's type and weight. The fee for most diesel passenger vehicles (effective from 15th October 2010) was $44.31 per 1,000km, which means than the cost of running a diesel car is around the same as a petrol-driven car (when the better diesel fuel efficiency is taken into account). A vehicle must be continuously licensed, which means that you must buy a new license before you've driven all the distance covered by the existing license.

If you're buying a used vehicle that is subject to RUC, make sure it's displaying a current RUC license – if it doesn't you'll be liable for any outstanding charges. You can call the RUC contact centre (☏ 0800-655 644, Mon-Fri, 8am to 6pm) to find out whether an RUC license is current.

CAR INSPECTION

All vehicles used on public roads are subject to an official inspection test, called a Warrant of Fitness (WoF) inspection. Vehicles first registered less than six years ago must have a WoF inspection every 12 months, while all other vehicles must have one every six months. The test is carried out at government testing stations and approved garages, where checks are made mainly for basic roadworthiness, covering such things as brakes, lights and tyres. The test isn't as stringent as either the British MOT or German TUV inspections and is similar to those carried out in most US states.

A WoF costs from around $40 for a light motor vehicle and around $30 for a motorcycle, which varies depending on the location (AA members get a discount at an AA inspection centre). Shop around for the best price.

When a vehicle passes its WoF check, a WoF label is attached to the inside of the front windscreen on the same side as the steering wheel. The circle showing the month the WoF expires is punched out when the WoF is issued, and it must be re-tested before the expiry date.

It's illegal to drive a car on public roads without a valid WoF label, for which there's a $200 penalty.

BUYING A CAR

There have never been any indigenous New Zealand cars. Honda, Mitsubishi, Nissan and Toyota used to have local plants where cars were assembled from imported parts in order to circumvent duty and tax on imported vehicles, but these have now closed, making the country entirely reliant on imports. Since the government's policy of restricting imported cars was abandoned, the New Zealand car market has been dominated by Japanese vehicles. This isn't surprising, given New Zealand's proximity to Japan and the fact that Japanese cars are well made, reliable and offer good value for money. Japanese car dealerships (particularly Honda, Nissan and Toyota) are found in most towns and offer most models, including family and luxury saloons, estate cars (station wagons) and sports cars.

It's possible to buy most European makes in New Zealand, although they are expensive and therefore most family cars are Japanese. The main non-Japanese makes are Ford, which are variants of Australian models (rather than American or European), and Holden, which are made in Australia by General Motors. The top ten vehicle manufacturers in New Zealand are Toyota, Ford, Holden, Mitsubishi, Nissan, Honda, Mazda, Hyundai, Subaru and Volkswagen.

Lovers of classic cars will be delighted to see many old British-made cars such as Minis and Morris Minors still in daily use in New Zealand. These date back to the days when 'patriotic' local car buyers imported British cars and kept them for 'ever' due to the high cost of new vehicles.

New Cars

New cars used to be astronomically expensive in New Zealand. However, reductions in import taxes, increasing competition and cheap Japanese imports have brought prices down to a more reasonable level. Nowadays prices are similar to those in Europe and many people can now afford to buy a new car, which was previously something of a luxury. New car prices start at around $15,000 for a small Japanese or Korean car, $30,000 for a small European family car and up to $100,000 for a luxury saloon such as BMW 5 Series.

You should shop around when buying a car in New Zealand and be prepared to haggle over the price. Although cars are officially sold at list price, there's usually a discount to be had somewhere, whether by inflating the allowance paid for a part exchange vehicle or in the form of a cash discount. In recent years, new car prices have been at an all-time low. Ensure that the price you're quoted includes GST (15 per cent) and registration (see above). If you want a new car but don't have the cash and don't want hire purchase or a bank loan, you can lease one, which usually requires a deposit of around 25 per cent of the cost and a monthly

fee (which depends on a car's value) of from around $300 per month.

The best-selling car magazine in New Zealand is *Auto Car*, which reports motor industry news, previews new models, performs road tests and provides a survey of prices, while the AA (see **Motoring Oganisations** on page 185) magazine *Directions* also contains a comprehensive listing of new car prices. Information about new cars is also available on *Trade Me* (🖥 www.trademe.co.nz/trade-me-motors/new-cars).

Used Cars

Price reductions in the new car market in New Zealand have had a knock-on effect of reducing used car prices and also accelerating depreciation. In recent years, used cars have been excellent value due to the recession, and cheap secondhand cars can be purchased for a few thousand dollars. There's no GST on private sales.

The easiest way to buy a used car is from a dealer, although it's wise to ask a colleague or neighbour whether they can recommend one. When buying a car from a dealer, you should check that he's a member of the Motor Trade Association (MTA, 🖥 www.mta.org.nz). The Association has around 4,500 members, who must comply with fair trading practice and abide by a strict code of ethics. Anyone who sells or exchanges more than six vehicles within a 12-month period must be licensed, although small dealers without MTA membership often pose as private sellers (which is illegal).

An alternative is to check the local newspapers (such as the *NZ Herald* on Wednesday and *The Dominion* on Saturday), *Auto Trader* magazine (🖥 www.autotrader.co.nz – the leading website for buying/selling cars) or *Trade Me* (🖥 www.trademe.co.nz/motors/used-cars) magazines, which list thousands of cars for sale (most accompanied by a photograph), both private sales and from dealers. Used car dealers and private sellers also advertise cars for sale via the internet, e.g. 🖥 www.autonet.co.nz and 🖥 www.sella.co.nz (in addition to those above).

In some towns there are weekend car markets where private sellers offer their cars for sale, such as the Manukau and Ellerslie

Racecourse car fair in Auckland (arrive before 9am for the best choice). Car auctions, often held several times a week, are also popular, e.g. 🖳 www.turners.co.nz/vehicles/cars.

See also **Imported Used Cars** below.

Important Precautions

As in most countries, buying a used car in New Zealand requires caution, and the vehicle and seller should be carefully scrutinised, including the following:

♦ Ensure that the seller owns a vehicle or is entitled to sell it. If it's a private sale, ask to see the vehicle registration certificate together with some additional proof of the seller's address. If the addresses match, this gives you an indication that the seller is probably who he says he is.

♦ Inspect the bodywork carefully for damage, as a lot of cars in New Zealand have been involved in accidents. A car with a few minor cosmetic knocks is preferable to one that looks immaculate, but which has been poorly (or even dangerously) repaired following a major accident.

♦ Try to confirm that the odometer reading is correct, as odometer tampering is common. Service records from a main dealership and repair invoices showing the km reading are a good way of doing this.

If you know little or nothing about cars, it's wise to arrange an inspection by a competent engineer. The AA provides this service (from around $100) and there are often car inspection services provided at car fairs and auctions. Before buying a used vehicle, you should also ensure that it isn't subject to a hire purchase or leasing arrangement, has not been pledged as security or has been reported stolen. There are a number of companies that provide this service, including 🖳 www. aalemoncheck.co.nz and www.autocheckextra. co.nz. This doesn't, however, guarantee that a vehicle hasn't suffered serious accident damage or that the kilometre reading is correct.

The New Zealand Transport Agency (🖳 www.nzta.govt.nz) publishes comprehensive information for car buyers.

Warranties & Guarantees

Used car dealers usually provide warranties and guarantees. All car sellers (including private sellers) are legally obliged to sell cars in a roadworthy condition. If you buy a car and find that it isn't roadworthy, a threat to report the seller to the police may secure you a refund (always assuming that you can find him!).

If you have a complaint about a new or used car purchased from a dealer, you can take it up with the Motor Vehicle Disputes Tribunal (MVDT, 🖳 www.justice.govt.nz/ tribunals/motor-vehicle-disputes-tribunal). If the tribunal finds that your complaint is justified, they can order the dealer to fix the problem, award compensation (up to $100,000) or take the car back and refund your money.

Imported Used Cars

A particular area of concern for buyers of used cars in New Zealand is that of imported used cars, i.e. vehicles that have been used in another country and then exported to New Zealand, as opposed to used cars which were purchased new in New Zealand. There have been problems in recent years with cars that have been stolen, usually in the UK, and shipped to New Zealand and resold. This mainly applies to prestige and executive cars. If you're offered a used vehicle such as a Mercedes or BMW at a temptingly low price, you should check its history very carefully. A popular (and probably apocryphal) bar-room tale in New Zealand tells of the Pom (Briton) who emigrated and bought back his BMW which had been stolen in London six months previously!

A problem can also occur with used cars imported from Japan, which are imported legally by dealers and sold at low prices (used cars are worth little in Japan), often with low mileage. However, several dealers have been convicted for winding back the odometers of cars on their sea journey from Japan, thereby defrauding buyers. Even with genuine used cars imported from Japan, there's often concern that the wear and tear on the engine is greater than the kilometre reading may suggest (Japanese cars spend most of their life crawling in traffic jams). On the other hand, several dealers have been caught winding the odometers of imported used cars *forward*, in order to reduce their value and cut the import taxes payable (thus defrauding customs). In summary, it's fair to say that buying a used car in New Zealand is something of a minefield, although it's no different from most other countries in this respect.

SELLING A CAR

Before selling a car in New Zealand, you must obtain a new Vehicle Inspection Certificate (VIC – see **Car Inspections** above) from a local garage, unless your current VIC was issued in the previous month. You then give the buyer the VIC, which he'll need to register the car in his name, which can be done by post or in person at a PostShop. Other things to do when selling a car include the following:

◆ Inform your insurance company.

◆ Notify the New Zealand Transport Agency (⌨ www.nzta.govt.nz – the buyer and seller must do so independently) of the sale by lodging an MR13A form within seven days. Don't rely on the buyer to lodge the form because if he doesn't (accidentally or deliberately) you'll be liable for any parking tickets and fines he incurs. Many people have found themselves liable for hundreds of dollars in fines plus high lawyer's fees, and it's time-consuming to sort out.

◆ When selling a car privately, insist on payment in cash or with a banker's draft (cashier's cheque), which is standard practice in New Zealand. If you accept a personal cheque, make sure that it clears before you part with the vehicle.

The best places to advertise a car for sale are in local newspapers or the *Auto Trader* magazine (⌨ www.autotrader.co.nz) or *Trade Me* (⌨ www.trademe.co.nz/motors/used-cars).

Some people sell a car at a car market or put a 'for sale' notice in the window with a phone number and park it in a prominent position.

CAR RENTAL

Many companies in New Zealand rent out cars by the day or week, including the ubiquitous multinationals such as Avis, Budget and Hertz, plus a large number of local firms. The multinationals offer better insurance and the newest cars, but are much more expensive than local and budget companies, which usually offer older cars (see below). One big advantage of renting from a national firm is that you can pick up a car in one town and drop it off in another, whereas local firms usually insist that a car is returned to the same place.

Note that many car rental firms don't allow you to take a car from the North to the South Island (or vice versa) on the ferry and those that do impose a stiff surcharge. This, together with the cost of taking a car on the ferry, means it's usually cheaper to drop a rental car off at the ferry terminal (where major rental companies have offices), travel as a foot passenger, and rent another car on the other island. Auckland has the most competitive car rental rates in the country.

☑ SURVIVAL TIP

It's important to note that no matter how comprehensive the insurance cover, you're unlikely to be covered for damage caused by driving on unsealed (gravel or compacted earth) roads, even if a vehicle has four-wheel-drive. Some companies forbid their cars to be driven on unsealed roads.

Typical models and daily rental costs (including GST) from a multinational such as Avis are around $70 per day for a sub compact (e.g. Toyota Yaris) and up to $100 per day for a full size vehicle (e.g. Holden Commodore), including the collision damage waiver (CDW – also called loss damage waiver/LCD and damage excess waiver/DEW), but excluding extra insurance, satnav, surcharge and GST. Tax and extras can easily add another $10-20 per day. If it isn't included, CDW will add another $10-20 per day, which removes any liability for damage caused to a rented vehicle. If you don't have CDW you must leave a hefty cash or credit card deposit. Extras that can be ordered with a rental car include child seats (compulsory in New Zealand), satnav, roof/ski racks and snow chains (recommended when venturing into a mountainous area during winter).

The minimum age for renting a car in New Zealand is usually 21 and a full license must have been held for at least 12 months, although some rental companies have a minimum age of 25. Rental companies may also levy a supplement for larger vehicles when the driver's under 25, and under 25s also incur a larger insurance excess with most rental companies.

You can save a lot of money renting a vehicle from a budget rental company, where rates on older vehicles (typically ten years old with 100,000-200,000km on the clock) start from around $10 per day or $20-30 per day including insurance. Many companies bump up the cost by charging a hefty fee for CDW insurance, therefore always obtain quotes inclusive of CDW when comparing rates. Among the many budget rental companies are 🖥 www.acerentals.co.nz, www.discount-car-rental.co.nz, www.jucy.co.nz and www.rentadent.co.nz. One company the author can personally recommend is Road Runner Rentals in Christchurch (☎ 0800-800 708, 🖥 www.roadrunnerrentals.co.nz), who have excellent rates on both cars and campervans and won't rip you off on insurance.

A number of car and motorhome rental companies offer a GPS tour guide from Tourism Radio (🖥 www.tourismradio.co.nz), which uses an integrated GPS system in rental vehicles to broadcast information about your surroundings draw your attention to prominent landmarks and highlights as you approach them.

Hiring a Campervan or Motorhome

Many visitors buy or hire a campervan or motorhome (RVs or recreation vehicles), which is the cheapest and best way to see the country and much more popular than touring caravans (towed behind a car).

Vehicles vary from luxuriously appointed American-style, Winnebago-type vehicles, which can accommodate six people in luxury, to conversions of small Japanese vans with room for just two (who need to be on intimate terms!).

Rental fees are from as little as $30 a day for a small 2-berth campervan to over $300 a day for a six-berth luxury motorhome; there are usually discounts for rentals of longer than 21 days. Rates should include goods & services tax (GST), unlimited kilometres, third party insurance, all drivers' fees, a one-way fee (if applicable), cleaning fee, full equipment (usually includes a camping table and chairs), full gas bottle(s), 24-hour breakdown assistance and a travel information pack.

Rates include basic third party insurance, although there's an extra charge for collision damage waiver (CDW) of $20 to $40 per day, which reduced the excess should any damage be caused to the vehicle. If you don't have CDW you must leave a bond (e.g. a credit card deposit) as security against damage.

There's usually a minimum rental period of around three days (which may depend on the kind of vehicle) and a minimum age limit of 21; some companies offer discounts to those aged over 55. Vehicles may be diesel or petrol, 2WD or 4WD, and manual or automatic (many vehicles are only available with a manual gearbox/stick shift). All companies offer one-way hire.

There's a huge number of campervan and motorhome rental companies in New Zealand, ranging from the log-established major (and most expensive) companies such as Britz

(🖥 www.britz.co.nz) and Maui (🖥 www.maui.co.nz), to many smaller and cheaper ones with older and smaller vehicles, such as 🖥 www.backpackercampervans.co.nz, www.escaperentals.co.nz, www.jucy.co.nz and www.roadrunnerrentals.co.nz (Christchurch).

There are a number of books for those touring New Zealand, including *31 Days in a Campervan: Trolling Around New Zealand*, Pete Buckley (Trafford Publishing), *Explore New Zealand: Over 60 Scenic Driving Tours*, John Cobb (New Holland), *New Zealand by Motorhome*, Shore and Campbell (Pelican Publishing Company) and *Motorhome Magic: Paradise Found in New Zealand*, Jane Dunn (Vanguard Press).

DRIVING LICENSE

The minimum age for driving in New Zealand is 15, which dates back to the days when the school leaving age was 15 and school-leavers were often required to drive vehicles on farms, although 15-year-olds are entitled only to a learner license and don't receive a full license until at least two years later. Nevertheless, many people think the young age at which teenagers can drive is a major contributor to accidents in New Zealand. In recent years, there have been proposals to raise the minimum licensing age to 17 or 18, but nothing has materialised due to objections from those living in rural and remote areas.

> The driving license system in New Zealand is unique and has three stages: learner license, restricted license and full license, each of which must be passed by prospective drivers.

A learner license ($48.20, blue plastic card) is issued after you've passed a theoretical and practical test (fee $45.70). With a learner license you can only drive a car when accompanied by an experienced driver and the car must display 'L' plates. Learner license drivers under the age of 20 are subject to additional license restrictions, including a lower blood alcohol limit (30mg of alcohol per 100ml of blood, which in practice means they cannot drink and drive at all).

The second stage, the restricted license (fee $48.20 red plastic card), is issued after a minimum of six months as a learner driver and an additional practical test (fee $86.60). With a restricted license you can drive alone but can carry no passengers other than your spouse and/or dependants (the only ones brave enough?), and you cannot drive at night. The full license (fee $49.60, green plastic card) is the third and final stage, awarded after you've held a restricted license for six months if you're aged 25 or over or after 18 months if you're under 25, and after passing further theoretical and practical tests (fee $59.90). To obtain a full license therefore takes at least a year and costs $338.20 (including test fees). Note that you require an eyesight test to obtain a New Zealand driving license.

If you already have a driving license issued in another country, it can be used in New Zealand for up to one year, provided it's written in English. If it isn't, it must be accompanied by an international driver's permit (IDP), which you can obtain from a motoring organisation in your home country. After a year, your foreign driving license must be exchanged for a New Zealand license (application fee $52.10). If your driving license was issued in Australia, Canada, the European Union, Norway, South Africa, Switzerland or the USA, you may be exempt from the practical driving test, but must take a theory test (fee $45.70). Driving license holders from other countries must also take a driving test (fee $86.60). Licenses are issued in plastic card form, which you're required to carry with your vehicle papers when driving in New Zealand.

At age 75, motorists are required to make an 'older driver license renewal' application (fee $18.70), produce a medical certificate and undergo an eyesight test to have their license renewed, and may also be required to take a on-road safety test (fee $41.80) if recommended by a doctor. Free 'Safe With Age' courses make an assessment of your driving skills and a free booklet, *Keeping Moving – The Positive Guide for Mature Road Users*, is published by the NZ Transport Agency (🖥 www.nzta.govt.nz).

Before taking to the road in New Zealand, you should familiarise yourself with the official guide to driving rules and regulations, known as the *Road Code*, which is New Zealand's best-selling book (amazingly – considering that nobody reads it!). It's also available on a CD-ROM, which includes details of driving tests, practice tests, first aid information and demonstrations of how to manoeuvre a vehicle, and via the internet (www.nzta.govt.nz/resources/roadcode).

CAR INSURANCE

In most countries, motorists are required to have at least third party insurance so that if they injure or kill another road user their insurance company pays compensation. This isn't legally required in New Zealand where a vehicle's registration fee (see above) covers any injury or medical claims if you're at fault in an accident, but it doesn't cover any damage to vehicles or property.

The debate about whether to make third party insurance compulsory has been raging for some time, with those in favour citing not only its economic benefits, but the benefits to road safety. A major argument of proponents of change is that young, inexperienced drivers with powerful modified vehicles wouldn't be able to afford the insurance premiums, and therefore fewer high risk drivers would be on the roads.

Most people, however, take out extra car insurance. The cost of car insurance varies depending on the extent of cover (e.g. third party, third party fire & theft or fully comprehensive); the make and type of vehicle; the driver's age (under 25-year-olds pay higher premiums and excesses), experience and accident record; and where you live (Aucklanders pay up to 30 per cent more than other city dwellers, while those who live in rural areas may pay even less).

New Zealand has the following three types of car insurance:

♦ **Third party property:** This covers you against damage to any third parties' property and/or vehicles if an accident occurs in which you're at fault. This is the cheapest form of car insurance.

♦ **Third party fire & theft:** This covers theft of your vehicle and damage by fire, in addition to third party property damage.

♦ **Fully comprehensive or all risks:** This covers you against accidental loss or damage to your own vehicle, irrespective of fault, and also includes third party fire & theft. Many comprehensive policies also include benefits such as towing costs from the scene of an accident and the provision of a rental car while your car is being repaired. Comprehensive insurance is generally compulsory for vehicles purchase with finance (hire purchase) or on lease.

The average fully comprehensive insurance premium is around $850 per year, and with most policies you must pay an excess (deductible) of around $250. Generally, the larger the excess, the lower your premiums. Young drivers under age 25 pay a higher excess, as do drivers with a poor driving record and those with driving convictions.

If you have third party, fire & theft or comprehensive insurance, you should check whether an insurance company offers an 'agreed value' or a 'market value' policy. With an agreed value policy, you agree up front exactly how much you'll be paid if your car is written off (i.e. a total loss) or stolen. Whereas with a market value policy, you're paid what the insurance company thinks your car is worth at the time of the claim, based on an independent valuation, which is often less than you expect.

A no-claims bonus (or discount) system operates in New Zealand, whereby you're required to provide a letter from your previous

Oops!

motor insurance company stating your no-claims bonus. In New Zealand you usually receive a no-claims bonus of 30 per cent after one year up to a maximum of around 60 per cent after four or five years. Some insurance companies (e.g. the AA) protect your bonus if you have an accident.

The major car insurance companies include the AA (🖥 www.aainsurance.co.nz) and State (🖥 www.state.co.nz), and many people also insure with their banks, although this isn't the cheapest option.

Motor Breakdown Insurance

When you buy a new or used car from a dealer, you usually receive an insurance-based warranty package as part of the deal, which covers the costs of a breakdown (e.g. garage fees and towing) and the cost of repairing most major components. However, warranties are riddled with loopholes and even if you get past the exclusions and excesses, you'll probably find the pay-out is minimal. The best way to 'insure' against breakdowns is to join the New Zealand Automobile Association (see page 185), who will attend to minor repairs on the spot or arrange for a vehicle to be taken to a garage.

GENERAL ROAD RULES

Newcomers may be forgiven for thinking that there are no road rules in New Zealand! Obviously this isn't the case, although not everybody adheres to them. Some of the most important rules are listed below:

◆ Among the many odd customs of New Zealanders is that of driving on the left-hand side of the road, as in Australia, Japan and the UK (and many other countries). You may find this a bit strange if you come from a country where traffic drives on the right; however, it saves a lot of confusion if you do likewise. It's helpful to have a reminder (e.g. 'think left!') on your car's dashboard (many rented cars have a fluorescent sticker stating 'DRIVE ON THE LEFT' on the dashboard). Take extra care when pulling out of junctions, one-way streets and at roundabouts. (Remember to look first to the *right* when crossing the road on foot.) If you're unused to driving on the left, you

should be prepared for some disorientation (or blind panic), although most people have few problems adjusting to it.

◆ At crossroads and junctions where no right of way is assigned, traffic coming from the right has priority. At major junctions, right of way is indicated by a triangular 'GIVE WAY' (yield) sign or an octagonal red 'STOP' sign. There are also usually road markings. When faced with a stop sign, you must stop completely (all four wheels must come to rest) before pulling out onto a major road, even if you can see that no traffic is approaching. At a give way sign you aren't required to stop, but must give priority to traffic already on a major road. You must also give way to traffic coming from your right when entering a motorway or dual carriageway from a slip road.

▲ Caution

One of New Zealand's strangest and most confusing rules is that of giving way to an oncoming vehicle that's turning right at cross roads and T-junctions, i.e. turning across your path **when you're turning left into the same road.** This is the opposite of the rule in every other country and is blamed for many of the 2,500 intersection crashes reach year.

◆ At roundabouts (traffic circles), vehicles on the roundabout have priority and not those entering it. Traffic flows clockwise around roundabouts and not anti-clockwise, as in countries where traffic drives on the right. Some roundabouts have a filter lane which is reserved for traffic turning left. You should stay in the lane in which you entered the roundabout, follow the lane markings and signal as you approach the exit you plan to take. There are many roundabouts in New Zealand, which, although they are a bit of a free-for-all, speed up traffic considerably and are usually preferable to traffic lights, particularly outside rush hours (although some busy roundabouts also have traffic lights).

◆ Where fitted, the use of seatbelts is compulsory for all passengers and children must be properly restrained by an approved child restraint or adult seatbelt, where fitted. In the absence of an approved restraint or seatbelt, children must travel in the back of a car. A child must *never* travel in the front seat without using a child restraint or seatbelt, even when the back seat is full. Seatbelts or restraints must be approved (to the requisite New Zealand standard) and be appropriate for the age and weight of a child. Babies aged up to six months must occupy an infant seat and children up to four must use a child's seat. Older children may use either a child seat or an adult seatbelt. Expectant mothers should use a maternity seatbelt, which helps protect unborn babies. It's estimated that seatbelts would prevent around 75 per cent of deaths and 90 per cent of injuries suffered by those involved in accidents who weren't wearing seat belts. In addition to the risk of death or injury, you can receive a fine for ignoring the seatbelt laws. Note that it's the driver's responsibility to ensure that children are properly restrained. If you're exempt from using a seatbelt for medical reasons, a safety belt exemption certificate is required from your GP.

◆ Be particularly wary of cyclists, moped riders and motorcyclists. It isn't always easy to see them, particularly when they're hidden by the blind spots of a car or when cyclists are riding at night without lights. **When overtaking, ALWAYS give them a wide . . . WIDE berth.** If you knock them off their bikes, you may have a difficult time convincing the police that it wasn't your fault; far better to avoid them (and the police). Cyclists must wear an approved safety helmet and must use lights when it's dark. Bicycles are classified as vehicles under NZ road rules and must observe the same rules where applicable. There are cycle lanes in towns and cities, which motor vehicles are prohibited from using. See 🖳 www.landtransport.govt.nz/road-user-safety/walking-and-cycling for further information.

◆ If you needed spectacles or contact lenses to pass your sight test, you must always wear them when driving. It's wise to carry a spare pair of glasses or contact lenses in your car.

◆ White or yellow markings are painted on the road surface in towns and cities, e.g. arrows

rush hour in New Zealand

to indicate the direction traffic must travel in a particular lane. You should stay in the centre of the lane in which you're driving or, where there are no lane markings, keep to the left side of the road. White lines mark the separation of traffic lanes. A solid single line or two solid lines means no overtaking in either direction. A solid line to the left of the centre line, i.e. on your side of the road, means that overtaking is prohibited in your direction. You may overtake only when there's a single broken line in the middle of the road or double lines with a broken line on your side.

◆ Headlights must be used when driving between sunset and sunrise or at any time when there's insufficient daylight to be able to see a person wearing dark clothing at a distance of 100 metres (so keep an eye out for people in dark clothing). It's illegal to drive on side (parking) lights, and headlights must usually be dipped (low beam) when driving in built-up areas where there's street lighting.

Headlamps must also be dipped within 200 metres of an approaching vehicle, immediately an oncoming vehicle has dipped its headlights and when travelling within 200 metres behind another vehicle. Headlight flashing has a different meaning in different countries. In some countries it means 'after you', while in others it means 'get out of my way'. It can even mean 'I'm driving a new car and haven't worked out what the switches are for yet'! In New Zealand, headlamp flashing has only one legal use – to warn another vehicle of your presence, although most people use it to give priority to another vehicle, e.g. when someone is waiting to exit from a junction. Note that it's illegal to warn other vehicles that they're approaching a speed trap or police road block by flashing your lights (although many drivers do it). Hazard warning lights – all indicators operating simultaneously – are used to warn other drivers of an obstruction, e.g. an accident or a traffic jam (they aren't an excuse to park illegally).

The sequence of New Zealand traffic lights is green, amber, red and back to green. Amber means stop at the stop line; you may proceed only if the amber light appears after you've crossed the stop line or when stopping may cause an accident. A green filter light may be shown in addition to the full lamp signals, which means you may travel in the direction shown by the arrow, irrespective of other lights showing. Cameras may be installed at busy traffic lights to detect motorists driving through red lights (a favourite pastime of some motorists). There are three and even four-way traffic lights in towns.

Always approach pedestrian crossings with caution and don't park or overtake another vehicle on the approach to a crossing. At some crossings a flashing amber light follows the red light, to warn you to give way to pedestrians before proceeding. Where a road crosses a public footpath, e.g. at the entrance to a property or car park bordering a road, motorists *must* give way to pedestrians.

⚠ Caution

Note that pedestrians have the right of way once they've stepped onto a crossing without traffic lights and you MUST STOP (it isn't optional as in many other countries). Motorists who don't stop are liable to heavy penalties.

 Tail-gating (driving close to the vehicle in front) is commonplace in New Zealand, where few drivers have any idea of safe stopping distances (including thinking distance, i.e. the time it takes a driver to react). In good conditions you should leave a gap equal to three seconds between your vehicle and the one in front in order to be able to stop in an emergency. Note that the three-second rule applies to cars with good brakes and tyres, on dry roads, in good visibility and with an *alert driver*. If you're half asleep and driving an old banger on a wet or icy road, you had better not exceed 20kph (12mph), or you'll never stop in an emergency! As a safety precaution, try to leave a large gap between you and the vehicle in front. This isn't just to allow you more time to stop, should the vehicles in front decide to come together, but also to give a 'tail-gater' behind you more time to stop. **The closer a car is behind you, the further you should be from the vehicle in front.**

◆ Watch out for pedestrianised streets in city centres (which are closed to traffic during certain periods indicated by a sign). Note that bicycles may not be ridden, and sometimes even wheeled, in pedestrianised streets.

◆ Keep an eye out for animals on roads in rural areas, where fields are often unfenced and livestock are free to graze at will. Many motorists are injured after collisions with animals, particularly at night.

◆ The nearest fire hydrant (FH) may be indicated by a yellow triangle which points to the left or right (the side of the road where the FH is) and a blue cat's eye which can be seen at night.

◆ Snow chains may be used on snow-covered roads, but should be removed as soon as the road is clear.

◆ Surprisingly, New Zealand is one of the few developed countries that still permits drivers to use mobile phones when driving, which is banned in most countries where it has proved to increase the likelihood of accidents manyfold. **Do it at your peril!**

ROAD SIGNS

Road signs in New Zealand can be extremely variable. In most cities and towns there are extensive road signs to most destinations and local facilities such as car parks, schools and swimming pools. However, outside towns, signposting can be 'discreet' and you frequently won't find any signs at all at junctions. The main reason for this is that there's often only one major road between cities and towns. For example, if you leave the Interislander ferry at Picton heading for Christchurch and keep to the major road at every junction, the only place you can end up is Christchurch. If you're stuck for directions, simply stop and ask. Most locals will be pleased to help you and, unlike in some countries, it's usually quite safe to stop anywhere at any time of the day or night.

On short stretches of motorway, signs usually indicate the street to which an exit leads, rather than a town or suburb. For example, when heading north to Auckland on the southern motorway and wishing to travel to the suburb of Newmarket, you're advised to take the exit marked Broadway, the main road that passes through Newmarket. Therefore check the name of the street before setting out. Some roads are promoted as tourist attractions (indicated by blue and white signs), for example the Pacific Coast Highway, which runs from Auckland to Hastings.

Roadside information signs in New Zealand traditionally contained written instructions, for example 'SHARP BEND' or 'MAJOR ROAD AHEAD', and there are still many of these signs around (which may puzzle visitors from America who must wonder how a bend can be sharp). However, international pictorial signs are becoming commonplace, although in some cases they are still accompanied by written explanations, e.g. 'no entry' signs consist of a red circle with a white bar accompanied by the words 'No Entry'. An inverted red triangle on a white background means give way or yield and is marked 'Give Way' just to remind you (not that most New Zealand motorists take too much notice of it!).

One sign that's peculiar to New Zealand is the 'LSZ' sign, consisting of black lettering on a white border surrounded by a red circle. This means Limited Speed Zone and is found where a major road runs through a town or village (often so small that you don't notice it, which is why the sign is there to remind you). The sign literally means 'slow down, take care and look out for pedestrians and animals'. Instructions are also sometimes marked on the road, but in the reverse order so that motorists can read the message in the correct sequence, e.g. 'Give' followed by 'Way' a little further down the road means that you're approaching a junction where you must yield right of way.

SPEED LIMITS

The speed limits in New Zealand couldn't be simpler: 50kph (31mph) in built-up areas and 100kph (62mph) in rural areas, except where (rarely) a different limit is indicated. The rural limit is reduced to 90kph (55mph) for buses and heavy lorries, and to 80kph (50mph) for school buses and vehicles towing trailers. In some areas there's an LSZ sign (Limited Speed Zone), which means that the speed limit is reduced to 50kph (31mph) under certain conditions such as bad weather.

Speed limits of 20, 30 or 40kph (12, 19 or 25mph) may be set for local roads under certain conditions. You must slow to 20kph when passing or approaching a school bus.

Although speed limits are low compared with many other countries, speeding is the direct cause of over one in five road deaths (second

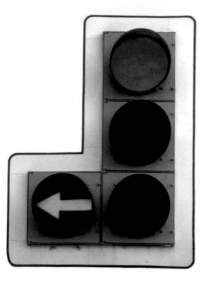

license is suspended immediately for 28 days. Demerit points for speeding range from 10 points for exceeding the speed limit by up to 10kph to 50 points for exceeding the speed limit by 36kph or more. If you receive a total of 100 demerit points in a two-year period, you're suspended from driving for three months.

TRAFFIC POLICE

The policing of road traffic and drivers in New Zealand comes under the authority of the Traffic Safety Service (TSS), which is jointly operated by the police and the Ministry of Transport. TSS officers drive black and white cars to distinguish them from police officers and like most police officers in New Zealand, they aren't armed. In late 2000, Specialist Highway Patrols were introduced to clamp down on speeding on major roads, which are patrolled by around 180 units. These and other officers deploy a range of radar and laser apparatus to detect speeding motorists, and carry out frequent roadside checks, random roadblocks (stopping motorists or filtering out 'suspicious looking' ones), checking documents and vehicles, and administering breath tests (see **Driving & Drinking** on page 182).

Officers cannot impose on-the-spot fines other than for minor violations (such as illegal parking or not displaying a valid VIC) and traffic offenders are usually issued with a traffic infringement notice and summoned to appear at a district court. Fines can be up to $1,000 for 'minor' offences and up to $6,000 for serious offences (such as dangerous driving), for which you can also be imprisoned for up to two years.

only to alcohol abuse), and the authorities are taking increasing steps to reduce and control vehicle speeds. There are many road signs designed to get motorists to slow down, many showing graveyard crosses and messages, such as 'The faster you go, the bigger the mess', but they have had little effect. Speed traps are common and employ a variety of methods to detect speeders, including radar and laser detectors. (Many speeding drivers employ radar detectors, although they are illegal.)

One device that the road safety authorities have taken to enthusiastically in their bid to persuade (or force) motorists to slow down is the speed camera, which measures the speed of passing vehicles and takes a photograph of the number plate of those that are speeding. These devices exist, of course, in other countries, but they aren't usually employed with the fervour that they are in New Zealand, where they raise over $50m annually ('spotting the speed camera' has become a national pastime). Speeding has been dramatically reduced since the introduction of cameras, as have speed-related crashes (by over 5 per cent a year). Even so, New Zealanders aren't about to be beaten by 'big brother' and it isn't uncommon for a friendly local to put up a hand-written 'Speed Camera Ahead' sign by the side of the road.

There are fines for speeding as well as demerit points and, if you're caught driving at more than 50kph above the speed limit, your

NEW ZEALAND ROADS

Roads in New Zealand are divided into three main categories: Motorways, state highways and secondary roads. Motorways are found only in the major cities, where they provide a direct route from the suburbs to the centre and consist of two or more lanes in each direction. In Auckland, motorways have three lanes in each direction and are known as the Northern, Southern and North-western motorways, and radiate out from the city centre in their respective directions. The Wellington Urban Motorway runs northwards from the city centre.

Special rules apply on motorways, which cannot be used by pedestrians, cyclists, animals or small-engined motorcycles. You may stop only in an emergency, when you must use the near-side verge or hard shoulder. Motorways are identified by signs with white letters on a green background, and junctions are numbered. In 2004, a new system was introduced which numbered junctions according to their distance in kilometres from a given point of the motorway (usually the start), rather than in numerical order. For example, junction ten is 10km (6ml) from the given point.

The Northern Gateway Toll Road is the last stage of the realignment and extension of the Northern Motorway between Albany and Puhoi to the north of Auckland. It's New Zealand's first toll road and perhaps a sign of things to come. (You can avoid the toll road by using the Hibiscus Coast Highway/SH17 or State Highway 16.) The Tariff Is $2 for cars. Motorcycles and light commercial vehicles and $4 for heavy vehicles exceeding 3.5 tonnes (motorcycles are free).

There's an electronic toll collection system for frequent users, whereby tolls are paid automatically after you set up a pre-pay account, which can be done via the toll road website (🖳 http://tollroad.govt.nz). Payment can also be made by credit or debit card via phone (☎ 0800-402 020) or by credit or debit card or cash at a self-service kiosk situated before the toll road (at the BP service centre at Dairy Flat or just off Highway 1 around 1km before the Waiwera exit). If you don't pay in advance, you have three days to pay the toll, whether by phone, internet or at a kiosk; there are penalties for late payment.

State highways are major trunk roads, usually with just one lane in each direction, on which you can expect to average around 55 to 65kmh when travelling cross-country. They're marked in red on maps and identified by a shield symbol, both on road signs and maps. There are eight principal state highways in New Zealand, shown in the table below.

Secondary routes are marked in yellow on most maps and by a shield symbol on maps and road signs. They're identified by a two-digit number and in most cases the first digit indicates that the road starts or finishes (as the case may be) on the state highway with the same number. All other roads are unclassified and unnumbered, and indicated by white lines on most maps, but have no special identification or road signs. They're usually of reasonable quality and sealed (tarmac), unless they're specifically marked on a map or signposted as 'unsealed' or 'not tar sealed', which means that they're gravel or compacted earth. They're passable by standard two-wheel-drive cars in good weather and four-wheel-drive vehicles at any time. When travelling in rural areas, keep a lookout for one-way bridges, narrow roads with passing sections, unsealed roads and dangerous roads (marked with a black silhouette of a car and skid marks on a yellow background).

New Zealand's roads rarely have special facilities such as service areas or rest stops, although they're well served by cafés, motels, petrol stations and restaurants (most state highways pass through towns rather than

State Highways

Highway	Route
No.1	Awanui-Auckland-Wellington-Picton-Christchurch-Invercargill
No.2	Auckland-Tauranga-Gisborne-Napier-Wellington
No.3	Hamilton-New Plymouth-Palmerston North
No.4	Te Kuiti-Wanganui
No.5	Putaruru-Napier
No.6	Blenheim-Invercargill (via the Southern Alps)
No.7	Greymouth-Waipara (near Christchurch)
No.8	Timaru-Milton (inland route)

bypassing them), where you can stop for accommodation, food, fuel and repairs. The only exception to this is in remote parts of the country, mainly in the South Island, where you should use a map to plan overnight stays, refuelling and rest stops.

Parking is never easy in major city centres, where rush hours are between 7.30 and 9am and 4.30 and 6.30pm, although outside the major cities there's no such thing as a rush hour. Roads are naturally busier during holiday periods, particularly between December and February. The beginning of summer school holidays (the end of the first week in December) and the week before Christmas are the only times when it's wise to think twice before making a long journey by road, as everyone else will be doing the same.

Auckland harbour bridge is a huge bottleneck, where there are long tailbacks during rush hours. Traffic has increased around twenty-fold since it opened in 1959 and four additional lanes were added through bolt-on sections ('Nippon clip-ons') in 1969, when the number of lanes increased from four to eight. Take care to get into the correct lane when exiting, as exits aren't shown as towns or suburbs but as street names.

Most roads are passable year round, except in the more inhospitable areas of the South Island, where some roads, particularly state highway 6 through the Southern Alps, are rendered impassable by snowfalls and icy conditions. In winter, you should check to make sure that you can reach your destination before setting out. On some roads there are automatic warning signs that indicate if there's a road closure further along the highway. Don't be tempted to ignore them, as each year many people are stranded and a number lose their lives by doing this. In the North Island, several main roads are subject to flooding during heavy rain, particularly where they pass through the volcanic plateaux.

NEW ZEALAND DRIVERS

In normal circumstances New Zealanders are friendly and polite. However, this changes the minute they get behind the wheel of a car, when they become uncharacteristically aggressive, impatient, discourteous and intolerant. The average New Zealander's attitude is to reach his destination as fast as possible with little regard for other road users. There are, on average, around ten road deaths each week, together with over 20,000 convictions annually for careless or dangerous driving. Being a foreigner doesn't exempt you from this carnage, although Land Transport New Zealand estimates that less than 3 per cent of fatal accidents are caused by foreign drivers.

New Zealand has a plague of boy-racers who love muscle cars and modified, personalised cars with personal number plates, paint jobs, engine mods, raunchy exhaust systems, loud stereo systems and 'go-faster' body kits. Insurance is relatively inexpensive or isn't even required in New Zealand and therefore doesn't deter young and inexperienced drivers from driving powerful cars (as it does in most other countries).

The three greatest threats to road safety are drunk driving (see below), excessive speed (see page 177) and reckless overtaking. Another problem is lane discipline, and changing lanes without indicating is a significant problem in New Zealand, where there are few multi-lane roads. Young men tend to be the worst offenders, although even young women and mature drivers compete in New Zealand's 'drink the pub dry and get home first at all costs' road race. It's advisable never to drink and drive in New Zealand or accept a ride with anyone who has been drinking. Road rage is the latest trend to emerge in New Zealand and there have been several cases of motorists who, after having been hit by a car, have remonstrated with the offending driver only to be hit again – this time in the face!

The above shouldn't put you off driving in New Zealand, where you'll experience breathtaking scenery (best admired by stopping the car), even on the most routine trip to the office or the shops. Best of all, roads are relatively uncrowded outside the major cities, so your chances of meeting kamikaze drivers are slim.

MOTORCYCLES

Motorcycling is popular in New Zealand, both as a means of transport and as a leisure pursuit. Motorcycle licenses come under class 6 and the licensing system is the same three-stage process as for car licenses with the same fees (see page 166). You must be aged at least 15 before you can apply for a learner's motorcycle license.

Like cars, motorcycles must be registered and licensed. The cost of motorcycle registration and license fees (from 1st May 2011) is shown below:

Motorcycle Registration		
Engine Size	**Period**	
	6 months	**12 months**
under 61cc	$246.26	$443.97
61-600cc	$273.86	$477.32
Over 600cc	$330.91	$591.42

Motorcycle License			
Engine Size	**Period**		
	3 months	**6 months**	**12 months**
under 61cc	$69.99	$131.76	$255.96
above 61cc	$72.50	$137.39	$267.21

Motorcycling in New Zealand can be a relatively dangerous undertaking, partly because drivers of other vehicles have little regard for motorcyclists (usually they don't even notice them) and because many motorcyclists take advantage of New Zealand's wide open roads to reach some incredible speeds. Crash helmets must be worn and riders must use dipped headlamps at all times. It also pays to wear bright, fluorescent or reflective clothing but, even then, don't expect car drivers to see you. In recent years, motorcycle deaths and injuries have been reduced thanks to helmets, better bikes and protective riding gear, better training and defensive riding by bikers. In general, the laws that apply to cars also apply to motorcycles.

It's possible to buy (or rent) a wide range of motorbikes in New Zealand, ranging from lovingly preserved British classics to the latest German and Japanese superbikes. A motorcycle can also be imported on the same terms as a car (see page 163).

ACCIDENTS

New Zealanders aren't generally perturbed by road accidents and many people delight in recounting the details of their latest scrape over dinner or in the pub. If you're unfortunate enough to be involved in a car accident in New Zealand, the procedure is as follows:

1. Stop immediately. Switch on your hazard warning lights. In bad visibility, at night or in a blind spot, try to warn oncoming traffic of the danger by sending someone ahead to flag down oncoming cars.

2. In the case of minor accidents, try to move your car off the road immediately. Many serious accidents are caused by other drivers running into vehicles that have had a minor bump.

3. If anyone is injured, call an ambulance and/or the fire service immediately by dialling 111. If there isn't a mobile or public phone, ask at the nearest house.

4. Don't move an injured person unless it's absolutely necessary to save him from further injury, and don't leave him alone except to call an ambulance. Cover him with a blanket or coat to keep him warm.

5. If there are no injuries and damage to vehicles or property isn't serious, it's unnecessary to call the police to the accident scene. Contacting the police may result in someone being fined or

prosecuted for a driving offence. If another driver has obviously been drinking or appears incapable of driving, call the police.

6. If either you or the other driver(s) involved decide to call the police, don't move your vehicle or allow other vehicles to be moved. If it's necessary to move vehicles to unblock the road, mark their positions with chalk. Alternatively, take photographs of the accident scene or make a drawing showing the position of all the vehicles involved before moving them.

7. Check whether there are any witnesses to the accident and note their names and addresses, particularly those who support your version of what happened. Note the registration numbers of the vehicles involved and their drivers' names, addresses and insurance details. If asked, give any other drivers involved your name, address and insurance details. Bear in mind, however, that motorists aren't legally required to have insurance, so don't be too surprised if the other driver doesn't have any!

8. If you've caused material damage, you must inform the owner of the damaged property as soon as possible. If you cannot reach him, contact the nearest police station (this also applies to damage caused to stationary vehicles, e.g. when parking).

9. If you're detained by the police, ask someone you're travelling with to contact anyone necessary as soon as you realise that you're going to be detained. Don't sign a statement unless you're certain you understand and agree with every word.

10. In the case of an accident involving two or more vehicles, it's normal practice for drivers to complete a standard accident report form provided by insurance companies. Each driver completes a form, which is then countersigned by the other and a copy exchanged. It isn't necessary for the two drivers' versions of the event to agree.

11. Your insurance company must be notified of an accident as soon as possible.

Claims for personal injury where the other driver is wholly or partly at fault can be directed to the government's Accident Compensation Corporation (ACC – see page 192). If your claim is complex, you may need to hire a lawyer to help you with it. You must, at the very least, have the registration number of the other vehicle(s) if you're to succeed with a claim.

DRIVING & DRINKING

It's estimated that alcohol is a factor in 30 per cent of motoring accidents in New Zealand (plus many due to drunken walking) and this is acknowledged as one of the country's most pressing social problems. It's still socially acceptable in New Zealand to drive after a 'few drinks' and the limited licensing hours for 'hotels' (pubs) often encourage people to travel in search of a drink when their local pub is closed on a Sunday or they live in a 'dry' area.

Drunken driving is endemic at all levels, from older drivers, who consider they're experienced enough to drive after drinking, to cocky young drivers who may even encourage their mates to drive when drunk.

Drunk drivers in New Zealand are often very drunk indeed. One driver who ended up in court on a drunk driving charge was reported to have so much alcohol in his body that a medical expert at his trial reckoned he should have been 'brain dead'.

In recent years, children as young as 14 have been caught drink-driving, prompting road

safety officials to admit that their multi-million dollar awareness campaigns aren't working. Despite the Government ploughing $millions into anti drink-driving campaigns in 2008 alone, the number of offenders skyrocketed and is now at record levels. Recent police figures reveal that the overall number of drink-drivers soared by a third between 2003 and 2008, to around 100 a day. In the under-18 age group, the number of offences almost doubled between 1998 and 2008, although the worst drink-driving offenders are 15 to 24-year-olds.

 Caution

The latest threat on New Zealand's roads is driving under the influence of drugs. Although there are no official figures, a significant number of drivers are believed to be under the influence of illegal drugs (mainly cannabis) when driving, and the government plans to introduce roadside drug testing when a reliable test is available.

The alcohol limit for motorists in New Zealand is 80mg per 100ml of blood (0.08 per cent), the same as the UK but higher than many other European countries. For motorists under 20 years of age, the limit is 30mg. Police and TSS officers can breathalyse drivers at any time without a reason, and drivers involved in accidents, however minor, are routinely breathalysed. Random breath tests are common, and roadblocks can be set up or moved at a moment's notice. All motorists stopped are tested and those with a reading above 400mcg of alcohol per litre of breath are given a blood test, after which, if they're still over the limit, they're charged with drunken driving.

Drunk driving is a serious offence and motorists caught driving over the legal limit can be fined up to $1,500 or be imprisoned for up to six months. The penalty for a third offence can be a fine of up to $6,000, a two-year prison sentence and a one-year disqualification from driving. Drink-driving causing injury or death carries fines of between $10,000 and $20,000. Your car can also be confiscated, although this usually applies only to repeat offenders.

Each year, over 30,000 New Zealanders are convicted of drunken driving, although few are jailed.

CAR THEFT

Usually when you leave your property unattended in New Zealand, you can expect it to be in the same place when you return. This doesn't, however, always apply to cars (or motorcycles and bicycles for that matter), as New Zealand has a surprisingly high incidence of car theft considering the fairly low general crime rate. There's a huge variation in the incidence of car crime between city and country areas, and while Auckland is the car crime capital of New Zealand, in most country areas, car theft is rare and even a theft *from* a car may make headline news.

It's rare for a stolen car to disappear completely in New Zealand, however, as there's no easy way for a thief to take a car abroad and most are unlikely to pay the inter-island ferry fare to spirit your car to the other island. Therefore, if your car is stolen, you're likely to get it back. The bad news, however, is that many cars are stolen by joy-riders or petty criminals, and when they are found they are often damaged or completely wrecked. Fast cars such as the Nissan Silvia (and 200SX), Subaru Impreza (and others) and BMW coupés are criminals' favourites.

To reduce the chance of theft, don't take unnecessary risks, and always lock your car, engage your steering lock and completely close all windows. Never leave your keys in the ignition, even when filling up at a petrol station or when parking in your drive. Put any valuables (including clothes) in the boot or out of sight and don't leave your vehicle registration papers or any form of identification in the car. When parking overnight or when it's dark, park in a well-lit area, which helps deter car thieves. Bear in mind, however, that almost half of all car thefts are from or near owners' homes.

Car theft has spawned a huge car security business in the (losing) battle to prevent or deter car thieves. This includes a multitude of alarms, immobilisers, locks, locking wheel nuts and petrol caps, removable/coded stereo systems (a favourite target of thieves), wheel clamps and window etching with a car's registration number. If you drive a new or valuable car, it's wise to have it fitted with an alarm, an engine immobiliser (preferably of the rolling code variety with a transponder arming key) or other anti-theft device, and to use a visible deterrent such as a steering or gear change lock. You can also have a tracking device fitted, which will help the police locate a stolen vehicle and may also reduce your insurance.

Although a good security system won't stop someone from breaking into your car (which usually takes a 'professional' a matter of seconds) or prevent it being stolen, it will make it more difficult and may prompt a thief to look for an easier target. If you plan to buy an expensive stereo system, buy one with a removable unit or control panel/fascia.

If your car is stolen, report it to the police and your insurance company as soon as possible. Don't, however, expect the police to find it or even take any interest in your loss (police give stolen cars a very low priority).

PETROL

There are generally two kinds of petrol sold in New Zealand: 91 unleaded and super unleaded 96 (unleaded 98 is available at some petrol stations). In early 2012, the average price of fuel per litre in the Auckland region was: 91 octane ($2.10), 95/96 octane ($2.20), 98 octane ($2.25) and diesel ($1.50). Fuel dockets from supermarkets (e.g. New World) can save you 4¢ a litre.

> You can check the price of petrol in your area via Price Watch (www.pricewatch.co.nz).

In recent years supermarkets have opened petrol stations selling fuel at discount prices, which has created something of a price war in some areas. Although diesel fuel is over 50¢ a litre cheaper than petrol, you must pay a Road User Charge, which negates any price advantage and extra mileage. New Zealand doesn't have a great number of diesel powered cars and it's mainly used in commercial vehicles, although many campervans are diesel powered.

Another kind of fuel available in New Zealand is Liquid Petroleum Gas (LPG) or Compressed Natural Gas (CNG), which can be used only in specially converted cars. Liquid gas is cheaper than petrol (around $1.25 per litre) and provides slightly better fuel consumption, although it's currently available only in the North Island and isn't widely sold.

There are plenty of petrol stations in towns and cities, but they can be few and far between in rural areas, particularly in the South Island. It's wise to plan your fuel stops on long trips using a reliable map – when you see a 'last fuel for 70 miles' sign, it may well be true and not just a cynical marketing ploy! Also note that many petrol stations close at 6pm and are closed on Saturday afternoons and all day Sundays, although now it's at least *possible* to buy petrol in New Zealand on a Sunday.

GARAGES

When buying a car in New Zealand (or before importing a car), you would be wise to take into account the local service facilities. There are plenty of Ford, Holden, Honda, Mazda and Toyota dealers in large towns, although dealers for other makes may be few and far between. It's difficult to find garages that can repair many European cars (which are often considered specialist or luxury cars) and the nearest dealer may be located a long way from your home or workplace. If you drive a rare car, it's wise to carry a basic selection of spare parts, as service stations in New Zealand may not stock them and you may need to wait several days (or even weeks) for them to arrive from Auckland or even from abroad. Kiwi mechanics, however, have a reputation for being able to improvise a repair on virtually any vehicle, given a few nuts and bolts and a couple of pieces of wire!

Garages in New Zealand usually charge an hourly rate for their work, which varies considerably between main dealers and small country garages. Some franchised dealers operate a 'menu pricing' system, charging a fixed fee for a particular job, irrespective of how long it takes. However, it's generally much cheaper to have your car serviced at a local country garage than at a main dealer, although they may lack expertise in such areas as automatic transmissions and ABS. If you have an accident and you car needs body repairs, it's usually best and cheaper to take it to a specialist body shop, of which there are many in New Zealand (not surprisingly!).

When a car is under warranty, it must usually be serviced regularly by an approved dealer in order not to invalidate the warranty. However, if you need urgent assistance, particularly with an exotic foreign car, you're more likely to receive sympathetic help from a small local garage than a large dealer. Garages in New Zealand generally open from 8am to 5pm, Mondays to Fridays, and may also open on Saturday mornings, but are closed on Saturday afternoons and all day on Sundays. In most areas there's a 24-hour breakdown service, although it's expensive and it may pay you to join a motoring organisation such as the AA (see below).

Service stations in New Zealand don't usually provide a free 'loan car' while yours is being serviced or repaired, although some garages are agents for local hire services which are cheaper than national companies. A garage may collect your car from your home or office and deliver it after a service, or drop you off at a bus station or in a local town and pick you up again when your car is ready for collection.

When choosing a garage, you may be better off choosing one that's a member of the Motor Trade Association (MTA, 🖵 www.mta.org.nz) or the AA (see below), through which you'll have some form of redress if things go wrong.

MOTORING ORGANISATIONS

The Automobile Association (☎ 0800-500 444, 🖵 www.aa.co.nz) is the major motoring organisation in New Zealand with over 1m members. It's similar to the British organisation of the same name (it even uses the same logo of black 'AA' letters on a yellow background), but shouldn't be confused with Alcoholics Anonymous! The AA

provides technical and legal advice, route planning, traffic information and a variety of maps and motoring books, as well as an emergency breakdown service.

Visitors who are members of most major foreign motoring organisations can use all AA services *except* the breakdown service.

Standard annual membership for the first year costs $89 in the Auckland area and $79 in the rest of New Zealand, reducing in subsequent years. Or you can choose AA Plus for an extra $49 a year, which offers additional benefits which may be worthwhile if you do high mileage or travel a lot.

The AA will send a mechanic to repair your car at the roadside or, if this proves impossible, have it taken to the nearest garage. Extra services, such as a 'get you home' service, loan car and hotel accommodation can be provided for an extra fee. Membership of the AA also entitles you to free maps and accommodation guides. The AA publishes a popular magazine (also available online) called *AA Directions,* which is useful for keeping abreast of the latest motoring news.

Several other organisations in New Zealand provide motoring breakdown cover, although most won't send a mechanic when you break down. Instead you must arrange your own repairs and the service then pays the bill up to a maximum amount.

ROAD MAPS & GUIDES

A variety of motoring maps is available in New Zealand, including the *AA New Zealand Road Atlas,* which is the best selling general map.

The AA (see above) also publishes 1:350,000 district maps, which are free to members, and it also has an online mapping tool (🖳 http://maps.aa.co.nz). If you want a more comprehensive guide, one of the best maps available is the *Explore New Zealand Motoring Guide* (New Holland Publishers), which shows motorways, state and secondary highways and unsealed roads, town maps with one-way streets, railway lines and stations, airports, public toilets and hospitals. It also provides historic information about a number of towns and cities, geological features, national and forest parks, campervan and camping sites, hot springs and skiing areas.

Good maps are also produced by the major oil companies (available from petrol stations) and many other publishers. Free maps of New Zealand are also available from Visitor Information Network (VIN) centres or I-SITE Visitor Centres, libraries and car rental companies. Local town maps are available from tourist offices. Maps are also available via the internet, including those showing major roads and towns produced by Land Information New Zealand (🖳 www.linz.govt.nz).

There are several books on driving in New Zealand, including *Signpost Guide New Zealand: Your Guide to Great Drives* by G. Powell (Thomas Cook Publishing), *4WD North Island* by Andy Cockroft and *4WD South Island* by Sibly & Wilson.

PARKING

Parking is becoming more of a problem in New Zealand, particularly in Auckland and Wellington. Street parking can also be difficult in other city centres during the day, although there are off-street (including multi-storey) car parks in most towns. Many hotels and public buildings have underground car parks that are open to the general public. Car parks are indicated by the internationally recognised 'P' symbol, and several cities publish a Guide to Parking, which you can pick up at local tourist (VIN) offices. Take care when using car parks as they are one of the most common places to have an accident.

On-street parking is usually pay-and-display, where you buy a ticket from a machine and display it behind the windscreen of your car.

In towns where there's free parking, it may be restricted to 90, 120 or 180 minutes, shown by a 'P' sign with a number beneath it, e.g. P 90.

Most public car parks have extra-wide, easy-access spaces for disabled drivers and offer free or reduced cost parking; to use them you need a Mobility Parking Scheme card, which is available from New Zealand CCS (PO Box 6349, Wellington, ☎ 04-384 5677, 🖳 www.ccs.org.nz). Applications must be supported by a certificate of disability from a doctor.

No Parking Zones

Restricted, on-road parking zones are indicated by yellow lines painted at the roadside. A nearby sign will explain whether parking is banned at all times or within certain hours only, and whether a time limit applies, e.g. on freeways (main streets) parking may be prohibited during rush hours, e.g. between 7am and 9am. Where parking is restricted, rather than prohibited at all times, restrictions usually apply between 8am and 6pm, Mondays to Fridays. Restrictions don't apply on Sundays, but are usually in force on Saturdays, e.g. from 8am to 1pm. In areas where there's late night shopping or night-time entertainment (e.g. restaurants or theatres), parking limitations often apply until 9pm. If this is so, expect them to be enforced with the same vigour as they are during the day. Where parking is permitted, you should park on the left-hand side of the road facing the direction of the traffic flow.

Charges & Fines

Most city and town centres have meter zones. The charge, together with the maximum permitted parking period, varies depending on the location but is usually from around $1 for half an hour (a nearby sign will explain the charges). Meters take 20¢, 50¢ and $1 coins. and credit cards. Some cities (such as Wellington) are experimenting with free weekend parking in an attempt to entice shoppers back to city centres and away from out-of-town shopping centres. Check carefully, however, as schemes change frequently. Car parks are relatively expensive and cost from $2 to $5 for half an hour and from $7 to $20 for a whole day, depending on the city.

Parking offenders receive fines of up to $60 for parking illegally (e.g. on a broken yellow line) and progressive fines for exceeding time limits, depending on the length of the unpaid period of parking, e.g. in Wellington fines are from $12 for up to 30 minutes, up to a maximum of $57 for over six hours.

Town and city councils employ a veritable army of parking wardens who are eager to give you a ticket or tow your vehicle away if you park in a dangerous place or park illegally.

PEDESTRIAN ROAD RULES

As in all countries, you should take great care when crossing the road. Pedestrian crossings in towns are indicated by white stripes and yellow flashing beacons. Once you're on the crossing, drivers must stop, but it's wise to give them warning rather than leaping out when vehicles are just a few feet away. Unlike in many other countries, drivers in New Zealand are very quick to stop at crossings – at least in towns. There are also crossings controlled by traffic lights.

Take extra care when with children, many of whom are killed or injured by speeding, drunk or dangerous drivers each year. Never let them play on a road, however quiet. Bear in mind that young children are unable to judge traffic speeds accurately and should usually be escorted to and from school. Take particular care in country areas where there are no footpaths, and wear bright coloured clothing and carry a torch (flashlight) at night. It's best to step off the road (jump into the ditch!) when you hear or see a vehicle approaching, even though it's legal to walk on a road without a footpath.

Take care when using pedestrianised streets, some of which allow access to vehicles at certain times or may be used by delivery vehicles and buses (cyclists also use pedestrianised streets, although it's illegal). When using footpaths, keep an eye open for skateboarders and rollerbladers (as well as cyclists). Many city authorities have banned skateboarding on footpaths and roads, but it remains a hazard despite the fact that offenders face a fine of up to $500.

personalised number plates

12.
HEALTH

At its best, the quality of healthcare in New Zealand – which spends almost 10 per cent of its GDP on health – is excellent and comparable with other developed countries. Most illnesses and chronic conditions can be treated in New Zealand hospitals, with the exception of a few highly specialist areas (such as certain transplants), when it may be necessary to travel abroad. The standard of public health is generally high, although there are some differences between racial groups, with Maori in particular suffering ill health more often than those of European origin. New Zealanders tend to suffer more from alcohol-related diseases than Europeans, but less from smoking-related diseases.

The infant mortality rate was 3.8 deaths per 1,000 live births in 2010 (well below average for OECD countries and falling) and life expectancy 82.6 years for a woman and 78.6 years for a man, although Maori life expectancy is lower at around 75 years for a woman and 70 years for a man (partly due to their higher smoking rates).

Obesity is a huge and growing problem in New Zealand, where around a quarter of men and women and 10 per cent of children are clinically obese, with many more over-weight. The nation is addicted to fast foods, and many parents don't know how to cook and live on pre-packaged foods which are high in fat, salt and sugar; the problem is so serious that there have been calls to tax fast foods or even ban them altogether! Diabetes is also a huge problem, with over 250,000 sufferers – and the number is likely to double by 2025. A disturbing trend in recent years has been that diseases associated with poverty, such as rickets and TB in children, are on the increase after being virtually wiped out.

Alternative therapies are popular in New Zealand, usually for conditions for which people had been seeing a GP. The most popular alternative therapies are chiropractic, herbal medicine, homeopathy and osteopathy. New Zealand GPs are generally sympathetic to these therapies and occasionally refer patients to alternative practitioners.

There are many useful health websites in New Zealand, including Everybody (🖳 www. everybody.co.nz) and NZ Doctor (🖳 www. nzdoctor.co.nz).

EMERGENCIES

In a medical emergency in New Zealand, simply dial 111 and ask for an ambulance, which will be dispatched to take you to the nearest hospital. The ambulance service is free in most regions and is provided by various organisations depending on the region, e.g. Wellington Free Ambulance (🖳 www.wellingtonfreeambulance.org.nz) in the capital. The international voluntary organisation St John (🖳 www.stjohn.org. nz) provides emergency and non-emergency ambulance services for some 85 per cent of New Zealand's population. In most regions, the ambulance service has paramedic teams and also uses helicopter ambulances. In remote areas, specially trained search-and-rescue teams are available, and usually include a doctor who can administer treatment and perform minor operations on the spot.

If you're physically able, you should go to the accident and emergency (A&E) department of your nearest hospital. When you move to a new area, it's wise to find out where your nearest emergency hospital is situated, as a number have closed or merged their A&E departments in recent years or operate them only part-time. Therefore, while there will always be an A&E facility in your area, not every hospital is equipped to handle emergencies. If your condition isn't serious enough to warrant a hospital visit, you should consult your family GP. In towns and cities there are also 'after-hours' clinics where you can see a doctor with minor ailments when your GP's surgery is closed (see **Doctors** below).

A private company, Accident Info Services (☎ 0800-263 345 or 09-529 0488), provides a telephone information service and advises callers about how to access New Zealand's health system. It can advise you on local doctors and hospitals or arrange for a doctor to visit you at home, and is particularly useful when medical help other than immediate hospital treatment is necessary.

STATE HEALTHCARE

New Zealand provides 'free' or subsidised healthcare to its citizens, permanent residents and certain visitors. The system is comparable to those in European countries such as France or Germany, where the state covers the bulk of the cost of medical treatment but expects most patients to make a contribution. 'Free' care isn't as comprehensive as under the British National Health Service, which aims to provide free care to almost everyone, including emergency treatment for visitors. On the other hand, it's a far cry from that in the USA, where every last pill, potion and sticking plaster must be paid for.

The Ministry of Health is responsible for funding and providing state healthcare, which it delegates to 21 District Health Boards (DHBs), which were established in 2001 when the New Zealand Public Health and Disability Act 2000 came into force. DHBs plan, manage, provide and purchase services for the population of their district. This includes funding for primary care, public health services, aged care, and services provided by other non-government health providers. DHBs use their funding to 'buy' healthcare services from various 'suppliers', including family GPs, hospitals,

nursing homes and other health organisations. Each of the 21 DHBs has substantial freedom to adopt its own system and framework and there tends to be a lack of consistency throughout the country.

Primary Health Organisations (PHOs) were established in 2002 and are funded by District Health Boards (DHBs) to provide essential primary health care services to those enrolled with the PHO. The 81 PHOs bring together doctors, nurses and other health professionals (such as Maori health workers, health promotion workers, dieticians, pharmacists, physiotherapists, psychologists and midwives) in the community to serve the health needs of their patients.

For information about public health services contact the Ministry of Health (PO Box 5013, Wellington, ☎ 04-496 2000, 💻 www.moh.govt.nz). See also Social Security on page 206.

Entitlements

All citizens and permanent residents are automatically entitled to state healthcare and it isn't necessary to establish a contributions record. If you're a visitor or temporary migrant and a national of a country with which New Zealand has a reciprocal agreement (e.g. Australia and the UK), you can also receive state health benefits. Others must pay the full cost of healthcare. New Zealand doesn't deduct social security health contributions from salaries and the cost of providing public health services is largely met from general taxation.

The basic principle of state healthcare is that hospital in-patient treatment is provided free, whereas the cost of out-patient and non-hospital treatment (e.g. consultations with a family GP and prescribed medicines) require a contribution to be paid by patients, although services are subsidised. A flat rate is levied for each visit to a GP, irrespective of the nature of the visit (see below).

Free healthcare includes:

♦ Hospital treatment, including 24-hour accident and emergency (A&E) clinics. There are some exceptions, such as for cosmetic surgery.

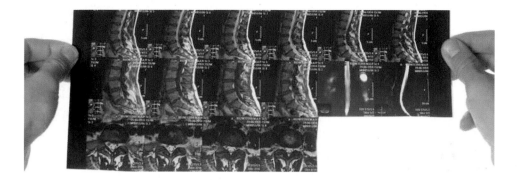

♦ Children's immunisations.

♦ Prescription medicines for children under six and those with a prescription subsidy card and a high use health card or Community Services Card (see below).

♦ Prescription medicines for all public hospital patients.

♦ Most laboratory tests and x-rays, except at privately-operated clinics.

♦ Healthcare during pregnancy and childbirth. This covers everything from the diagnosis of pregnancy to pre- and post-natal care for mother and baby. There's no charge for hospital stays.

♦ General practitioner (GP) referrals to a public hospital for treatment.

♦ Check-ups and basic dental treatment for schoolchildren.

♦ Breast-screening for women aged 50 to 64.

♦ Acute or chronic medical conditions (in some circumstances, a financial contribution may be required).

The following healthcare is subsidised but not free:

♦ Visits to general practitioners (see **Doctors** below).

♦ Prescription items (see **Medicines** below).

♦ Visits to physiotherapists, chiropractors and osteopaths when referred by a GP.

♦ Ambulance services (in some areas).

Those on low incomes can apply for a Community Services Card (CSC) which entitles them to a discount on healthcare costs (☎ 0800-999 999 for information). There's no automatic reduction in charges for special groups (although free GPs' services are provided for children under six) and pensioners aren't automatically entitled to reduced-cost services unless they have a low income. Note that dental treatment and optical services are largely outside the scope of the state health scheme.

Healthcare Problems

Like many countries, the state health system has huge and growing problems providing universal health care, including chronic staff shortages (it loses hundreds of doctors and nurses to Australia and further afield each year), a shortage of hospital beds, overcrowded emergency departments, rising costs (equipment, drugs, staff, etc.), limited services in rural areas and underfunding. Added to which, preventive medicine is minimal, many people do little or no exercise and eat badly, leading to an epidemic of obesity and associated health problems, and the country has an ageing population – in 2026, it's estimated that one in five New Zealanders will be 65 or older.

The state healthcare system has come under huge pressure in recent years due to an increasing demand for services amid severe financial constraints, as politicians have sought to reduce the spiralling health budget in order to fund tax cuts. A number of hospitals have been closed and the number of people on waiting lists for non-emergency treatment, once unknown in New Zealand, has soared to over 100,000.

An increasing problem is the tens of thousands of patients who fail to turn up for specialist appointments or operations, for which no penalty is incurred. Some analysts have suggested a pre-paid deposit to deter no-shows. At Auckland hospital, patients must reconfirm an appointment 24 hours in advance, otherwise the appointment is given to someone else.

There have also been various disruptions to healthcare services, as successive governments have experimented with various measures aimed at providing a better service for less money (a formidable task). The latest healthcare innovation is the Health Information Strategy for New Zealand – launched in August 2005 – which aims to deal with current challenges, including the ageing population, the rising incidence of chronic diseases such as diabetes and cardiovascular disease, the emergence of new infectious diseases such as SARS, and the high cost of new technology and treatments.

The New Zealand public and media are concerned at a perceived lack of funding of the country's state healthcare, and medical staff generally feel that they're underpaid and obliged to work with over-stretched resources. There have been several high-profile cases of people needing urgent treatment who have had to wait too long. The New Zealand Medical Association (🖳 www.nzma.org.nz) also highlights the shortage of rural GPs and professionals in some specialist areas, such as psychiatry, as well as the 'brain drain' of doctors from New Zealand who accumulate vast student debts and are then enticed overseas by higher salaries and better working conditions.

In the 2011 budget the government earmarked an additional $1.7bn for health services between 2011-12 and 2014-15. Spending on health will be $13.95bn in 2011-12. Priority health targets include shorter waiting times for emergency department treatment, reducing smoking and diabetes, additional immunisation and cardiovascular services, as well as reduced waiting times for critical cancer treatment and elective surgery.

☑ SURVIVAL TIP

Most people who can afford to take out private health insurance to circumvent the public health waiting lists for non-emergency specialist appointments and hospital treatment (see Private Health Care below and Health Insurance on page 211).

Accident Compensation Scheme

Medical treatment required as the result of an accident isn't covered by the state healthcare scheme but by the accident compensation scheme operated by the Accident Compensation Corporation (ACC, 🖳 www. acc.co.nz – see page 203). Medical benefits paid by the ACC are more comprehensive than the basic state health scheme and include all treatment, including surgery, hospital care, specialists, doctors' fees and medicines, irrespective of where or how the accident occurred and who was to blame.

Under the Injury Prevention and Rehabilitation Act of 2000, medical expenses are paid in full and claimants are paid a weekly allowance, but must go through comprehensive monitored rehabilitation before they receive a lump sum compensation. Compensation is paid only after the claimant's condition has stabilised or after two years, provided the claimant has 'whole person impairment'.

The advantages of this scheme, which is unique, are that you don't need to buy private accident insurance (although you can if you wish) or sue a guilty party for compensation (in fact the law forbids you to do this). The main disadvantage is that the benefits aren't as generous as they would be with private insurance, or compensation as high as you could receive as a result of taking legal action against someone who causes an accident.

PRIVATE HEALTHCARE

Private health practitioners operate both hand-in-hand with the public health service and independently of it. In addition to specialist appointments and hospital treatment, people commonly use private health treatment to obtain second opinions, health checks and screening, and for complementary medicine (which isn't usually available under the public health service). If you need to see a GP or specialist privately, you (or your insurance company) must pay the full fee. Most patients who receive private health treatment in New Zealand have private health insurance (see page 211), usually in order to circumvent the public health waiting lists for non-emergency specialist appointments and hospital treatment. Private patients are free to choose their own specialist and hospital, and are usually accommodated in a single, hotel style room with a radio, telephone, colour TV, en suite bathroom and room service.

You should check that a doctor or medical practitioner is qualified to provide the treatment you require and, when choosing a private specialist or clinic, only go to one that has been recommended by someone you trust. It's sometimes wise to obtain a second opinion, particularly if you're diagnosed as having a serious illness or require a major operation (but don't expect your GP or specialist to approve).

Although it isn't common in New Zealand, unnecessary operations aren't unknown.

The quality of private treatment isn't any better than that provided by the public health service and you shouldn't assume that because a doctor (or any other medical practitioner) is in private practice, he's more competent than his public health counterpart. In fact you'll often see the same specialist or be treated by the same surgeon under the public health service and privately.

DOCTORS

New Zealand has a community-based system of healthcare, where your first point of contact for any medical problem is your family doctor or general practitioner (GP), who treats minor conditions and refers more serious cases to specialists or hospitals. It's advisable to find and register with a GP as soon as you arrive in New Zealand or move to a new area. Most GPs belong to a Primary Health Organisation (PHO), which charges lower fees. Note, however, that it can sometimes take about three months after submitting an application to receive lower priced care, therefore it's advisable to enrol with a PHO sooner rather than later.

You can choose any GP, although it's obviously more convenient to use one near your home. Telephone directories contain a list of local GPs in the preface. Just go along to the practice of your choice with your passport or residence visa and tell them you wish to register as a patient.

Most GPs' surgeries are well equipped and often take the form of health centres or group practices where several doctors practise together and specialise in different areas, such as obstetrics or paediatrics. Many also have their own nurses who you can consult for minor problems and treatment, which is cheaper than seeing a doctor. Nurses are highly trained and qualified in New Zealand, and are authorised to prescribe certain drugs and administer treatments (such as intravenous injections) which aren't permitted in many other countries.

Under the state healthcare scheme, a flat rate is levied for each visit to a doctor, irrespective of the nature of the visit. GPs set their own rates and you can usually find

GP fees on District Health Board websites (although doctors are coy about publishing them, so you may have to hunt around or even ring the surgery). Most GPs don't charge for under six-year-olds, while others may charge a small fee. Doctors' fees in some regions are also affected by the different PHO subsidies available to different socioeconomic groups.

The basic consultation fee varies and is usually from $45 to $65 between 8.30am and 5.30pm, while visits at night and weekends cost $10 to $15 extra. GP visits for children are subsidised by $15 for those aged 6 to 17 and by $35 for children under six. GP's fee are lower if a doctor is a member of a PHO; for example those aged 18-24 pay around $25 a visit, while some 60 per cent of practices provide free GP visits for children under six.

Healthline (☎ 0800-611 116, 🖥 www.moh. govt.nz/healthline) is a free, 24-hour, seven days a week, telephone advice service (which includes the Well Child service) provided by trained nurses, who assess a person's condition and health and recommend the best course of action.

Adults who visit the doctor often or who receive social benefits receive a $15 subsidy. If you have a means-tested Community Services Card/CSC, a doctor's visit costs around $15 for an adult and $10 for a child over six. If you need to visit the doctor frequently (at least 12 times a year), you can obtain a High Use Health Card (HUHC) from your GP, which entitles you to the same reductions as a CSC.

Surgery hours are usually 8.30am to 5.30pm, Mondays to Fridays, although it's necessary to make an appointment; most GP's will usually see you on the day you make an appointment. Some family GPs provide a service outside surgery hours and make house calls, although this is rare; in cities, calls outside surgery hours are directed to an after-hours clinic. If you don't know where your nearest after-hours clinic is located, call your doctor's regular number and your call will be diverted (or a recorded message will tell you where the clinic is).

If you need to see a specialist, which is free, you must be referred by your GP. However, there are waiting times, which vary according to the region, urgency and treatment involved. If you prefer not to wait and opt to see a specialist privately, you (or your private health insurance) must pay the fee.

MEDICINES

Medicines are sold in pharmacies, also known as chemists, which may be part of another business. The vast majority of pharmacies belong to national chains, which include Amcal (🖥 www.amcal.co.nz), Life Pharmacy (🖥 www. lifepharmacy.co.nz), Radius Pharmacy (🖥 www. radiuspharmacy.co.nz) and Unichem (🖥 www. unichem.co.nz), most of which also sell online.

Pharmacies sell prescription and non-prescription medicines, and other products such as cosmetics and toiletries, but don't usually carry such an extensive range of goods as an American drugstore. Normal opening hours are 9am to 5.30pm, Mondays to Fridays (occasionally later on Thursdays or Fridays), and possibly Saturday mornings. In most areas there's a duty or 'urgent' pharmacy, which is open longer hours or an emergency contact number is provided for those needing medicines in an emergency (details are displayed in pharmacy windows).

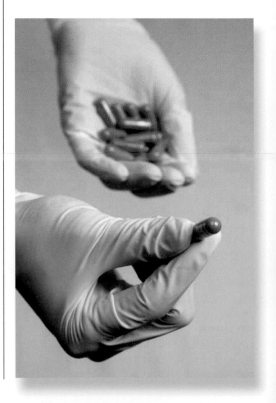

Drugs tend to fall into four classifications: Prescription medicines which are available only from a pharmacy with a prescription; restricted or pharmacy-only medicines for minor complaints, available without a prescription but not displayed on shelves; and pharmacy (e.g. own-brand) medicines available only in pharmacies. The final category is unrestricted general sale medicines, such as aspirin, which are widely available in general stores and supermarkets, where they may be cheaper than in pharmacies.

The cost of medicines that are fully subsidised by the government agency, Pharmac (🖥 www.pharmac.govt.nz), is a maximum of $15 per item for adults, $10 for a child aged 6 to 17 years and free for children under six. If you're enrolled in a Primary Health Organisation (PHO), are a Care Plus patient (i.e. someone with a chronic health condition), or have a CSC or HUHC card (see above), you pay $3 for a subsidised prescription. Once you've paid for 20 prescription items in a year, you're entitled to apply for a Prescription Subsidy Card (PSC), irrespective of your income, which entitles you to receive further prescriptions for $2 each for the rest of the year (or free if you have a CSC). You can apply for a PSC at your chemist.

Pharmac periodically adds and removes medicines from its subsidised list. If a prescribed medicine isn't on the subsidised list, you must pay a supplement, which includes PSC and CSC holders. If you're obtaining a prescription item from a pharmacy, you pay the same price everywhere. However, the cost of non-prescription items can vary considerably and may be cheaper at a supermarket than a pharmacy. You can check whether a medicine requires a prescription at www.medsafe.govt.nz.

Most pharmacists provide general advice about the best medicines for particular conditions, and some are specially trained to provide individual consultations and advice under the Comprehensive Pharmaceutical Care Service. Many patients use this system as a cheaper alternative to visiting a doctor, with the result that some pharmacists charge $30 to $50 for consultations, plus the cost of medicines! However, it's possible to find a pharmacist who dispenses free advice, which in the case of minor ailments can save you the cost of a visit to a doctor. Pharmacists can also tell you which drugs can be purchased over the counter for less than the $15 prescription charge.

HOSPITALS & CLINICS

Members of the public can use hospitals without a GP's referral only in the case of accidents and emergencies, when you visit or are taken directly to an A&E department. In all other cases your first point of contact is your family GP, who will refer you to the appropriate hospital as necessary.

The main criticism of healthcare reforms in recent years has related to the increase in hospital waiting lists, which are long and growing longer (and vary from region to region).

There have been many horror stories in recent years of patients requiring urgent hospital treatment having to wait ten hours (often on a trolley in a corridor) or more for a bed, or patients with chronic symptoms even being sent home. The public hospital system bears the brunt of the failures of the health service, and long waiting lists and a shortage of beds, specialist doctors and nurses is widespread. In hospitals with a shortage of beds, elderly patients may be required to share rooms with members of the opposite sex.

Under the current system, regional health authorities must 'buy' the services you require (e.g. an operation) from the most cost-effective source, which is usually your local hospital. However, if you're willing to travel to another (or any) hospital, you should inform your GP, as he may be able to book you into a hospital where the waiting list is shorter.

Once you're given a bed in a public hospital, the standard of medical and nursing care is as good as you're likely to find anywhere. New Zealand hospitals provide free in-patient healthcare, which includes medical and nursing care, medicines and accommodation. (The government experimented with a $50 per day 'hotel charge' for in-patients between 1991 and 1993, but this was dropped after public opposition.) Out-patient treatment in accident and emergency (A&E) departments isn't free and is paid for in the same way as visits to a family GP (CSC holders pay reduced fees).

It can be difficult to identify hospitals since the 1993 changes to the state healthcare system, when they became known by various euphemisms such as 'healthcare centres', 'mental care units' (mental hospitals) or 'elder care units' (geriatric hospitals). In addition to public hospitals, there are also many private hospitals in New Zealand, which allow the wealthy and those with medical insurance to circumvent the public sector waiting lists.

Many private hospitals are owned by the medical insurance companies (as public hospitals don't accept private patients) and accommodation may be more luxurious than in public hospitals, although the standard of medical care is generally the same and hospitals are often served by many of the same doctors. Some private hospitals receive government subsidies and there are a number of projects where the public and private sectors co-operate to provide specialist services such as coronary care. Some charities also provide health services, e.g. community clinics, which are partially funded by the government. There are also private hospitals and clinics that specialise in non-essential, cosmetic surgery.

CHILDBIRTH & ABORTION

The first port of call for pregnant women in New Zealand is their family GP. He can undertake preliminary tests and checks, and refer you for ante-natal and (subsequently) post-natal care, either within the practice itself or at a nearby clinic (where you're attended to by a 'lead maternity carer' who may be either a midwife or a doctor). It's usual for a birth to take place in a local hospital, where you stay for up to five days, although it's possible to have a baby at home attended by a midwife. This is more common in rural areas, where the nearest hospital may be a considerable distance away. All maternity and childbirth treatment within the state system is free.

Abortion is legal in New Zealand under certain conditions, such as when continuing with a pregnancy would pose a threat to the physical or mental well-being of the mother,

or when a child is likely to be born seriously handicapped. Two specially approved doctors or counsellors must authorise an abortion.

CHILDREN'S HEALTH

Family GPs provide a health service for children and where necessary refer them to consultants and specialists at an appropriate hospital. Child immunisation is free and actively encouraged for diphtheria, hepatitis B, HIB, measles, mumps, poliomyelitis, rubella, tetanus and whooping cough, although the country lags behind in immunisation for MMR. Public health nurses visit primary schools to conduct regular hearing and eye tests.

A national non-profit organisation, the Royal New Zealand Plunket Society (PO Box 5474, Wellington, ☎ 04-471 0177, 💻 www.plunket. org.nz), provides free check-ups for children, advice, information and support. Plunket, which is run by professionals and volunteers and aims to provide children with access to the best healthcare, fills any gaps in the state child healthcare system. It also works closely with Maori and ethnic groups.

New Zealand's leading children's hospital, with a similar status to London's famous Great Ormond Street Children's Hospital, is Auckland's Starship Children's Hospital (💻 www.starship.org.nz). It caused an outcry among doctors and dieticians for allowing McDonald's to open a fast food outlet in the foyer, although it went down well with the kids; ironically it closed in February 2005, by which time some nutritionists were grudgingly in favour of its new menu's fruit and salads.

New Zealand has a tradition of promoting access to the great outdoors for children and there are 'health camps' throughout the country for children aged under 13 with special needs, who can attend for up to six weeks. Children are referred to the camps by doctors, social workers and teachers, and they undertake a programme of remedial and health education, sports and games, in addition to learning 'life skills'. Camps also have psychologists who counsel children with behavioural problems.

Health camps are largely financed by special 'health postage stamps' issued by NZ Post in the spring, from which a donation is made to help fund camps. Health authorities also operate various health education and development programmes for children.

DENTISTS

There are excellent dentists throughout New Zealand; indeed New Zealanders travelling abroad often search high and low in cities such as London and New York for a New Zealand dentist. If you wish, you may be able to find a British or American dentist in Auckland or Wellington, although they all inflict the same torture irrespective of nationality! Most dentists are in private practice, as the public health scheme doesn't extend to dentistry, except in the case of children.

Children at primary schools see a school dental nurse and many primary schools have a dental surgery on the premises. Children are entitled to see a school dentist every 12 months, although a backlog has been developing for several years resulting in most children seeing a dentist only once every 18 months (they don't seem to mind!). All children up to the age of 16 (18 if still at school) are entitled to free treatment by the dentist of their choice, assuming that he participates in the 'free dental scheme'; however, many dentists have withdrawn from the scheme due to the 'inadequate' fees paid by the Ministry of Health.

To find a dentist, obtain recommendations from neighbours, colleagues and friends, or consult your local telephone directory. It's wise to shop around, as charges can vary considerably, particularly for extensive repair work. However, most dentists, unless they target wealthy patients, charge fees that are affordable to the average person (although it can still be an expensive business). It's wise to obtain a quotation before having 'expensive' treatment – many dentists have 'menu pricing', although this should only be regarded as a guide.

Dental costs are highest in Auckland, where they are up to 50 per cent more than in other towns and cities. Typical dental fees are $75 for an examination, $110 for an examination and clean, and $125-150 for a small filling, while

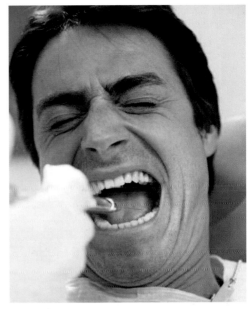

say AARGH!

a ceramic crown or porcelain laminate veneer will set you back around $1,250. Information about dentists can be obtained from the Dental Council of New Zealand (☎ 04-499 4820, 🖥 www.dentalcouncil.org.nz).

It's possible to take out special insurance against dental costs, and cover for dental treatment may also be included in general medical insurance policies, which can be purchased from medical insurance companies and dentists (see **Chapter 13**).

OPTICIANS

Opticians in New Zealand are known as optometrists and have 'surgeries' (more often shops) in most towns and cities, where they provide eye tests and sell spectacle lenses, frames and contact lenses. Optometry is a private business in New Zealand and outside the scope of the public health system. Nowadays many independent opticians have been replaced by chain stores, which sell a wide range of frames, including top international brands, at competitive prices. Major chains include OPSM (☎ 0800-696 776, www.opsm.co.nz), Specsavers (🖥 www.specsavers.co.nz), which claims to be the best value for money, and Visique (☎ 0800-847 478, 🖥 www.visique.co.nz). You can also find an optometrist through the New Zealand Association of Optometrists (☎ 0800-439 322, 💻 www.nzao.co.nz).

Prices vary considerably for both frames and lenses, therefore you need to shop around for the best deal. A standard pair of spectacles and lenses costs around $300 to $400 plus $50 for the cost of an eye test, although a basic deal is available countrywide for around $200 plus $50 for the eye test required for a driving licence. (When the requirement was introduced, many New Zealanders were shocked to discover that not only couldn't they see well enough to drive, but they also had to pay for new glasses!)

Optometrists should carry out free tests for glaucoma as part of an eye test; if their tests indicate a problem, you should take their report to your GP and ask him to refer you to a specialist, in which case any treatment necessary will be provided free of charge.

COUNSELLING & SOCIAL SERVICES

Counselling and assistance for health and social problems are available under the public health system and from many local community groups and volunteer organisations, ranging from national associations to small local groups (including self-help groups). Local authorities provide social workers to advise and support those requiring help within their community. If you need to find help locally, you can contact your local council, local voluntary services or a Citizens' Advice Bureau (☎ 0800-367 222, 💻 www.cab.org.nz). A list of 24-hour emergency services (including many counselling services) is included in telephone directories, plus community help and welfare services, and help for young people.

Many colleges and educational establishments provide a counselling service for students, and general hospitals usually have a psychiatrist on call 24 hours a day. Problems for which help is available are numerous and include alcoholism (e.g. Alcoholics Anonymous), attempted suicide and psychiatric problems, battered children and women, dieting (e.g. Weight Watchers), drug rehabilitation, gambling, homosexual

related problems, marriage and relationship counselling, rape, smoking and youth problems.

A number of voluntary organisations and local authorities run refuges for battered wives (and their children) or maltreated children whose conditions have become intolerable (some provide 24-hour emergency phone numbers). If you or a member of your family are the victims of a violent crime, the police will put you in touch with a local victim support scheme. For information about help and advice to disabled people, see below.

HELP FOR THE HANDICAPPED

Official government statistics show that around 20 per cent of New Zealanders have some kind of 'handicap', varying from a serious physical disability to a minor visual impairment (curiously the rate is much higher in the South Island than in the North Island). All public offices and businesses are required to make special provision for handicapped people (e.g. special access ramps, facilities for the hard of hearing, etc.), although provision of these services is patchy, because a lot of older buildings cannot be modified.

Most buses cannot accommodate those with mobility problems, although a small number of taxis can. There are several organisations that provide help to the handicapped in New Zealand, which includes practical help, financial assistance and advice, e.g. about state benefits. The main organisations include:

♦ Enable New Zealand (☎ 0800-171 981, 🖥 www.enable.co.nz) facilitates and delivers quality access to resources for people with identified health and disability support needs, plus a range of services for older people and disabled people.

♦ CCS Disability Action (☎ 0800-227 2255, 🖥 www.ccsdisabilityaction.org.nz) provides information, advocacy and support to children, youth, adults, their families and whanau (extended family).

♦ Weka (🖥 www.weka.net.nz) is New Zealand's disability information website, for people with disabilities, their families, whanau and caregivers, health professionals and disability information providers.

In addition to the above, many local councils have a disability information service, such as Christchurch (☎ 03-366 6189, 🖥 www.disinfo. co.nz).

Invalids benefit is payable to those unable to work because of a physical or mental disability, while those who are handicapped as a result of an accident receive payments from the Accident Compensation Corporation (see page 203).

SEXUALLY TRANSMITTED DISEASES

Like most countries, New Zealand has its share of sexually transmitted diseases (STDs), including Acquired Immune Deficiency Syndrome (Aids). Fortunately, New Zealand has one of the lowest occurrences of Aids in the developed world, although it has risen in recent years. Aids is transmitted by sexual contact, needle sharing among drug addicts, and less commonly, through transfused blood or its components. All blood used in transfusions in New Zealand is screened for HIV (human immunodeficiency virus), the virus which usually leads to Aids.

The furore over Aids has died down in the past few years, which many fear may cause those most at risk to be lulled into a false sense of security (many teenagers still practise unprotected sex). The explosion of Aids predicted by 'experts' in Western countries

hasn't materialised, particularly among the heterosexual population, although the number of heterosexual cases is increasing.

In an attempt to combat Aids, the use of condoms has been widely encouraged through a comprehensive (if obscure) advertising campaign, although it has taken a long time to get the message across about safe sex. Condom machines can be found in various public places (there's an on-going debate about whether they should be installed in secondary schools) and purchased from chemists and other outlets (but they aren't cheap). Some positive news for sufferers is that several Aids-inhibiting drugs have been placed on the subsidised drugs list in recent years (see **Medicines** above).

Family GPs can provide basic information about STD prevention and can refer those with particular problems and worries to specialists. There are also specialist clinics throughout the country, such as those run by the Auckland Sexual Health Service (☎ 0800-739 432, 🖥 www.ashs.org.nz/nz_clinics.html), and gay and other organisations are also active in providing help and advice.

SMOKING & DRUGS

New Zealand has become one of the world's leading countries in the battle against smoking, which has resulted in a lower death rate from lung disease and other smoking-related diseases than, for example, in some European countries. Smoking is directly responsible for some 5,000 deaths a year and costs the public health service some $2bn a year. Around 18 per cent of the population are smokers, although rates are 50 per cent among Maori.

Cigarettes have become increasingly expensive thanks to sharp tax rises in the last few years. The government spends tens of millions of dollars a year on anti-smoking programmes aimed principally at children and Maori, although the figure represents only a fraction of the amount raised in tobacco taxes (a strange situation, in which the government is spending money in order to try to *reduce* its income!).

Cigarette packets contain bi-lingual (English and Maori) warnings about the perils of smoking. Those under 18 are prohibited from purchasing tobacco products and the penalty for selling tobacco to anyone under age is $2,000. The government plans to ban retailers from selling tobacco if they have several convictions for selling tobacco to minors. The Quit Group provides advice and support for those trying to give up smoking (☎ 0800-778 778, www.quit.org.nz).

Smoking is officially banned in most public places and you may not smoke in most public buildings or on buses, coaches, trains and aircraft. Most workplaces have banned smoking altogether, although some have a small smoking area. Quite apart from anti-smoking legislation, smoking is considered socially unacceptable in New Zealand; even when indulging perfectly legally you may attract angry glances, remarks, or even requests to stub it out if your smoke is causing annoyance to others.

New Zealand was the third country (after Norway and Ireland) in the world to ban smoking in public places (in 2004), such as bars, restaurants, casinos, clubs and school grounds, although many countries have since followed suit.

'Recreational' smoking of cannabis, which is widely grown in New Zealand, is widespread, although it's illegal, and the use of ecstasy and hard drugs such as heroin and cocaine is on the increase. However, drug abuse is less of a problem than in many other countries and New Zealand's border controls are relatively effective in keeping out illicit substances.

A number of organisations provide help for those with alcohol, drug and other addictions, including 💻 www.addictionshelp.org.nz, www.alcoholdrughelp.org.nz and www.carenz.co.nz, while the NZS website provides links to numerous support organisations (💻 www.nzs.com/health/addiction).

BIRTHS & DEATHS

Births in New Zealand must be registered 'as soon as possible' at your local registry office for births, marriages and deaths. You'll be provided with a copy of the entry in the register, otherwise known as a birth certificate (necessary for official purposes such as claiming benefits and school registration). Deaths should be registered at the same office (within three working days after the burial or cremation) with a copy of the death certificate provided by the hospital or doctor attending the death. This is usually carried out by the undertaker. As anywhere, dying is a major expense in New Zealand, where an average funeral and burial costs around $8,800 and possibly much more with 'extras' such as cars and flowers. The cost of shipping a body to another country for burial is considerable and is to be avoided if at all possible.

Most medical insurance policies provide cover for funeral expenses (with the amount of benefit linked to the cost of the policy). It's also possible to take out a funeral plan to cover these expenses. For those without insurance or private resources, Work and Income New Zealand (WINZ) provides a funeral grant of up to $1,925.34, which depends on the means and assets of the deceased and his next of kin (it's generally only available to those who already receive social security benefits) and the Accident Compensation Corporation (see page 203) provides a funeral grant of up to $5,788.92 for deaths that occur as a result of an accident or medical misadventure (up to $10,000 for crime victims). You cannot, however, claim a grant from WINZ and the ACC.

MEDICAL TREATMENT ABROAD

If you're a visitor to New Zealand and a resident of a country with a reciprocal health agreement with New Zealand (including Australia and the UK), you can take advantage of public healthcare services in New Zealand, including free hospital in-patient treatment and free medicines while in hospital. When visiting a doctor, you'll be charged at the same rate as New Zealanders for consultations and will also be able to purchase subsidised prescriptions (see page 194). To claim these benefits, simply show your passport to the doctor or chemist. There's no entitlement to subsidised dentistry (except for children) or optical services and you aren't entitled to free treatment for conditions which existed before you entered

New Zealand (if you knew or could reasonably have been expected to know about them).

If you're entitled to social security health benefits in New Zealand, you can take advantage of reciprocal healthcare arrangements in other countries with which New Zealand has such an agreement, including Australia, and the UK, where you're entitled to the same public health benefits as citizens and residents, simply by producing your New Zealand passport or migration documents. In Australia you receive free hospital treatment and subsidised prescriptions through the Medicare system, while in the UK you receive most medical treatment free, paying only prescription and subsidised dental charges.

Aotearoa (land of the long white cloud)

13.

INSURANCE

New Zealand has an innovative approach to insurance, which is quite different from that in, for example, the USA and most Western European countries. In these countries there are state schemes which pay health, sickness and unemployment benefits; however, unlike most other countries, New Zealand's system isn't largely insurance based and individuals aren't required to make contributions in order to benefit. Although, as the substantial costs are funded by general taxation, they cannot be said to be free to taxpayers. New Zealand has also taken the concept of state insurance a step further than most other countries and provides universal accident benefits to all citizens, residents and visitors alike (see below).

Note, however, that the situation regarding 'free' insurance in New Zealand doesn't mean that you don't need to take out private insurance. The state schemes don't, by any means, cover every eventuality and neither are the benefits generous, meaning private insurance is recommended, if not essential.

General information about insurance is provided by the Insurance Council of New Zealand (💻 www.icnz.org.nz). See also **Car Insurance** and **Motor Breakdown Insurance** in **Chapter 11**.

ACCIDENT COMPENSATION SCHEME

If you have an accident in New Zealand, e.g. at work or on the roads, you'll be compensated by the government-run Accident Compensation Corporation (ACC, ☎ 0800 101 996, 💻 www. acc.co.nz), irrespective of who was to blame or whether you've paid any contributions. The ACC operates what's essentially a mandatory accident insurance system, financed both through taxes and (unlike most other state benefits) a levy on earnings. However, entitlement to benefits isn't based on contributions as it would be with a commercial insurance scheme.

Visitors are also covered by the ACC scheme, without the need to make contributions. If you should suffer an accident and make a claim, the ACC will cover your medical and associated expenses in New Zealand, but it won't cover repatriation or medical expenses arising abroad in connection with an accident or loss of earnings abroad. Note that, as the ACC isn't a social security scheme, continuing to pay into the social security scheme in your home country (which you're usually entitled to do) doesn't exempt you from paying the ACC levy on your earnings in New Zealand.

The aim of the accident compensation scheme was originally to provide New Zealanders with accident insurance at low cost by taking the commercialism out of insurance. The scheme has gone through many changes in recent years, including a period of two years when employers were permitted to take out accident compensation insurance with private companies, instead of with the state ACC. However, since 2000 workplace insurance could only be provided by ACC. Payments made under the ACC scheme used to be generous and consisted of lump sum payments on a fixed scale, but this resulted in large amounts of money being paid to people with relatively minor injuries.

The Injury Prevention and Rehabilitation Act of 2000 resulted in a general tightening of the ACC budget, and the emphasis now lies on injury prevention and rehabilitation, rather than the payment of compensation, as was previously the case. Compensation ranges from a minimum of $2,500 to a maximum of $100,000. The aim of the Act, which also established a 'code of claimants' rights', is to prevent fraud and to ensure that the more seriously injured claimants receive greater compensation than the less seriously injured. The Act has come in for much criticism, particularly from employers, but the ACC scheme is much more generous than most other countries' public schemes, most of which don't pay out a penny to accident victims, certainly not without a long legal struggle.

Note that suing the party who caused an accident isn't usually possible under New Zealand law – a situation that that would have grossly overpaid personal injury lawyers in the USA gasping in horror!

You must simply accept the payment awarded by the ACC, which, although it means that you're unlikely to receive a multi-million dollar payout, ensures that a lot of money isn't wasted on long drawn out court cases (and it prevents fraud, reduces premiums, etc.). However, if you wish, you can take out personal injury insurance, which is likely to pay considerably higher compensation in the case of an accident and may also compensate you for damage to property (which the ACC doesn't).

Expenses covered by the ACC are comprehensive and include medical and hospital treatment, hospital surgery, loss of earnings, loss of future earnings, physiotherapy, home nursing care, expenses involved with rehabilitation or future disability, and an allowance if you're unable to work. For information about ACC health benefits, see **Accident Compensation Scheme** on page 192. For further information, contact the Accident Compensation Corporate Office (☎ 04-918 7700, 🖳 www.acc.co.nz).

Contributions

Although New Zealand doesn't require employees to make social security contributions, you must contribute to the ACC scheme. Employees' ACC contributions, known as the 'earner's levy', are used to pay compensation for accidents occurring outside the workplace. They're fixed annually and deducted from your salary by your employer, who will automatically register you for the ACC levy when you start work. ACC contributions (which are changed periodically) for employees were $2.04 (2011-2012) for each $100 of liable income, up to a maximum earnings limit of $111,669 (i.e. a maximum contribution of $2,278.04). Employees don't have a choice of ACC schemes.

Your employer also makes a contribution to the scheme, known as the 'employer's levy', which is used to provide compensation for accidents in the workplace. It's illegal (punishable by a $5,000 fine) for an employer to try to recover the employer's levy from employees, either by a direct deduction or any kind of informal agreement.

The self-employed pay the same ACC levy as employees, although they're exempt if their liable earnings are less than $26,520 per year (expenses are deductible) up to maximum earnings of $110,018 (2011-12).

Further information and advice about ACC contributions can be obtained from your local Inland Revenue Department (IRD, 🖳 www.ird.govt.nz) office or from the ACC (☎ 04-918 7700, 🖳 www.acc.co.nz).

INSURANCE COMPANIES

There are numerous insurance companies to choose from in New Zealand, which either provide a range of insurance services or specialise in certain sectors only. You can buy insurance from many sources, including traditional insurance companies selling through their own salesmen or independent brokers, direct insurance companies (selling directly to the public), banks and other financial institutions, and motoring organisations.

An increasingly common trend in New Zealand is for banks to offer property, life and motor insurance to their customers, which they do on an agency basis, i.e. they don't compare prices from various companies to find you the cheapest policy, although their premiums are usually competitive. If you're tempted to insure with your bank, you should compare their policies with the AA (🖳 www.aainsurance.co.nz) and State (🖳 www.state.co.nz), two of New Zealand's largest insurers. The major insurance companies have offices or agents (brokers) throughout the country, most of whom will provide a free analysis of your family or business insurance needs.

Two organisations that offer useful information and advice about insurance are the Insurance Company of New Zealand, which publishes several guides to different types of insurance (PO Box 474, Wellington, ☎ 04-472 5230, 🖳 www.icnz.org.nz), and the Citizens' Advice Bureau (CAB), which has offices in most large towns and cities (☎ 0800-367 222, 🖳 www.cab.org.nz). Independent information is also available online, e.g. 🖳 www.my-insurance-guide.co.nz and www.insurancenz.net. New Zealand also has an insurance ombudsman who deals with complaints about insurance companies and services (PO Box 10-845, Wellington, ☎ 04-499 7612, 🖳 www.iombudsman.org.nz).

Brokers

If you choose a broker, you should use one who's independent and sells policies from a range of insurance companies. Some brokers or agents are tied to a particular insurance company and sell policies only from that company (which includes most banks). An

independent broker should research the whole market and take into account your individual requirements, why you're investing (if applicable), the various companies' financial performance, what you can afford and the kind of policy that's best for you. He mustn't offer you a policy because it pays him the highest commission, which, incidentally, you should ask him about (particularly regarding life insurance).

Direct Insurance

In recent years many insurance companies have begun operating by 'direct response' (i.e. bypassing brokers), which has resulted in huge savings for consumers, particularly for car, building and home contents insurance Direct response companies provide quotations over the telephone and often you aren't even required to complete a proposal form. You should compare premiums from a number of direct response insurance companies with the best deals from brokers before choosing a policy.

Shop Around

When buying insurance, you should shop 'til you drop and then shop around some more! Premiums vary considerably (e.g. by 100 per cent or more), although you must ensure that you're comparing similar policies and that important benefits haven't been omitted. Bear in mind that the cheapest policy isn't necessarily the best, particularly regarding the prompt payment of claims. Many analysts believe that it's better to pay for independent insurance advice rather than accept 'free' advice, which may be more expensive in the long run.

You should obtain a number of quotations for each insurance need and shouldn't assume that your existing insurance company is the best choice for a new insurance requirement. Buy only the insurance that you *want* and *need* and ensure that you can afford the payments.

INSURANCE CONTRACTS

Read insurance contracts carefully before signing them. If you don't understand everything, ask a friend or colleague to 'translate' it or obtain professional advice.

Policies often contain traps and legal loopholes in the small print. If a policy has pages of legal jargon and gobbledegook in *very* small print, you have a right to be suspicious, particularly as it's common practice nowadays to be as brief as possible and write clearly and concisely in language which doesn't require a doctorate in law. Note that an insurance certificate or schedule won't list all the conditions and exclusions, which are listed only in the full policy document.

Many of the new direct response companies handle quotations, enquiries and claims by telephone on a paperless basis, so you may never see a form or document explaining your policy. This saves companies money, which they supposedly pass on to policyholders in the form of lower premiums. Take care how you answer questions in an insurance proposal form, because even if you mistakenly provide false information, an insurance company can refuse to pay out when you make a claim.

Most insurance policies run for a calendar year from the date on which you take out a policy. All insurance policy premiums should be paid punctually, as late payment can affect your benefits or a claim, although if this is so it should be noted in your policy. Before signing an insurance policy, you should shop around and take a day or two to think it over; never sign on the spot, as you may regret it later. With some insurance contracts, you may have a 'cooling off' period, e.g. 10 to 14 days, during which you can cancel a policy without penalty.

Claims

Although insurance companies are keen to take your money, many aren't nearly so happy to settle claims. As in other countries, some insurance companies will do almost anything to avoid paying out in the event of a claim and will use any available loophole. Fraud is estimated to cost the insurance industry millions of dollars a year (particularly motor insurance fraud) and staff may be trained to automatically assume that claims are fraudulent.

If you wish to make a claim, you must usually inform your insurance company in writing by registered letter within a number of days of an incident (possibly within 24 hours in the case of theft). Failure to do so will render your claim void!

Don't send original bills or documents regarding a claim to your insurance company unless it's essential (you can send a certified copy). Keep a copy of bills, documents and correspondence, and send letters by recorded or registered post so that your insurance company cannot deny receipt.

Don't bank a cheque received in settlement of a claim if you think it's insufficient, as you may be deemed to have accepted it as full and final settlement. It's also unwise to accept the first offer, as many insurance companies try to get away with making a low settlement (if an insurer pays what you've claimed without a quibble, you probably claimed too little!). When dealing with insurance companies, perseverance often pays off. Insurers are increasingly refusing to pay up on the flimsiest of pretexts, as they know that many people won't pursue their cases, even when they have a valid claim. Don't give up on a claim if you have a good case, but persist until you have exhausted every avenue.

SOCIAL SECURITY

New Zealand has a comprehensive social security system that provides a wide range of benefits to cover sickness and invalidity, unemployment and old age. Around one in four New Zealanders receives some kind of social security payment. As in many other countries, the social security system has suffered a funding crisis in recent years and (in real terms) benefits are being reduced, even though they're officially increased each year. Benefits are reviewed annually, with increases taking effect in January. The government spends around a third of its annual budget on social security benefits, most of which aren't based on contributions or previous earnings, but on a flat rate set by the government. On average this provides claimants receiving benefits with around 40 to 50 per cent of the average annual weekly wage, which is barely enough to live on.

The government has introduced a number of schemes in recent years to try to ensure that benefits are paid only to those in genuine need and, even then, only for as long as they are necessary. An increasing number of benefits are paid only after means-testing (an appraisal of an applicant's savings and other financial circumstances). In many cases, claimants are regularly called to account and expected to prove that they still need a benefit and cannot manage without it. Despite this increasingly tough stance on paying out government (or rather taxpayers') money, the authorities still encourage people to claim benefits to which they may be entitled on a 'we may turn you down but you're welcome to try' basis.

Eligibility

New Zealand nationals, permanent residents and foreign workers temporarily employed in New Zealand are covered by social security, without the requirement to make social security contributions. (They must, however, make contributions to the ACC scheme – see above) Benefits are normally paid only after a minimum period of residence, e.g. unemployment benefit is available only after you've lived in New Zealand for two years, and national superannuation (the state pension) usually requires a ten-year residence period.

New Zealand has reciprocal agreements with certain countries (including Australia, Canada, Denmark, Greece, Guernsey, Ireland, Jersey, the Netherlands and the UK), under which those migrating from these countries can apply for New Zealand social security benefits as soon as they arrive to take up permanent residence. It's important to note that a reciprocal agreement entitles you only to *apply* for benefits; whether or not a benefit is paid may depend on other criteria. Not all residents

are eligible for all benefits, as various 'tests' (e.g. income and other means) may be used to determine whether you're entitled to them.

For further information, contact Work and Income (National Office, Level 8, Bowen State Building, Bowen Street, PO Box 12-136, Wellington, ☎ 0800-559 009 or 09-913 0300, 🖳 www. workandincome.govt.nz).

Benefits

Social security benefits are paid (where applicable) at a flat rate, irrespective of your previous income. Benefits are taxable, assuming you earn enough to pay tax, and the Department of Social Welfare deducts the tax due before paying benefits. If you receive a benefit for the first time and aren't registered for tax, you should contact your local IRD office, which will issue you with an IRD number. This is required by Work and Income in order to deduct tax before paying your benefits. Those who receive no income other than benefits receive an 'M' tax code.

Health Benefit

Your entitlement to health benefit in New Zealand doesn't depend on having established a contributions record. If you're either a New Zealand citizen or a permanent resident you're automatically entitled to state healthcare (see page 190). If you're a visitor or temporary migrant and a national of a country (see above) with which New Zealand has a reciprocal agreement, you can also receive health benefit. Otherwise you must pay the full cost of healthcare.

Sickness & Maternity Benefits

Sickness benefit is payable to those who are unable to work due to illness on a temporary basis, whereas invalid's benefit (see below) is a permanent or semi-permanent benefit. With regard to social security, pregnancy also counts as a 'sickness' in that expectant mothers can apply for sickness benefit when they're unable to work, both during and after a pregnancy (you can claim from the 27th week of the pregnancy, or earlier if you have complications, and for up to 13 weeks after birth). Sickness benefit is payable weekly at various rates (from 1st April 2011), ranging from $134.26 (single aged 18-19), $288.47 (single parent) and $167.83 each for a couple after tax, i.e. net.

Parental leave is paid at a maximum of $458.82 per week (from 1st July 2011) before tax and is paid for up to 14 weeks, although some mothers (such as the self-employed) don't qualify. However, there's a minimum parental leave payment for the self-employed of $130 per week.

Accidental Injury Benefit

If you have an accident at work or elsewhere in New Zealand (including when motoring), all expenses and appropriate compensation are paid by the ACC scheme (see above).

Invalid's Benefit

Invalid's benefit is payable to those permanently unable to work due to a physical or mental disability, and provides a weekly payment equivalent to around half the average wage. Invalid's benefit is granted following a medical examination and is based on the opinion of the examining doctor. As in other countries, there has been concern that many people receiving this kind of benefit aren't incapable of work. The eligibility criteria have therefore been tightened and those receiving the benefit are periodically re-examined to ensure that they still qualify. Net (after tax) weekly rates range from $203.71 for a single person aged 16-17, $330.70 for a sole parent and $209.78 each for a couple.

Minimum Family Tax Credits & Other Family Benefits

The **minimum family tax credit** is paid to ensure that the annual income (before tax) of a family with dependant children aged 18 or younger doesn't fall below $22,204 from 1st April 2011. To qualify, couples must work at least 30 hours a week between them, and sole parents must work at least 20 hours a week. It ensures that families have a minimum income of $427 a week after tax. How much you receive depends on your total family income before tax.

A **parental tax credit** is paid to families with a newborn baby for the first 56 days (eight weeks)

after the baby is born. How much you receive depends on your total family income before tax, the number of dependant children in your care, the age of the children and the number of newborn children per year. You receive up to $150 a week for the first eight weeks (total $1,200) or 56 days after the baby is born.

An **Out of School Care and Recreation** (OSCAR) subsidy is a payment which helps families with the costs of before- and after-school programmes (up to 20 hours a week), and school holiday programmes (up to 50 hours a week). You may qualify for an OSCAR subsidy if you're the main carer of a dependant child, don't have a partner who can provide childcare, and are a New Zealand citizen or permanent resident. It also depends on how much you and your spouse or partner earn. Payments are from $29.60 to $76.80 per child during term time (20 hours per week) to $74 to $192 per child during holidays (50 hours per week), depending on the number of children you have and your gross weekly income.

For further information, see 🖥 www.workingforfamilies.govt.nz.

Domestic Purposes Benefit (DPB)

Domestic purposes benefit is mainly intended for single parents with dependant children who don't receive maintenance or support from a partner, although it's also sometimes paid to eligible widows and widowers, and those caring for sick or disabled relatives at home. It's generally payable only to those on low incomes (although there are various eligibility criteria) and only to New Zealand citizens and permanent residents, although under a reciprocal agreement, those moving from Australia and the UK can apply for the benefit immediately. From 1st April 2011, DPB was paid at the following rates:

Domestic Purposes Benefit	
Category	**Net Weekly Rate ($)**
Sole Parent	$288.47
Hospital Rate*	$41.64
* when an in-patient	

Widow's Benefit

Widow's benefit is payable to women whose husband or partner has died. The benefit is mainly to help widows with children to support. It's a means tested benefit payable only to those of limited means, and if the widow remarries she's no longer eligible. In 2011-2012 the weekly net widow's benefit was $209.78 for a single person with no children and $288.47 for a sole parent.

Funeral Grant

A funeral grant of up to $1,925.34 is payable to those who suffer a death in the family. It is, however, a means tested benefit payable only to those with limited resources. The assets of the deceased person are also taken into account when assessing whether it's payable.

See also **Births & Deaths** on page 200.

Unemployment Benefit

Some 6.3 per cent (around 150,000) of the working population were registered as unemployed in New Zealand in early 2012. New Zealand citizens and permanent residents can apply for unemployment benefit (or 'dole'), and no history of contributions or tax deductions is required to make a claim. However, newcomers must wait two years (unless in hardship) before they can apply for unemployment benefit, and those who resign from their jobs or are dismissed must wait 13 weeks before they can receive benefits.

The unemployment benefit service is operated by Work and Income, the section of the Department of Labour that provides a job-finding (or 'vacancy-filling') service to employees and employers. A much tougher approach than in the past is being taken regarding unemployment benefit, and claimants are required to register with Work and Income and make a 'Job Seeker Agreement', under which they're obliged to look for full-time work or training and take a suitable job if offered one. Claimants are also required to have regular meetings to determine what they're doing to find work, and to ensure that they aren't working while claiming benefit!

Those who fail to meet their obligations without a good reason can have their benefit suspended; and after the third failure, benefit may be stopped for 13 weeks. There are exceptions for those with children under 14 or those caring for a disabled or dependant relative. The benefit is paid at a flat rate irrespective of your previous income, although there are variations depending on your age and family status (and you also may be eligible for other benefits).

Rates from 1st April 2011 were as follows:

Unemployment Benefit	
Category	Net Weekly Rate ($)
Single, aged 18-19	
- living at home	$134.26
- living away from home	$167.83
Single, aged 20-24	$167.83
Single, aged 25+	$201.40
Married couple (each)	$167.83
Sole parent	$288.47

National Superannuation

New Zealand provides a retirement pension known as national superannuation or New Zealand Superannuation (NZS) – 'super' for short – which is funded from general taxation, rather than individual contributions. To qualify you must:

◆ be aged 65 or over;

◆ be a legal resident of New Zealand and normally live there;

◆ have lived in New Zealand for ten years since the age of 20 (five of those years must have been since your 50th birthday).

If you come to New Zealand from a country with a reciprocal social security agreement (including Australia, Canada, Ireland and the UK), you can claim national superannuation without a minimum period of residence, provided you would have been entitled to a state pension in your home country, although your overseas pension will probably be deducted from New Zealand superannuation.

Work and Income have special freephone contact numbers for overseas entitlements; Australia ☎ 0800-777 227, Ireland and the UK ☎ 0800-771 001, all other countries ☎ 0800-777 117.

National superannuation payments are made every two weeks. At 1st April 2011, the maximum net rates (after tax) were at follows:

Superannuation

Status	Fortnightly Benefit
Married (both partners qualify)	$1,045.92
Married (only one partner qualifies)	$994.04
Single (living alone)	$679.84
Single (sharing)	$627.56

Superannuation is intended to provide a basic standard of living only. There are, however, several additional allowances available to those on superannuation, including Disability Allowance, Accommodation Allowance, a Community Services Card (entitling the holder to reduced doctor and prescription costs), a High Use Health Card (for a reduction in doctor costs if you visit the doctor more than 12 times a year) and a Pharmaceutical Subsidy Card (see **Chapter 12**). Contact Work and Income for further details.

If you're an employer, you must make contributions to employee superannuation funds, which are subject to a superannuation contribution withholding tax.

For further information about national superannuation, contact Work and Income (☎ 0800-559 009, 🖳 www.workandincome. govt.nz), which publishes a useful booklet, *New Zealand Superannuation* (also downloadable).

There are Super Centres in most large towns and cities where you can obtain information and advice. Those receiving superannuation (superannuitants) are issued with a Super Card, which can be used as proof of age and to obtain discounts offered by private organisations (e.g. public transport).

New Zealand has an ageing society, in which a falling number of workers will need to fund an increasing number of retirees in future – how to resolve this problem is an increasing problem for many countries. Government plans to abolish the national superannuation scheme and replace it with a system of private pensions were defeated overwhelmingly in a referendum in 1997. However, in order to reduce the cost of NZS, the government introduced a voluntary workplace savings scheme, KiwiSaver, in 2007, which is described below.

KiwiSaver

In 2007, the government introduced KiwiSaver (🖳 www.kiwisaver.govt.nz), a voluntary workplace savings scheme to help people save for their retirement. You'll be able to access your savings when you're eligible for NZ Super (currently at age 65) or after five years' membership (if you joined after age 60), whichever is later. Being a KiwiSaver member won't affect your eligibility for NZ Super.

Employees are automatically enrolled in KiwiSaver (although they can opt out), which invests your money in a personal account. If you earn a salary or wages, contributions, at either 2, 4 or 8 per cent of salary (you choose), are deducted automatically from your pay. If you don't earn a salary or wages from which PAYE is deducted, for example if you're self-employed or a stay-at-home parent, you agree with your scheme provider how much you're going to contribute, which may be an annual sum or monthly/quarterly payments.

To induce people to sign up to KiwiSaver, the Government provides a $1,000 kick-start, an annual tax credit, and, for those who qualify, a first home deposit subsidy.

KiwiSaver contributions are calculated on your gross pay (i.e. your total salary, including bonuses, commission, overtime, gratuities or any other kind of remuneration) at the rate of 2, 4 or 8 per cent. However, contributions aren't tax deductible and you must still pay tax on your total gross pay. For example, if you earn $100 and have 4 per cent ($4) KiwiSaver contributions deducted, you must pay tax on the full $100.

Existing employer schemes have the option of merging with the KiwiSaver scheme and members of occupational schemes can also choose to join KiwiSaver instead of, or in addition to, their current pension scheme. However, automatic enrolment doesn't apply to workers where their employer already provides a pension fund that's transferable to another scheme, open to all employees, and has a total contribution rate of at least 4 per cent. Employers must make compulsory contributions of 2 per cent of the gross salary of employees aged 18 to 64 who are KiwiSaver members, if they don't already pay into another eligible registered superannuation scheme. Your employer can also choose to make voluntary contributions to your KiwiSaver account over and above the compulsory employer contribution rate.

For further information about KiwiSaver, see 🖳 www.kiwisaver.govt.nz. The Retirement Commission (🖳 www.retirement.org.nz) publishes a free 'Sorted KiwiSaver Decision Guide', available in English and several other languages, which is designed to help you decide whether it's advantageous to sign up to KiwiSaver.

PRIVATE PENSIONS

Private pensions are common in New Zealand, as national superannuation (see above) provides only sufficient income to maintain a basic standard of living, and fewer than 15 per cent of employees are enrolled in a company scheme. If your employer doesn't have a company scheme, you would be wise to consider taking out a private pension. These are available from a variety of insurance companies and are also offered by many banks (shop around). Most private pensions are based on a savings scheme, which accumulates a lump sum that, on retirement, is used to purchase an annuity which provides a regular income. In recent years, many retirees' retirement dreams have been shattered, as many nest eggs have been worth much less than expected. There's no tax relief on private pension contributions, which was abolished in 1987.

If you don't plan to remain in New Zealand indefinitely, you should ensure that you can take your private pension with you when you leave. Generally, you cannot 'export' a private pension from New Zealand to another country unless you've been paying contributions for at least two years.

The Retirement Commission is an autonomous crown entity that helps New Zealanders prepare financially for their retirement. For more information, see 🖳 www.retirement.org.nz.

HEALTH INSURANCE

Everyone who's resident in New Zealand, or a visitor from a country with which New Zealand has a reciprocal agreement, is covered by the national healthcare scheme, which provides either free or reduced cost medical treatment. However, while treatment under the state health scheme is considered adequate, many people also have private health insurance. The main purpose of this is to pay the cost of doctor's consultations, prescriptions and dentistry (which aren't covered

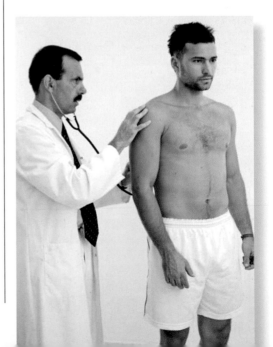

by the state healthcare system), and also to pay for specialist consultations and treatment in private hospitals, thus circumventing public hospital waiting lists. Private health insurance schemes also provide other benefits, such as cover for loss of earnings due to illness.

Nearly half of all New Zealanders have some form of private health insurance, which can be purchased from a variety of insurance companies, including Southern Cross Healthcare (☎ 0800-800 181, www.southerncross.co.nz), the country's largest private healthcare group. Alternatively you can contact a broker such as Medical Direct (☎ 09-473 8010, ⌨ www.medicaldirect.co.nz), one of New Zealand's leading independent medical insurance and private health cover brokers.

Premiums vary considerably depending on what's covered and which company you insure with. For a family of four, a hospital-only policy costs from around $1,000 to $2,000 per year and a comprehensive policy up to $4,000 per year. Premiums may depend on your lifestyle, such as whether you smoke, how much alcohol you drink, your diet and how much exercise you take. Private health insurance costs have rocketed in recent years, as more people make claims to avoid waiting for treatment at public hospitals, and they're likely to continue increasing at a rate well above inflation, particularly for the elderly.

The Consumers' Institute (⌨ www.consumer.org.nz) publishes useful information about health insurance, including advice on whether you really need it.

Checklist

When comparing the level of cover provided by different health insurance schemes, the following points should be considered:

◆ Does the scheme have a wide range of premium levels and are discounts or special rates available for families or children?

◆ Is private hospital cover available and are there private rooms at local hospitals? What are the costs? Is there a limit on the time you can spend in hospital?

◆ Is dental cover included? What exactly does it include? Can it be extended to include

extra treatment? Dental insurance usually contains numerous limitations and doesn't cover cosmetic treatment.

◆ Are there restrictions regarding hospitalisation, either in New Zealand or abroad?

◆ What is the qualification period for special benefits or services?

◆ What level of cover is provided outside New Zealand and what are the limitations?

◆ What is the cover regarding pregnancy, hospital births and associated costs? What is the position if conception occurred before joining the insurance scheme?

◆ Are medicines included?

◆ Are convalescent homes or spa treatments covered when prescribed by a doctor?

◆ What are the restrictions on complementary medicine, e.g. acupuncture, chiropractic, massage, naturopathy and osteopathy? Are they covered? Must a referral be made by a doctor?

◆ Is life insurance or a disability pension included, possibly as an option?

◆ Are extra costs likely? If so, what for?

◆ Are spectacles or contact lenses covered, and if so, how much can be claimed and how frequently?

◆ Is the provision and repair of artificial limbs and similar health aids covered?

 ⚠ Caution

It's important to check what the rules are regarding pre-existing conditions, for which you usually aren't covered for a period, e.g. two years. If they can, insurance companies will happily blame an illness on an undisclosed pre-existing condition, thus avoiding paying out.

If you're planning to change your health insurance company, you should ensure that no important benefits are lost. If you change your health insurance company, it's wise to inform your old health insurance company if you have any outstanding bills for which they're liable.

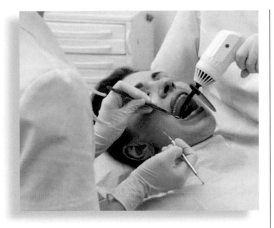

DENTAL INSURANCE

With the exception of school children and emergency dental treatment for those on low incomes, dental treatment isn't provided free under the state healthcare system. It's possible to take out special insurance to cover dental costs, although it's unusual to have full dental insurance in New Zealand, as the cost is prohibitive. The cost of dental insurance varies depending on the state of your teeth and what treatment is covered. Most people find that it's cheaper not to have dental insurance, but to put a little money aside for dental costs and pay bills from their own pocket.

However, cover for dental treatment may be included in general health insurance policies, which can be purchased from medical insurance companies and from dentists. Basic dental care such as check-ups, X-rays and cleaning are usually included in the standard premium, and some companies offer more comprehensive dental cover as an optional extra. Some international health policies also include basic dental care, and most offer optional (or additional) dental cover, although there are many restrictions and cosmetic treatment is excluded. The amount paid by a health insurance policy for a particular item of treatment is usually fixed and depends on your level of dental insurance. A detailed schedule of refunds is available from insurance companies.

If you have healthy teeth and rarely need more than a scale and polish, then dental insurance is a waste of money.

HOUSEHOLD INSURANCE

As when living anywhere, it's important to ensure that your home and its contents are fully insured in New Zealand. Premiums are modest in most areas, particularly for home contents insurance (a reflection of the country's modest crime rate). However, your insurance company will probably claw back the savings on buildings insurance, as damage caused by severe weather (particularly flooding) isn't uncommon in certain parts of the country, and subsidence can also be a problem in some areas.

When insuring your home (rather than its contents), you're offered a choice between fully comprehensive insurance (known as 'accident damage insurance'), which covers all risks, and 'defined risk insurance', which covers specific risks only. Defined risk insurance is the cheaper option, particularly in an area subject to subsidence or flooding, where these risks are expensive to insure against and can be excluded from a policy (although you should ask yourself why you want to live there in the first place!).

You're also offered a choice between a policy that pays out at replacement value and one that pays at indemnity value. Under a replacement value policy, a destroyed home is replaced with a new building of similar quality, while an indemnity value policy pays out the market value of your home. If the market value of your home is less than the cost of rebuilding, an indemnity value policy is cheaper, although it should cover the purchase of a property of similar age and quality. In all cases, the value of the land on which your home is built is excluded.

Contents Insurance

Home contents insurance is usually separate from buildings insurance, although most people have buildings and contents insurance with the same company. It covers home contents up to a specified figure against risks such as theft, fire and accidental damage. If you have particularly valuable possessions, you should take out extra cover, which usually requires high-value items to be detailed, and photographs and documentation (e.g. a receipt or valuation) provided. When claiming for contents, you should produce the original bills if possible (always keep bills for expensive items), and bear in mind that replacing imported items may cost more than their original price.

Contents policies usually contain security clauses, and, if you don't adhere to them, a claim won't be considered.

Most policies don't cover possessions (such as cameras and musical instruments) when they're used outside your home, although you can usually pay an extra premium to cover this.

Earthquake Insurance

As the earthquakes in the Canterbury region in 2010-11 tragically demonstrated, New Zealand is situated within an earthquake zone and minor (usually unnoticeable) tremors occur almost monthly, although serious quakes are relatively rare. As the consequences of a major earthquake are usually catastrophic and no insurance company could possibly cover them, the New Zealand government assumes the responsibility of providing earthquake insurance.

The Earthquake Commission (EQC) operates an insurance scheme, which is funded through a small levy on property insurance policies. EQC pays out on claims from residential property owners for damage caused by earthquake, natural landslip, volcanic eruption, hydrothermal activity, tsunami; in the case of residential land, a storm or flood; or fire caused by any of these.

In the event that an earthquake devastates your property, the EQC will pay you compensation up to a maximum of $100,000 (on a replacement value basis) for a property and $20,000 for personal effects. If your property is insured for less, you'll receive only the sum insured. The EQC pays no compensation for boats, jewellery, money, vehicles or works of art. This scheme ensures that, in the event of an earthquake, most property owners are compensated, even if the government goes bust as a result! (The EQC reserve fund of some $6bn was wiped out by the Christchurch earthquakes.)

Because $100,000 is unlikely to be sufficient to rebuild anything other than a modest home (or a garage in Auckland), most insurance companies offer top-up insurance to cover the difference between the $100,000 paid by the government and the value of your home, which is essential for owners of valuable properties. Further information is available from the Earthquake Commission

earthquake damage, Christchurch

(PO Box 311, Wellington, ☎ 04-978-6400, 🖳 www.eqc.govt.nz).

You can learn how to prepare for an earthquake or any of the other natural disaster the EQC covers at the EQ-IQ website (🖳 www.eq-iq.org.nz/iqhome.aspx).

HOLIDAY & TRAVEL INSURANCE

Travel insurance is recommended for anyone who doesn't wish to risk having his holiday or travel marred by financial problems or to arrive home broke. As you're no doubt aware, many things can, and often do, go wrong with a holiday, sometimes before you even reach the airport or port (particularly when you don't have insurance). In addition, New Zealand has some fairly dangerous roads, is home to dangerous (and downright suicidal) sports and is in an earthquake zone (see above). If you don't fall victim to bungee jumping or a crazed New Zealand motorist, there's always the possibility of falling into boiling mud (it has happened to hapless hikers on a number of occasions!).

> **☑ SURVIVAL TIP**
>
> Bear in mind that some travel insurance doesn't cover you for costs or losses arising from the failure of accommodation providers, airlines or other carriers, tour operators and travel agents. You should check your policy carefully and use a credit card to pay for holidays and travel, which offers added protection.

Travel insurance is available from many sources, including travel agents, insurance agents, motoring organisations, transport companies and direct from insurance companies. Package holiday companies also offer insurance policies, although most don't provide adequate cover. Before taking out travel insurance, carefully consider the level of cover you require and compare policies. Most policies include cover for loss of deposit or holiday cancellation, missed flights, departure delay at both the start and end of a holiday (a common occurrence), delayed and lost baggage and personal effects, medical

expenses and accidents (including repatriation if necessary), loss or theft of money, personal liability, legal expenses and, in some cases, a tour operator going bust.

Extent of Cover

Medical expenses are an important aspect of travel insurance, and you shouldn't rely on reciprocal health arrangements, assuming you're entitled to them (Americans, among others, aren't). It's also unwise to rely on travel insurance provided by charge and credit card companies, household policies or even private medical insurance, most of which don't provide adequate cover (although you should take advantage of what they offer). The minimum medical insurance recommended by experts when travelling to New Zealand is $2m. If applicable, check whether pregnancy-related claims are covered and whether there are restrictions for those aged over 65 or 70.

Check any exclusion clauses in contracts by obtaining a copy of the full policy document, as all relevant information won't be included in the insurance leaflet. Skiing and other winter sports aren't usually covered unless you take out a policy specifically for this purpose (widely available but expensive). 'Dangerous' activities such as bungee jumping and parachuting aren't covered by standard travel insurance policies, and it's often difficult to obtain cover at any price.

When participating in a dangerous sport, check what (if any) insurance cover the organisers provide, as many include (or will sell you) dangerous sports insurance, although it may cover you only for third party liability (e.g. if you sky-dive through someone's roof) and may not cover personal injury. You may, however, be covered under New Zealand's ACC scheme (see page 203) if you have an accident, but the pay-out may be inadequate if your injuries are serious, and it won't pay for repatriation, medical expenses or loss of income abroad.

Annual Policies

For people who travel overseas frequently, whether for business or pleasure, an annual travel policy is often an excellent idea, costing around $250 to $350 per year for worldwide cover for an unlimited number of trips.

However, always carefully check exactly what's included and read the small print (some insist that travel is by air). Most annual policies don't cover you for travel within New Zealand and there's a maximum limit on the length of each individual trip, e.g. 90 days.

Claims

Although travel insurance companies gladly take your money, they aren't so keen to pay claims and you may need to persevere before they pay up. Be persistent and make a claim irrespective of any small print, as this may be unreasonable and therefore invalid in law. Insurance companies usually require you to report a loss (or any incident for which you intend to make a claim) to the local police (or carriers) within 24 hours and obtain a written report. Failure to do this may mean that a claim won't be considered. Bear in mind that it's difficult or impossible to sue for compensation for personal injuries in New Zealand, although if you have taken out insurance in another country you may have a better chance of obtaining compensation.

LIFE INSURANCE

Although there are worse things in life than death (like spending an evening with a life insurance salesman), your dependants may rate your death *without* life insurance high on their list. You can take out a life insurance policy with dozens of companies in New Zealand, although it's important to shop around before doing so. Be extremely wary of insurance sales people (whose credibility is on a par with used car salesmen, estate agents and politicians), some of whom use dubious hard-sell methods to hook customers. You have no guarantee of receiving good or independent advice or indeed any advice at all. When buying life insurance, you're usually better off dealing with an independent insurance adviser or broker who does business with a number of insurance companies. Most banks are unable to provide independent advice on life policies, as many are tied to a particular insurance company.

Some companies provide free life insurance as an employment benefit (although it may be accident life insurance only), and a private pension scheme may provide a death-in-service benefit. A life insurance policy can be used as security for a bank loan and can be limited to cover the period of the loan. Most companies offer a variety of life insurance policies, e.g. term or whole life.

Note that although it's often referred to as life *insurance*, life policies are usually for life *assurance*. Assurance is a policy which covers an eventuality which is certain to occur (for example, like it or not, you'll die one day). Thus a life assurance policy is valid until you die. An insurance policy covers a risk which *may* happen, but isn't a certainty, for example, accident insurance (unless you're exceptionally accident prone).

Commissions & Charges

One disadvantage of life insurance policies is the large commissions paid to salesmen, which may be equivalent to a year's premiums, therefore it pays to shop around and ask salesmen or brokers about their rates of commission. Added to commissions are expenses, including management and administration fees. Performance tables are published regularly in financial magazines showing the best-performing unit trusts, pension funds and other long-term investments. You would be wise to consult them and other independent sources of information before taking out a policy from which you expect either a lump sum on maturity or a regular income, as choosing the wrong investment can be *very* costly. Try to ensure that you have a cooling-off period, during which you can cancel a policy without incurring a penalty.

Health

Whether you need to undergo a medical examination depends on the insurance company, your age, state of health and the amount of insurance required. You must complete a medical questionnaire and, depending on your age and health record, your GP may be required to provide a medical report. If you have no family GP or previous medical history, you may be required to have a medical examination. Many policies don't pay out when death is the result of certain illnesses, e.g. an AIDS-related illness. If you're a clean living, non-smoking teetotaller, you may be able to obtain cheaper life insurance than an alcoholic, sensation-seeking, chain-smoker (although you'll probably die early of boredom!).

☑ SURVIVAL TIP

It's advisable to keep a copy of all insurance policies with your will (see page 234) and with your lawyer. If you don't have a lawyer, keep a copy in a safe deposit box. A life insurance policy must usually be sent to the insurance company upon the death of the insured, with a copy of the death certificate.

14.

FINANCE

Although lagging behind Australia, most European Union countries and the USA, New Zealand is a relatively wealthy country, with a Gross Domestic Product (GDP) per head in 2011 of US$29,350 (*The Economist*). The economy experienced its longest sustained period of growth in three decades between 1999 and 2008, averaging almost 3.3. per cent annually. However, the economy fell into recession before the start of the global financial crisis and contracted for five consecutive quarters in 2008-09, posting a 1.7 per cent decline in 2009. The country pulled out of recession late in 2009 and achieved 2.1 per cent growth in 2010 and around 2 per cent in 2011. Inflation was 2.5 per cent in February 2012.

New Zealand has a relatively large current account deficit, which stood at just over 6 per cent of GDP in 1999 and has since fluctuated between 2.5 and 8.5 per cent (2008), and is a constant source of concern for policymakers. The deficit was $8.7bn (4.3 per cent of GDP) for the year ended September 2011. The average New Zealander has been living beyond his means for years (household debt is high) and many people purchased property with foreign currency loans in the boom years, against which the NZ$ fell sharply.

New Zealand has fewer extremes of wealth and poverty than many other developed countries, with a large middle class and comparatively few poor people, while very wealthy people are rare enough for them to be 'famous' (or notorious). New Zealanders are generally restrained when discussing money, much the same as the British, although the '80s saw the creation of a 'yuppy' class who did well in business and the professions, and didn't mind flaunting their wealth.

The New Zealand banking and financial sector is modern and efficient. For example, it's possible to clear cheques virtually instantaneously in New Zealand – something which isn't even possible in the UK or USA (although this is a deliberate policy on the part of banks in these countries). Wide use is made

of electronic banking, rather than shuffling pieces of paper around the country, and New Zealanders have taken enthusiastically to the cashless economy – the use of credit and debit cards is widespread, while cheques are becoming much less popular. This isn't because New Zealanders are enthusiastic about credit, but simply that it's so convenient. The banking sector is dominated by a relatively small number of large institutions, although there's quite a lot of competition.

When you arrive to take up residence in New Zealand, it's advisable to have a bank account already in place with funds on deposit, plus some New Zealand currency for immediate use. If you're planning to invest in property or a business financed with funds from abroad, it's important to consider both the present and possible future exchange rates (don't be too optimistic). On the other hand, if your income is in New Zealand dollars, this may affect your commitments abroad, particularly if the New Zealand dollar weakens.

If you plan to live and work in New Zealand you should ensure that your income is (and will remain) sufficient to live on, bearing in mind the cost of living (see below). If you're receiving a pension from abroad you should be cautious, as you'll be at the mercy of not only exchange rate fluctuations, but also the fact that pensions are usually calculated according to the cost of living in your *home* country, and may be inadequate to support you in New Zealand.

A number of websites provide comprehensive financial information; two of the best are 💻 www.interest.co.nz and www.sorted.org.nz.

COST OF LIVING

It's useful to try to estimate how far your dollars will stretch and how much money you'll have left (if any) after paying your bills. The inflation rate in New Zealand is relatively low at around 2.5 per cent in February 2012. Prices of many imported goods have fallen in real terms in recent years, particularly cars and electrical appliances, while the price of food has increased (in the year to June 2011, food prices rose 7.5 per cent). Housing costs have soared in the last decade or so, although prices have been flat or fallen slightly in most regions in the last four years (although they are high for migrants due to the high value of the NZ$).

In general, New Zealanders enjoy a high standard of living, although salaries are lower than in Australia, North America and many European countries. Most migrants will be shocked at the relatively high cost of living in New Zealand, although on paper – and in surveys – it's doesn't appear so high. In the Economist Intelligence Unit 2011 survey, Auckland and Wellington – where the cost of living has doubled in the last decade – were as expensive as London!

> The fundamental flaw with most cost of living surveys is that they convert local prices into $US, which means that ranking positions are as much (or more) the result of currency fluctuations than price inflation. Therefore in the last few years, the Eurozone, Australia and New Zealand, with their harder currencies, have become more expensive in dollar terms, while the UK and the USA have become relatively cheaper (on paper).

In the Mercer 2011 Cost of Living Survey (💻 www.mercer.com/costofliving) of 214 cities worldwide – one of the most respected annual surveys – Auckland was ranked 118th (up from 149 in 2010) and Wellington 136th (163 in 2010); Christchurch was not ranked. British cities ranked were London (18). Aberdeen (144), Glasgow (148), Birmingham (150) and Belfast (178). Other selected rankings included Tokyo (2), Singapore (8), Hong Kong (9), Sydney (14), Beijing (20), Melbourne (21), Tel Aviv (24), Perth (30), New York (32 – the only US city in the top 50), Canberra (34), Adelaide (46), Toronto (59), Vancouver (65), Los Angeles (77), Montreal (79), Calgary (96), Chicago (=108), Washington (=108) and Ottawa (114).

It's also possible to compare the cost of living between various cities, using websites such as the Economist Intelligence Unit (💻 http://eiu.enumerate.com/asp/wcol_wcolhome.asp), for which a fee is payable. There are also websites that give you an idea of living costs in New Zealand, such as 💻 www.numbeo.com/cost-of-living/country_result.jsp?country=new+zealand. However, bear in mind that information should be taken with a pinch of salt, as it may not be up to date, and price comparisons with other countries are often wildly inaccurate (and often include irrelevant items which distort the results).

It's difficult to estimate an average cost of living in New Zealand, as it depends on where you live as well as your lifestyle. The cost of living in rural areas is, not surprisingly, lower than in the major cities (particularly housing). If you live in Auckland, drive a BMW and dine in expensive restaurants, your cost of living will be much higher than if you live in a rural part of the South Island, drive a small Japanese car, and live on lamb and kiwi fruit. You can live relatively inexpensively by buying New Zealand produce where possible and avoiding expensive imported goods.

Quality of Life

In Mercer's 2011 Quality of Living survey, Auckland was ranked 3rd, beaten only by Vienna and Zurich worldwide. Among other Australasian cities, Sydney was in 11th position, followed by Wellington (13), Melbourne (18), Perth (21), Canberra (26), Adelaide (30) and Brisbane (37). London was in 38th position and was the only UK city in the top 50. In Mercer's 'Personal Safety Rating' – based on measures of internal stability, crime levels, law enforcement effectiveness and international relations – Auckland and Wellington were rated equal 9th.

New Zealand was judged the second most-peaceful nation (behind Iceland) in the 2011 Global Peace Index (💻 www.visionofhumanity.org/gpi-data/#/2011/scor) report, prepared for the Australia-based Institute for Economics and Peace in conjunction with the Economist Intelligence Unit, which ranked 153 countries in a league table of peacefulness.

NEW ZEALAND CURRENCY

The New Zealand unit of currency is the New Zealand dollar, affectionately know as the 'Kiwi dollar' or just the 'Kiwi'. The dollar is usually identified by the international $ sign and is rarely prefixed by NZ, except in some banking documents involving currency exchange and in international trade (in this book a $ sign refers to the NZ$, unless otherwise stated).

In recent years the NZ$ has soared against most foreign currencies – it hit a 30-year high againt the US$ in 2011 – and is now one of the world's strongest currencies. In February 2012, the NZ$ exchange rate (💻 www.xe.com) was US$1.18 and GB£1.89. This means that British migrants get one third fewer NZ$ for their GB£ than they did around three years ago!

The New Zealand dollar is divided into 100 cents. Banknotes are issued in denominations of 100, 50, 20, 10 and 5 dollars, and coins are minted in one and two dollars, 50, 20, 10 and 5 cents. (The 5 cent coin is colloquially known as

the 'pest'.) The cent is identified by the symbol ¢, although occasionally you'll see it expressed as a decimal, e.g. $0.75, or values in dollars expressed as cents, e.g. 115¢, neither of which is officially correct.

Until 1992, Her Majesty Queen Elizabeth II appeared on all New Zealand banknotes, but she was 'retired' (despite protests from many people) and now appears only on the $20 note. Famous New Zealanders have been installed on other notes: Lord Rutherford ('Father of the Atom') on the $100, Apirana Ngata (a Maori statesman) on the $50, Kate Sheppard (a suffragette) on the $10 and Sir Edmund Hillary (one of the first two men to climb Mount Everest) on the $5 note.

Note that 20¢ and 10¢ coins are difficult to distinguish from Australian coins of the same value, and Australian coins occasionally turn up in your change in New Zealand (you can either save them for a trip to Oz or use them in parking meters).

It's wise to obtain some New Zealand currency before your arrival in the country. However, because international *bureaux de change* don't usually handle coins, the smallest unit of currency you'll be able to obtain outside New Zealand is $5. Ask for a selection of $5, $10 and $20 notes, which are the most useful. Many shops, taxi drivers and small businesses are reluctant to accept $50 and $100 notes; legally they cannot reject any notes or coins, but if you proffer a $100 note, they're likely to have no change. These notes also attract most scrutiny, as they're more likely to be the target of forgers, although counterfeit currency isn't a serious problem in New Zealand.

FOREIGN CURRENCY

Exchange controls operated in New Zealand between 1938 and 1984 but have since been abolished and there are now no restrictions on the import or export of funds. A resident is permitted to open a bank account in any country and to export unlimited funds from New Zealand. It's also possible to transmit funds to New Zealand without being hindered by bureaucratic procedures.

While the exchange rate is so unfavourable, some financial experts advise migrants to import (or at least exchange) as little foreign currency as possible – and postpone buying a home and other expensive items – until the exchange rate improves.

Transferring Money

When transferring or sending money to (or from) New Zealand, you should be aware of the alternatives. The safest method of transferring money is to make an electronic transfer between banks, which can be completed within a few hours. However, bear in mind that (because of the time difference) banks in New Zealand close for the day before they open in Europe or the USA, so it will be at least the next day before funds are available in New Zealand.

The transfer process is usually faster and less likely to come unstuck when it's between branches of the same or affiliated banks (in any case, any delays are more likely to be overseas than in New Zealand). The Commonwealth Bank of Australia, which has branches in Europe and the USA, can transfer funds almost instantaneously to its branches in New Zealand, although its branch network there (around 130) isn't the most extensive.

The cost of transfers varies considerably – not only commission and exchange rates, but also transfer charges (shop around and compare rates). Usually the faster the transfer, the more it costs. Transfer fees may also vary depending on the amount being transferred, and there are usually minimum and maximum fees. For example, banks in the UK charge between £15 and £45 for electronic transfers.

When you have money transferred to a bank in New Zealand, ensure that you give the name, account number, branch number and the bank sort code. Bear in mind that the names of some New Zealand banks (and towns) are strikingly similar, so always double check your instructions. If you plan to send a large amount of money to New Zealand or overseas for a business transaction, such as buying property, you should ensure that you receive the commercial rate of exchange rather than the tourist rate. Check charges and rates in advance and agree them with your bank (you may be able to negotiate a lower charge or a better exchange rate). You can also transfer money using a specialist company such as HIFX (🖳 www.hifx.co.uk) and Moneycorp (🖳 www.moneycorp.com).

CREDIT RATING

Whether you're able to obtain credit (or how much) in New Zealand usually depends on your credit rating (or credit score), which is becoming increasingly important in today's credit-driven financial world. Most financial institutions use some kind of credit scoring system and request a credit reference agency report to find out whether you're 'worthy' of having money lent to you.

⚠ Caution

If you're a new arrival in New Zealand, a lender may request a report from an agency in your previous country of residence. You may be asked to provide written consent to having your credit rating checked.

Your credit rating depends on many factors, such as your age, occupation and marital status, how long you've held your current job, whether you're a homeowner, where you live, whether you're on the electoral roll, whether you have a telephone and, not least, your credit record. In recent years, lenders have been increasingly deciding on credit based on where you live; if you live in an area where there's a high number of defaulters you may not be offered the best deals on home loans (South Auckland and Canterbury are high risk areas). If you're refused credit because of a credit report, you'll be informed and can ask to see the report and challenge anything that's incorrect. You can check your own credit rating online at www.mycreditfile.co.nz.

If you have a bad credit rating it may be impossible to obtain credit in New Zealand unless you're able to provide collateral, i.e. security such as a property. A life assurance policy can be used to provide collateral for a loan. If you're refused credit, look on the bright side: You cannot run up any debts!

BANKS

There are officially just two kinds of financial institution in New Zealand: Registered banks and what are euphemistically known as 'other financial institutions'. The main exception is the

Reserve Bank of New Zealand (📧 www.rbnz.govt.nz), which doesn't fit into either of these categories and is the country's central bank, performing a role similar to the Bank of England or the Federal Reserve Bank in the USA. It has a range of functions, including managing the money supply, supervising commercial banks, implementing the government's financial policy, controlling the exchange rate, providing a banking service to the government and acting as a registrar for government stocks. Most New Zealand banks are diversified and well capitalised and have weathered the credit storm well, with most having an AA- rating (Standard & Poor's).

Savings banks in New Zealand were traditionally mutual organisations owned by their members or investors, which concentrated on personal savings accounts and mortgages for residential property. In this respect they were much like building societies in the UK and savings and loan organisations in the USA. However, deregulation in the financial sector during the '80s allowed commercial banks to enter this market. With their greater financial clout and marketing expertise, they've managed to take it over, and as a result many savings banks have either converted to registered banks or been taken over by them.

Changes in the banking system over the last few years have meant that most individuals and businesses in New Zealand carry out their banking, including savings, loans, mortgages and day-to-day transactions, with one of the registered commercial banks. Banks operating in this sector include Australia New Zealand Bank (ANZ, 📧 www.anz.co.nz) and ASB (📧 www.asbbank.co.nz), formerly the Auckland Savings Bank. Not surprisingly, the ASB is strongest in Auckland, but it's also popular throughout the rest of the country and is routinely rated New Zealand's number one major bank in terms of customer satisfaction in a recent University of Auckland survey of bank customers.

The Bank of New Zealand (BNZ, 📧 www.bnz.co.nz) is New Zealand's largest bank in asset terms and, despite its name, is wholly Australian-owned. Other banks include the National Bank (📧 www.nationalbank.co.nz) and Westpac NZ (📧 www.westpac.co.nz), which has the largest market share (over 1.3m customers) and is also the government's banker.

It's estimated that less than 15 per cent of the New Zealand banking market is operated by indigenous banks. Note that the banking operations of Australian banks in New Zealand are completely separate, therefore customers of Australian Westpac, for example, cannot access their Australian accounts at Westpac in New Zealand, or vice versa.

Some banks are mainly telephone and internet-based, e.g. Bank Direct (📧 www.bankdirect.co.nz), owned by ASB, PSIS (📧 www.psis.co.nz), a co-operative bank, and TSB (📧 www.tsb.co.nz), which is 100 per cent New Zealand owned. The large insurance group, AMP (📧 www.amp.co.nz), also offers banking services, as does the New Zealand Post Office (at PostShops) under the name Kiwibank (see page 112).

In addition to locally registered banks, there are also many international banks in New Zealand, which are mainly located in the financial district of Wellington, and don't have extensive branch networks throughout the country. Other financial institutions that aren't registered banks include merchant banks and leasing companies, which mainly serve the business sector. They aren't authorised to accept deposits from the public and, in any case, registered banks offer a more comprehensive range of services. Finance companies aren't registered banks, but provide consumer credit such as loans and hire purchase (or time purchase as it's also known in New Zealand).

All New Zealand banks are efficient and highly automated. You'll find that staff, who are generally friendly and informal, work behind low counters or desks rather than armoured glass. This isn't to say that banks in New Zealand aren't robbed (they most certainly are), but the transition towards cashless banking has done much to reduce the amount of cash shuffled across bank counters (and used in shops and other businesses).

If you have a complaint that you cannot resolve with your bank, you can refer it to the Office of the Banking Ombudsman (Freepost 218002, PO Box 10573, The Terrace, Wellington 6143, ☎ 0800-805 950, 🖳 www.bankombudsman.org.nz).

Opening Hours

Normal banking hours are from 9am until 4.30pm, Mondays to Fridays, although banks stay open later on one evening a week (which is the exception rather than the rule). Banks don't usually open at weekends, with the exception of the Kiwibank (see page 112) which opens on Saturdays, and they are also closed on public holidays.

Opening an Account

You can open a bank account from outside the country or after your arrival, although given the widespread use of cashless transactions in New Zealand, it's better to open an account before you arrive. To open an account while overseas, you can contact any office of a New Zealand bank, e.g. via the internet. There are also branches of the major New Zealand banks in most major cities in Europe, North America and Asia. You don't usually need to visit a branch in person, as an account can be opened by telephone, post or even via the internet.

To open a bank account, simply choose a branch of any of the registered banks that's convenient to your home or place of work (or where you hope to live or work). Different banks may require different documentation, therefore you should check exactly what's required beforehand; typically you'll need two

forms of identification, your Inland Revenue Department (IRD) number and possibly statements from your current or a previous bank. Note that if you don't have an IRD number when you open an account, you'll be charged resident withholding tax (see page 233).

If you think that you may want to apply for an overdraft, loan or mortgage in New Zealand at some time, it's wise to obtain a reference from your overseas bank manager to the effect that your account has been maintained in good order.

Current Accounts

The normal account for day-to-day transactions in New Zealand is a current or cheque account. You receive a cheque book within a week of opening your account, even though cheques are becoming less widely used in New Zealand, where most people pay bills in shops with debit or credit cards and pay their regular household bills by direct debit. There are no cheque guarantee cards in New Zealand, which is why you may be asked to produce a driving licence or credit card as proof of identity when paying by cheque. Not surprisingly, many shops and businesses are reluctant to take personal cheques (there may be a notice to this effect).

The design of cheques is basically the same as that in most other countries; you enter the name of the payee, the date, the amount in words and figures, and sign it. All cheques should be crossed, although crossed cheques are a fairly recent innovation in New Zealand. A crossed cheque can only be paid into a bank account in the name of the payee and cannot be cashed. The use of a cheque incurs cheque duty of 5¢, which is automatically deducted by your bank.

Cheque clearing in New Zealand is highly efficient and a cheque paid into your account is usually credited the next day (occasionally the same day if it's at the same branch or bank). A cheque drawn on your account and given to someone else may also be debited from your account on the same or next day as there isn't a delay of between three and ten days as in some other countries. Nevertheless, when paying a cheque into your account, it's probably best to wait a few days to spend the

money just in case the drawer didn't have sufficient funds to cover the cheque. On the other hand, you should assume that a cheque drawn on your account will be debited on the same day.

Account statements are usually provided monthly, although you can ask to have them sent weekly. It's also possible to obtain details of your most recent transactions, request a mini-statement or make a balance enquiry at an automated teller machine (ATM), commonly referred to as a cash dispenser. Although you can withdraw cash from your account at any branch of your own bank by writing a cheque, it's much easier to use a debit card in an ATM (it's also possible to pay cash or cheques into your account at some machines).

Savings Accounts

You can open a savings (or deposit) account with any registered or savings bank. Over the last few years registered banks have become more competitive in this sector and have largely taken over the functions of the savings banks. Most financial institutions offer a range

of savings accounts with interest rates varying depending on the amount deposited, the period for which the money must be left on deposit, and the notice which must be given before you can withdraw it.

An account with a minimum deposit period is known as a term deposit account, with terms ranging from one month to five years (the longer the term, the higher the interest paid). The interest rate may fluctuate according to the bank rate, be fixed for the entire term, or escalate (where the rate of interest paid rises annually irrespective of general interest rates).

Bank Charges

As in many countries, banks in New Zealand make charges for most transactions, which are highly unpopular with clients (a recent survey showed that some 75 per cent of bank customers find bank charges excessive) and are the major reason why people change banks. Most banks charge a monthly base fee for some accounts of up to $10 unless you meet certain conditions, such as maintaining a minimum monthly balance, e.g. $5,000. Electronic transaction and cheque fees are around 30-50¢ and staff-assisted (manual) transactions may cost as much as $3. Most banks also charge around $1.50 for the use of a rival bank's ATM.

In order to reduce your bank charges, the Citizens' Advice Bureau (☎ 0800-367 222, 🖳 www.cab.org.nz) offers the following advice:

◆ Reduce the number of transactions you make, e.g. when you pay with a debit card, get some cash at the same time.

◆ Use electronic banking which is cheaper than over-the-counter.

◆ Ask if there's a flat-fee option, which may be cheaper if you have a lot of monthly transactions, and negotiate the best deal with your bank.

You should also compare a bank's fees with Kiwibank (see page 112), which doesn't charge account or transaction fees.

General Information

The following points are applicable to most New Zealand banks:

♦ All regular bills such as electricity, gas, telephone, mortgage or rent, can be paid automatically by direct debit from your bank account. The creditor or your bank will provide the necessary form for you to complete and return to them. You're protected against loss as a result of error or fraud in the system.

♦ To stop a cheque, contact your bank. If your cheque book or debit/credit card is lost or stolen, inform your bank immediately.

♦ Safety deposit boxes are provided at most branches and are an effective way of keeping your valuables secure. The annual rental charge for a small box is usually $50 to $100, plus a key deposit (bond). Most banks conduct extensive security checks, including fingerprinting, when you use a deposit box.

♦ Registered banks offer a range of investments in addition to regular savings accounts, including stocks and shares, bonds and securities. Although you can also buy these through a stockbroker, banks offer competitive fees, particularly for small transactions. You don't need to use your own bank and may be able to find a cheaper stock and share service elsewhere, e.g. via the internet.

♦ Most registered banks offer a range of non-banking services, such as insurance and pensions. Charges and premiums are usually competitive compared with similar products available from other sources, such as insurance brokers. However, it's important to shop around, as some banks sell only their own products or those from certain companies, rather than choosing the best deal from the whole range available (which an independent broker should do).

DEBIT CARDS

When opening a bank account you should request a debit card, also known as a cashpoint card, where payments are debited directly from your account. The use of debit cards is widespread in New Zealand, much more so than in many European countries, and most businesses accept them. A debit card can be used to withdraw cash from ATMs throughout the country and overseas, for which you need a PIN number (which is usually sent

automatically and separately from the card itself).

Guard your debit card and PIN carefully, and if the card is lost or stolen inform your bank immediately so that it can be cancelled. If your card is lost or stolen, you won't be responsible for any more than a token amount (and even then it isn't usually charged), provided you've used your card properly and informed your bank as soon as you discovered it was missing.

You aren't usually charged a fee when using a debit card in a shop or other outlet, although it's legal for shops to charge a fee to cover their costs. Those that do must display a notice advising you of the fee, which is usually 50¢ or $1. When using a debit card to withdraw cash from an ATM, you aren't usually charged a fee if the cash dispenser belongs to your own bank. Most banks have arrangements with other banks whereby their debit cards can be used in other banks' ATMs, although where this is possible you may be charged a fee of up to $3.

In recent years, banks have been promoting cash cards or cash passports, where you load money onto a card for travelling. You can use these to lock in exchange rates and keep money in a variety of currencies such as NZ$, Aus$, $US, £sterling and Euros. You can reload a card via internet banking from a savings or current account. The drawback is that no interest is paid and you need to pay withdrawal and reload fees – you should compare the benefits with the cost of using a standard debit card from a current account, for which there are fees for overseas cash withdrawals.

CREDIT & CHARGE CARDS

New Zealanders are enthusiastic users of credit and charge cards, although many prefer debit cards, where payments are debited from an account. Credit and charge cards are issued by most banks (although some will only give you a credit card if you have a certain type of account with them, e.g. a mortgage loan) and are accepted almost anywhere (although small shops may not accept credit cards), and can also be used to withdraw cash from ATMs or over the counter at banks (note that there's a fee of from $1.50 to $4 and interest is levied from the day of the withdrawal). To use ATMs you require a PIN number.

Most international credit and charge cards are widely accepted in New Zealand, particularly MasterCard and Visa; American Express and Diners Club are less popular and may only be accepted in up-market establishments. Most businesses in New Zealand accept both MasterCard and Visa, therefore you're unlikely to be stuck if you possess only one card.

Annual fees are between around $20 and $100, depending on the type of card, and interest fees can be high (over 20 per cent APR) if you don't pay off the balance each month. Most credit cards offer loyalty schemes with various bonuses, such as frequent flyer points with Qantas or Air New Zealand or cash rewards ('cashback'), which are popular.

Some large store groups in New Zealand issue their own charge cards, although you should note that they usually charge a significantly higher interest rate than most credit cards – which is *really* high!

Credit card fraud is a huge problem in New Zealand. If you lose your credit or charge card, you must report it to the issuer immediately by telephone. The law protects you from liability for any losses when a card is lost or stolen, unless it has been misused with your consent (e.g. by a friend), in which case you're liable.

MORTGAGES

Mortgages (home loans) are available from New Zealand banks, mortgage brokers and some direct response (i.e. via telephone or the internet) lenders, although the number of lenders has contracted in the last few years and many non-bank lenders are no longer in the market. The central bank lending rate has fallen in the last year and was 2.5 per cent in February 2012, although lenders have increased the deposits required, which are now a minimum of around 20 per cent for the best deals. So, although it's easier to repay a mortgage it's harder to get on the housing ladder; it takes 15-20 years for the average person or couple to save a 20 per cent deposit, depending on the region or city where they live. In early 2012, mortgages rates were around 6 per cent.

Generally, there's little difference between the interest rates charged by different lenders, although there's a variety of mortgage plans with different repayment methods, terms and fees, therefore it's necessary to shop around for the best deal. You can check the best mortgage deals via ☐ www.interest.co.nz/mortgages. asp. Some of the best deals are available from Kiwibank (☎ 0800-000 654, ☐ www.kiwibank. co.nz).

Many people use a mortgage broker to find the best mortgage, which accounts for around a third of the market. If you use a mortgage broker, you should ensure that he's a member of the New Zealand Mortgage Brokers Association (☎ 09-912 1000, ☐ www. nzmba.co.nz), whose members must have professional indemnity insurance and work with at least six different lenders. Among the leading mortgage brokers are ☐ www. nzhomeloans.co.nz and www.mikepero.co.nz. Many websites, such as ☐ www.interest.co.nz/ calculator, have an online mortgage calculator where you can compare mortgages and check the repayments.

There are no fixed lending criteria in New Zealand, where the maximum mortgage you can obtain usually depends on your income – repayments must usually be no more than 30 per cent of your net income (which is combined for a couple). Unlike most countries, 100 per cent mortgages used to be widely available in New Zealand, but disappeared during the credit crunch and nowadays 80 per cent is the maximum you can borrow if you want

reduce over the years as the capital owed reduces. Information about the various mortgage products is available from lenders and brokers, and also from the independent Consumer organisation (💻 www.consumer.org.nz/reports/mortgage-strategies).

Interest on a New Zealand mortgage is either 'floating' (variable), so that it varies with the central bank interest rate, or fixed for the period of the loan, the repayment period being adjusted accordingly. A recent trend is for lenders to offer mortgages that are fixed (at a lower interest rate) for a period, such as one to five years, and then revert to a floating rate. These offer a temptingly cheap opportunity to get a foot on the property ladder, provided you budget for the fact that your repayments are likely to increase after the fixed rate period expires, depending on how interest rates change in the meantime. You can, of course, always take out another short-term fixed rate mortgage.

Some 80 per cent of homeowners have fixed rate mortgages, many at much higher interest rates than are available today. These mortgages can be 'broken' for which there's a (usually high) termination fee, although this can save you a lot of money in interest payments and reduce your monthly payments considerably. However, it's important to obtain expert independent advice before breaking a mortgage.

A New Zealand mortgage usually provides a high degree of flexibility. Lenders usually allow you to convert from one type of mortgage to another, increase or decrease your payments, take a payment 'holiday' for a few months, or repay part of the capital early (thus reducing your repayments or the term of the mortgage). It's also possible to transfer your mortgage to another property. In fact, provided you keep making the repayments, you're likely to find your lender accommodating.

Mortgages can be obtained for any period up to 25 years, although the trend nowadays is for people to take 20 or even 15-year mortgages. Although the repayments on a shorter mortgage are higher, you pay much less interest. Many New Zealanders take out

the best rates. However, some lenders offer larger mortgages (e.g. 90 per cent) at higher interest rates, which usually include mortgage guarantee insurance (which guarantees that the lender gets his money back if you default on your repayments).

Kiwibank offers 100 per cent home loans through the Government's Welcome Home Loan scheme, whereby the Government, in the form of Housing New Zealand (💻 www.hnzc.co.nz), guarantees the loan. Welcome Home Loans are for those who can afford the mortgage repayments but don't have a deposit. Kiwibank's best interest rates are only available on lending up to 80 per cent of a home's value, above which the borrower pays more to cover the cost of mortgage insurance.

Types of Mortgage

The two main kinds of mortgage offered in New Zealand are a 'table mortgage' (equivalent to a repayment mortgage in other countries), where you make equal repayments of capital and interest throughout the period of the loan, and interest-only mortgages, where you pay only the interest on the sum borrowed and are required to repay the original capital sum at the end of the term. Some lenders require you to take out an insurance policy to guarantee repayment of the loan, and in this way an interest-only mortgage is similar to an endowment mortgage offered in some other countries.

A third kind of mortgage that's sometimes offered is a 'straight line' (or reducing) mortgage, where you repay capital and interest throughout the term and repayments a second mortgage in order to pay for their children's education or buy a holiday home.

Should you need to, it's usually quite easy to re-mortgage your property and gain access to some of the equity you've built up in it (assuming that property prices have risen since you purchased it!). It's also possible to have a mortgage linked to a revolving line of credit, where the difference between the capital borrowed and the value of your property can be advanced for other uses, such as home improvements, a car purchase or a holiday. This is a cheap way of borrowing, as the mortgage interest rate is usually much lower than that for a personal loan. Many New Zealanders use one of these methods to finance the purchase of a holiday home (bach or crib), which, because of their often 'flimsy' construction, don't qualify for a standard mortgage.

Conditions & Fees

Once a loan has been agreed in principle, a lender will provide you with a conditional offer of a loan outlining the terms. You need to provide proof of your income and outgoings, such as mortgage or rental payments, loans, credit card debts, and other regular commitments (e.g. bills). Proof of income includes three months' pay slips for employees; if you're self-employed, you require an audited copy of your trading accounts for the past three years. If you decide to accept the offer, you must usually pay a deposit (likely to be at least $500) to your mortgage lender. If the purchase doesn't go ahead for any reason, the deposit should be refundable, although many lenders charge a 'discontinued application fee' which is deducted from the deposit. Therefore it isn't wise to accept a mortgage offer unless you're certain you want to go ahead with a property purchase.

There are various fees associated with mortgages and it's necessary to compare the fees and up-front costs, plus ongoing and discharge (termination) fees, from a number of lenders. Most lenders charge an application fee for processing a loan, usually 1 per cent of the loan amount or from $150 to $600 (you won't be charged all of this sum if your application is rejected). There's usually a minimum fee and there may also be a maximum, although many mortgage lenders will negotiate the fees.

In addition there's a land transfer registration fee. It isn't usually necessary to have a survey unless you're borrowing over 80 per cent of the value of a property, although it may be wise to have one, particularly for an old property.

If you fail to maintain your mortgage repayments, your property can be repossessed and sold at auction, although this rarely happens in New Zealand, as most lenders will arrange lower repayments when borrowers get into financial difficulties. In 2008, banks promised to relax mortgage repayment conditions for struggling home-owners as part of a deal with the government guaranteeing their overseas debts. If a customer is having trouble, the lender can help by changing the timing and frequency of payments, extending the term giving the lender longer to repay the mortgage, or changing repayments to interest only. It's best to contact your lender immediately if you have repayment problems, rather than wait until a huge debt has accumulated.

Foreign Currency Mortgages

It isn't unusual in New Zealand for property buyers to take out a foreign currency mortgage, i.e. in a currency other than New Zealand dollars, particularly if interest rates are lower in another country. However, you should be wary of doing so, as interest rate gains can be wiped out overnight by currency swings and devaluations. When choosing between a New Zealand dollar and a foreign currency loan, be sure to take into account all costs, fees and possible currency fluctuations. If you have a foreign currency mortgage, you must usually pay commission charges each time you transfer money into the foreign currency to meet your mortgage repayments, although some lenders do this free of charge.

▲ Caution

Taking out a foreign currency mortgage is a risky business and, while it can save you a small fortune, it can just as easily cost you one (which happened in the last few years when the NZ$ fell heavily against many foreign currencies).

GOODS & SERVICES TAX

A goods and services tax (GST) is levied in New Zealand, which is essentially the same as the value added tax levied in European Union countries, but isn't a sales tax as in the USA. GST is the second-largest component of tax revenue and is levied at a single rate of 15 per cent on most goods and services, although some are exempt, e.g. the letting of residential accommodation. When you import goods into New Zealand, GST (and in some cases also customs duty) is assessed on their value, unless they're exempt or imported under a tax-free arrangement. Immigrants can import their personal possessions free of duty and tax, provided they've been owned and used prior to their arrival.

All businesses with a turnover of $60,000 or more within a 12-month period must register for GST with the Inland Revenue Department and must levy GST on goods and services supplied (unless they're exempt). Similarly, businesses can reclaim GST paid on goods and services used in their business. A GST return must usually be filed every two months, although businesses with a turnover of less than $250,000 a year can choose to file a return every six months, while those with an annual turnover of over $24m must file monthly. A penalty of 1 per cent of the tax due is levied if a return isn't filed by the due date, plus a further 4 per cent if there's still unpaid tax a week later. Thereafter, a further 1 per cent per month is added to any unpaid amount. For further information about GST, contact the Inland Revenue (☎ 0800-377 776, 🖳 www.ird. govt.nz).

INCOME TAX

Generally speaking, income tax in New Zealand is below average for a developed country. During the '90s most people saw their income tax reduced, but in the 21st century income taxes have increased. Most New Zealanders are resigned to paying taxes (tax evasion isn't a national sport as it is in some other countries), and in any case the country has a system of pay-as-you-earn (PAYE) that ensures that tax is deducted at source from employees' salaries. The tax system in New Zealand isn't particularly complicated. It's designed so that most people can prepare and file their own tax returns, although if your tax situation is complicated you may need to seek advice from an accountant.

Information

The IRD operates a comprehensive help service and publishes numerous factsheets and leaflets for taxpayers. It also has a number of helplines, including the following:

◆ Income tax and general enquiries: 0800-227 774 or 04-978 0779;

◆ General employee enquiries: ☎ 0800-377 772;

◆ Non-resident general enquiries: ☎ 03-951 2020.

The IRD also has a comprehensive website (🖳 www.ird.govt.nz), which includes downloadable factsheets and forms.

Liability

Your country of domicile determines whether you're liable to pay New Zealand income tax. Residents are taxed on their worldwide income, while non-residents are subject to income tax only on income derived from New Zealand. To determine 'domicile' the tax authorities apply what's known as the 'permanent place of abode test', although this is arbitrary and isn't enshrined in New Zealand

tax law. Usually anyone who's present in New Zealand for more than 183 days in a 12-month period is considered resident there and liable to pay taxes.

You don't need to be a permanent resident to be liable, and the existence of financial and social ties (including bank accounts and club memberships) may be taken as evidence of domicile. You're usually considered exempt from New Zealand taxes only if you aren't present in the country for 325 days in a 12-month period. However, if you maintain a home in the country, you cannot be considered non-resident, no matter how brief your stay. If you decide to leave New Zealand, you should inform your local IRD office. Note that the 325-day time limit doesn't start until the IRD has confirmed that you've ceased to be a resident.

> Income that's subject to tax in New Zealand includes commissions, dividends, interest, profits or gains from a business, rents, royalties, salary and wages, and trust distributions.

Double Taxation

New Zealand has double taxation treaties with over 30 countries including: Australia, Austria, Belgium, Canada, Chile, China, Czech Republic, Denmark, Fiji, Finland, France, Germany, Hong Kong, India, Indonesia, Ireland, Italy, Japan, (South) Korea, Malaysia, Mexico, the Netherlands, Norway, the Philippines, Poland, Russia, Singapore, South Africa, Spain, Sweden, Switzerland, Taiwan, Thailand, Turkey, the UAE, the UK and the USA.

Double taxation treaties are designed to ensure that income which has been taxed in one treaty country isn't taxed again in another. A treaty establishes a tax credit or exemption on certain kinds of income, either in the taxpayer's country of residence or in the country where the income is earned. Where applicable, a double taxation treaty prevails over local law.

Tax Code

Taxpayers in New Zealand are required to complete a Tax Code Declaration (form IR 330) when they start employment and if there are any changes in their employment circumstances, e.g. if their working hours are reduced. You should be given the form by your employer, who sends the completed form to the IRD. The tax code for most employees is M. It's important that you complete the form correctly, as the amount of tax you pay is based on the information provided.

Tax Return & Tax Bill

When you start work in New Zealand, you should register with your local IRD office, who will issue you with an IRD or tax file number, which must be quoted on tax documents and enquiries. If you don't have an IRD number, tax will be deducted at a no-declaration rate, which is higher than the normal deduction rate. To apply for an IRD number you must complete an IRD form and send a copy of your passport (☎ 0000-227 774, 💻 www.ird.govt.nz). IRD numbers are usually issued within five working days.

Recent changes in tax legislation have made tax calculations simpler and more accurate, and tax returns easier to complete. Until recently, everyone who earned an income in New Zealand had to file an income tax return annually with the Commissioner of the Inland Revenue Department. However, under new tax legislation, tax returns have been eliminated for individuals who only receive income from employment that's subject to PAYE or from interest and dividends subject to Resident Withholding Tax (RWT – see below).

All individuals who derive income that isn't taxed at the time of payment or who are in business must file an annual return. The return, known as an IR3, is sent to you automatically each year. The New Zealand tax year runs from 1st April to 31st March of the following year, and returns must be filed by 7th July. The IRD then issues a tax assessment (i.e. a tax bill) showing the amount of income tax payable.

Payments for due tax can be made in a variety of ways, including cheque, electronic payment or direct debit from your bank, via cash or cheque at any branch of the Westpac Trust bank, or online via the internet banking facility at any major New Zealand bank.

Personal Tax Summaries

Employees whose income tax is deducted at source by their employer under PAYE and who don't have any other income, receive a Personal Tax Summary from the IRD based on information provided by employers, and shouldn't have any additional income tax to pay. The Personal Tax Summary states your tax code – check with the IRD that you're using the correct one (see above).

You'll also receive a Personal Tax Summary if you receive family assistance payments from IRD or from Work and Income, and earn over $20,000, have a student loan and qualify for an interest write-off, or if you have paid too little or too much tax. The Personal Tax Summary shows whether you're entitled to a tax refund or have tax to pay. If you have tax to pay, you must pay it by 7th February for those without a tax agent, or by 7th April for those with an agent and a time extension.

If you're entitled to a refund, it will be paid when you've confirmed your Personal Tax Summary or within 30 days if the amount owing is less than $200. If you wish to claim certain tax credits (see below) or you earn under $48,000 but your dividend income was taxed at 33 per cent, you should request a Personal Tax Summary.

You can check whether you're entitled to a tax refund for tax paid in the last five years by using a specialist company such as ⌨ www.myrefund.co.nz or www.taxrefunds.co.nz, which charge a capped fee for filing a refund claim.

Tax Rates

It has become common practice in recent years for the rates or income bands to be adjusted annually in the budget. There are four tax rates in New Zealand (from 1st April 2011), which are as shown in the table below.

Tax Credits

Before you're liable for income tax, you can deduct certain tax rebates (formerly known as rebates) from your gross salary, which reduce your tax bill. Key tax credits include:

♦ **independent earner tax credit (IETC)**, for individuals whose annual income is between $24,000 and $44,000;

♦ **tax credit for children**, available for children under 19 and still at school;

♦ **housekeeper rebate**, if you paid above a certain sum for childcare or a housekeeper;

♦ **payroll donations rebate**, on charitable donations above a certain sum;

♦ **tax credit for income under $9,880**, for those working 20 hours or more per week.

For information about the above tax credits, contact the IRD or see their website (⌨ www.ird.govt.nz).

Tax credits must be claimed by 30th September following the end of the relevant tax year. Expenses associated with employment (such as clothing or travel to work) cannot usually be claimed as a tax allowance. However, the self-employed can claim legitimate business expenses. Interest on a mortgage cannot be claimed as a tax allowance.

Resident Withholding Tax

Interest on bank and other savings accounts is paid after deduction of resident withholding tax (RWT) at a rate equivalent to the standard rate of income tax (17.5 per cent). If, however, you don't provide your IRD or tax file number (see above) to a bank when opening an account, it's taxed at the higher rate (33 per cent). The standard RWT rate for companies is 33 per cent.

For further information, contact an IRD office or ☎ 0800-800 468.

Businesses & Self-employment

Income tax for the self-employed and small businesses is broadly similar to wage and salary earners. You're sent a tax return (form IR3) at the end of your financial year, which you must complete and return by the 7th day of the fourth month following the end of your financial year. If your financial year is the same as

Tax Rates		
Taxable Income ($)	Tax Rate (%)	Cumulative Tax ($)
0-14,000	10.5%	$1,470
14,001-48,000	17.5%	$5,950
48,001-70,000	30%	$6,600
over 70,000	33%	

are often carried out by the company Quotable Value New Zealand (⌨ www.qv.co.nz).

Bills are sent out at the beginning of the rating year, which may not coincide with the calendar year, and are payable by whoever occupies the property, whether it's the owner or a tenant. If you occupy a property for only part of a year, then only a proportion of the tax is payable. The annual bill for an average family house is between $2,000 and $3,000. It isn't uncommon for residents, either individually or collectively, to appeal against property valuations in order to obtain a tax reduction. Rates may be paid in instalments; for example in Wellington, rates are billed in four instalments due on 1st September, 1st December, 1st March and 1st June. There may be a penalty, e.g. 10 per cent, if taxes aren't paid by the due date.

Property taxes pay for local services such as street cleaning, lighting and subsidies paid to local public transport companies. They usually include rubbish collection (although an extra charge is levied in some areas), recycling collection and water, although in some areas such as Auckland, water is billed separately. Auckland residents have been protesting against water charges and rates for the last few years, because although water charges were recently excluded from their rates, they weren't reduced! As a result, Auckland residents pay more or less the same as before in rates as well as expensive water charges (most households pay over $800 per year).

the tax year (April to March), your tax return must be filed by 7th July each year. You can apply to have a financial year that differs from the tax year.

The self-employed are required to pay a proportion of their estimated tax on a monthly basis, which is based on their previous year's liability. When your tax return is submitted, the IRD reconciles the tax due with the sum already paid and issues a tax assessment for any tax payable or a refund if you've over-paid. Company tax is levied at a flat rate of 33 per cent, whether a company is resident or non-resident.

PROPERTY TAXES

Property taxes (rates) are levied by local authorities and are based on the capital value (CV) of properties and the land use, e.g. residential or commercial. There has been an increase in property rates in the last decade due to a sharp increase in property values, although property prices have been stable or have fallen by 5 to 10 per cent in the last few years in most regions. The CV is an assessment of the probable price that would have been paid, including land and buildings, on a certain date, which is reviewed periodically, e.g. every three years in Auckland. It isn't the market value of a property. Capital valuations are assessed independently and

OTHER TAXES

There are no local income taxes, wealth tax, capital gains tax or estate taxes (inheritance taxes) in New Zealand. However, income tax may be levied on income derived from any undertaking or scheme entered into or devised for the purpose of making a profit. For example, income from the sale of property and land if the principal purpose of purchasing it was to resell it or if your business is dealing in property. In addition, gains resulting from certain investments, such as debentures and some preference shares, options and leases, may be taxable irrespective of whether the nature of the gain is capital or income.

Gift Duty

Gift duty (known as gift tax in other countries) is imposed at fixed rates on certain gifts, including property in New Zealand or elsewhere if the donor was domiciled in New Zealand at the time of the gift. Gifts that aren't dutiable include those made to charities, gifts for the maintenance or education of your immediate family, and gifts of up to $2,000 per year to an individual if they're made as part of the donor's normal expenditure, e.g. birthday and Christmas presents. Any person who makes gifts with a combined total value of over $12,000 in any 12-month period must complete a gift statement (IR196) and forward it to Inland Revenue within three months of making the gift.

The rates of gift duty are shown in the table below:

Value of Gift	Rate of Duty	Tax on Band
below $27,000	zero	
$27,001 to 36,000	5%	$450
$36,001 to $54,000	10%	$1,800
$54,001 to $72,000	20%	$3,600
over $72,000	25%	

Fringe Benefits Tax (FBT)

Fringe Benefits Tax (FBT) is payable by employers on the value of most fringe benefits paid to employees in New Zealand. You can choose to pay FBT at one of three rates: Single rate, alternate rate or short form alternate rate, depending on how you choose to declare it. Benefits that attract fringe benefits tax include motor vehicles; low-interest loans; free, subsidised or discounted goods and services; and employer contributions to funds, insurance, health insurance and superannuation schemes.

For further information, see the *Fringe benefit tax return guide* (IR 425) available from the Inland Revenue Department (www.ird. govt.nz).

Income such as interest, rents, dividends and royalties are taxable under income tax in New Zealand, rather than separately, as is the case in some other countries.

WILLS

It's an unfortunate fact of life, but you're unable to take your worldly goods with you when you take your final bow (even if you have plans to return in a later life). Once you've accepted that you're mortal (the one statistic you can confidently rely on is that 100 per cent of all human beings eventually die), it's wise to make a will leaving your estate to someone or something you love, rather than leaving it to the government or leaving a mess which everyone will fight over (unless that's your intention).

Many people in New Zealand die intestate, i.e. without making a will, in which case their property is subject to New Zealand's intestacy laws. In general, these divide your estate equally between your spouse and children. If you die in New Zealand without making a will and aren't domiciled there, the intestacy laws of your home country will apply to the disposal of your estate.

As a general rule, New Zealand law entitles you to make a will according to the law of any country and in any language. If you're a foreign national and don't want your estate to be subject to New Zealand law, you may be eligible to state in your will that it's to be interpreted under the law of another country. To avoid being subject to New Zealand inheritance laws, you must establish your domicile in another country. If you don't specify in your will that the law of another country applies to your estate, then New Zealand law will apply. A legal foreign will made in an overseas country dealing with overseas assets is valid in New Zealand and will be accepted for probate there. However, you should have a New Zealand will to deal with your New Zealand assets.

It isn't a legal requirement in New Zealand to use a lawyer to prepare your will, although the relatively small fee (e.g. $200) may save problems later. If you want to make your own will, you can simply write your instructions and sign them, which is known as a holographic will and doesn't need to be witnessed. If your circumstances change dramatically, e.g. you get married, you must make a new will, as under New Zealand law marriage automatically annuls an existing will. A husband and wife should make separate 'mirror' wills. Similarly, if you separate or are divorced, you should consider making a new will, although divorce doesn't automatically annul a will.

A new bequest or a change can be made to an existing will through a document called a codicil. You should check your will every few years to make sure it still fulfils your wishes and circumstances (your assets may also increase dramatically in value). A will can be revoked simply by tearing it up.

You also need someone to act as the executor of your estate, which can be relatively costly for modest estates. Your bank, building society, solicitor or other professional will usually act as the executor, although this should be avoided if possible, as fees can be *very* high. If you appoint a professional as the executor of your estate, check the fees in advance (and whether they could increase in future). The good news about dying in New Zealand (at least for your beneficiaries) is that there's no inheritance tax or death duties.

Keep a copy of your will in a safe place (e.g. a bank) and another copy with your solicitor or the executor of your estate. It's useful to leave an updated list of your assets with your will to assist the executor in distributing your estate. You should keep information regarding bank accounts and insurance policies with your will(s) – but don't forget to tell someone where they are!

Homer Simpson?

Christchurch Art Gallery

15.
LEISURE

New Zealand is one of the most beautiful and scenic countries in the world, with a surprisingly varied landscape, therefore when it comes to leisure, both residents and visitors take full advantage of the natural environment and the great outdoors. New Zealanders and most tourists spend a great deal of time touring or hiking (tramping) around the country or simply sitting back and admiring its beauty over a few drinks. Whether your idea of leisure involves the beach, mountains, forests or the strange thermal areas where forces deep in the centre of the earth make their presence felt, you'll never be short of something to see and do. New Zealanders take their leisure time seriously and city dwellers (although many cities are little more than country towns by European and North American standards) cannot wait for the weekend to arrive so that they can take off to their cabins in the country, known as 'baches' in the North Island and 'cribs' in the South Island.

In comparison with many other countries, New Zealand doesn't offer a great variety of organised leisure activities, particularly cultural events. However, things have improved in recent years and many cities now boast impressive theatres and arts festivals. Nevertheless, if you're a lover of the arts you'll generally need to travel to the major cities and even then the choice of activities won't be as great as in many other countries. Rural New Zealand has little to offer in the way of culture and even Australians – who aren't generally known for their cultural awareness – make jokes about the backwardness of small-town New Zealand. The New Zealanders' description of themselves as a nation of 'rugby, racing and beer' isn't wholly accurate, but there's rarely smoke without fire!

One of the compensations of this reliance on outdoor activities is that there's much to be enjoyed that's inexpensive or free. The American and European trend for massive Disneyland-style theme parks, where it's possible for a family of four to spend a week's wages in one day, is unlikely to overwhelm New Zealand, although Auckland does have a modest amusement park (situated at the quaintly named, Rainbow's End).

Information about local events and entertainment is available from tourist offices, Visitor Information Network (VIN) centres or i-SITE Visitor Centres (see below), and is also published in local newspapers and magazines. In the major cities there are magazines and newspapers devoted to entertainment, and free weekly or monthly programmes are published by tourist organisations in the major cities and tourist centres. Many city newspapers also publish weekly magazines or supplements containing a detailed programme of local events and entertainment.

The main aim of this chapter, and indeed the purpose of the whole book, is to provide information that isn't found in general guide books. General information about New Zealand is available in many excellent guide books including *Fodor's New Zealand*, *Frommer's New Zealand*, *Let's Go New Zealand*, *Lonely Planet New Zealand*, *New Zealand* (Eyewitness Travel Guides) and the *Rough Guide New Zealand* (see **Appendix B** for a comprehensive list). There are also many guides to the major cities.

There are numerous websites that provide information for tourists and travellers, including 💻 www.newzealand.com, the official website of Tourism New Zealand, 💻 www.discovernewzealand.com, www.greatnewzealand.co.nz, www.nz.com and www.tourism.net.nz.

TOURIST INFORMATION

All cities, towns and popular tourist spots in New Zealand have a tourist office, known as a Visitor Information Network (VIN) centre or an i-SITE Visitor Centre, of which there are over 80 in New Zealand (there are ten in Auckland alone). Tourist offices or VIN centres are usually located in a prominent position, for example in the city hall or another public building; railway stations don't usually have tourist offices, although you'll find them at airports. Look for the internationally recognised (green) 'i' symbol. Opening hours vary considerably and during the winter months (April to October) even major city offices are open for limited hours, e.g. 10am to 4pm, and small town and resort offices are usually closed completely (except in winter sports resorts).

Tourist offices provide a wealth of information about local attractions, restaurants, accommodation, sporting events and facilities, package holidays, tours, public transport, car rental and much more. Offices can provide information on a wide range of leisure activities and sports, therefore you should mention any special interests when making enquiries. They can also book your accommodation, although unless you plan to arrive late or don't have time to look around, you can usually find accommodation on the spot (except in major cities). If you book through a tourist office you'll pay the full rate and probably also a booking fee, while if you book direct you won't only save the booking fee, but may also pay a lower rate.

Tourist offices use the latest technology and VIN centres can access the NZ Host National Tourism database at the touch of a button and print information. An increasing number of tourist offices are also equipped to deal with enquiries by e-mail. Most cities and regions publish free entertainment magazines and newspapers containing maps and a plethora of information about local attractions and events, distributed by tourist offices, hotels, transport companies and information bureaux.

> New Zealand is promoted overseas by Tourism New Zealand (💻 www.newzealand.com), which is a mine of information and has offices in Asia (China, Hong Kong, India, Japan, Korea, Singapore and Thailand), Australia, the UK (London) and the USA.

HOTELS

In New Zealand the term hotel can be rather confusing for the newcomer. As in Australia, a public house or a bar is usually called a hotel, when in fact it doesn't provide accommodation. Or rather, it may keep a bedroom or two 'for rent' to satisfy a 'quaint' old law that says hotels must offer accommodation, but you aren't expected to ask to stay there! However, you'll be pleased to hear that New Zealand has a plethora of 'proper' hotels with accommodation ranging from the most basic to the most luxurious. Standards and service are usually high, and an increasing number of hotel staff have completed the nationally-recognised 'Kiwi Host' customer service workshop.

Many businesses have adopted the Qualmark Rating system (💻 www.qualmark.co.nz), similar to the key rating in the UK, where properties are inspected annually by trained assessors. The system awards stars on a scale of one to five, where one star indicates that a property meets minimum requirements and is clean and comfortable, and five stars indicate that the accommodation is the best available in its class. Properties participating in the system display a sign with the Qualmark system logo (a capital Q in navy and green) together with the number of stars awarded.

You can book a hotel in New Zealand via numerous international hotel websites (e.g. Expedia and Travelocity), plus dedicated local websites such as 💻 www.mainstay.co.nz and www.millenniumhotels.co.nz.

Luxury Hotels

Top hotels in New Zealand are comparable with those in any other country, both in terms of facilities and room rates, and can be found in major cities and resort areas. Many leading international names have hotels in New Zealand including Carlton, Hilton, Hyatt, Parkroyal, Sheraton, Southern Pacific and Stamford Plaza. There are also privately-owned luxury hotels. You should expect to pay between $200 and $1,250 per night for a double room in a luxury hotel.

Sporting Lodges

Sporting lodges are rural country house hotels and are a unique feature of the luxury hotel business in New Zealand. They're invariably set in superb locations in the mountains, by lakes or near the sea. Each lodge is individually styled and many are noted for their excellent cuisine. Lodges usually offer fishing (e.g. brown or rainbow trout in a nearby river or lake, or sea-fishing for marlin and other big game fish) and golf (New Zealand has over 400 courses), hence the name 'sporting'. Many also offer other sports facilities such as diving, jet-boating, rafting, riding, sailing, skiing, snorkelling, trekking or water-skiing. Rates for sporting lodges range from between around $250 and $1,250 per night for a double room, although tariffs include meals. The New Zealand Lodge Association publishes a catalogue containing details of lodges, *New Zealand Lodges – Luxury Lodges and Sporting Retreats* (🖥 www.lodgesofnz.co.nz).

Mid-range Hotels

For those unable to afford the indulgence of a sporting lodge, there are plenty of mid-range hotels in both cities and resort areas. These may not be in such prime locations but they usually have good facilities, including a bar and restaurant (usually open to non-residents), and possibly a swimming pool and health club. Room rates in a mid-range hotel are usually between $80 to $200 per night for a double room. Many motels (see below) fall into the mid-range price bracket, plus chains such as Kingsgate, Mainstay, Pacifica and Scenic Circle.

Motels

Motels are found throughout New Zealand, even in quite remote areas, and although they aren't always located in prime positions, they're usually easily accessible on or near major roads. One unique feature of a New Zealand motel is that most accommodation is more like an apartment than a hotel room, with one or two bedrooms, a living area, kitchenette and a full-sized bathroom. Motels are so well equipped that New Zealanders frequently use them as holiday bases and not just for the odd one- or two-night stay. Some have restaurants, bars and swimming pools on site, although they aren't generally as well appointed as hotels. A refreshing change is that chain motels (which can be soulless in other countries) are often family-run in New Zealand, and while of a consistent standard, also offer genuine, friendly, personal service (including free milk!).

Another feature of motels is that they frequently operate 'all in' pricing, which means that you pay a fixed room rate no matter how many people occupy it. You're unlikely to find more than $5 or $10 difference between the rate for a single room and a double or family room, and therefore they're an economical place for families to stay. The main motel chains in New Zealand include Best Western, Budget, Flag and Golden Chain. Most motels are excellent value for money, with the price for a double room from $100 to $150 per night. Some chains, such as Best Western (🖥 www.bestwestern.co.nz), offer 'last-minute international special' rates, which guarantee you their lowest rates.

The Motel 'bible' in New Zealand is *Jasons Motels, Motor Lodges & Apartments* (🖥 www.jasons.com/guides/new-zealand) and the

Motel Association of New Zealand has a comprehensive website (💻 www.nzmotels. co.nz).

Prices

Hotel prices are quoted inclusive of tax (GST at 15 per cent), and in line with New Zealand's no-tipping policy, you won't be charged extra for service. Hotels in popular resorts may have slightly higher room rates during the summer and a minimum stay of three nights, although outside the high season, hotels may offer a discount for stays of three nights or longer. Many offer low season discounts, particularly during the winter and early spring months, which may include three nights for the price of two or two nights for the price of one at weekends.

Hotels in New Zealand frequently have 'special offer' rates which include meals, although you won't be obliged to pay for meals if you only require a room. In smaller hotels and motels without a restaurant, you can usually order breakfast, which will be deliveed to your room.

Facilities

Although facilities vary considerably depending on the price and category of accommodation, you can usually expect en suite facilities (bath or shower) in a New Zealand hotel. Hotel and motel rooms are usually equipped with a telephone, radio and TV (including cable or satellite TV in top hotels), plus tea and coffee-making facilities, and a small fridge (even in modestly priced hotels) complete with a complimentary bottle of milk – a peculiar

New Zealand tradition. More expensive hotels provide room service and a mini-bar, which is expensive. Power points are usually provided and there's often a razor socket in the bathroom (you'll need an adapter to use any appliance without a local plug). Most hotels (except those in city centres) have private parking, and when they don't there's usually on-street parking or a secure off-road car park nearby.

In general, New Zealand hotels don't cater particularly for business travellers, as relatively few people make a lot of overnight business trips. Business centres (possibly with secretarial staff and translation services) are usually confined to a few luxury and business-class hotels in Auckland and other major cities, although most hotels offer in-room internet, usually broadband, for which there's usually a fee. Some have swimming pools and health and sports facilities such as gymnasiums, and most top class hotels have a restaurant, coffee shop and bar, although you can often obtain a better and cheaper meal at a local restaurant.

Booking

It isn't usually necessary to book far ahead in New Zealand, except in summer or on public holiday weekends, and during international trade fairs, conventions and festivals in the major cities. In any case, if your chosen hotel or motel isn't available there's usually something similar nearby. The only exception to this is if you're venturing to the more remote tip of the South Island, where it's wise to book as accommodation is more scarce. You won't usually be shown a room unless you ask and it's usually safe to accept a room without inspecting it. In the case of an international hotel or motel chain, your room will have the same facilities as a similarly priced establishment in Manchester or Miami and may even be decorated in the same 'international' style.

Checkout time is usually 11am or noon at the latest, and if you stay any later you can be charged for an extra day. If you're staying in a small hotel or guest house and wish to leave early in the morning, it's wise to pay your bill the evening before and tell the proprietor when you plan to leave; otherwise you may find your hosts are still in bed and the door locked!

BED & BREAKFAST

New Zealand has a long tradition of providing bed and breakfast (B&B) accommodation (the country's largest category of tourist accommodation), also known as guest houses, which in rural areas are often on working farms. The cost is similar to inexpensive hotels, although B&Bs offer a more individual service. However, there has been a trend toward more up-market B&Bs in recent years and many are now quite luxurious – with prices to match.

The price of a B&B (obviously) includes a hearty breakfast, which isn't usually the case in a hotel, therefore the price is actually more reasonable than it looks. Expect to pay from around $80 per night for a single room and from $120 for a double room. Not all B&B rooms have en suite facilities, although they're available nearby and the owners usually allow guests access to most of the facilities of their home, so in many ways a B&B is often better served than a hotel. In modest B&Bs you may find the facilities are rather worn or 'homely', but if you need anything such as extra blankets or pillows, you need only ask your host.

You can find B&Bs through local tourist offices and VIN centres, via the Federation of Bed and Breakfast Hotels (52 Armagh Street, Christchurch, ☎ 06-358 6928, 🖳 www.nzbnbhotels.com – from where you can download their brochure), and from books such as *The New Zealand Bed and Breakfast Book* (Moonshine Press, 🖳 www.bnb.co.nz), published annually, and *Jasons Selections NZ Bed & Breakfast Directory* (🖳 www.jasons.com/guides/new-zealand). There are also dozens of websites where you can book B&Bs, including 🖳 www.bed-and-breakfast.co.nz, www.kiwibedandbreakfast.com and www.travelwise.co.nz.

HOMESTAYS

It's possible to stay in private homes in New Zealand as a 'guest' of a family. If you're travelling by public transport, your hosts will usually pick you up from the nearest town or village. The difference between this kind of accommodation and a guest house is that you're treated as a member of the family and invited to join them at mealtimes and in other activities around the house (like doing the housework!). Homestay hosts don't usually accept more than one group of guests at a time and most offer homestays as a way of meeting people, rather than simply making money.

As many homestays are on farms, you may be able to try your hand at sheep-shearing or roam the wide open spaces on a tractor or horse, while your children help raise new-born lambs. The duration of a stay can be anything from one night to three weeks or more, with the cost between $125 to $450 per night for two people, including all meals (homestays shouldn't be considered as a cheap form of accommodation).

Various organisations arrange homestays, including New Zealand Farm Holidays (PO Box 74, Kumeu, Auckland, ☎ 09-412 9649, 🖳 www.nzfarmholidays.co.nz) and Rural Holidays New Zealand Ltd. (PO Box 2155, Christchurch 8140, ☎ 03-355 6218, 🖳 www.ruralholidays.co.nz). A useful publication is *50 Great Farmstays in New Zealand*.

HOSTELS

There's a variety of inexpensive accommodation in New Zealand, including youth and other hostels. These include privately-owned hostels and hostels owned by the Youth Hostel Association of New Zealand (YHANZ), affiliated to Hostelling International (HI). It's necessary to be a member of HI to use YHA hostels. You can join on a night-by-night basis when you arrive at a hostel, although it's cheaper to take out annual membership, either abroad or in New Zealand (where it costs $42 for those aged over 18). The YHANZ (🖳 www.yha.co.nz) publishes the *YHA NZ Hostel Accommodation Guide*, containing hostel addresses.

There are no age restrictions at New Zealand hostels. Hostels fill up early in summer, so you should book well in advance if possible, although some hostels don't accept reservations and restrict stays to a maximum of three or four nights. Linen is sometimes provided and where it isn't it can be hired. Hostels vary considerably in size from around 10 to 300 beds, with the larger hostels usually having dormitories, although rooms for one to four people are available in many hostels.

A dormitory bed costs from around $25 per person, per night (rooms may be single sex or mixed and have up ten beds), a double/twin private room in the region of $75 per room, per night, and a single private room around $70 per night, e.g. in Auckland. There are usually discounts of around 25 to 30 per cent for those aged 5 to 17; children under five may only be accommodated at a hostel's discretion, therefore check in advance.

Hostel hosts are an excellent source of information about the surrounding area and will gladly tell you about places to see and things to do (or even about temporary employment opportunities, which are often posted on hostel notice boards). They will also usually book your next night's hostel accommodation.

Backpackers

New Zealand is a pioneer and leader in backpacker accommodation and almost every tourist spot in the country has at least one backpacker hostel. Hostels offer much the same accommodation as youth hostels and some belong to backpacker groups, while others are independent. The main backpacker group operating in the country is Budget Backpacker Hostels (☏ 03-379 3014, 🖳 www.bbh.co.nz – generally considered to be *the* backpacker's website in New Zealand), membership of which not only qualifies you for accommodation discounts, but also to discounts on transport and activities.

Other useful websites for backpackers include 🖳 www.backpackerboard.co.nz, www.backpackerbus.co.nz and www.stayatbase.com.

CAMPING & CARAVANNING

Camping and caravanning are extremely popular with New Zealanders and tourists, who flock to the country each year to enjoy holidays in the open air. Campsites in New Zealand are among the best in the world and are often in prime beauty spots. They vary considerably, from small wilderness sites with fairly basic facilities (or even no facilities) to luxury establishments with a wide range of amenities. Rates range from around $15 per night (usually from noon to noon) at a basic site, and up to $65 or more at a four-star site for a family of four, a car and a caravan site or camping space. Some sites charge extra for the use of showers, sports facilities (such as tennis courts), and amenities such as ironing or the use of a freezer. Most sites have different rates for high and low seasons.

Permission is required to park or camp on private property or anywhere outside official campsites. Whether or not it's legal to camp in the countryside depends on the attitude of the local authority (VIN centres can advise you). In rural areas, camping by the roadside is a popular practice, although elsewhere the availability of campsites makes 'rough camping' less popular than in some other countries. Note that areas where there are no campsites may be remote, with even facilities such as clean drinking water difficult to find; rough camping may be discouraged, particularly if the area is so remote as to make rescue difficult, e.g. in case of a medical emergency. Camping isn't usually permitted alongside walking trails (for which New Zealand is famous), although huts are available in most areas with bunk beds, cooking facilities, toilets and possibly showers, for a fee of from $10 per night.

Holiday Accommodation Parks of New Zealand (HAPNZ) produces a directory describing the facilities at over 295 member sites, including sites with cabins to rent.

It's available from HAPNZ (PO Box 394, Paraparaumu, ☎ 04-298 3283, 💻 www. holidayparks.co.nz), and from bookshops and camping, caravanning and motoring organisations in New Zealand. HAPNZ also offers caravan and travel insurance, travel services, rallies, holidays, reservations and a range of other benefits for members.

The Department of Conservation (DOC, www.doc.govt.nz) operates around 120 camping grounds in New Zealand, usually in national parks or reserves. These offer only basic facilities and there's usually a standard charge (around $5 per adult), although DOC informal camping grounds are free. DOC offices around the country can provide lists of camping grounds.

Information about camping is available from *Jasons NZ Holiday Parks & Campgrounds Accommodation Directory* (💻 www.jasons. com/new-zealand) and a number of websites, including 💻 www.camping.org.nz and www. nzcamping.co.nz.

SELF-CATERING

New Zealand offers an abundance of self-catering accommodation and a wide choice of 'mobile' homes, including cabins, condominiums, serviced motels and tourist flats. The most luxurious dwellings have private swimming pools, tennis courts and acres of private grounds, although you may need to take out a second mortgage to pay the bill! Standards vary considerably, from basic, no-frills cabins to luxury apartments with every modern convenience.

> There are a number of books for self-caterers, including Boutique Lodgings of New Zealand by Emma Fowler (Catherine Stewart) and Charming Places to Stay in New Zealand, by Uli Newman (Travelwise, 💻 www.travelwise.co.nz).

Cabins

One particular feature of self-catering accommodation in New Zealand is the cabin, which is usually basic, containing only beds and essential furniture, but a step up from a tent. You must provide your own bedding or sleeping bag. In addition to dedicated cabin sites, cabins are also available at many camping and caravanning sites, from between $35 to $70 per night. Holiday Accommodation Parks of New Zealand (💻 www.holidayparks.co.nz) publishes a directory containing details of over 295 member sites.

Tourist Flats

A tourist flat is the New Zealand term for a holiday apartment. Unlike cabins they're usually located in purpose-built buildings and can vary from fairly basic one-room studios to two or three-bedroom apartments. They usually contain bedding and linen and a well-equipped kitchen, while better quality flats are fully serviced and contain washing machines, dishwashers and TVs (they also provide the use of swimming pools and sporting facilities). A tourist flat typically costs between $75 and $100 per night, depending on the facilities and location.

Condominiums

An increasingly popular trend in New Zealand is for American-style condominiums, which are essentially the same as tourist flats but more luxurious. They're sometimes found in the grounds of luxury hotels and sporting lodges, and include the use of swimming pools, spas, tennis courts and extensive gardens. The cost ranges from $1,000 to $2,000 per week, per unit.

It isn't usually necessary to book far in advance for self-catering accommodation, as there's a wide choice and there isn't much of a peak holiday season in New Zealand. However, if you wish to stay in a particular unit for a particular week during the summer, you should certainly book, although if you're flexible you need to book only a week or two in advance or can simply turn up and find somewhere on the spot; if your preferred accommodation isn't available, there's usually somewhere similar nearby.

Various organisations publish guides to self-catering accommodation and an excellent *Where to Stay Guide* is also published by Tourism New Zealand, listing the different accommodation options in New Zealand. It's available free from tourist offices, although a charge is made if you want the guide posted to you. Other good guides include *Jasons Budget Accommodation* and *Motels and Motor Lodges* (www.jasons.com/new-zealand), the New Zealand equivalent of a Michelin guide.

There are numerous websites for renting privately-owned holiday homes, including 💻 www.bookabach.co.nz, www.holidayhomes.co.nz and www.nzholidayhomes.co.nz.

MUSEUMS & GALLERIES

Most exhibits in New Zealand museums and galleries are from recent history, although you can enjoy ancient treasures and old masters at art galleries in the major cities. However, there's definitely a preference for more contemporary works and many of the exhibits are by present-day Maori and *Pākehā* (a local term for white, European settlers) artists. The standard of museums and art galleries is generally high (many have living or interactive displays) and even in small towns you're likely to find a local museum where you can learn something about local history and culture. Admission is usually free, except for collections housed in historic buildings, where a small charge is made. The New Zealand Historic Places Trust (💻 www.historic.org.nz) maintains 43 sites and collections around the country.

Among the most famous museums and galleries in New Zealand are the Auckland Art Gallery, the New Zealand Maritime Museum (also in Auckland), the Te Papa or Museum of New Zealand in Wellington (which has excellent displays of Pacific and Maori cultures, as well as exhibits about New Zealand history and European settlement, 💻 www.tepapa.govt.nz), the Canterbury Museum, and the Christchurch Art Gallery Te Puna o Waiwhetu (💻 www.christchurchartgallery.org.nz – closed until mid-2013 due to the earthquake), one of the few galleries to exhibit European masters. For information contact Museums Aotearoa (PO Box 10 928, Wellington 6143, ☎ 04-499 1313, 💻 www.museums-aotearoa.org.nz).

It's also possible to visit many businesses in New Zealand, particularly those in the food and drink industry, including breweries, dairies, distilleries, farms, mineral water springs and vineyards. Technology enthusiasts may also wish to visit a hydroelectric power plant or a mine.

Disabled Access

Like many countries, New Zealand has started to take access for the disabled seriously only within the last decade. The law now requires that new buildings and redevelopment projects incorporate 'reasonable and adequate' access for disabled people. There are, however, still a lot of old public buildings that cannot be modified for practical or aesthetic reasons. Commercial operators tend to be more forward thinking and most leisure attractions provide disabled access, and hotels and motels are required to provide at least a few units with wheelchair access.

THEATRE, OPERA & BALLET

New Zealand has resident professional theatre companies in a number of major cities and repertory theatre groups throughout the country, even in smaller towns. Among New Zealand's best known playwrights are Bruce Mason, Joe Musaphia, Greg McGee and Roger Hall, whose play 'Middle Age Spread' was a major success in London's West End. Wellingtonians are particularly noted for their love of theatre and the city hosts an International Festival of Arts (💻 www.aucklandfestival.co.nz) biennially (in odd numbered years). Auckland, Christchurch and Dunedin also have active theatre scenes.

The New Zealand Opera Company (💻 www.nzopera.com) dates back to 1954 and the National Opera was established in 1979. New Zealand Opera is more famous outside the country than within, although opera singer Dame Kiri te Kanawa is revered in New Zealand (mainly because she's a New Zealander who has made it on the world stage, rather than because of the average Kiwi's interest in opera). Auckland stages an 'Opera in the Park' season annually in January.

The Royal New Zealand Ballet (💻 www.nzballet.org.nz) was founded in 1953 and the National School of Ballet (now part of the New Zealand School of Dance, 💻 www.nzschoolofdance.co.nz) was established in 1968. Like its counterparts in opera, the Royal New Zealand Ballet has an excellent repertoire of 19th century and more modern works, and performs regularly in New Zealand and abroad.

MUSIC

New Zealand's Symphony Orchestra (www.nzso.co.nz) regularly tours the country and undertakes overseas tours, particularly to Australia and Japan. Most major cities also have their own symphony

and concert orchestras. Prominent New Zealand musicians include concert organist Gillian Weir and pianists Michael Houston and Maurice Till. New Zealand is also noted for its metropolitan brass bands (a local tradition), which frequently take part in international competitions and have been world champions on several occasions.

There are few well-known New Zealand rock and pop bands, Crowded House being one of the few to attain international fame, although most groups leave for Europe as soon as they achieve some success. Internationally known rock and pop stars do, however, tour New Zealand on a regular basis, mainly in November and December, with tickets for top acts costing at least $50. There are rock, folk and jazz clubs in most cities, although these tend to be quieter and less cosmopolitan than those found in Europe and North America.

CINEMA

New Zealand produces a number of home-grown feature films, which are popular with local cinema-goers, and some, such as Roger Donaldson's *Sleeping Dogs* and Jane Campion's *The Piano* (highly acclaimed at Cannes and the Academy Awards), have received international recognition. Other acclaimed films include *Goodbye Pork Pie* (1981), one of New Zealand's most popular films, and the recent comedy, *Second Hand Wedding* (2008). The three highest-grossing New Zealand films are *The World's Fastest Indian*, *Once Were Warriors* and *Whale Rider*.

However, New Zealand's largest cinema triumph in many a year came in December 2001, with the blockbuster *Lord of the Rings* trilogy, filmed entirely on location in New Zealand and produced by Kiwi Peter Jackson. Extensive marketing campaigns have capitalised on the exposure from the trilogy and NZ Post has even issued commemorative stamps!

Cinema-lovers are well-catered for as most of the world's blockbuster movies are released in New Zealand sooner or later (sometimes before Europe). There are several popular annual film festivals in New Zealand, including the International Film Festival held in Auckland and the 'Incredible Film Festival' showing B-grade and other unusual films.

There are cinemas in the major cities and most towns of any size, including multi-screen centres in the major cities, and Auckland has an IMAX screen at its Force Entertainment Centre. Tickets cost $10-15 for adults and $7.50-10 for children (prices increase at weekends). Children aged from 3 to 15 must show ID cards when buying tickets. There are also concessions for senior citizens and the disabled, plus special offers.

Films are graded by censors according to a unique classification system, shown below.

Note that only R16 and R18 films are restricted by law to the relevant audience. The censors

Film Grading	
Classification	**Audience**
G	general viewing
PG (parent guidance)	parents should decide whether the film is suitable for younger viewers
M	only those aged 16 or over
R16	only those aged 16 or over
R18	only those aged 18 or over

frequently add a descriptive tag to their rating, such as 'violent content' or 'explicit sexual content', which gives additional guidance and makes it easier for parents to decide which films their children shouldn't see (or conversely, which films children will do anything to try to see!).

BARS & PUBS

As befits a nation in which drinking is virtually an obsession, New Zealand has a vast choice of drinking establishments. Every town of any size has at least one pub or bar, and in many town and city suburbs there's one on every corner. Dunedin is generally considered to have the country's best pub scene. However, despite (or perhaps because of) the popularity of drinking, New Zealand has some of the world's more bizarre licensing laws.

The traditional New Zealand drinking place is the local 'hotel', which is roughly equivalent to a pub in the UK or a bar elsewhere. Despite being called hotels, they rarely offer accommodation. At its most basic, a New Zealand hotel can be very rudimentary indeed, with plastic chairs, fluorescent lighting and no music, although the larger establishments offer a choice between public and lounge bars (a lounge bar is more attractively furnished but drinks are up to 50 per cent more expensive). Some country hotels even have beer gardens. Most traditional hotels don't serve food and those that do have a rather limited menu. All hotels have a so-called bottle sales counter where you can buy alcohol to take away, which is a consequence of the licensing laws that allow shops and supermarkets to sell beer and wine, but not spirits.

New Zealand hotels are public houses in the true sense of the word, in that usually all-comers are served. Women drinking in a public bar may attract a few stares in remote places, but are unlikely to meet with disapproval. In country areas you may initially feel that you're intruding upon the locals' private territory, but you'll usually be warmly welcomed and engaged in conversation. Indeed, you should make an attempt to talk to the regulars, as it may be considered rude not to do so.

Bars are generally more up-market establishments and are usually found in cities and large towns, where you can choose from French-influenced bars, café-bars, brasseries, wine bars and pavement cafés. These places offer none of

the traditional New Zealand atmosphere, but as in other countries, are fashionable places to see and be seen. Drinks are invariably more expensive than in a hotel and bars may also serve food.

Licensing Hours

Until 1967 hotels could serve alcohol only until 6pm and, although licensing hours have been liberalised in recent years, the 5 to 6pm 'swill' is still often the busiest time for drinking. The same liberalisation has also resulted in a confusing array of licensing hours that apply to different premises in different places. In theory, drinking establishments can apply for a 24-hour licence allowing them to open day and night except on Sundays, when they must close by 3am. In practice, most hotels and bars are open daily from 11am to 10pm and until 10.30pm on Fridays and Saturdays. Even establishments with a 24-hour licence may be closed by 1am, simply due to a lack of demand for late-night drinking. Establishments that don't serve food aren't usually allowed to sell alcohol on Sundays, although Sunday drinking is permitted in night-clubs, private clubs and places of entertainment (in addition to restaurants).

A few areas of Auckland, Wellington and Christchurch have licensing authorities which don't license any establishments to serve alcohol and are therefore effectively 'dry' (there's still a strong temperance movement in New

Zealand). The main effect of this, however, is to encourage drinking and driving, as drinkers are forced to travel to other areas to quench their thirst.

The legal age for drinking in public establishments in New Zealand was reduced in 1999 (after much public debate) from 20 to 18, although it remains controversial, as statistics show teenage drinking to be on the increase. The country's youth drinking culture includes mindless violence and property damage, which has led to liquor bans on public streets and beaches throughout New Zealand.

On-the-spot fines for under-age drinking have been introduced, and are up to $200 for the offender and up to $10,000 for the establishment that sold the alcohol. Identity cards, such as a passport or driving licence, must be shown on request.

Beer

The most popular drink in New Zealand is beer, which is usually sold in draught form and is similar in taste and strength to British bitter. There are two major breweries in the country, NZ Breweries and DB Breweries (formerly Dominion Breweries), which together also own the vast majority of drinking establishments, and produce a range of beers and lagers.

There are a number of independent breweries and micro (tiny) breweries producing their own draught and bottled brands. Imported and locally brewed versions of foreign beers are available in larger hotels and trendier establishments.

Beer is sold in a wide variety of measures, which may vary with the city or region. Glasses are designed to hold metric quantities, although beer can also be ordered in imperial quantities, e.g. if you ask for a pint or half pint, you'll get around 500ml to 600ml or 250ml to 300ml respectively. The most common measures are a 'seven' (originally 7oz but now 200ml), a 'twelve' (originally 12oz but now 350ml), a 'handle' (500ml) and a jug (containing one or two litres). If in doubt, just ask for a 'small' or 'large' beer. In any case, in most places 'free pouring' is the norm and measures tend to be somewhat academic!

Wine

New Zealand wine production has boomed in the last decade or so and there are now eight major wine regions and over 600 vineyards (or wineries), with more than 30,000 hectares in vines in 2012. Wine production was a record 221m litres in 2011, with exports worth $1.1bn. The UK (34 per cent) is the largest export market, closely followed by Australia (29.5 per cent) and the USA (21 per cent).

The major wine producing areas are Marlborough (which is home to half of the country's wineries), Hawke's Bay and Gisborne. Most vineyards are open to the public and offer free or inexpensive tastings to encourage visitors to buy a few cases. In recent years, wineries have increased in popularity as places to enjoy a drink or meal with friends, and many now have cafés and excellent restaurants. Some also hold wine festivals, which are very popular, particularly when free samples are provided! Information about vineyards and wine festivals can be obtained via the internet (see 🖥 www.winesofnz.com and www.nzwine.com).

New Zealand wines have earned an excellent international reputation for quality in the last decade or so. The best wines have traditionally been white, made from sauvignon blanc and chardonnay grapes, although red wines are increasingly important and in recent years the country has become a major producer of high quality pinot noir (which now exceeds Chardonnay in the area in vine). You rarely find a bad New Zealand wine, although the poorer brands tend to be inflicted on the home market rather than sent overseas to taint the reputation of New Zealand exports. The country also produces (inevitably?) kiwi fruit wine, which, not surprisingly, is an acquired taste!

Foreign wines are also available in New Zealand, although apart from Australian wines – which can be excellent value and may be cheaper than in Australia – they're usually more expensive, due to duty and shipping fees. You can buy wine by the glass in hotels (pubs), although they're invariably dominated by beer-swilling men and generally offer a poor selection. Domestic wine consumption has increased over the last decade, but it's still only some 15 litres per capita, per year, which is far behind beer.

Further information about New Zealand's wines can be obtained from the New Zealand Wine Institute (🖥 www.nzwine.com) and from a number of books and magazines including *Wine NZ* magazine (🖥 www.winenzmagazine.co.nz) and Michael Cooper's *Buyer's Guide to New Zealand Wines* and *Wine Atlas of New Zealand* (Hodder Moa).

Spirits

Spirits are available in most hotels and bars, although the choice may be limited and they are relatively expensive, which is why most people drink beer or wine. New Zealand's only indigenous spirit is kiwi fruit liqueur, which is similar to fruit liqueurs found in other countries.

CAFÉS & RESTAURANTS

New Zealand cuisine is largely driven by local ingredients and seasonal variations. Thanks to its predominantly agricultural economy and vast coastline, New Zealanders enjoy superb local produce from land and sea. Similar to Australia, New Zealand's cuisine is often described as Pacific Rim, drawing inspiration from Europe, Asia and Polynesia. This blend of influences has created a mouth-watering range of flavours and food in cafés and restaurants nationwide. To complement its superb produce, New Zealand produces a wealth of home-grown wines, including world-class sauvignon blanc and pinot noir, from almost 400 wineries.

New Zealand food takes its techniques and ingredients from far and wide, not least from the Maori culture, New American cuisine, the Mediterranean, and Chinese and Indian dishes. Traditional hearty 'settlers' dishes, now dubbed *Kwisine Kiwiana*, remain popular, particularly in the more traditional parts of the country, and include staples such as roasts (rack of lamb is superb), fish and chips (invariably excellent) and meat pies (delicious gourmet venison pies!). For dishes that have a distinctly New Zealand style, there's lamb, pork and venison, salmon, crayfish (lobster), Bluff oysters, paua (abalone), mussels, scallops, pipis and tuatua (types of shellfish), kumara (sweet potato), kiwifruit, tamarillo and pavlova.

The national pudding is pavlova (or 'pav'), the invention of which is claimed by both Australia and New Zealand, named after the famous Russian ballet dancer. It's an air-filled concoction of meringue, cream and fruit (often topped with kiwifruit), which is traditionally served on high holidays. However, the weight-obsessed needn't despair; salads are also popular, particularly those featuring exotic ingredients.

Food culture and fashions in New Zealand tend to follow Australia and many Kiwi chefs endeavour to learn from their trans-Tasman cousins. However, that's not to say that New Zealand doesn't have its own innovative and ground-breaking chefs – in recent years many New Zealanders have exported their cooking expertise to Australia and farther afield. This foodie mini-boom has been stimulated by the nation's love of travelling, as generations of Kiwis have experienced dining in the world's great culinary capitals. It's also a response to the demands and tastes of tourists who visit New Zealand, plus the fact that the country's cuisine and choice of restaurants has been vastly enriched by immigrants.

New Zealand has become something of a Mecca for 'foodies' in recent years (particularly the major cities), where the interest in food is reflected by the wealth of food magazines, cookbooks (which regularly feature in the bestseller lists) and cookery programmes which attract large audiences. Food and wine magazines include *Cuisine*, (🖥 www.cuisine.co.nz), a foodies delight, *Dish*, the *Healthy Food Guide*, *Taste* and *Wine NZ*.

Wine and food festivals are popular throughout the country and are held annually in Auckland, Hawke's Bay, Martinborough, Nelson, Canterbury and Queenstown. Of particular interest for adventurous foodies is the Wildfoods Festival (Hokitika, South Island, March), where you can try a wide range of odd and interesting food.

Cafés

New Zealanders take after the British and drink a lot of tea and an increasing amount of coffee. Café society (and caffeine culture) has become popular in New Zealand in the last few decades and there are even *Café* and *Coffee Culture* magazines! There's a huge number and variety of coffee shops, which are important places for socialising even in small towns, which have largely replaced the traditional tearooms (many of which have converted to cafés). However, the habit of eating cakes and pastries hasn't diminished, and most cafés offer a huge variety of home-baked, diet-busting delights.

Coffee is served in a mind boggling variety in a plethora of coffee shops and cafés. If you just want a regular white coffee, it's best to stick with an 'Americano' or a 'flat white'. Coffee also comes in various sizes including short (small – large enough for most people unless you want to swim in it) and long (very large), which may be served in a cup (usually) or a glass. The cost of a coffee is usually between $3 and $3.50. You normally order and pay at the counter in a café and may be given a number to put on your table, with your order being delivered when it's ready (although, disappointingly, it's often lukewarm).

The more usual types of coffee offered in New Zealand include those listed in the table below; the list isn't definitive and the names, descriptions and ingredients/style may vary depending on the establishment.

Coffee Culture	
Name	**Description**
Affogato	a single or double espresso poured over vanilla ice cream
Americano	an espresso diluted with an equal portion of hot water (with milk)
Café au lait	coffee and heated milk in latte proportions, but using 'regular' coffee instead of espresso
Cappuccino	a single shot of espresso with frothy milk, topped with a pinch of powdered chocolate
Espresso	a black strong coffee prepared in the Italian way by forcing steam through dark-roast coffee beans – can be short (single shot, also called a short black) or long (double shot, also called a long black)
Filter	a method for brewing coffee which involves pouring water over coffee contained in a filter. Not considered real coffee (except by Americans) and may be left to stew in a jug. It may be available in caffeinated and decaffeinated (decaf) versions
Flat White	made with one-third espresso and two-thirds steamed milk and similar to the ingredients in a latte. Can be a single or double (i.e. an extra shot)
Latte	an espresso with steamed milk and a cap of foam
Long Black	a double-shot espresso topped with hot water
Macchiato	a single espresso with a shot of cold or steamed milk (short macchiato) or a glass filled with hot frothed milk into which a double espresso is slowly dribbled (long macchiato)
Mocha	usually an espresso shot with steamed milk and chocolate
Mochaccino	an espresso with hot chocolate milk
Plunger	a one-person plunger or French press (cafétière) coffee
Short Black	a single-shot espresso
Vienna	a double shot espresso, laced with vanilla and topped with whipped cream

Restaurants

New Zealand has a wealth of restaurants of all shapes and sizes and price ranges, from 5-star fine dining establishments to fast-food outlets, award-winning city eateries to al fresco rural and beachside restaurants, traditional Kiwi fare to a plethora of ethnic delights. Modestly-priced restaurants and take-aways are widespread and increasingly favoured over home cooking, and include BYO ('bring your own') eateries where you can take your own wine.

Ethnic restaurants are common in New Zealand, thanks to the country's large number of immigrants. Asian restaurants are widespread and most towns have at least one Chinese restaurant, although the food is invariably of the westernised Chinese variety rather than authentic Chinese cuisine. You'll also find French, Indian, Italian, Japanese, Mexican and Thai (to mention just a few) restaurants in the major cities. However, although excellent value for money, ethnic food is often disappointing in New Zealand, where it tends to be at the bottom rather than at the top of the food chain.

If you're an enthusiastic epicure you need to head for the major cities, where you'll find excellent restaurants comparable with the best London, New York or Paris has to offer. Auckland and Wellington have a good choice of fine dining, with prices that are much lower than similar establishments abroad. However, outside the major cities there's a relative dearth of gastronomic excellence, with the notable exception of fish and seafood restaurants, where fresh seafood is prepared and cooked imaginatively, often with a strong Maori influence.

Eating *al fresco* is popular and indicative of the laidback Kiwi psyche, where everything is as relaxed and unaffected as possible. Summer sees many eating outdoors in cafés or at barbecues – a large part of Kiwi culture – where fare such as lamb, venison, lobster, fresh fish and shellfish is plentiful. Among the best places to eat *al fresco* are wineries, many of which have award-winning restaurants – and wines! It's also a good choice for smokers, as smoking is banned in restaurants.

One of the best things about dining out in New Zealand is the price. Ethnic meals range from $10-20 for lunch up to $40-50 for dinner with a glass of wine. Fine dining costs more but is still reasonable, at around $60 a head with wine. There's a relatively low mark-up on wine (around twice the supermarket price), which usually costs from around $8 or $9 a glass. Restaurants are good value by international standards, although the locals tend to think they are expensive, as salaries are much lower in New Zealand than in Europe or North America.

Although the food is invariably good or very good and the service efficient and friendly, the ambience and décor sometimes tend to be uninspiring, even in up-market establishments. The dress code for dining out in New Zealand is notably informal and Kiwis follow European table manners, but in a typically informal, relaxed way – nobody will be much concerned

if you're unsure which fork or spoon to use. Apart from a few pretentious places in the major cities that insist on a jacket or tie, most restaurants don't impose dress restrictions, although you may not be admitted to a top restaurant wearing shorts and a T-shirt! Most New Zealanders don't dress up to eat out and smart casual dress is usually adequate, even for the best restaurants.

Auckland is New Zealand's culinary capital, where the annual magazines, *Auckland's Great Restaurant Guide* and *Auckland's Great Café, Deli and Bar Guide* are popular. Jasons (🖳 www.jasons.com/guides/new-zealand) also publish a number of restaurant guides, including *Jasons Taste Traveller* and *Dining Guides* to Auckland, Christchurch, Queenstown, Rotorua and Wellington. There are also many online restaurant guides, including 💻 www.dineout.co.nz, www.eatout.co.nz, www.menumania.co.nz and www.time2dine.co.nz (Auckland).

The advantages of eating out in New Zealand include generous portions, friendly service and surprisingly low prices – you can enjoy an excellent three-course meal in a good restaurant for $50 a head, including drinks.

Bring-Your-Own (BYO) Restaurants

BYO restaurants date back to the days when alcohol licences were hard to come by and restaurants without a licence allowed customers to bring their own wine or other drinks. In return for a small fee (corkage), the waiter uncorks (and serves) your wine. Although not as widespread as they once were, as licences are easier to come by nowadays, many restaurants choose not to become licensed in order to allow customers to choose their own drinks at the price they want to pay (or can afford). Some licensed restaurants also allow customers to bring their own drinks, although the policy regarding this is variable and you should make enquiries in advance, particularly if you're inviting guests to dinner.

One drawback is that non-BYO restaurants fix their own corkage fee and you may find yourself paying as much for 'uncorking' as you paid for your bottle of supermarket plonk! Corkage charges in BYO restaurants start at around $2 a bottle in small establishments, with an average of around $5 per bottle, rising to $7.50 on Fridays and Saturdays.

Opening Hours

Restaurant opening hours reflect licensing hours, and as a result many restaurants don't open on Sundays, therefore it's wise to check if you plan to eat in a particular place. Some restaurants that open on Sundays close on Mondays. Booking isn't usually necessary, but it's recommended in the more fashionable places, particularly on Fridays and Saturdays. Note that many restaurants are closed on public holidays and over holiday periods such as Easter, Christmas and the New Year.

Tipping

As in other areas of New Zealand life (see page 300), a no-tipping policy usually applies in restaurants (if only other countries would follow suit!). You won't be expected to tip and, should you try to, it may be greeted with surprise and even embarrassment by your waiter. Neither is there usually a service charge. The menu price is the price you pay; no extra charges will be added to your bill and you won't be expected to add anything. However, in some tourist areas tipping has become more widespread, and not surprisingly is well-received by the staff, although you should only tip if you receive excellent service.

Note, however, that some restaurants charge a surcharge (similar to a service charge), e.g. 15 per cent, on public holidays to compensate for the additional staff costs (staff must be paid time and a half to work on public holidays).

Vegetarianism

New Zealanders used to have an unsympathetic attitude towards vegetarians, who were once thin on the ground. Not eating meat was considered almost unpatriotic in a country which earns millions of dollars from meat exports, and where the number of sheep makes lamb one of the cheapest and most frequently served dishes. Despite exhortations by the Ministry of Health for people to eat less meat and more cereals, fruit and vegetables, a high meat-based diet remains a part of Kiwi culture, albeit with a reduction in red meat consumption and more fish and chicken.

However, the attitude towards vegetarians has changed in recent years and at least one vegetarian option is now available in most restaurants. There are a number of vegetarian restaurants in the major cities and 'fishetarians' can enjoy many excellent seafood restaurants. Consult the NZ Vegetarian Society website for further information (💻 www.vegetarian.org.nz).

Smoking

Smoking in restaurants (and bars, casinos and clubs) has been prohibited since December 2004.

SOCIAL CLUBS

There are many social clubs and organisations in New Zealand, including Anglo-New Zealand Clubs, Business Clubs, International Men's and Women's Clubs, and Rotary Clubs. Expatriates from many countries have their own clubs in the major cities, a list of which is often maintained by embassies and consulates in New Zealand.

The Country Women's Institutes of New Zealand (💻 www.wi.org.nz) and Rural Women New Zealand (💻 www.ruralwomen.org) play an important part in the social life of women in rural areas, where there are few formal social facilities. All towns have a YMCA (💻 www.ymca.org.nz) and YWCA (💻 www.ywca.org.nz), many of which organise extensive social programmes. In keeping with the country's sporting heritage, there are a range of sports clubs in most towns, the most common of which are rugby, soccer, cricket, hockey and netball.

Many clubs organise activities and pastimes such as art, bridge, chess, music, outings, sports activities, and theatre and cinema trips. Joining a local club is one of the best ways to meet people, make friends and integrate into your local community or society in general. Ask your local library or community centre for details.

NIGHTLIFE

New Zealand nightlife varies considerably depending on the town or region, and in small towns you may be fortunate to find a bar with music. In contrast, some towns buzz with nightlife; for example Dunedin, with its large student population, is the country's live music and pub capital. New Zealand pubs are traditionally serious drinking places and many shun any trends towards making them more attractive with live music. In cities you'll find a wide range of attractions, including jazz clubs, discos, music clubs, karaoke bars, trendy bars, night-clubs and music halls.

Although some venues are fast-paced by New Zealand standards, you're unlikely to find a night-spot that's as dynamic as the top establishments in London, New York or Paris. All night clubs restrict entry to those aged over 20, which in part accounts for the more mature (i.e. conservative) atmosphere, where strict dress codes are often enforced. The most popular clubs change continually and are listed in newspapers and entertainment magazines. There are a few places in Auckland that keep going until the small hours, but you'll find that most establishments are closed by 1am simply because the revellers have all gone home.

There are many national and regional online entertainment and gig guides, including 💻 www.95bfm.co.nz/default,guides.sm, www.entry.co.nz and www.viewauckland.co.nz.

GAMBLING

Gambling is a national passion in New Zealand, where gamblers spend (lose) over $2bn annually. Gambling is strictly controlled by the state (gambling in some other countries seems completely unfettered in comparison), although compulsive gambling is on the increase. Slot machines and electronic amusement arcade gambling games have been legal only since 1987, but there are now over 20,000 gaming machines in New Zealand, which are responsible for the problems of the vast majority of compulsive gamblers (estimated to number over 100,000).

The national lottery (Lotto) is the most widespread form of gambling in New Zealand, where over two-thirds of the population buy a ticket each week. Tickets can be purchased at designated Lotto outlets, including most dairies (corner shops) and PostShops, and the draw is shown live on prime-time TV on Saturday evenings. The New Zealand Lotteries Commission is prepared to go to extraordinary lengths to make sure that as many New Zealanders as possible participate and offers 'multi-draw' entry options for people going on holiday (you can play for up to ten weeks in advance) and the facility to play Lotto by post if you live in a remote area without a Lotto outlet. Instant-win scratch cards, known as 'scratchies', can also be bought from the same outlets. Some of the proceeds of Lotto are donated to charity, including charities which help compulsive gamblers!

After Lotto, betting on horse racing is the next most popular gambling activity, with over 500 regular race meetings throughout the country each year (an average of ten a week). New Zealanders are even more passionate about horse racing (including harness racing or trotting and flat racing) than Australians, and bets are often huge. Bets can be placed at betting offices licensed by the Totalisator Agency Board (TAB, 💻 www.tab.co.nz), which also accepts bets on Australian races.

Those looking for a more genteel outlet for their gambling passions may like to try their hand at bingo, known locally as housie. Most pubs and clubs have a housie night at least once a week (some every night), where for around $10 you can buy a card entitling you to play some 40 games. Casinos have been legalised within the last few years and there are six in total, including the Sky City casino in Auckland with over 100 gaming tables, a Keno lounge and over 1,600 slot machines.

Sky City is housed in Sky Tower, one of New Zealand's most famous landmarks after the completion of the 328m (1,000ft) tower topped by a revolving restaurant, which has the added 'attraction' of swaying in high winds! Opening hours are 11am to 3am from Monday to Thursday, and continuously from 11am Thursday until 3am Monday morning.

All advertising for casinos in New Zealand is accompanied by a gambling 'health warning' and the number of an organisation which helps compulsive gamblers, Gamblers Helpline (☎ 0800-654 655, 💻 www.gamblingproblem. co.nz).

EVENING CLASSES

Evening classes are provided by various organisations in cities and large towns in New Zealand. In addition to formal adult and further education, evening classes offer courses and lectures in everything from astrology to zoology. The range and variety of subjects offered is endless and includes foreign languages, handicrafts, hobbies and sports, and business-related courses. Among the most popular classes are cookery, and motor and home maintenance.

New Zealanders have a long tradition of do-it-yourself dating back to the days of the early settlers and few people would dream of paying somebody to fix their home or car if they could do it themselves (an old New Zealand saying is 'you can fix it fine with binder twine' – the string used to bind bales of hay!). If you live in a remote area you may find it difficult to find a local tradesman to do odd jobs around your home, therefore classes have a practical as well as a leisure purpose.

LIBRARIES

Almost every town in New Zealand has a local library, which is generally excellent. New Zealanders are avid readers and the relatively high cost of books (there are relatively few local publishers and most books are imported from Australia, the UK or the USA) makes the library a popular place to stock up on reading material. Libraries in major towns and cities also lend CDs and DVDs.

Library opening hours and the range of books stocked vary considerably with the size of the town. Larger libraries offer a range of material and services, including archives, book reservation, newspapers and periodicals, photocopying and computers with internet access. Libraries are also an excellent source of information about the local community, including local services, groups and clubs. To join your local library you simply need to provide proof of your address, such as a utility bill or bank statement.

16.
SPORTS

New Zealand has the ideal climate and terrain for a wide range of sports, including world class skiing and surfing, both of which you can do on the same day, although why anyone would want to is another matter! Most New Zealanders are passionate about sport, which is a symbol of national pride, and New Zealand sports men and women are world renowned in a number of sports, notably rugby, sailing and equestrianism.

Over half of the adult population belongs to a sports or health club, although the New Zealander's love of exercise hasn't had much impact on the rate of heart disease, which kills around 6,000 people a year. Most towns have a leisure centre with a pool, gym and other sports facilities, where casual use costs around $5-10, which can be reduced by buying a multi-visit ticket. Many councils publish a Sport and Recreation Guide. The doctrine that sport is very much for 'the people' is illustrated by the fact that the majority of sports in New Zealand are played at amateur level, with little professional sport. The main exception is rugby, which is primarily a professional game at the top level and one of the few sports where professional athletes can earn the sort of telephone-number salaries that are common in many other countries.

While team sports are popular, there's also a large following for many solo sports, particularly those where competitors can pit their wits against the natural elements. Despite the dominance of traditional sports such as rugby, New Zealand is famous as the adventure sports 'capital of the world', with abseiling, bungee jumping (a Kiwi invention), jet boating, white-water rafting and aerial sports (e.g. para-sailing, hang-gliding and sky-diving) all hugely popular.

New Zealand is also noted for its (other) outdoor pursuits, including fishing (trout, sport), hunting (deer, game birds, pigs), boating/

sailing, horse-riding, trekking, rock and mountain climbing, cycling/mountain-biking, off-road/quad bike/ATV driving, canyoning and zorbing. If it's dangerous, New Zealanders somewhere will be doing it and inviting the world to participate. A useful book for thrill-seekers is *Jasons Encounter NZ Outdoor Activities Directory* (⌨ www.jasons.com/guides/new-zealand).

Sport and Recreation New Zealand (SPARC, ⌨ www.sparc.org.nz) works 'to ensure New Zealand remains a thriving, healthy, dynamic country'. It was formed in 2002 following the merger of the Hillary Commission, the New Zealand Sports Foundation and the policy arm of the Office of Tourism and Sport. SPARC works with community clubs, local authorities, schools and sports organisations to create opportunities for New Zealanders to reach their potential in their chosen sports.

Rugby is New Zealand's national sport and obsession, and in the past even the Prime Minister has become embroiled in the selection of the national rugby (union) team, the All Blacks.

RUGBY

While many New Zealanders are interested in playing and watching rugby, many more are supporters simply because the success of the national team brings New Zealand such fame and prestige around the world. Interest in rugby fell in the '70s and '80s, when the national team maintained links with apartheid South Africa, but following the demise of apartheid, its popularity and match attendances have soared, and the country shuts down to watch a rugby test match. Top players are as revered in New Zealand as top soccer players are in other countries. Rugby professionals have the opportunity to earn more through rugby than almost any other 'occupation' and an All Black's annual income can be up to $1m, although this is modest compared to what they can earn overseas, and several top New Zealand players play abroad.

The rugby season traditionally lasts from May until September, during which clubs play rugby union (🖥 www.nzrugby.co.nz) and rugby league (🖥 www.rugbyleaguenz. com) at all levels, including international, regional, representative, city and local. While primarily a men's game, New Zealand also has a small but enthusiastically supported women's rugby movement (the national team won the world cup in 1998, 2002, 2006 and 2010). Teams play in a huge variety of league and cup competitions, with the top divisions in both codes (the Super 12 and Super League) including teams from outside New Zealand.

Australia (the Wallabies) and South Africa (the Springboks or 'Boks') are the All Blacks' traditional arch enemies and they compete annually in the Tri-Nations (🖥 www. trinationsrugby.net) tournament, which is one of the country's major sporting events (it 2012 its became four nations, with the addition of Argentina). The All Blacks (🖥 www.allblacks. com) won it seven times between 2002-2011. Although rugby largely transcends racial groups, there's also a national Maori side at league level. Tickets to top rugby matches cost from around $75 to $150.

Sevens rugby is also popular and New Zealand competes in the world series (🖥 www. sevens.co.nz), which it hosts in Wellington in February – one of eight IRB World Series tournaments held around the globe each year. New Zealand were the winners in Auckland in 2012.

The Southern Hemisphere's top provincial tournament is the super 15 (🖥 www.superxv. com), which is played out between 15 teams; five from Australia, five from New Zealand and five from South Africa. The New Zealand teams are the Blues (Auckland, Northland), Chiefs (Waikato, Bay of Plenty), Crusaders (Canterbury, Tasman), Highlanders (Otago, Southland), and the Hurricanes (Wellington to Hawke's Bay). The 2011 tournament was won by the Reds (Queensland, Australia), with the Crusaders, Blues and Stormers occupying the next three places.

> Anyone with a keen interest in rugby will find they're warmly welcomed by local clubs and even those with absolutely no interest will find that they're unable to escape the country's passion for their national sport.

Success for the All Blacks results in almost non-stop coverage and much merriment and rejoicing, while failure may result in any mention of rugby being unofficially purged from the media, as if the sport had ceased to exist overnight. Expatriates report that an air of misery descends on the country following an All Blacks defeat, with sulking and moodiness lasting for several days. The good news is that the All Blacks triumphed on home soil in the 2011 World Cup.

Despite the game's supposedly gentlemanly image, rugby can be a dangerous sport. Post-match violence and drunkenness (as is associated with soccer in some other countries) occurs occasionally and being a rugby referee isn't without its risks, with attacks on referees during and after matches not uncommon.

Touch rugby is a lighter version of 'real' rugby and is popular throughout the country. It's played on a football pitch, the aim being to score a touchdown by passing the ball backwards and forwards to your team mates. Touch rugby teams must include at least two women or children and the game is supposed to be non-contact. Games are essentially social occasions with 'compulsory' beer and BBQ afterwards. Not only is it good fun, but it's an excellent way to meet people and you don't have to be a sports fanatic to join in (see 🖥 www.touchnz.co.nz).

It will come as no surprise to hear that the New Zealand Sports Academy (🖥 www.

nzsportsacademy.co.nz) is dedicated to nurturing future All Blacks – no other sport is important in New Zealand!

FOOTBALL

Football is widely played in New Zealand, although it's usually known as soccer to differentiate it from rugby football, which most New Zealanders consider 'proper' football. In New Zealand, the popularity of soccer lags way behind rugby and its cause hasn't been helped by some schools actually banning it in the past, in the fear that pupils would be tempted away from the 'superior' game. Interest in soccer boomed some years ago when the New Zealand national team, the All Whites, qualified for the World Cup. However, in recent times, the New Zealand team has been notably unsuccessful, particularly against the Australian national team, a country not noted for its prowess at soccer.

National, northern, central and southern soccer leagues operate in New Zealand, where soccer is played in both summer and winter, although the 'official' soccer season runs from May to September. New Zealand soccer 'stars' are nonentities compared with the cult status of top rugby players and the game is light years away from the standard seen in top European leagues or even second-rate countries. Local clubs occasionally sign foreign players and the signing of a British player from a second or third division side makes headline news. Interest is, however, growing at the amateur level and there are local leagues in most areas. A combined New Zealand team has been formed to play in the Australian soccer league and it's hoped this will increase the competitiveness and general standard of soccer in New Zealand.

CRICKET

Cricket is a national passion in New Zealand, as it is in many countries that derive their national heritage from the UK. There's wide support for the national team and it's popular among participants and spectators at all levels. International one-day matches between New Zealand and England attract crowds of 25,000 at Christchurch's floodlit Lancaster

Park Stadium. Top cricket players are held in almost as high a regard as rugby stars, although support for cricket declined a few years ago and most young people have a preference for rugby.

The national cricket team, known as the Black Caps (💻 www.blackcaps.co.nz), has a good international reputation (they are ranked number four in the world) and punches well above its weight.

The Black Caps reached the semi-final of the World Cup (💻 http://icc-cricket.yahoo.net) in India in 2011, where they were beaten by Sri Lanka – the sixth time the Kiwis have lost in the semi-finals.

The cricket season runs from November to April, and tickets for major international matches cost from around $15. There's also a small but significant women's cricket movement in New Zealand, and the national team's matches are followed keenly. In June 2010, New Zealand were runners-up to Australia in the final of the women's T20 World Cup.

TREKKING

Trekking (or tramping) is New Zealand's name for hiking, which is an institution enjoyed by

New Zealanders of all ages, from toddlers to pensioners. Trekking encompasses everything from a leisurely afternoon walk to an endurance-testing, near-military, route march lasting several days or weeks. The advantage of trekking is that you can make it as easy or as demanding as you wish, and there are plenty of places to trek, even close to major cities. A vast proportion of the country is made up of parks (e.g. national, forest and maritime parks) and there's always somewhere new to explore, which in the more remote areas includes many breathtaking spots that are accessible only on foot.

Despite its allusion to wilderness ways, trekking is highly organised and the whole country is criss-crossed with numerous tracks, some of which are internationally famous and attract hikers from around the world. These are known as the Great Walks and are often quite crowded, especially in summer (a pass is required). The more popular tracks are well signposted (look for 'W' signs) and maintained and often radiate out from the city suburbs. The more demanding tracks may not be signposted but are marked on trekking maps.

Some of the longer tracks are legendary, including the South Island's Abel Tasman (three to four days), Greenstone (two to three days), Heaphy (four to five days), Hollyford (five to six days), Kepler (four to five days,) Milford (four days) and Routeburn (usually a three-day trek through rain forests, mountains and alpine passes), and the North Island's Whirinaki Track (three to four days). Some tracks, such as the Abel Tasman, can be walked year round, while others such as the Routeburn are at higher altitudes and may be impassable in winter. October to April is unofficially regarded as the trekking season and some of the most popular routes can be quite congested in January and February.

As well as the well-known tracks, there are numerous less-popular tracks, which are just as enjoyable and spectacular in their own right. The Department of Conservation (DOC, 🖥 www.doc.govt.nz) can provide information and advice about tracks, and also maintains visitor centres and publishes numerous useful pamphlets. Each of the roughly 50 national, forest and marine parks has its own DOC headquarters, where you can obtain information about local tracks.

Although many trekkers (or should they be called trekkies?) take to the tracks independently, it's possible to take a trekking package holiday, which is ideal for the slightly less adventurous. Companies specialising in trekking holidays provide an experienced guide and accommodation in luxury lodges, mountain huts or tent camps, with hot showers and meals. The cost of guided treks ranges from $500 to $1,500 for a five-day trek. If you don't wish to take a full package tour, you can hire an experienced local guide to show you a route and provide commentary on the flora and fauna.

When trekking independently you need to carry your own food and equipment (take plenty of warm clothing even in summer). Accommodation can be found in DOC huts (there are over 950) situated along tracks, which may be free or require a modest fee (e.g. between $5 and $45 per night depending on the category), where bunks, cooking facilities and clean water are provided. There's no charge for children under 11, while older children are charged half-price provided they have a 'youth ticket'.

DOC also sells an annual huts pass, although this isn't valid for huts on the Great Walks. Accommodation in DOC huts is basic

and is provided on a first-come, first-served basis. Some independent trekkers prefer to take tents, which can usually be pitched near huts, but cannot usually be pitched alongside tracks in order to protect the character of treks.

You must pre-book to walk the Great Walks and obtain a special Great Walks Pass, even when walking independently. The pass is sold at DOC offices and national park offices. See www.doc.govt.nz/parks-and-recreation/tracks-and-walks/great-walks for information.

The most popular trekking season is, not surprisingly, the summer, when many of the Great Walks may be disappointingly crowded, although it's relatively easy to find a quieter, lesser known track. The best time of year to trek as far as the weather goes, is from November to March/April. You should avoid trekking in winter, particularly in the South Island, when weather conditions can be severe on high-altitude walks and some are closed due to the danger of avalanches. Whatever the season, you should always check the weather forecast and conditions before setting out, as a fine sunny day can quickly become wet and foggy. It's worth bearing in mind that although thousands of people trek safely each year in New Zealand, a number of people die each year in the mountains.

As well as the comprehensive DOC guides and leaflets, there are numerous trekking guides available, including Lonely Planet's *Tramping in New Zealand*, the definitive book on the subject, *New Zealand's Top Ten Tracks* by Mark Pickering, which describes many of the Great Walks, and *Wild Walks – North Island* and *Wild Walks – South Island*, both of which describe lesser-known tracks. There are also many hiking websites, including www.hikingnewzealand.com, www.nztramping.com and http://tramper.co.nz.

General Information

The following notes may help you survive a tramp in the mountains:

◆ If you're going to take up hiking seriously, a good pair of walking shoes or boots is mandatory (available from sports and trekking shops). Always wear proper walking shoes or boots where the terrain is rough. Unfortunately, walking boots are sometimes uncomfortable or hurt your feet after a few hours (if they don't hurt, it isn't doing you any good). Wearing two pairs of socks can help prevent blisters. It's advisable to break in a new pair of boots on some *gentle* hikes before setting out on a marathon hike around the country.

◆ Don't over-exert yourself, particularly at high altitudes where the air is thinner. Mountain sickness usually occurs only above 4,000 metres, but can also happen at lower altitudes. A few words of warning for those who aren't particularly fit: **Take it easy and set a slow pace.** It's easy to over-exert yourself and underestimate the duration or difficulty of a hike. Start slowly and build up to those weekend marathons. If the most exercise you usually get is walking to the pub and crawling back, you can use chair-lifts and cable-cars to reach high altitudes in some areas.

 Caution

Don't attempt a major hike alone. Notify someone of your route, destination and estimated time of return, and give them a mobile phone number on which you can be contacted (or can call for help if necessary – but bear in mind that reception may be impossible in some areas unless you have a satellite phone).

◆ It's advisable to inform the nearest DOC office of your intentions and ask for their advice before setting out. Check the conditions along your route and the times of any public transport connections (set out early to avoid missing the last bus). Take into account the time required for both ascents and descents. If you're unable to return by the time expected, let somebody know. If you realise that you're unable to reach your destination, for example due to tiredness or bad weather, turn back in good time or take a shorter route. If you get caught in a heavy storm, descend as quickly as possible or seek protection, e.g. in a DOC hut.

◆ Check the weather forecast, which is usually available from the local tourist office.

Generally, the higher the altitude, the more unpredictable the weather.

♦ Hiking, even in lowland areas, can be dangerous, so don't take any unnecessary risks. There are enough natural hazards, including avalanches, bad weather, rock-falls, rough terrain, snow and ice, and wet grass, without adding to them.

♦ Don't walk on closed tracks at any time (they're signposted). This is particularly important in the spring, when there's a danger of avalanches or rock-falls, and when tracks may be closed due to forestry work. If you're in doubt about a particular route, ask in advance at the local tourist office.

♦ Wear loose-fitting clothes and not, for example, tight jeans, which can become uncomfortable when you get warmed up. Shorts (short pants to Americans) are excellent in hot weather. Light cotton trousers are comfortable unless it's cold. You can wear your shorts underneath your trousers and remove your trousers when you've warmed up.

♦ Take a warm pullover, gloves (in winter) and a raincoat or cape. Mountain weather can change suddenly, and even in summer it's sometimes cold at high altitudes. A first-aid kit (for cuts and grazes), compass, identification, maps, small torch, a pocket knife and a mobile phone may also come in handy. A pair of binoculars is useful for spotting wildlife. Take a rucksack to carry your survival rations. A 35 to 40-litre capacity rucksack is best for day trips or a 65-litre capacity for longer hikes.

♦ Take sun protection, e.g. a hat, sunglasses and sun barrier cream, as you'll burn more easily at high altitudes (the ozone layer is thin in New Zealand and the sun can be very strong). Use a total sunblock cream on your lips, nose and eyelids, and take a scarf or handkerchief to protect your neck. You may also need to protect yourself against ticks and mosquitoes in some areas.

♦ Take water to prevent dehydration. This will also prove welcome when you discover that the restaurant or hotel that was 'just around the corner' is still miles away because you took a wrong turning.

♦ Don't take young children on difficult hikes unless you enjoy carrying them.

Impress upon children the importance of not wandering off on their own. If you lose anyone, particularly children, seek help as soon as possible and before nightfall. It's wise to equip children with a loud whistle, some warm clothing and a mobile phone (provided they are old enough to use it), in case they get lost.

Trekking Rules

Hikers are asked to observe the following general rules:

– Take care not to damage trees, flowers and bushes.
– Leave animals in peace (e.g. dogs mustn't be allowed to disturb farm animals).
– Be careful with fire and never start a fire in a forbidden area.
– Watch where you walk and keep to paths.
– Keep streams and lakes pure.
– Don't litter the countryside.
– Think of others.
– Close gates after use.

FISHING

Fishing, whether in the sea, rivers, streams or lakes, is one of the most popular participation sports in New Zealand and one of the few that doesn't involve a great deal of exertion

(unless you're fighting a 500kg marlin). Salmon and trout (brown and rainbow weighing up to 5kg) are plentiful in the country's lakes and rivers, and are the most popular freshwater catches. There are two species of salmon in New Zealand: Landlocked quinnats (which spawn near the source of the country's main rivers), which can weigh up to 11kg, and sea-run quinnats (which emerge from the sea to spawn in river estuaries) that rarely exceed 1kg.

Fishing Licences		
	Period	
For	Whole Season	24-hour
Family	$151	
Adult	$116	$23
Junior	$23	$7

*Juniors aged 12-17, under 12s free

The fishing season varies, depending on the area and the catch, and usually starts around 1st October and finishes some time between 30th April and 30th June. Signs showing what you can catch, the limits and the season, are displayed on beaches throughout the country.

Fishing tackle can be imported into New Zealand without restriction (and can be purchased in the USA via the internet at huge savings over local prices), although it's wise not to import fishing flies, as they must be fumigated before passing through customs (at your expense), which can be frustrating bearing in mind their relatively small cost.

All anglers require a fishing licence, which is valid from 1st October until 30th September of the following year. They can be purchased from tackle and sports shops, although Maori claim they have the right (enshrined in the Treaty of Waitangi) to fish without a licence and this has occasionally been upheld by the courts. Note that you must have the licence with you when fishing and obey the rules and regulations (there are huge fines for not doing so!). An adult is anyone aged 18 or over (on 1st October for the following season), a junior is someone aged 12-17, while children under 12 can fish for free. A family consists of two adults and up to five children or juniors, You can buy a licence online from Fish & Game New Zealand (⌨ www.fishandgame.org.nz) – the cost (2011-2012 season) is shown in the table opposite.

A fishing licence allows you to fish in any area except Lake Taupo, where you must buy a local licence. There are heavy fines for unlicenced anglers plus court costs.

New Zealand's clear coastal waters are ideal for sea fishing; deep-sea fishing is also popular, although it's naturally more expensive as it requires the hire of a boat and special equipment. The best location for deep-sea fishing is the north-east of the North Island, while other good spots include the Bay of Islands around Russell, Mercury Bay, Tutukaka near Whangari, Tauranga and Whakatane. Some avid fishermen even venture as far as the Chatham Islands, 850km (528mi) east of New Zealand. Boats and tackle can be hired throughout New Zealand, and no licence is required for game or deep-sea fishing. Popular catches include hammerhead, mako and thresher sharks; black, Pacific blue and striped marlin; kingfish (yellowtail), broadbill swordfish and tuna (which is also the Maori word for eel).

It's possible to hire a local guide (ask for a quotation first) to find the best local fishing spots. The New Zealand Professional Fishing Guides Association (PO Box 213, 295 Gladstone Road, Gisborne, ☎ 06-867 7874, ⌨ www.nzpfga.com) can also provide information and assistance. There are several good books about fishing in New Zealand, including the *North Island Trout Fishing Guide* and the *South Island Trout Fishing Guide*, both by John Kent (Pacific Island Books), and a number of magazines including *NZ Fishing News* and *NZ Fishing World*. There are also numerous websites for anglers, including ⌨ www.fishing.net.nz, www.flyfishingnz.co.nz, www.nzfishing.com and www.sportfishingnz.com.

Rock-fishing enthusiasts should wear a lifejacket at all times, as it's easy to get swept out to sea.

WATERSPORTS

New Zealand is a Mecca for watersports, the most popular of which are outlined below. All instructors and operators of organised watersports in New Zealand must comply with

Ministry of Transport safety codes, but it's wise to check that they do before booking.

There has been a spate of fatal boating and watersport-related accidents in recent years, many of which could have been avoided had the safety regulations been followed. All watersport participants should wear a lifejacket (which alone would prevent some 70 per cent of fatalities) and ensure that children wear them at ALL times. **A buoyancy vest isn't a substitute for a lifejacket!**

Jet-skiing

New Zealand invented jet-skiing (jet-boating) and it's enjoyed by people of all ages. A jet-ski (or jet-boat) is a propeller-less, LPG-powered craft which can reach up to 70kph (43mph), turn through 360 degrees within its own length and plane over just a few inches of water. Jet-skiing is usually done in coastal waters and on lakes, although jet-skis can also negotiate shallow river gorges that are inaccessible to most other craft. The most popular areas for jet-skiing pleasure rides are Waimakariri near Christchurch, the Buller and Makaroa regions, the Rangitaiki River gorges, and the Wanganui and Waikato River below the Huka Falls. Jet-skis can be hired in many beach resorts and on some inland lakes, where there are usually restrictions on their use.

⚠ Caution

Note that if you aren't an experienced rider it's wise to steer well clear of jet-skis, which are deadly in the wrong hands, both to riders and anyone who's unfortunate enough to come into contact with them.

Kayaking

Kayaking is broadly similar to canoeing and is a popular watersport, particularly among the less well-off watersports enthusiasts. Kayaking is enjoyed in coastal waters and on lakes and rivers, and can range from a sedate paddle along a lakeside to negotiating the torrents of a raging river gorge. Kayaks and safety equipment (a helmet should always be worn) can be bought or hired in most popular kayaking areas. Further information can be obtained from the New

Zealand Recreational Canoeing Association (NZRCA, PO Box 284, Wellington, ☎ 04-560 3590, 🖥 http://rivers.org.nz).

Rafting

Rafting is a slightly more challenging alternative to kayaking, entailing the navigation of often hostile white-water in a large inflatable raft accommodating four to eight people, and is an extremely popular sport in New Zealand. The most popular (and safe) way to raft is to take part in an organised trip, which includes a qualified guide and tuition. Trips cost between $75 and $150 per person per day, and range from short trips of an hour or two to expeditions of two to five days, with food and camping equipment included. Rafting is also a popular winter sport, when a wetsuit is considered essential. Rivers are graded on a scale I (gentle) to VI (unraftable), the best of which are generally considered to be the Kawarau, Rangitata and Shotover, all in the South Island. **Bear in mind that rafting is a high risk sport.**

For information, contact the New Zealand Rafting Association (🖥 www.nz-rafting.co.nz).

Rowing

New Zealanders are enthusiastic rowers and there are plenty of lakes and rivers on which to practise this sport in all its guises, including leisure and competitive rowing. The country also fields a team in dragon boat racing, which is particularly popular in south-east Asia.

Sailing

Sailing is one of New Zealand's favourite sports (the country boasts the highest per capita boat ownership in the world) and Auckland has even gone so far as to dub itself the 'City of Sails', and like Wellington (the windy city) has a reputation for being windy. (Land yachting is also popular in New Zealand, which is a major producer of land yachts.) Yacht harbours are found throughout the country, the most popular of which include the Bay of Islands, Hauraki Gulf and the Marlborough Sounds. More adventurous yachtsmen venture to the Pacific islands, which, with their idyllic climate and unspoilt beauty, make ideal yachting destinations.

Sailing isn't necessarily a pursuit just for the wealthy (unless you yearn to own an ocean-going luxury yacht), as there are numerous opportunities to hire a boat and spend some time on the ocean waves or pottering around the coastline. A variety of boats are available for 'bare-boating', where a hire company provides the yacht and sailing equipment and you provide the crew and provisions. For less intrepid sailors, it's possible to hire a professionally-crewed yacht, where the crew also wait on you.

There are sailing clubs throughout the country, details of which can be obtained from Yachting New Zealand (PO Box 33-789, Takapuna, Auckland, ☎ 09-488 9325, 🖥 www.yachtingnz.org.nz). Another useful organisation is Sailing New Zealand (🖥 www.nzsailing.net), which provides coaching for beginners, advanced sailing tips, and resources for sailing clubs and experts.

New Zealand secured an impressive and unexpected victory in the 1995 America's Cup and successfully defended the title in the Hauraki Gulf in 2000 (it has also contested the last two finals – the most recent in Valencia, Spain in 2007 – losing to Alinghi, Switzerland each time).

Sailors must observe all warning signs and never go to sea in an unseaworthy boat, which should be regularly serviced and have sufficient fuel (running out of fuel in bad weather can prove fatal). Other vital equipment includes a radio/cellphone, flares, first-aid kit, whistle, water, survival rations and a secondary form of propulsion. Also bear in mind that the weather conditions around the coast can change in minutes. You can check the coastal weather conditions and the state of rivers and lakes via the Met Service (☎ 0900-999 + area code or 🖥 www.metservice.co.nz).

Scuba Diving & Snorkelling

New Zealand is a paradise for scuba divers and snorkellers, and the country's waters are teeming with exotic fish and plant life. Jacques Cousteau rated New Zealand's waters as one of the top ten diving destinations in the world. Popular diving spots include the Poor Knights Islands near Whangerei (where the waters are particularly clear), the South Island fjords (famous for their unusual red and black coral) and the kelp forests

off Stewart Island (with their huge paua shell fish). The main diving season is from February to June, although in the warmer, more sheltered waters off the Bay of Islands near Auckland, it's possible to dive year round. The former Greenpeace flagship 'Rainbow Warrior' (sunk by French secret service agents in an operation against anti-nuclear protestors) has been scuttled in this area to provide a haven for sea life.

Along the coast there are numerous dive stores providing tuition, equipment rental, the filling of air bottles, and information on dive locations and organised trips. Divers need a Professional Association of Diving Instructors (PADI) certificate, and tuition is offered in most diving areas in New Zealand. Always learn with a qualified and reputable outfit and avoid 'cowboy' operators. Further information can be obtained from the New Zealand Underwater Association (PO Box 875, Auckland, ☎ 09-623 3252, 🖥 www.nzunderwater.org.nz).

A good book for divers is *Top New Zealand Dive Sites* by Gillian & Darryl Torckler (Penguin).

Surfing

New Zealanders don't quite share the passion for surfing of their Australian neighbours, although it's a popular pursuit. Many coastal areas have a surf lifesaving club (SLSC) for children and adults, where surfing, swimming and surf rescue combine as a sport, leisure pursuit and public service, i.e. lifesavers on beaches and at swimming pools. The best surfing areas are around Auckland and Dunedin. Windsurfing and river surfing are also popular in New Zealand.

Information can be obtained from Surfing New Zealand (Private Bag 1, PA Bow Street, Raglan, New Zealand, ☎ 07-825 0018, 💻 www.surfingnz.co.nz).

Swimming

Most New Zealanders are taught to swim at an early age, and swimming is a popular leisure and competitive sport. Despite the country's abundance of coastal waters, rivers and lakes, it isn't necessary to head for the great outdoors if you're a keen swimmer. Most towns have at least one public indoor swimming pool, some of which are equipped with waterchutes, wave machines and a range of other facilities, such as saunas and Jacuzzis.

In several places it's possible to swim with dolphins, which, apart from the thrill, is claimed to have valuable therapeutic powers. 'Dolphin swimming' is possible (subject to dolphins being able to fit in with your schedule) in the Bay of Islands, Kaikoura and Whakatane in the South Island.

Some 80 beaches are patrolled by members of Surf Life Saving New Zealand (💻 www.slsnz.org.nz), which has over 3,500 volunteer lifeguards and makes some 350,000 safety interventions during the summer season. On patrolled beaches (officially from 10am to 5pm) you should always swim within the yellow and red flags, which indicate the safest swimming area in the prevailing conditions and also the area under closest scrutiny by lifesavers. Surf-lifesaving sports are also popular and there are national championships and international competitions.

Swimmers are urged by lifesaving associations never to swim outside patrolled areas – most beach drownings occur on unpatrolled beaches.

Take care not to venture too far out, as it isn't uncommon for swimmers to be swept out to sea. Beware of unpatrolled beaches with rips – channels (often indicated by darker water) where the water flows faster out to sea than the average swimmer can handle – which are the biggest killers and can lurk beneath the most calm seas. There's a danger of stinging jellyfish and sharks in some waters, although your chance of encountering either on patrolled beaches is small. Shark attacks occur every few years around New Zealand's coastline, but very few prove fatal. If you get into trouble while swimming off a beach manned by lifesavers, you should raise one arm in the air, which will alert the lifesavers.

Before swimming in public waters, you may wish to check the water quality, which varies considerably, which you can do via the Consumer Institute website (💻 www.consumer.org.nz/reports/swimming-water-quality) or by contacting the relevant council.

For information about swimming clubs, lessons and competitions in New Zealand, see 💻 www.swimmingnz.org.nz and www.swiminfo.co.nz.

SKIING

Few people associate New Zealand with snow, but its first commercial ski slopes opened in 1947 and the country is internationally recognised as a top skiing destination. The skiing season extends throughout the European and North American summer, beginning in June and ending in November, and professional skiers and ski bums from the northern hemisphere often ski and train in New Zealand out of their season.

There are 14 commercial skiing areas, in both the North and the South Islands, all accessible by road. All skiing areas have ski lifts, ski schools and equipment rental facilities, and offer a choice of accommodation from guest houses to good quality hotels. However, few skiing areas have accommodation virtually on-piste, as is common in Europe, and a short journey is usually necessary to reach the slopes. A number of package tour operators offer skiing package holidays.

If you're travelling independently, full day lift passes in the 2011 season cost from $95 (child from $52) per day for the Treble Cone/Coronet

Peak region. Bear in mind that usually the more expensive the pass, the more crowded the skiing – you pay for the better facilities and piste grooming. Equipment rental is around $50 per day (skis, poles and boots) and lessons around $50 for a half-day group class. Nordic (cross-country) skiing is also possible in New Zealand, where there's one Nordic skiing area and 12 club fields (open to the public) with more basic facilities.

Helicopter and glacier-skiing are increasingly popular in the South Island, although both are only for the experienced and are expensive. Several operators offer off-piste heli-skiing in the southern Alps and you can glacier-ski the Tasman Glacier, although this will cost you $1,000 or more. An unusual feature of New Zealand skiing is that a range of facilities not usually associated with skiing is also offered in (or near) ski resorts, including bungee-jumping, canoeing, jet-skiing, rafting and trekking. These are usually available in the valleys, which may be free of snow.

> ☑ SURVIVAL TIP
>
> If you're planning to go off-peak skiing, you should have an avalanche transceiver or a personal locator distress beacon (see 🖳 www.beacons.org.nz) in case of an accident or avalanche.

Safety information is available from the New Zealand Mountain Safety Council (PO Box 6027, Wellington, ☎ 04-385 7162, 🖳 www.mountainsafety.org.nz). For general information about skiing in New Zealand, see 🖳 http://snow.co.nz, www.nzski.com and www.ski-newzealand.co.nz.

North Island

Whakapapa, Tukino and Turoa are the North Island's main skiing areas, situated on Mount Ruapehu (an active volcano) around four hours by road from Auckland (23km northeast of Ohakune). They attract around 500,000 visitors a year and the high altitude (2,800m/9,186ft) means that skiing is possible from June to well into November.

South Island

One of the most popular ski resorts in the South Island is Mount Hutt, which is around an hour by road from Christchurch. Its location and advanced snow-making system mean that it's often the first resort to open and the last to close. Other resorts include Lake Wanaka, located in New Zealand's 'Alpine' zone, five hours from Christchurch, which includes Cardrona, Snow Farm, Snow Park and Treble Cone. It's the country's premier winter resort, with slopes suitable for beginners and experts, plus facilities for heli-skiing. The powder snow and demanding terrain have also made the area popular with snowboarders. Wanaka is also the only ski resort in New Zealand where it's possible to find accommodation on the mountain.

Queenstown has the best all-round facilities, in addition to two world-class ski areas, the Remarkables and Coronet Peak, both within 30 minutes' drive of the town. Queenstown boasts over 100 restaurants, night-clubs, cafés and bars, several large hotels and good shopping. It's also possible to enjoy trout fishing, or go wine tasting in the nearby Otago vineyards.

The free (in New Zealand) *NZ Ski and Snowboard Guide* published annually by Brown Bear (🖳 www.brownbear.co.nz/ski) offers a wealth of useful information.

CYCLING

Cycle touring is a popular sport and pastime in New Zealand, although it's some way behind countries such as France. While it's true that much of the terrain is mountainous or hilly, roads are generally well surfaced and largely traffic-free. The hilly terrain is a boon for mountain biking, which is also popular, although it's banned in New Zealand's national parks. Helmets must be worn when cycling anywhere in New Zealand.

It's hardly worthwhile taking your own bicycle to New Zealand, where a wide range of new and used bikes are available at reasonable prices. It's also possible to hire touring cycles, mountain bikes and even tandems in many areas. Organised cycling package holidays are popular, and in some areas (such as Mount Ruapehu on the Otago Peninsula) there are shuttle bus services that take you to the top of the mountains or extinct volcanoes. These allow you to experience the pleasure of the downhill descent, without the pain of the uphill journey.

One contradiction to New Zealand's otherwise cyclist-friendly culture is that cycles cannot be taken on most buses or trains. Long-distance

coaches accept bikes (for a fee of around $10), but usually only if you remove the pedals and wrap the chain (e.g. in newspaper) – see **Chapter 10**. Note also that, despite New Zealand's relatively low crime rate, the theft of bicycles is high and care should be taken to secure your bike when it isn't in use, particularly if it's an expensive model.

Useful books on cycling include the *Pedallers' Paradise* series and Lonely Planet's, *Cycling NZ*. Further information can be obtained from Cycling NZ (💻 http://cyclingnz.com) and Mountain Bike NZ (PO Box 1057, Wellington, ☎ 04-473 8386, 💻 www.mountainbike.co.nz).

GOLF

Golf is the one of most popular participant sports in New Zealand, with over 500,000 players and around 125,000 club members. The country has over 400 golf courses – it's said that nowhere in New Zealand is more than 50km/31mi from a course – including some of the most beautiful in the world. Several courses have gained international recognition, including Cape Kidnappers (Hawke's Bay), Millbrook (Queenstown), Oreti Sands (Invercargill), Paraparaumu Beach (north of Wellington), Royal Wellington (Wellington), Titirangi (Auckland) and Wairakei International (Taupo).

Courses are relatively uncrowded, which makes them increasingly popular with visitors, particularly Japanese golfers who, coming from such a densely populated land, are unaccustomed to the choice and space of New Zealand's golf courses. An added attraction for most golfers (certainly those of more modest means) is the relatively liberal attitude of most golf clubs, which, with the exception of a few top clubs, don't have long waiting lists or high membership fees.

However, it isn't a cheap sport, even in New Zealand. The vast majority of clubs also welcome non-members, a round costing anything from $50 to well over $100, although players who are members of other New Zealand clubs or Australian clubs play for a lower 'affiliate' fee. The larger clubs have resident professionals, and clubs, carts (known as trundlers) and motorised buggies for hire, while smaller clubs offer fewer facilities – you may even be expected to leave your green fees in an honesty box! Typical fees for equipment hire are electric cart ($40), club hire ($50), shoes ($10) and golf bag cart/trundler ($10).

The tourist authorities can provide information about golf in New Zealand or you can contact New Zealand Golf (PO Box 331678, Takapuna, North Shore City 0740, ☎ 09-485 3230, 💻 www.nzgolf.org.nz). Interesting publications for golfers include, *100 Essential New Zealand Golf Holes* by Tom Hyde (Awa Press) and the *New Zealand Golf Guide* (💻 http://nzgolfguide.myshopify.com), which offers up to 50 per cent discount on green fees at over 260 North and South Island golf courses. Interesting websites for golfers include 💻 www.bestofgolfnewzealand.com, www.golf.co.nz and www.golfnewzealand.com.

CLIMBING & MOUNTAINEERING

New Zealand's greatest sporting hero is Sir Edmund Hillary (1919-2008), one of the first two people to conquer Everest. The country is home to some of the highest peaks in the southern hemisphere, offering challenges for even the most experienced mountaineers. Most mountaineers head for the Southern Alps, where it's usual to hire a guide or take advice from a local Alpine club, of which there are several. Rock climbing is also popular. In the

North Island, popular climbing areas include the Mount Eden Quarry near Auckland, Whanganui Bay and Motuoapa near Lake Taupo. The Wharepape rock climbing field near Te Awamutu offers over 40 different climbs suitable for both advanced climbers and beginners. In the South Island, Port Hills near Christchurch and Castle Hill are popular climbing spots. Tuition and equipment (for sale and hire) are available in climbing areas.

Note that a number of climbers are killed each year in New Zealand, many of whom are inexperienced and reckless, and others owe their survival to rescuers who risk their own lives to rescue them.

 Caution

It's extremely foolish, not to mention highly dangerous, to venture into the mountains without an experienced guide, proper preparation, excellent physical condition, sufficient training and the appropriate equipment and supplies.

Useful addresses for mountaineers and climbers include the New Zealand Alpine Club (PO Box 786, Christchurch 8140, ☎ 03-377 7595, 🖳 http://alpineclub.org.nz) and the NZ Mountain Guides Association (PO Box 10, Aoraki, Mount Cook, ☎ 03-435 0336, 🖳 www. nzmga.org.nz). A useful website for climbers and mountaineers is 🖳 www.climb.co.nz, which includes information about equipment, mountain safety and weather conditions.

ADVENTURE SPORTS

Although New Zealand may have a rather staid reputation (undeservedly) in certain areas, this certainly isn't true when it comes to adventure sports. The New Zealanders' passion for dangerous sports, which often involve throwing yourself from great heights or challenging the forces of nature, is virtually unparalleled. Sporting daredevils certainly need never be short of challenges in New Zealand, where ever more risky adventure sports are continually being invented by thrill-seeking (or should it be suicidal?) New Zealanders.

Adventure sports include the following:

Abseiling & Rap Jumping

Abseiling is popular in New Zealand and can be done throughout the country. Rap jumping is a New Zealand invention and much like abseiling, except that it involves descending a cliff face head first rather than feet first. The Bay of Islands, Queenstown and Wanaka are popular rap jumping areas, where instructors are available to initiate newcomers into the sport.

Bungee Jumping

New Zealand (Bungy land) invented bungy (or bungee) jumping – entrusting your life to an elasticated rope. Queenstown is the main centre, where you can jump from the Kawarau River Bridge (43m) or the Skippers Bridge (71m). If those aren't high enough, you can try jumping from the 102m Pipeline or from a helicopter (but preferably not when coming in to land!). Bungy jumping can also be experienced in many other locations throughout the country (see 🖳 www.bungy.co.nz).

Caving & Cave Rafting

Caving is a popular sport and there are numerous clubs. However, New Zealanders have also invented cave rafting, whereby intrepid cavers float through underground cave systems on large inner tubes. Cave rafting is possible at Waitomo (North Island), and Westport and Greymouth (South Island).

Flightseeing

When New Zealanders aren't scrambling over their country's terrain or wading through its water, they enjoy nothing more than taking to the air and admiring it from above, a pursuit which has been dubbed flightseeing. You can take a trip (or learn to fly) in a sea- or float-plane, a helicopter, a vintage aircraft or even a hot air balloon, from airfields (or fields) throughout the country.

Glacier Walking

A walk along a glacier is one way to appreciate one of the most incredible feats of nature. The Fox, Franz Josef and Tasman Glaciers in the Southern Alps are open to walkers, although it's best to join a guided tour if you aren't an experienced mountaineer. Never ignore warning signs or get too close to glaciers, as ice falls can prove fatal (as some Australian tourists discovered in 2008).

Hang Gliding & Paragliding

Hang Gliding and Paragliding (also called parapenting) are popular in New Zealand, particular in mountainous areas such as Queenstown and Wanaka. It's possible to try tandem hang gliding or paragliding (with or attached to an instructor) if you don't have the time or inclination to undergo training. For information, see the New Zealand Hang Gliding and Paragliding Association website (💻 www. nzhgpa.org.nz).

Parachuting & Sky-diving

Both solo and tandem parachuting and sky-diving are available in New Zealand, where there are centres near Auckland, Greymouth, Mount Hutt, Napier, Nelson, Queenstown and Taupo.

See 💻 www.nzskydive.com for information.

Parasailing

Parasailing involves being towed behind a fast moving boat while attached to a parachute. When the driver accelerates, you ascend into the air from a launching platform at the back of the boat. Unlike paragliding, it can be enjoyed by absolute beginners without being strapped to an instructor.

OTHER SPORTS

The following is a selection of other popular sports in New Zealand:

Baseball

Baseball has been popular for many years in New Zealand, where it's played only at amateur level.

Basketball

Basketball is growing in popularity and is widely played in schools. There's also a national basketball league, the season commencing in April and finishing around October. The national basketball team is named the Tall Blacks, a tongue-in-cheek pun on the name of the national rugby team. See 💻 www.basketball.org.nz for more information.

Bowls

Lawn bowls is a sport enjoyed mainly, but not exclusively, by older people in New Zealand. There are outdoor bowling greens in most towns and also indoor bowling greens in some areas, which are in use all year round. Bowling clubs often serve tea and cucumber sandwiches in the British tradition, which tells you something about the kind of members they tend to attract. New Zealand is one of the world's leading bowls nations (see 💻 www. bowlsnz.co.nz).

Hockey

Hockey is played to a high standard in New Zealand by both men and women, although it loses out to more popular sports in terms of media coverage. There are club and national teams, and the New Zealand women's team has been particularly successful in recent years. For more information, see 💻 www.hockeynz.co.nz. You can also play underwater hockey in New Zealand, also called octopush.

Horse Riding

New Zealand has a worldwide reputation for breeding high quality bloodstock, and horses still have a working role on many farms, where horse-riding remains the best means of crossing the often rough terrain. Although competitive riding is common in New Zealand, the most popular form of riding is 'trekking', which involves spending anything from a day to a week or more riding across the country's beaches, farmland, forests and hills. Stables are found in all areas, where it's possible to hire a horse and tack (or stable your own horse) and join an organised trip. A hard hat must always be worn when riding.

For information, see 💻 www.nzequestrian. org.nz and www.horsetalk.co.nz.

New Zealand has produced a number of world class show-jumping riders and achieved notable success in international competitions and the Olympics (although the nearest most New Zealanders ever get to a horse is losing their shirt on them).

Hunting

Despite New Zealand's conservation-minded image, hunting has a large following, and there are few inhibitions about bagging the local wildlife. Sika stags are hunted in the North Island and red stags in the North and the South Islands, while in the more mountainous areas, hunters take pot-shots at wily tahr and chamois. Most hunters hire a local guide to lead them to their prey, due to the difficult terrain and unpredictable weather in the main hunting areas.

On a more modest level, ducks, geese, pheasant, quail and swans are the main game birds in New Zealand. The only drawback for the keen hunter (or good news for their quarry) is that a short season is enforced, commencing the first weekend in May and extending for a maximum of eight weeks. A permit is required to own a gun in New Zealand. Further information can be obtained from the NZ Shooting Federation (PO Box 72-846, Papakura, Auckland, ☎ 09-296 1308, 🖳 www.nzshootingfed.org.nz). Boar hunting is also very popular in New Zealand (see 🖳 http://go-the-wholehog.com), where there's even a *NZ Pig Hunter* magazine.

For more information, see www.fishnhunt.co.nz, www.huntingandfishing.co.nz and www.nzhuntinginfo.com.

Marching

Marching is a traditional New Zealand female sport which dates back to the 1930s and is still popular today. It's taken seriously and participants are divided into four grades: Adults (16+), junior (12 to 16 years), midget (7 to 12 years) and introductory (unborn).

Netball

Although most New Zealand sports have a predominantly masculine image, women participate in most sporting activities and also have their own sports. One of the most popular women's sports in New Zealand is (English) netball, which is generally taken much more seriously here than in the 'mother' country. New Zealand netball is known for its precision and strict adherence to the rules and traditions, which makes it much more than just a casual pastime. The national netball team (the Silver Ferns) has enjoyed considerable success in international competitions. See www.mynetball.co.nz for further information.

Tennis & Squash

Tennis is played throughout New Zealand and is particularly popular in the more fashionable suburbs of Auckland and Wellington. Most places aren't far from public courts or a private club. If you wish to join a private club, you won't find it particularly expensive or conservative, although most have strict dress codes. For information, see 🖳 www.tennisnz.com.

Squash is also a popular sport, in which New Zealand has produced a number of world-class players, including world champions Susan Devoy, Leilani Joyce and Ross Norman. Details are available from Squash New Zealand (☎ 09-815 0970, 🖳 www.squashnz.co.nz).

Triathlon

The triathlon, a gruelling combination of swimming, running and cycling (carried out consecutively on the same day), is as popular in New Zealand as it is in Australia. Many New Zealanders participate in triathlon events simply as a way of keeping (super) fit, although there are also many highly regarded competitive triathlons for athletes of all abilities and both sexes. See 🖳 www.triathlon.org.nz for more information.

17.
SHOPPING

Historically, New Zealand hasn't been noted for providing a very interesting or exciting shopping experience. Traditionally, many New Zealanders were largely self-sufficient and shopped only for the basic necessities that they couldn't grow or make themselves, and they still have a preference for making and growing things themselves wherever possible, particularly in rural areas. However, this has changed considerably in recent decades as the country has become more affluent, with an influx of international chain stores and designer shops in towns and cities. Naturally, you won't find the same comprehensive choice of shops or merchandise on offer in New Zealand as in the USA, the UK or even Australia, because the market is so much smaller than in those countries. However, a shopping trip in New Zealand is now a much more enjoyable and rewarding experience than was previously the case.

Although New Zealand shoppers complain endlessly about increasing prices – which are an increasing concern – they generally get a better deal than they did in the past. The removal or reduction of punitive taxes on imported goods (such as cars and high-tech consumer products) has made many goods better value, although they've risen in price in dollar terms, and increased competition has also helped reduce prices. Competition has additionally forced retailers to take more care in the quality of goods and services they offer and how they present their wares, which in the past was at best uninspired and at worst poor.

Those from the UK will recognise several names on the New Zealand high street, although it's important to note that stores don't sell the same goods as their British equivalents. Australians will also find some of their favourite stores in New Zealand, many of which operate on a franchise basis. As in most other Western countries, modern shopping centres have sprung up outside towns, with the result that many stores have moved out of town centres and left them run-down and neglected.

Credit cards (e.g. Visa and MasterCard) are widely accepted in shops in New Zealand, even in out of the way places, although debit cards are the preferred method of payment (some stores also provide charge cards). Cheques may also be accepted in some stores, although most are reluctant to accept them as there are no cheque guarantee cards in New Zealand.

Goods and services tax (GST) at 15 per cent is levied on almost everything you buy in New Zealand. You can assume that tax is included in the price unless it's indicated otherwise.

SHOPPING HOURS

The standard shopping hours in New Zealand are 9am until 5pm, Mondays to Fridays. Many stores also open on Saturdays and some open on Sundays. In resorts you'll also find most stores open in the evenings. Most shops have late night opening one day a week (usually Thursday or Friday), when they open until 8.30 or 9pm. A limited amount of Sunday shopping is permitted in New Zealand, but because many shops stay closed while others open, planning a Sunday shopping trip is a hit and miss affair.

As in other countries, supermarkets tend to buck the trend and most are open seven days a week, e.g. from 7am to 10pm. You'll also find that the traditional New Zealand 'dairy' (see below) operates an open-all-hours policy, remaining open from when the proprietor gets up until he's too tired to continue (usually until 9 or 10pm).

All shops are required to close under the Shop Trading Hours Repeal Act 1990 on Christmas Day, Good Friday and Easter Sunday, and on ANew ZealandAC Day until 1pm (see 🖥 www.ers.govt.nz/audienceinfo/shop.html).

LOCAL SHOPS & SERVICES

Despite the proliferation of out-of-town shopping centres, there are still plenty of small local shops in most towns and city suburbs in New Zealand, although fewer than previously. Shops tend to follow the British pattern, with a baker, butcher, chemist (pharmacy), greengrocer (fruit and vegetables) and grocer (general provisions). Some shopping centres in towns offer two or three hours' free parking, to attract shoppers and deter them from going to out of town shopping centres. Most suburban shopping streets have a Pacific Island shop selling housewares, toys, and assorted other household essentials and bric-a-brac. A curiosity left over from New Zealand's British heritage, although becoming less common, is that fresh milk is delivered to homes each morning in most cities (although no longer in bottles).

In smart suburbs in major cities, many shops that used to sell everyday goods (such as food) have been taken over by outlets selling arts and crafts, gifts, stationery, and Maori and Polynesian artifacts and reproductions (Qualmark – 🖥 www.qualmark.co.nz – is New Zealand tourism's official quality mark). Although interesting for visitors, these are of little use to residents, who often need to visit shopping centres and supermarkets for the essentials. This is particularly true in many shopping arcades in Auckland and Wellington.

In common with other countries, petrol (gas) stations sell a selection of basic grocery items, and are handy in the evenings and on Saturday afternoons and Sundays when most shops are closed.

Dairies

The dairy is a great New Zealand tradition. It isn't just a dairy – in fact in most cases it isn't a dairy at all (there appear to be few New Zealanders who can remember when dairies made butter and cheese) – and a more accurate description of a dairy nowadays is a corner shop, convenience store or mini-market. The dairy was once the mainstay of communities, where everyone did most of their daily shopping.

Nowadays, with the proliferation of supermarkets, most tend to be patronised only for odds and ends that have been forgotten at the supermarket or in emergencies, and most are suffering from declining trade and look rather run down. However, the traditional dairy soldiers on and is the one local outlet where you can be sure of buying essentials on Sundays, when most other stores are closed. Dairies are also a focal point for the local community and an excellent source of help, information, advice and local gossip.

Dairies sell a 'little bit of everything', particularly tinned and packet foods, plus fresh fruit, vegetables and meat, perhaps locally produced. There's usually a display of confectionery (lollies), a variety of soft drinks (but generally no alcohol) and an impressive range of ice cream, which is of excellent quality and consumed enthusiastically in New Zealand. A dairy is also often the best place to buy snacks (at any time of day) and usually offers a choice of sandwiches and pies, although they may be limited to meat (lamb mince) or bacon and egg. In country areas, you may also find hardware and clothing (although you shouldn't expect much choice). Dairies are also a good place to buy the local newspaper and a selection of magazines, and they also distribute free newspapers and real estate 'magazines'.

Dairies are noted for their personal service (they're usually owner-operated) and if there's anything you particularly want, the friendly proprietor will usually obtain it for you, although prices are inevitably higher than in supermarkets.

SUPERMARKETS

Most New Zealanders do the bulk of their shopping at supermarkets, which offer convenient one-stop shopping, longer opening hours (e.g. 7am to 10pm), a wide choice of products (although not as large as in other Western countries) and free parking. In addition to food, supermarkets sell household and cleaning products, toiletries, newspapers and a selection of magazines, stationery, DVDs and books. Supermarkets also sell wine and beer, but don't sell any other alcohol, which you must buy from a liquor store (see below). The better quality supermarkets offer some popular brands from Australia, Europe and the US, although shipping costs make these prohibitively expensive and there's usually a local New Zealand equivalent that's just as good.

Countdown offer an online shopping service (🖥 http://shop.countdown.co.nz) in various parts of the country, where orders can be placed by computer and delivered to your home. Deliveries cost from around $8.25 to over $20, depending on how much you spend and where you live.

The largest supermarket chain is Countdown (🖥 www.countdown.co.nz), which has rebranded its Foodtown and Woolworths (which it bought in 2002) stores in the last few years. It's part of the Australian-owned Progressive Enterprises Ltd. (🖥 www.progressive.co.nz) which operates some 160 stores nationwide.

New World (🖥 www.newworld.co.nz) is Countdown's main competitor and an excellent, up-market supermarket chain with over 130 stores countrywide (voted 'Most Trusted Supermarket' by *Readers Digest*). It offers a good choice of fresh food, excellent meat, a delicatessen section and a wide choice of reasonably-priced wines (mainly from NZ and Australia). There's also a useful self-serve section for nuts, sweets, dried fruit, etc., where you just fill a plastic bag and write the number on it with the pen provided. New World offers 'Fly Buys' points (which you can trade for goods – 🖥 www.flybuys.co.nz) and fuel dockets, but doesn't offer online shopping or home deliveries.

Some supermarkets, such as Pak 'n' Save (🖥 www.paknsave.co.nz), operate on a pile-'em-high-and-sell-'em-cheap basis, which means you can expect warehouse-style decor (i.e. none), less choice, budget brands and minimal service – but rock-bottom prices. Good for stocking up on basics, but not so good for meat and produce.

In the Consumer's Institute (🖥 www.consumer.org.nz) annual price surveys, Pak 'n Save (no checkout bags) consistently comes out cheapest, followed by Countdown, New World and Warehouse Extra (🖥 www.thewarehouse.co.nz). The larger Countdown stores provide the widest choice of food, including organic food.

Some supermarkets (e.g. New World) offer self checkout desks, with attendants on hand, which use a scale in the bagging area to confirm that the products purchased have been correctly scanned. New World also provides bag-packers, although they don't take your bags to your car, which you do in a trolley (called a trundler in New Zealand).

FOOD

One of the pleasures of living in New Zealand is the wide range of fresh food that's available at affordable prices. Shopping for most foods, particularly fruit and vegetables, tends to be seasonal, as most shops sell only what's available from local farmers. Unlike in Europe and North America, you cannot usually buy most produce out of season (e.g. strawberries in mid-winter) and when available, imported produce is expensive. The authorities are also careful about what they allow into the country as a precaution against importing pests and diseases.

New Zealand is a major food producer (and exporter), particularly in meat, dairy produce and fruit, and although the choice isn't as large as in some other countries (particularly prepared meals), the quality is excellent and prices competitive. In recent years New Zealanders have become more cosmopolitan in their approach to food and cooking, a consequence of which is that there are numerous delis, specialist food stores and an increasing number of deli counters in supermarkets.

However, although supermarkets, particularly New World, now sell a wider selection of quality foods that were once the preserve of delis and posh food shops, you're unlikely to find many knowledgeable staff, and specialist food stores invariably define and keep redefining the things that are special. Artisanal foods rarely turn up in a supermarket and although a specialist food store may cost more, it can make you feel good – something a supermarket will rarely do. Other good places to buy artisanal foods are farmers' markets (🖥 www.farmersmarket.org.nz).

An influx of Asian immigrants has led to the easy availability of a wide variety of Asian foods such as noodles, shitake mushrooms and pak choi (bok choy), especially in the major cities, which also have Asian supermarkets. The latter are common in areas with high Asian populations, particularly Auckland, and stock a variety of imported canned and preserved foods and a mixture of imported and local fruit and vegetables. In small towns you can usually buy some foreign foods at a deli and large supermarkets also stock a selection.

Food prices have risen in New Zealand in recent years, with the cost of imported food impacted by the fall in the value of the NZ$, while food manufacturers were also hit by high commodity costs. In the year to June 2011, food prices rose 7.5 per cent, but by January 2012 the annual increase was just 1 per cent (source: Statistics NZ – 🖥 www.stats.govt.nz). The apparent discrepancy is largely due to seasonal fluctuations in prices, although in the real world most people believe the increase is much higher. However, food inflation is relatively low compared with many other countries, with most produce being seasonal and home grown and not a lot imported.

Those from the UK and USA should note that foodstuffs in New Zealand shops are sold in metric quantities, although it's still common for older people to ask for half a pound of butter or two pounds of potatoes. This is a foreign language to the ears of young shop assistants, who have never heard of Imperial weights and measures. Conversion tables are shown in **Appendix D**.

A price guide for the most popular foods is published by Statistics New Zealand (🖥 www.stats.govt.nz).

Meat

Meat is usually good value in New Zealand, as it's one of the country's major industries, and most families can afford to serve meat at each meal. There are over 40m sheep in New Zealand and the country exports $1bn of lamb annually. Not surprisingly, lamb is good value and all joints are inexpensive and readily available, plus a range of lamb products such as burgers, paté, pies and sausages (known as snarlers). Hogget is one-year-old lamb, i.e. it actually is a lamb and not mutton sold as lamb, as in many other countries. If you have the freezer space, you may wish to consider buying a whole lamb (bought either whole or jointed as preferred), which, with prices starting as low as $100, represents good value.

Poultry, pork and beef are also common, but less popular than lamb, although New Zealanders like their steak, which is excellent quality (it's sometimes served garnished with oysters, known as a 'carpetbagger'). Venison is also an increasingly popular meat and is available from many butchers and supermarkets (New Zealand has become a major exporter in recent years).

You can buy meat from a supermarket or a local butcher, where it may be fresher and locally produced – the grazing lamb you passed on your way to work in the morning could be riding home in your car in the evening! However, be wary of buying cheap meat, particularly special buys, at some of the cheaper supermarkets, which can be of poor quality. The two main chains of 'family' butchers are the Mad Butcher (☏ 09-531 5911, 🖥 www.madbutcher.co.nz), with 37 stores nationwide, and the Aussie Butcher (eight stores, North Island only, 🖥 http://theaussiebutcher.com).

Dairy Products

Dairy products are plentiful and cheap in New Zealand, so much so that motels leave a free carton of milk in rooms. They're one of the country's major exports and it even exports to Caribbean countries. The quality and variety of dairy produce is good, with excellent butter, cheese and yoghurt. The country now produces a much broader range of cheese, including many delicious creamy blue cheeses, which are a local speciality, and goats' and sheeps' cheese. It's also possible to buy New Zealand versions of soft cheeses such as Brie and Camembert, plus imported cheeses, although these are expensive and must usually be purchased from a delicatessen rather than a dairy or supermarket.

Fruit & Vegetables

New Zealand greengrocers (and supermarket fruit and vegetable departments) offer a relatively wide choice of fruit and vegetables, which is midway between what you would find in Western Europe and a street market in the Pacific islands. Among the more commonplace Gala apples, pears, potatoes, strawberries and tomatoes, you'll also find a variety of exotic fruits and vegetables. Unusual produce includes boysenberries, feijoa (a lemon-like fruit with a much sweeter flavour), kiwano melons, the ubiquitous kiwi fruit (green and gold), kumara (a sweet potato and a staple of the Maori diet) and tamarillos, which have a subtle, slightly tart flavour.

In most regions you'll find roadside stalls selling fresh fruit (never pass up the chance to buy fresh cherries!) and vegetables, and you can also pick your own produce at many farms. Stalls often operate on the honour system – when they're unattended you leave the money for what you take in a box. This is a good way to buy kiwi fruit, which can be bought for just a few cents each when there's a bumper crop.

Seafood

A wide range of seafood is available in New Zealand, appealing to all tastes. If you want 'international' species such as cod and haddock, you can find them, but there's also a huge variety of local fish available. Local seafood includes green-lipped mussels, Pacific oysters, smoked eel, pipis, paua, toheroas (local clams) and shark (sometimes known as lemon fish). Note that New Zealand whitebait isn't the same fish as whitebait in other countries, but is a tiny, thread-like, transparent fish with a subtle flavour.

Generally, seafood isn't such good value as meat, as much of New Zealand's catch goes for export and the country's fish wholesalers often buy fish from South America to satisfy local demand. It's illegal to deal in trout commercially, therefore if you enjoy trout you usually need to catch it yourself. This isn't difficult, as the country's rivers, lakes and streams are teeming with brown and rainbow trout. The same applies to wild oysters, which are frequently found in New Zealand's clear waters, but which you aren't permitted to harvest.

Bakery & Confectionery

New Zealand bakers and supermarkets sell a fairly predictable range of bread and confectionery. You can buy white and brown loaves (sliced or unsliced) together with a variety of rolls in different shapes and sizes and pink iced buns, which are a national tradition. As anywhere, shop bread varies between delicious and tasteless, and it's usually a matter of looking around until you find a baker you like.

In some of the more adventurous bakeries and supermarkets (e.g. New World) you can also find French-style baguettes, croissants and Italian-style ciabatta bread. The 'national dessert' is pavlova (or 'pav'), named after the famous Russian ballerina. It consists of meringue, cream and fruit (usually kiwi fruit) and is available in all shapes and sizes, baked in-store and 'factory' made.

The largest bakery chains in New Zealand include Bakers Delight (☎ 03-9811 6111, 🖳 www.bakersdelight.co.nz) and Brumby's Bakeries (🖳 www.brumbys.com.au/brumbys/stores/?c=&s=nz). There are small family-owned bakers and patisseries in most towns, of which Pandoro Panetteria (☎ 09-588 5000, 🖳 www.pandoro.co.nz), with stores in Auckland and Wellington, deserves a special mention.

To find a good local baker, you can check the results of the 'bakery of the year' competition organised by the Baking Industry Association (🖳 www.bianz.co.nz).

MARKETS

Most towns have markets on one or two days a week, and in the major cities there may be a market (or a number) on most days. Markets are cheap, colourful and interesting, although you need to be careful what you buy. Items commonly for sale in markets include arts and crafts, books, clothes, fish, fruit and vegetables, household goods, jewellery and meat.

Food and farmers' markets (🖳 www.farmersmarket.org.nz) are usually the best place to buy fresh food. In areas with a large Maori community, there are Polynesian markets selling ethnic foodstuffs, seafood and textiles. Arts and crafts markets are also common in major cities and resort towns, where artisans can often be seen at work, although prices may be substantially higher than at local shops.

Flea markets are popular in the major cities and sell secondhand goods, including antiques, books, clothes, records and miscellaneous bric-a-brac. In some places you may find that what are advertised as markets are actually indoor mini-shopping centres, where the area is divided into small shop units operated on a permanent basis. Note that haggling isn't usual in New Zealand markets, where prices are displayed, although produce is sold off cheaper later in the day (when a cheeky offer may also be accepted). Check with your local council or tourist office for information about local markets.

DEPARTMENT & CHAIN STORES

New Zealand has a variety of department and chain stores. with branches in most major towns and cities. For the uninitiated, a department store is a large store, usually with several floors, which sells almost everything and may also include a food hall. In a large department store, each floor may be dedicated to a particular type of goods, such as ladies' or men's fashions, or furniture and furnishings. Leading department stores include Smith and Caughey's (🖳 www.smithandcaughey.co.nz) in Queen Street and Newmarket in Auckland, Kirkcaldie & Stains (🖳 www.kirkcaldies.co.nz) in Wellington and Ballantynes (🖳 www.ballantynes.co.nz) in Christchurch. Chain stores are simply stores with a number of branches, usually in different towns and cities.

One of the major New Zealand department stores is Farmers (🖳 www.farmers.co.nz), nothing to do with farming, which sells almost everything and offers medium quality goods at affordable prices, although its stores and products are uninspiring. Kmart (🖳 www.

kmart.co.nz) is another cheap-and-cheerful, sell-anything store, as is Warehouse (💻 www.thewarehouse.co.nz), whose slogan is 'where everyone gets a bargain'. Warehouse, similar to Wal-Mart in the US, is the country's largest discount chain store with over 250 huge, red, barn-like stores (colloquially referred to as 'The Red Shed', 'The Wuds' and 'WareWhare' – *whare* is Maori for house) throughout the country. Bond & Bond (💻 www.bondandbond.co.nz) and Noel Leeming (💻 www.noelleeming.co.nz) are chain stores selling a wide variety of products, including household goods, electrical appliances and computers.

Recent years have seen a trend towards huge shopping centres, known as 'mega-centres', found in major suburban areas, which house most of the country's major chain stores plus restaurants, cafés and cinema complexes. The Australian company, Westfield, has recently bought and refurbished nine centres in key locations. Shopping centres are popular, and visiting them constitutes a major 'leisure' activity in New Zealand.

ALCOHOL

New Zealand has some of the world's more bizarre licensing laws, which date back to the UK's oppressive licensing laws during the First World War, when workers were kept as far away from alcohol as possible lest their performance in the munitions factories was affected (or they caused an explosion!). New Zealand's laws have been reformed at a much slower pace than in the UK, although plans for liberalisation seem to slip back further each time there's an outbreak of drunken behaviour at a cricket or rugby match. Less than ten years ago you couldn't buy alcohol on a Sunday and supermarkets couldn't sell alcohol at all, while the legal age for buying and drinking alcohol was 20 (now 18).

Nowadays you can buy alcohol from supermarkets (but not spirits), bottle shops, wine shops and pubs. Pubs (known as hotels) usually have a 'bottle sales counter' or a separate 'bottle shop' (equivalent to a USA liquor store or a UK off-licence) on the premises, although these have limited opening hours, high prices and a poor selection compared with similar establishments in other countries. Dairies and grocery shops can also obtain a licence to sell beer and wine, although few do. Bottle shops or liquor stores usually have a good choice of beer, but the selection of wines and spirits is usually limited.

> The major liquor chains include The Mill (☎ 0800-843 6455, 💻 www.themill.co.nz) and Liquor King (☎ 0800-455 347, www.liquorking.co.nz), both with around 40 stores nationwide. Another good chain of wine stores is Glengarry (☎ 0800-733 505, 💻 www.glengarry.co.nz) in Auckland and Wellington. All liquor chains sell online (there's a delivery charge) and Countdown (see Supermarkets above) also sell beer and wine online.

Supermarkets have entered the alcohol market in recent years but are permitted to sell only wine and beer (of which they stock a wide variety at competitive prices) but not spirits. They're easily the cheapest place to buy wine and even cheaper than buying direct from vineyards (known as wineries), most of which tend to sell their wines at full price. If you want to find a retailer of a particular wine or compare prices, you can do it online at 💻 www.wine-searcher.com.

The majority of New Zealand wine is white and made from the Sauvignon Blanc grape, although Chardonnay is also popular, as are aromatics such as Gewürztraminer, Pinot Gris and Riesling. New Zealand is also noted for its Pinot Noir, which rates among the best in the world, and Syrah (Shiraz), although the latter isn't usually as good as Australian Shiraz. There are also excellent Bordeaux-style wines made from a variety of grapes, which have a good reputation (and prices to match). You can also choose from a wide selection of Australian wines and a limited choice of wines from farther afield.

Wine is sold in 75cl bottles, wine boxes and barrels (casks) of varying capacities, although buying wine in bulk (by the case – 12 bottles) usually saves you around 10 per cent. Beer is sold in cans of 440ml, usually in trays of 24 known as a 'two dozen lot' (Kiwis have a way with words), although bottled beer is much more popular. You can also buy a flagon containing 2.25 litres, which is sometimes still known as a 'half g' (half gallon) because it's equivalent to four pints. You should expect to pay $15-20 for a decent bottle of wine (cheaper wines are available for under $10 a bottle), $5 to $15 for a six-pack of beer, depending on the brand, and $30 to $60 for a bottle of spirits.

New Zealanders aren't big spirits drinkers, partly because spirits aren't widely available and are expensive. However, if you miss your favourite tipple, most major brands are available, including whisky (e.g. American, Canadian and Scotch) and local gin, which is relatively good value.

TOBACCO

New Zealanders aren't generally heavy smokers, which is just as well, as it's fast becoming socially unacceptable (see page 199) and has been banned in many places. As in most other countries, tobacco is becoming ever more expensive. The government grabs over 80 per cent of the cost of a packet of cigarettes in duty, ostensibly to promote good health and encourage people to give up. International and local brands are available, with the price of a pack of 20 starting at around $12. A recent test found that New Zealand brands contained twice as much nicotine as American and Canadian brands. Rolling tobacco is even more expensive than cigarettes (the government believes it's more damaging to your health), costing around $32.50 for 50g.

CLOTHING & SHOES

New Zealanders aren't noted for their fashion-consciousness, although a wide range of clothing (locally made and imported) is available. It used to be necessary for Kiwis to go to Australia or further afield to find the latest fashions, although it's now possible to buy the latest (or almost the latest) fashions in New Zealand, and the country also has many home-grown designers and manufacturers.

As in any country, prices vary considerably depending on the quality and where you shop, although clothes are generally more expensive than in Europe and North America. The cheapest clothing is available from chain stores, such as Kmart or Farmers, where you'll find uninspiring designs but plenty of choice. Millers Fashion Club is a leading chain of women's clothing stores which has done much to make women's clothing more competitive (like many New Zealand retailers, it originated in Australia). Glassons, Max, Ricochet and Jean Jones are also popular nationwide chains, while Ezibuy (🖥 www.ezibuy.co.nz) is a good mail-order retailer.

A number of retailers cater especially for larger women, including the Carpenter's Daughter (🖥 www.tcd.co.nz) and Real Women (🖥 www.realwomen.co.nz) – a euphemism for 'large'. A good children's clothes chain is Pumpkin Patch (🖥 www.pumpkinpatch.co.nz).

> Fashion-conscious shoppers may wish to check out department stores, such as Smith & Caughey in Auckland, Kirkcaldies & Stains in Wellington and Ballantynes in Christchurch (see Department & Chain Stores above), which stock a range of designer names.

Major cities such as Auckland and Wellington have an increasing number of trendy boutiques and designer stores, where you'll find brands from leading American, Australian and European designers, with correspondingly high prices. There are also several prominent local designers, including Amanda Nicolle, Chrissie Potter and Karen Walker. One of the leading innovators in New Zealand fashion is World (🖥 www.worldbrand.co.nz), which has stores in Auckland and Wellington.

New Zealand fashion has achieved record sales since it first participated in the London Fashion Week in 1999, and since 2001 has held its own annual Fashion Week (🖥 www.nzfashionweek.com) in Auckland in September, which receives international acclaim. However, unless you're a fashion 'victim' or move in the trendiest circles, it isn't usually worthwhile buying designer clothing in New Zealand, where most people aren't prone to label snobbery. Casual clothing is acceptable for most occasions, and country or sports clothing is particularly fashionable, even among those who spend all their time in cities.

Despite the ready availability of wool, woollen garments can be expensive, although anything in sheepskin is a bargain (you never know, it may come back into fashion one day!). Hand-knitted garments are popular. Cotton clothes are the cheapest and most popular in New Zealand, as they're cool in summer and warm in winter, particularly when worn in layers. Canterbury (💻 www.canterburynz.com) is famous for its rugby shirts, which can be worn for any occasion, while Swanndri (💻 www.swanndri.co.nz) is a well known brand of woollen shirts and jackets, which have become something of a classic (affectionately known as 'swannis').

There's also a wide choice of shoe shops in New Zealand, with prices to suit every budget, from plastic jandals (flip-flops) and beach shoes to the latest fashion statement from Jimmy Choo or Manolo Blahnik. A wide range of inexpensive shoes is available from chain stores such as Farmers, Kmart and The Warehouse (see above), while there's also a plethora of sports shoe shops in the major cities (such as the Shoe Clinic, 💻 www.shoeclinic.co.nz). International designer shoes are available from numerous boutique stores and the major department stores. Major retail chains include Overland Footwear (💻 www.overlandfootwear.co.nz), Number 1 Shoes (💻 www.no1shoes.co.nz), Footmark (💻 www.footmark.co.nz), a consortium of independent shoe shops, and Kumfs (see below).

New Zealand also has a number of home-grown shoe manufacturers, including Briarwood (💻 www.briarwood.co.nz), Minnie Cooper (💻 www.minniecooper.co.nz) for women, McKinlays (💻 www.mckinlays.co.nz) for men and Ziera (which was Kumfs – 💻 www.zierashoes.co.nz).

Factory Shops

Factory outlet shops are a growing influence in the clothing industry and include DressSmart (💻 www.dressmart.co.nz), which introduced the factory shopping mall concept into New Zealand in 1995 when their first mall opened in Auckland, followed by others in Christchurch (60 stores), Hamilton (36 stores) and Wellington (35 stores). The Auckland mall (Onehunga) is the largest with over 100 stores (open seven days a week from 10am to 5pm), featuring leading local and international brands at up to 70 per cent below normal retail price. The smaller Fox Outlet Centre (💻 www.foxoutletcentre.co.nz), with some 30 stores, is located on Auckland's North Shore in Northcote. There are also many independent factory shops, which can be found via 💻 www.factoryshops.co.nz and www.bargainshopping.co.nz.

FURNITURE & FURNISHINGS

The average New Zealand home is furnished much as it would be in Europe or North America. The staple items of furniture are the three-piece suite (usually called a lounge suite) and the dining table with four or six chairs. A wide range of furniture is available, from antique or reproduction to contemporary, with quality ranging from bargain-priced flat-pack or secondhand furniture, to exclusive handmade and designer items. Most homes in New Zealand have large fitted wardrobes in the American style, which are often walk-in rooms fitted with shelves and rails, thus rendering bedroom furniture other than a bed and a dressing table unnecessary. Fitted kitchens are also standard in new properties and basic appliances (oven, hob and refrigerator, and possibly also a washing machine and dishwasher) are usually included in the price of a new home.

The furniture market consists mainly of inexpensive pine and other timber furniture at the bottom end and a wide range of designer furniture and furnishings at the top end, with not a lot in the middle. Native hardwoods such as kauri, matai and rimu are rarely used to make furniture nowadays as they are too expensive, although recycled or fallen native timbers are used. It's common to have furniture custom made in New Zealand.

There's little affordable innovative furniture design in New Zealand, such as that provided by IKEA and similar manufacturers in many other countries.

Among the major furniture retailers in New Zealand are Farmers (🖳 www.farmers.co.nz), Freedom Furniture (🖳 www.freedomfurniture. co.nz), Harvey Norman (www.harveynorman. co.nz) and Target Furniture (🖳 www. targetfurniture.co.nz), while for beds there are Beds R Us (🖳 www.bedsrus.co.nz) and Sleepy Head (🖳 www.sleepyhead.co.nz). Boutique design stores usually offer an interior design service. You may wish to visit a home show for inspiration, such as the Auckland Home Show (🖳 www.aucklandhomeshow.co.nz), held in September and HomeShows in autumn in Auckland and Canterbury (see 🖳 www. homeshows.co.nz).

Antiques are popular, although relatively expensive, and mostly imported from the UK. If you have any good antique furniture, you may wish to bring it with you. You can buy secondhand furniture from dealers and via auction sites such as Trade Me (see **Secondhand Bargains** below).

HOUSEHOLD GOODS

New Zealand used to be notorious for the high cost of domestic appliances, as a result of prohibitive import taxes designed to protect local industries. In the '80s, however, the government decided to allow imports on more favourable terms, since when New Zealanders have been able to replace their ageing home appliances with modern equipment at more reasonable prices.

A wide choice of home appliances is available in New Zealand, and smaller appliances such as electric irons, grills, toasters and vacuum cleaners aren't expensive and are usually of good quality. All electrical goods sold in New Zealand must conform to local safety standards. It pays to shop around, as quality, reliability and prices vary considerably. Before buying household appliances, whether large or small, it's advisable to check the test reports in consumer magazines (see **Consumer Protection** below).

The major retailers of home appliances and white goods are Bond & Bond (🖳 www. bondandbond.co.nz) and Noel Leeming (🖳 www.noelleeming.co.nz), which are both owned by the same company, therefore prices are almost identical. The Warehouse and Kmart also carry limited ranges of cheap appliances, but are good for general household goods and homewares, as is Briscoes (🖳 www.briscoes. co.nz). One innovative New Zealand product is the double drawer dishwasher that allows you to do half-loads; they are available from a number of manufacturers, including NZ's own Fisher & Paykel (🖳 www.fisherpaykel.co.nz).

DIY is popular in New Zealand, where there are numerous DIY and hardware stores. The major chains include Bunnings Warehouse (🖳 www.bunnings.co.nz) and Mitre 10 (🖳 www. mitre10.co.nz), while Knobs 'n Knockers (🖳 www.knobsnknockers.co.nz) are popular in Auckland.

It isn't worthwhile shipping bulky domestic appliances to New Zealand, such as a dishwasher, refrigerator or washing machine, which, irrespective of the shipping expense, may not meet local safety regulations or fit into a local kitchen. However, if you own good quality, small household appliances, it's worthwhile bringing them to New Zealand, as all that's usually required is a change of plug, provided you're coming from a country with a 220/240V electricity supply (see page 99).

☑ SURVIVAL TIP

Don't bring a TV to New Zealand, other than from Australia, as it won't work.

SECONDHAND BARGAINS

There's a lively secondhand market for almost everything in New Zealand, from antiques to

cars, computers to photographic equipment. With such a large secondhand market there are often bargains to be found, particularly if you're quick off the mark. Many towns have a local secondhand or junk store and charity shops (e.g. Salvation Army and St Vincent Paul) selling new and secondhand articles (where most of your money goes to help those in need). In some places (e.g. Wellington) you can even buy goods which have been rescued from the city dump and which are displayed in a special warehouse at the site!

Some of the best sources for secondhand goods are auction websites such as Trade Me (⌨ www.trademe.co.nz), a national icon/obsession, and Sella (⌨ www.sella.co.nz). Cash Converters (⌨ www.cashconverters. co.nz), which has stores nationwide, plus Dollar Dealers (⌨ www.dollardealers.co.nz) with seven stores in Auckland, are also popular.

If you're looking for a particular item, such as a boat, car, camera, or motorcycle, you may be better off looking through the small advertisements in specialist magazines, rather than in more general newspapers or magazines. The classified advertisements in local newspapers are also a good source of bargains, particularly for items such as furniture and large household appliances.

Shopping centre and newsagent bulletin boards and company notice boards may also prove fruitful. Another place to pick up a bargain is at an auction, although it helps to have specialist knowledge about what you're buying (you'll be competing with experts). Auctions are held throughout the year for everything from antiques and paintings to cars and property.

There are antique shops and centres in most towns, and antique street markets and fairs are common in the major cities, where you can pick up interesting early New Zealand artifacts (Kiwiana) – but you must get up early to beat the dealers to the best buys. For information about local markets, ask at your local tourist or information office. Car boot (trunk) and garage (yard) sales, where people sell their surplus belongings at bargain prices, are also popular; sales may be advertised in local newspapers and signposted on local roads (they're usually held at weekends).

HOME SHOPPING

Mail-order catalogue shopping has long been popular in New Zealand, particularly among people living in remote areas, and internet shopping (see below) has soared in recent years. The country's most popular home shopping websites are Trade Me (see box) and Sella (⌨ www.sella.co.nz). Direct retailing is also fairly common, particularly for computers, electronics, office equipment and supplies, and financial services. TV shopping is also increasingly popular and there are a number of 24-hour shopping channels, where products are sold through 'infomercials'.

Internet Shopping

Internet shopping has mushroomed in New Zealand in recent years and now accounts for an increasing share of purchases. Most retailers have a website where they offer online shopping and there are also a number of online price comparison sites, including ⌨ www.priceme.co.nz, www.pricecomparison.co.nz, www.pricespy.co.nz and www.shopbot.co.nz. There's a number of dedicated online shopping sites, such as ⌨ www.fashionz.co.nz/online-shopping-2.html, www.shopnewzealand.co.nz, www.shophere.co.nz, and www.shopsafe.co.nz (a shopping portal that vets online vendors).

New Zealand's most successful website is Trade Me (⌨ www.trademe.co.nz) – the country's equivalent of eBay – which was sold to John Fairfax in 2006 for $700m!

All prices on websites selling to domestic buyers must include GST. GST and duty must also be paid on imported goods, although no GST is payable if the total amount owing is less than $50.

NEWSPAPERS, MAGAZINES & BOOKS

New Zealand doesn't offer a particularly wide choice of daily newspapers, a situation that has been exacerbated by the closure of a number of long-established newspapers in recent years. There are no national newspapers in New Zealand, where newspapers are regional (centred on the major cities) and aren't widely distributed throughout the country. As a result, most New Zealand newspapers tend to have a provincial feel, although they do contain both national and international news.

The most authoritative newspaper is the excellent *New Zealand Herald* (Auckland), which has a world view and includes many sections and weekly and weekend magazines. Other major newspapers include the *Dominion Post* (Wellington), *The Press* (Christchurch), the *Waikato Times* (Hamilton) and the *Otago Daily Times* (Dunedin). Most daily newspapers are published from Mondays to Saturdays and separate titles are published on Sundays, e.g. the *Sunday Star Times* in Auckland. Other popular publications include the weekly *National Business Review*, New Zealand's main business magazine, and *The Truth*, a weekly 'shock-horror' tabloid.

Most New Zealand and foreign newspapers can be accessed online via 🖥 www.world-newspapers.com and www.onlinenewspapers.com (listed A-Z by town/city). Note, however,

that you may need to subscribe to a newspaper to access most content.

Politically, most newspapers take an even-handed approach, as they're mainly independently owned. The content of most newspapers, which are usually broadsheets, is fairly standard and includes news, business, sport and TV programmes, while the Thursday, Friday and Saturday editions are the best for advertisements such as jobs, property and cars. Friday editions of most newspapers include a substantial 'what's on' entertainment section.

Newspapers are sold by dairies, newsagents and bookshops such as Whitcoulls (🖥 www.whitcoulls.co.nz) and Paper Plus (🖥 www.paperplus.co.nz), both of which sell newspapers, magazines, books and stationery. You can also buy them from street stands (where you leave the money in an honesty box) and vending machines, where depositing your money opens the door giving you access to the newspapers inside. If you buy a newspaper out of its local area, e.g. the *New Zealand Herald* (Auckland) in Christchurch, you pay a $0.50 surcharge (as sold by Whitcoulls). You can also have newspapers delivered to your home. Free local newspapers are distributed to homes in most cities and are useful for finding local services, jobs, property and cars.

British expatriates will be pleased to hear that they can buy the *International Express* and *Weekly Telegraph* in NZ, which are condensed weekly editions containing a summary of the week's most important news (the real news minus the showbiz gossip), available on subscription and from most newsagents and supermarkets in New Zealand.

New Zealand offers a surprisingly wide selection of excellent home-grown magazines, although sales have plunged during the recession, plus many from Australia, the UK and the US. Magazines cater for most tastes, including sports, hobbies, women's and men's interests, and home and business topics, totalling over 600 titles, of which *The TV Guide* has the largest circulation, followed by *New Zealand Woman's Day*. Magazines can be purchased on subscription from 🖳 www.isubscribe.co.nz and www.nzmagazineshop.co.nz.

Books

Most bookshops in New Zealand stock a wide selection of books, including many published in Australia, the UK and the USA. However, due to the relatively small print runs of New Zealand publishers and the cost of shipping books from other countries, they're relatively expensive (Americans will be horrified). Note that it's possible to buy books at reasonable prices via the internet from a number of international internet booksellers, the largest of which is Amazon (🖳 www.amazon.com). Local online sellers include 🖳 www.fishpond.co.nz, www.thenile.co.nz, www.goodbooks.com (where the profits go to Oxfam) and www.newzealandbooks.co.nz, which specialises in books published in New Zealand.

The book market in New Zealand is dominated by Whitcoulls (🖳 www.whitcoulls.co.nz), which has some 80 branches nationwide, and Paper Plus (🖳 www.paperplus.co.nz) and its smaller subsidiary Take Note (www.takenote.co.nz), which have a total of over 100 stores. There are also some stalwart independent stores and four branches of Australian booksellers Dymocks (🖳 www.dymocks.co.nz). The Warehouse (🖳 www.thewarehouse.co.nz) and supermarkets also sell a limited selection of the latest bestsellers and cut-price books.

> ☑ SURVIVAL TIP
>
> Second-hand bookshops thrive in the major towns, most of which allow you to part-exchange books for a small fee. See also Libraries on page 253.

DUTY-FREE & SHOPPING ABROAD

Apart from your personal effects, those aged over 17 entering New Zealand (whether as visitors or residents) are permitted to import a limited amount of goods duty-free (i.e. free of goods and services tax at 12.5 per cent). These include:

- 200 cigarettes or 250g tobacco or 50 cigars (or a mixture of all three provided they don't weigh more than 250g);
- three 1,125-litre bottles of spirit or liqueur;
- 4.5 litres of wine or beer (six 75cl bottles);
- other goods up to a value of $700.

When leaving New Zealand, you may purchase duty-free goods at duty-free shops in central Auckland, Wellington or Christchurch and at airports. If you buy duty-free goods from a city duty-free shop, they're delivered free to the airport in time for your departure and it isn't possible to take them with you when you leave the store. If you prefer, you can have your purchases shipped to an address abroad, which duty-free shops are happy to arrange.

Although buying goods duty-free saves you the 15 per cent GST, if you're travelling via the Far East or the USA you may be able to obtain a better deal there, depending on what you wish to buy. You can also buy duty-free goods at airports in New Zealand on arrival from overseas.

RECEIPTS & GUARANTEES

When shopping, you should always insist on a receipt and keep it until you've left the shop or reached home. This isn't only in case you need to return or exchange goods, which may be impossible without the receipt, but also to verify that you've paid if an automatic alarm goes off as you're leaving the shop or any other questions arise. If you're paying in cash, you should check receipts immediately (particularly in supermarkets), because if you're overcharged it's almost impossible to obtain redress later.

You may also need your receipt to return an item for repair or replacement (usually to the place of purchase) during the warranty period. It's wise to keep receipts and records of major purchases made while you're resident in New Zealand, particularly if you're staying for a short period only. This may save you time and money when you finally leave the country and are required to declare your belongings in your new country of residence.

CONSUMER PROTECTION

If you buy something which is faulty, damaged or doesn't work or measure up to the manufacturer's or vendor's claims, you can return it and obtain a replacement or your money back (unless you bought it at auction). Note that extended warranties or money-back guarantees don't affect your statutory rights as a purchaser, although the legal status of a warranty may be unclear. Some stores offer an exchange of goods or a money-back guarantee for any reason, which isn't required by law, although this guarantee is usually for a limited period only and goods must be returned unused and in 'as new' condition.

Some stores attempt to restrict your rights to a credit note or to replacement goods when an item is faulty or unfit for use, which is illegal. Signs such as 'no refunds given', 'no responsibility for loss or damage', 'goods left for repair at your own risk' and 'all care but no responsibility taken' are meaningless and unlawful. All goods must be of 'merchantable' (reasonable) quality and fit for the purpose for which they were sold, and it's illegal for sellers to include a clause in the conditions of sale that exempts them from liability for defects, product faults and lack of care. Most traders will back down once you show that you know the law and are determined to obtain your legal rights.

Consumer protection laws are monitored and enforced by the Ministry of Consumer Affairs (PO Box 1473, Wellington 6140, ☎ 04-474 2750, 🖳 www.consumer-ministry.govt.nz), which has local offices throughout the country. You can also obtain advice and assistance from a local Citizens' Advice Bureau (☎ 0800-367 222, 🖳 www.cab.org.nz).

The Consumer Institute publishes *Consumer* magazine, which is the country's most trusted source of consumer advice and information, whether in a supermarket or car yard, choosing insurance or investing for your future security. It's published monthly (11 issues annually) for $28 for online access for three months (including access to over 500 reports), $53 for the printed magazine for six months, or $67 for both the printed magazine and online access for six months. The magazine is also available from newsagents.

☑ SURVIVAL TIP

The New Zealand consumer champion is the Consumer Institute of New Zealand (☎ 0800-266 786, 🖳 www.consumer.org. nz), an independent, non-profit organisation established in 1959 with the sole aim of getting consumers a fairer deal.

Rainforest

18.
ODDS & ENDS

This chapter contains miscellaneous information. Although all topics aren't of vital importance, most are of interest to anyone planning to live or work in New Zealand, including everything you ever wanted to know (but were afraid to ask) about subjects such as tipping and toilets.

NEW ZEALAND CITIZENSHIP

Those who have received permanent residence since 21st April 2005 can apply for New Zealand citizenship after five years. Citizenship confers the right to vote in local elections and apply for a New Zealand passport. In order for your application to be successful, you must provide proof of good character, show your knowledge of the responsibilities and privileges of New Zealand citizenship, and speak and understand English. You must attend a citizenship ceremony and take an oath or affirmation of allegiance.

Children born of New Zealand residents automatically become New Zealand citizens and can hold dual nationality when it's permitted under the law of their parents' countries of birth or nationality. Foreign nationals who marry New Zealanders can apply for citizenship immediately they take up residence, and those who live with a New Zealand partner in a genuine de facto relationship can apply for citizenship after two years. The fee for the granting of citizenship is $470.20.

Enquiries regarding citizenship must be made to the Citizenship Office (☎ 0800-225 151, 💻 www.citizenship.govt.nz).

CLIMATE

Being an island nation, New Zealand's climate tends to be dominated by its ocean setting, although it experiences a variety of climatic patterns due to its mountainous terrain. Conditions vary considerably and include sub-tropical, sub-Antarctic, semi-arid (mainly in the Northland region), super-humid, frost-free, and sub-Alpine, with permanent snow and ice in the mountainous areas.

The eastern regions experience a drier climate than the west, due to prevailing westerly winds, the wettest area being the south-west (west of the Southern Alps). Being situated in the southern hemisphere, New Zealand's seasons are the opposite of those in the northern latitudes, i.e. summer (December to February), autumn (March to May), winter (June to August) and Spring (September to November). Unseasonal weather is rare.

The most important characteristic of New Zealand's weather is its unreliability; if there's one word that sums up the weather it's 'changeable'. Long-range (or even 24-hour) weather forecasts are a lottery and notoriously unreliable, particularly in the spring when the weather can change hourly from bright sunshine to downpours (extremes are commonplace). As the locals say, "if you want a weather forecast, look out of the window".

The North Island tends to be warmer and drier than the South Island, although the highest mountains often have snow on their peaks year round. The average rainfall in the North Island is around 1,300mm/51in. Daytime temperatures in Auckland average 23ºC (73ºF) in summer and 14ºC (57ºF) in winter, while in Wellington they range from 26ºC (79ºF) in summer to as low as 2ºC (35ºF) in winter.

Wellington is renowned for its extremely windy weather, which can also make the sea crossing between the two islands rough.

Variations in weather and temperature in the South Island are more pronounced, and the Southern Alps have 'wet' (west) and 'dry' (east) sides. On the east side of the Southern Alps rainfall can be as low as 300mm/11.8in (droughts are fairly common) and temperatures a lot higher than on the west side. Snow is a permanent feature on the highest peaks. Christchurch averages temperatures of around 22ºC (72ºF) in summer and 12ºC (54ºF) in winter, while Dunedin averages 19ºC (66ºF) in summer and 10ºC (50ºF) in winter.

Average temperatures, rainfall levels and sunshine hours for the major towns and cities are shown below. Bear in mind that the temperatures are averages and it can be much warmer or colder on some days:

The weather forecast is provided in daily newspapers, via the internet (e.g. 🖥 www. metservice.co.nz and www.nzweather.net), TV teletext services, and TV and radio weather reports. Note, however, that forecasts are often wildly inaccurate due to the ever-changing (and notoriously difficult to predict) climatic conditions of New Zealand's coastal and mountainous terrain, and planning a (hopefully)

sunny break in, for example, spring can be difficult.

CRIME

New Zealand has a reputation as a low-crime country and is safe by international standards, although violent crime has risen in recent years, including family-related violence, and drug and anti-social behaviour. There has also been an increase in racially-motivated violent attacks and rapes, particularly against Asians and Pacific Islanders, although it should be noted that, overall, race relations in New Zealand are excellent and the envy of many other countries. However, despite the crime figures, and with the exception of a few Auckland suburbs, you can safely walk anywhere at any time of day or night without fear of becoming a victim of crime.

Nevertheless, when choosing somewhere to live, it's worth checking the local crime statistics and avoiding high-crime areas! There's a huge difference between crime levels in some major city suburbs and rural areas, where it's still common for people not to lock their homes or cars, a practice which used to be common throughout New Zealand. In urban areas, however, good door and window locks

Climate in the Major Cities				
Town/City	Average Temp (ºC) Summer	Winter	Average Annual Rainfall (mm)	Annual Hours Sunshine
NORTH ISLAND:				
Bay of Islands	25	15	1,648	2,020
Auckland	23	14	1,268	2,140
Rotorua	23	12	1,511	1,940
Napier	24	13	780	2,270
Wellington	20	11	1,271	2,020
SOUTH ISLAND:				
Nelson	22	12	999	2,410
Christchurch	22	12	658	1,990
Queenstown	22	8	849	1,940
Dunedin	19	10	772	1,700
Invercargill	18	9	1,042	1,630

(and insurance) are considered essential. Car theft is also a problem in cities and it's wise to have an immobiliser and alarm system fitted to your car.

A Crime and Safety Survey carried out in recent years revealed that 1 in 14 houses had been broken into in the previous year and one in five people had been the victim of some kind of assault. In the light of these worrying findings and the general rise in crime, the government has introduced a series of measures designed to tackle crime (such as the DNA testing of criminals, including burglars, and greater police funding) and provide greater support for crime victims. Police have also been targeting low-level crime in some areas (zero tolerance), with more police officers on the beat, in an effort to prevent more serious offences.

Recent initiatives include a task force on youth offending, which is a particular problem in some cities. Recent crime statistics show that these measures have been at least partially successful; burglary and car theft rates have decreased by almost 15 per cent and the resolution of crime was the highest for a decade. Violent crime, however, is still on the increase, and convictions for domestic violence have risen significantly, although it's believed that this may be due to greater public awareness and because more domestic violence is reported to the police. Further information and statistics on crime can be obtained from the Minister of Justice (19 Aitken

Street, SX10088, Wellington, ☎ 04-918 8800, 🖳 www.justice.govt.nz).

Despite the statistics, you can safely walk almost anywhere at any time of the day or night in most parts of the country. However, it's important to take the same precautions as you would in any country. Beware of pickpockets and bag-snatchers in cities and keep a close eye on your belongings in shops and when using public transport, particularly trains and the Interislander ferry. If your luggage is stolen on public transport, you should make a claim to the relevant authority, as they may make an ex-gratia payment for lost, stolen or damaged baggage.

Most New Zealanders are law-abiding and their 'crimes' amount to little more than speeding, 'pulling a sickie' (i.e. taking a day off work to go to the beach), or exaggerating a road or workplace accident in order to secure a more generous payout from the ACC. (Insurance companies recently reported that insurance claims were believed to be inflated by at least $50m annually by otherwise law-abiding citizens.) White collar fraud and corruption have become a more serious problem in recent years, and a number of respected companies have been rocked by financial scandals, which were previously unheard of in New Zealand.

The New Zealand Police provides safety tips on its website (🖳 www.police.govt.nz/safety/index.html). However, don't expect the police to respond if you've been burgled, as such crimes are given a relatively low priority – the lack of response has been the cause of a huge increase in complaints in recent years.

Gangs

Gangs are a problem in some cities, particularly in poor inner-city areas of Auckland and Wellington, although there's some gang activity in most large towns. As the gangs main activity tends to be inter-gang warfare, most people rarely come into contact with them, except when a gang organises a 'convention' in a public place or at a major rock concert or sporting event. However, gang 'meets' are usually well publicised and characterised by a much larger than usual police presence. The best advice to newcomers is not to buy or rent a home in an area known for gang activity (or high crime), and to stay well away from events or areas where gangs are likely to congregate.

Prisons

Tougher sentencing in recent years has created something of a prison crisis in New Zealand, where the prison population in over 8,000, which is a rate of almost 200 per 100,000 population, which is very high by the standards of most Western countries except the USA. The authorities are experimenting with more liberal punishments, such as home detention, electronic tagging and community work.

Drugs

New Zealand has been described as having the perfect climate for the cultivation of cannabis, and plantations are tucked away in most parts of the country, particularly in Northland, which is dubbed New Zealand's 'cannabis capital'. Police regularly destroy plantations, but many more are believed to remain undiscovered, and this doesn't take into account plants that are grown literally on the window sills and balconies of homes throughout the country.

⚠ Caution

Recreational smoking of cannabis or marijuana ('electric puha' as it's known in some places) is commonplace, although it's illegal and its possession is punishable by a $1,000 fine and/or 12 months' imprisonment.

As in some other countries, there's pressure on the government to legalise cannabis, headed by the National Organisation For The Reform of Marijuana Laws (NORML, 🖳 www. norml.org.nz). While most people feel this is unlikely to happen, a plan to punish possession by on-the-spot fines, similar to parking tickets, has been seriously proposed in recent years. The police tend to concentrate on tracing and prosecuting growers (using helicopter patrols in rural areas) and dealers rather than casual users, and they rarely raid homes in search of small quantities. However, vehicles driven by

'likely looking' drug users (those with glazed eyes, fixed grins and flowers in their hair?) who are stopped for traffic offences may be searched for drugs.

Ecstasy is a popular alternative to cannabis, particularly among teenagers, and the use of hard drugs such as heroin and cocaine is increasing (the official 'Just Say No' anti-drugs campaign is often criticised for its lack of impact). New Zealand also has an increasing problem with methamphetamine, know colloquially as 'drug P' (sometimes use to lace cannabis), of which Kiwis are the world's largest users.

Despite the foregoing, drugs are generally much less of a problem than in the USA or Western Europe, as New Zealand maintains relatively effective border controls aimed at keeping 'nasties' (including illicit fruit and vegetables) out of the country.

For more information, visit the website of the New Zealand Drug Foundation (🖳 www. drugfoundation.org.nz).

GEOGRAPHY

New Zealand is comprised of two main islands, the North Island and the South Island (they were named in the 19th century by the British, who obviously exercised a great deal of effort and imagination in christening them). There are also numerous smaller islands, of which Stewart and Chatham are the most important, and a number of dependencies, including Ross Dependency (in Antarctica) and Niue, Tokelau and the Cook Islands (in the Pacific Ocean). New Zealand covers an area of 270,534km^2 (104,461mi^2), which makes it comparable in size to the UK.

New Zealand lies in the South Pacific Ocean, south-east of Australia, and, contrary to popular belief – and to the eternal relief of most New Zealanders – isn't 'just off the coast of Australia', but some 2,000km (1,250mi) away across the Tasman Sea.

New Zealand is a mountainous country, some 60 per cent of which is between around 200m (655ft) and 1,070m (3,500ft) above sea level, with over 220 mountains above 2,000m (6,550ft). The principal mountain ranges in the North Island extend along the eastern side, where the north central region has three active volcanic peaks: Mount Ruapehu (2,797m/9,176ft), the highest point on the island, Mount Ngauruhoe (2,291m/7,516ft) and Mount Tongariro (1,968m/6,456ft). Mount Taranaki (2,518m/8,261ft), a solitary extinct volcanic cone, is situated near the western extremity of the island.

The North Island also has numerous rivers, most of which rise in the eastern and central mountains, including the Waikato River (435km/270mi), the longest river in New Zealand. It flows north out of Lake Taupo (606km^2/233mi^2), the country's largest lake (where mineral springs are also found), into the Tasman Sea in the west. The North Island has an irregular coastline, particularly at its northern extremity, the Auckland Peninsula, where it's just 10km/6mi wide.

The South Island has a more regular coastline than the North Island and is characterised by deep fjords in the south-west. The chief mountain range of the South Island is the Southern Alps, a massive range extending from the south-west to the north-east almost the entire length of the island, with 17 peaks over 3,000m (9,842ft). Mount Cook (3,754m/12,316ft) is the highest point in New Zealand and rises from the centre of the range, which also contains a number of glaciers. Most of the rivers of the South Island, including the Clutha River (338km/210mi long), the longest river on the island, rise in the Southern Alps. The largest lake is Lake Te Anau (342km^2/132mi^2) in the southern part of the Southern Alps. The Canterbury plains in the east and the Southland plains in the extreme south are the only extensive flat areas in the South Island.

The islands of New Zealand emerged in the Tertiary period and contain a complete series of marine sedimentary rocks, some of which date from the early Paleozoic era. Much of the topography of New Zealand has resulted from warping and block faulting, although volcanic action has also played a part in its formation, particularly that of the North Island, where it continues to this day. Geysers and mineral hot springs occur in the volcanic area, particularly around Rotorua.

New Zealand lies within an earthquake zone – as the earthquakes in the South Island's Canterbury region in 2010-11 tragically demonstrated – and minor (usually unnoticeable) tremors occur almost monthly, although serious earthquakes are relatively rare. The Canterbury earthquake in September 2010 measured 7.1 on the Richter scale and resulted in widespread damage, but few serious injuries and no direct deaths. This was followed by a weaker (6.3) but more destructive earthquake – as it was centred close to Christchurch – on 22nd February 2011, which resulted in the deaths of 181 people. This was followed by a less powerful earthquake (5.8) on the 23rd December 2011, which caused realtively minor damage. Experts believe that the 'quakes could continue for some years.

The Geonet website (www.geonet.org.nz) contains a map showing the near real-time shaking intensity from New Zealand's network of seismographs and it also constantly monitors the country's volcanoes, the possibility of tsunamis and maintains a rapid

Champagne Pool, Waitopu, North Island

response to landslides (see also **Earthquake Insurance** on page 214).

Much New Zealand plant life is unique, and of the 2,000 indigenous species, some 1,500 are found only here, including the golden kowhai and the scarlet pohutukawa. The North Island is home to predominantly subtropical vegetation, including mangrove swamps in the north. The forest, or so-called bush, of the North Island is mainly evergreen, with a dense undergrowth of mosses and ferns. Evergreen trees include the kahikatea, kauri (the traditional wood used for house building in New Zealand), rimu and totara, all of which are excellent timber trees. The only extensive area of native grassland in the North Island is the central volcanic plain. The eastern part of the South Island is, for the most part, grassland up to an elevation of around 1,500m/4,921ft, while most forests are situated in the west (consisting mainly of native beech and Alpine vegetation at high altitudes).

With the exception of two species of bat, New Zealand has no indigenous mammals. The first white settlers (who arrived early in the 19th century) found a kind of dog and a black rat, both of which had been introduced by the Maori around 500 years earlier and are now almost extinct. All other wild mammals are descended from deer, ferrets, goats, opossums, pigs, rabbits and weasels, all of which were imported by early Western settlers. No snakes and few unusual species of insects inhabit New Zealand (unlike Australia, which is infested with them!), although it does boast the tuatara, a lizard-like reptile with a third eye believed to be a distant relative of the dinosaurs. New Zealand has a large population of wild birds, including 23 native species which include the bellbird and tui (songbirds) and flightless species such as the kakapo, kiwi (from which New Zealanders take their colloquial name), takahe and weka. The survival of flightless birds is attributed to the absence of predatory animals (with the exception of domestic cats). The blackbird, magpie, myna, skylark, sparrow and thrush are among the most prevalent imported species.

New Zealand's rivers and lakes contain a variety of native edible fish, including eel, freshwater crustaceans (particularly crayfish), lamprey and whitebait,. Trout and salmon have been introduced and are found in waters throughout the country. The surrounding ocean

waters are the habitat of blue cod, flounder, flying fish, hapuku, shark, snapper, swordfish, tarakihi and whales, in addition to a variety of shellfish including mussels, oysters and toheroas.

GOVERNMENT

New Zealand is a parliamentary democracy modelled on the British system. It is, however, unicameral, that is it has only one legislative body, the House of Representatives (🖥 www. parliament.nz), and no upper house, which was abolished in 1951.

> Members of Parliament (MPs) sit in the Parliament Building (Beehive) in Wellington, which is regarded by New Zealanders as the country's largest source of hot air, easily outperforming any of New Zealand's impressive geothermal geysers – not that it's any different from most other seats of government in this respect.

The executive branch of the government consists of the Prime Minister and his cabinet New Zealand has a Governor-General (G-G), who's appointed by the British Crown, although it's largely an honorary position and he rarely participates in government and usually intervenes only in constitutional matters. The G-G is appointed by the sovereign every five years on the recommendation of the government of the day and his most important (ceremonial) role is to dissolve the outgoing parliament and invite the leaders of the parties elected to power to form a new government.

For comprehensive information about the New Zealand government, see 🖥 newzealand.govt.nz.

Political Parties

Politics in New Zealand has traditionally been dominated by two parties: The National Party, which favours right-wing social policies and a market-orientated approach to the economy, and the left-wing Labour Party. The Labour Party traditionally favoured left-of-centre policies, including comprehensive social welfare spending, but during the '80s and '90s 'borrowed' what were previously thought to be National Party policies, including economic reform and financial market deregulation. Most elections attract a string of independents and minority parties, together with what can best be described as 'loony' parties (such as Legalise Cannabis and Natural Law).

The last general election was in November 2011, when the National Party were returned to power with John Key remaining as Prime Minister. The state of the parties in 2011 was: National Party 59 seats, Labour 34, Greens 14, New Zealand First 8, Maori Party 3, ACT 1, Mana 1 and United Future 1 (total 121 seats).

Voting & Elections

New Zealand changed (in 1993) to a system of proportional representation (PR) from the first-past-the-post (FPP) system previously used. The kind of PR used in New Zealand is known as a Mixed Member Proportional (MMP) system, which is designed to ensure that each political party's share of seats in parliament corresponds to its share of the vote. (In November 2011, the country voted in a referendum 58 to 42 per cent to retain the MMP voting system.) Voters have two votes; a 'party vote' for the party of their choice and a second vote for their preferred candidate. Parties are allocated seats in proportion to the number of party votes they receive and then candidates are allocated to those seats according to the votes they polled individually.

The House of Representatives consists of 121 MPs, one representing each of the 63 general electoral districts and 52 who are allocated according to the number of votes each party receives (selected from party lists). The final seven seats are reserved for candidates from Maori electoral districts. (The 2005 election created an 'overhang' of one extra seat, awarded to the party that wins more seats in electorates than the number of seats its proportion of the party vote would have awarded it – don't worry if you find this baffling, most Kiwis do also). Some politicians have recently proposed that the number of MPs be reduced to save money – a sensible idea, which would no doubt prove popular in most countries!

New Zealand's system of MMP, while generally being recognised as an improvement over FPP, has caused something of an upheaval in the political system and has allowed smaller parties to obtain a presence in parliament for the first time, although no party can obtain a seat in

The Beehive, Parliament building, Wellington

parliament unless it obtains at least 5 per cent of the total vote. It has also created a situation where it's impossible for a single party to obtain an overall majority and thus two or more parties are forced to co-operate in a coalition to form a government. Some politicians have argued for a return to FPP, although this is unlikely to happen.

Parliamentary elections are held every three years, although the government can call an early election at any time, although it rarely does, preferring to allow each parliament to run its course. Although many New Zealanders are apathetic about politics, they're usually keen to exercise their right to vote and the turnout in general elections is rarely less than 80 per cent (the 2011 turnout of just over 74 per cent was the lowest since 1887). Additionally, the New Zealand government doesn't hesitate to call referenda on subjects considered of great importance to the country. Recent referenda have included proportional representation (which was accepted by a small majority) and changes to the national superannuation system (which was rejected by a small percentage).

Legislative Process

New laws in New Zealand begin life as 'bills', which are 'read' to parliament. Bills undergo first and second readings before being passed to a select committee for discussion and consideration of submissions by interested parties. The select committee must report back to parliament within six months. A bill is then debated and the House of Representatives considers it on a clause-by-clause basis. After a third reading, it's passed to the Governor-General (G-G) for assent and then becomes law. In theory, the G-G can reject laws using reserve power, particularly if he feels that the government is acting unconstitutionally. However, in practice, he's bound by convention to follow the advice of the government and give his assent to bills.

Under the Constitution Act 1986, the British parliament is unable to make laws affecting New Zealand, although some British laws (the Imperial Acts, such as the Magna Carta and Habeas Corpus) are enshrined in New Zealand law.

Judiciary

New Zealand has a fiercely independent judiciary which, as with many other aspects of law and government, is modelled on the British system with some antipodean modifications. Judges are nominated from the ranks of the legal profession (barristers or solicitors with a minimum of seven years' service) and appointed by the G-G (not by the government or the electorate). Judges must retire on reaching the age of 68, although they may be re-appointed for up to two years.

The Judicial Committee of the Privy Council is New Zealand's highest legal authority. The highest court is the Court of Appeal, whose decisions are final unless leave is granted to appeal to the Privy Council. The principal trial courts are the high court, staffed by the chief justice and 32 high court judges, and the district courts. Justices of the peace may, in some cases, try minor criminal cases. Special courts and tribunals determine matters relating to family law, labour disputes, land rights and workers' compensation.

All registered electors between the ages of 20 and 65 can be summoned to serve on a jury, although those in certain occupations, e.g. police officers, and those with criminal convictions which resulted in more than three years' imprisonment, are excluded. Anyone called for jury service may apply to be excused on religious grounds or when service would cause unnecessary hardship.

Local Government

New Zealand is divided into 12 regional councils and 74 territorial authorities, of which 16 are city councils and 58 district councils. See the Local Government New Zealand website for further details (🖳 www.lgnz.co.nz).

LEGAL & GENERAL ADVICE

As in other developed countries, fees charged by solicitors and barristers are sky-high and legal fees for even a simple case, e.g. a breach of contract, can run into tens of thousands of dollars. Junior lawyers charge at least $125 an hour and advice from a senior lawyer is likely to cost at least $200 an hour. Most New Zealand lawyers are qualified both as solicitors and barristers, i.e. they can work as advocates in court and don't need to appoint a separate barrister to perform this task. New Zealand has a system of legal aid which provides assistance to those who cannot afford to pay a solicitor, although the budget is tight and changes are continually being made to the system in order to streamline it and make it more cost effective. Those requiring legal aid for civil cases may find it difficult to obtain free legal assistance.

The Legal Services Board (🖳 www.legalservicesboard.org.uk) also operates a 'duty solicitor' scheme, which provides free and immediate legal aid to anyone who's arrested by the police. If you're arrested, you're entitled to a consultation with a solicitor and to have him present during an interview. In most towns and cities, usually in poorer areas, there are community law centres (around 20 nationally) financed by public funds and other means, such as fund-raising. They provide free legal advice and representation to those who are unable to afford it, within the limits of their resources. Most towns also have a Citizens' Advice Bureau (☎ 0800-367 222, 🖳 www.cab.org.nz), where you can obtain free and confidential advice on a wide range of matters. Free legal advice is also provided by Outreach Centres in most towns.

MARRIAGE & DIVORCE

Like many countries, New Zealand has a declining marriage rate, although the divorce rate has fallen in the last few years after remaining stable at around 10,000 annually since 1996; and the average length of a marriage is around 15 years, which is longer than in most other Western countries. An increasing number of New Zealanders choose to marry later in life (the average age is 32 for men and 30 for women) or to remain single, with the number of marriages around 22,000 annually. The country also has many single mothers and one of the world's highest rates of unmarried teenage pregnancies, although many women are also single mothers by choice and happily juggle career and family. Women are choosing to wait to have families until later in life and the average childbearing age is around 30.

An increasing number of New Zealanders choose a simple civil ceremony rather than a church service, mainly because of the informality it provides and the much reduced cost. It's possible to marry anywhere in New Zealand, not just in a church or at a registry office, assuming that you can find a clergyman or registrar willing to perform the ceremony (a Dunedin couple married in the city's municipal swimming pool!).

New Zealand recognises de facto relationships, i.e. unmarried couples (both heterosexual and homosexual) living together, who enjoy most of the rights and responsibilities of married couples, including the same rights regarding the inheritance of property. De facto couples are also entitled to an equal share of the family home and other 'chattels', irrespective of who owns them, although the law applies only to relationships of three years or longer. Couples can also make alternative arrangements for the division of their property, which is known as 'contracting out'. Advice regarding legislation should be sought from a lawyer or your local community law centre (see **Legal & General Advice** above).

MILITARY SERVICE

There's no conscription (draft) in New Zealand, where members of the armed forces are volunteers. The minimum age for enlistment is 17, in line with United Nations guidelines on the enlistment of minors. The New Zealand Army, Royal New Zealand Air Force (RNZAF) and Royal New Zealand Navy (RNZN) are separate services under the control of the Ministry of Defence. The army numbers around 4,500 regular personnel, the air force around 2,700 and the navy around 2,000. In addition there's a part-time reserve force (around 2,500 troops) called the Territorial Army (or 'Terries'), which trains in the evenings and at weekends, and can be called upon to assist the regular forces in an emergency. New Zealand spent around 1 per cent of its GDP on defence or around $2.1bn in 2000-2010.

The size of New Zealand's military forces reflects the small size of the country, and there has been discussion about whether the navy and some other elements of the armed forces are viable on such a small scale, and whether they should be merged with the Australian armed services. Australia spends around 2 per cent of its GDP (double what New Zealand spends) on defending not only Australia, but also the surrounding region, and it periodically takes its smaller neighbour to task for spending what it considers too little on defence.

Members of the armed forces can expect to be posted to a new base every two to three years, a practice which may be changed, as it's believed to be largely responsible for the high number of service personnel who resign after their initial term. In a bid to make military life more attractive, the navy has recently (among other steps) introduced maternity uniform, which allows women to continue military service during a pregnancy! In line with the New Zealand government's 'e-solutions' policy, the defence ministry has introduced an 'e-recruiting' strategy, thought to be in the world's first in the armed forces. Prospective recruits can now sign up online, which it's hoped may encourage more people to enlist.

New Zealand is a signatory to a number of defence treaties, including the Five Power Defence Agreement with Australia, Malaysia, Singapore and the UK, and the ANZUS alliance with Australia and the USA. New Zealand contributed forces to the Western alliance during the Gulf War, contributes to peacekeeping duties around the world and has a particularly strong presence in East Timor, Mozambique and Sierra Leone, where New Zealand troops are in charge of de-mining operations. New Zealand operates a strict anti-nuclear defence policy and doesn't allow visits by foreign military forces carrying nuclear weapons, e.g. warships, which has caused friction with the US.

PETS

New Zealanders are enthusiastic animal lovers and many people keep dogs (it's a very dog-friendly country) and cats. If you plan to take a pet to New Zealand, it's important to check the latest regulations, which are complex. New Zealand has strict regulations regarding the importation of animals in order to prevent animal diseases entering the country, and pets and other animals cannot be imported without authorisation from customs. Only domesticated dogs and cats can usually be imported and if you have a non-traditional pet such as a bird, rabbit, ferret, hamster, guinea pig, rat or mouse it cannot be imported into New Zealand. Certain breeds of dogs (including cross-breeds) cannot be imported, including the American Pit Bull Terrier, Dogo Argentine, Japanese Tosa and Brazilian Fila.

Cats have received a 'bad press' in recent years, as they're believed to be responsible for the decimation of New Zealand's wildlife. They aren't indigenous to New Zealand and flightless birds such as the kiwi had few natural predators until the first European settlers landed their pets on the country's shores.

Unless you're travelling from Australia, shipping your pets to New Zealand entails a long journey, which is best entrusted to a specialist pet shipping company. The cost of transporting a pet from Europe or the USA can run into thousands of dollars, for example, from the UK flight costs are from around GB£600 for a cat and GB£1,500 to £3,500 for a dog, depending on its size! Shop around as costs vary. In addition, there are vet costs in your home country, the cost of an import permit ($130 for any number of pets), customs' clearance ($50) and quarantine accommodation costing from around $40 per day ($1,200 for a 30-day stay).

You must obtain an import permit, which is available from the Executive Co-ordinator (Biosecurity New Zealand, PO Box 2526, Wellington, ☎ 04-470 2754, 💻 www.biosecurity.govt.nz). If your pet needs to spend time in quarantine, the import permit will be approved only if it's accompanied by a letter from a MAF-approved quarantine establishment (there are only three) confirming that your cat or dog has a reserved place.

You require a 'zoo-sanitary certificate' and a health certificate from a veterinary surgeon in your home country, and your pet will need to undergo a period of quarantine after its arrival in New Zealand unless it's exempt. Cats and dogs imported from Australia, Hawaii, Norway, Singapore, Sweden and the UK needn't be quarantined, provided they're microchipped, are older than 16 weeks and have been resident in the exporting country for a minimum of six months before travel. Dogs from these countries must be isolated at the owner's home for 30 days. Dogs must be kept on a leash when in public areas, and on private property must be unable to get out and roam on their own.

If you're coming from a country where rabies is present, pets must be vaccinated against rabies and must have had a Rabies Neutralising Antibody Tritation test no less than six months before they enter quarantine. A repeat test must be done within 30 days of the start of quarantine. Dogs must also be immunised against distemper, hepatitis, Parvovirus, parainfluenza and kennel cough, and must have a blood test for diseases such as leptospira canola. Cats must also be immunised against a range of diseases.

All dogs have been required to be microchipped since 2006 (with a subcutaneous identity chip), which was introduced to control dangerous dogs and reduce attacks on humans. The details of dogs and their owners are kept on the National Dog Database (NDD) and any unregistered dog picked up is automatically registered and microchipped before release. There's a one-off cost for a microchip of between $15 and $20 plus an insertion and verification fee, which can cost up to $70. Some councils offer inexpensive microchip insertion services, either free or subsidised. Microchips inserted overseas must be compatible with New Zealand scanners.

For further information contact the Ministry of Agriculture and Forestry, PO Box 2526, Wellington (☎ 04-474 4100, 🖳 www.maf.govt. nz), a New Zealand diplomatic mission or NZ Customs (☎ 0800-428 786 or 09-300 5399 from abroad). Customs also has a comprehensive website (🖳 www.customs.govt.nz) or you can contact one of the following offices: Auckland International Airport, PO Box 73-003 (☎ 09-275 9059), Christchurch, PO Box 14-086 (☎ 03-358 0600) or Wellington, PO Box 2218 (☎ 04-473 6099).

Additional information about importing and keeping pets in New Zealand is available from the Department of Internal Affairs' (🖳 www.dia. govt.nz), the Royal New Zealand Society for the Prevention of Cruelty to Animals (RNZSPCA, 🖳 www.rnzspca.org.nz), the New Zealand Kennel Club (🖳 www.nzkc.org.nz) and Cats Incorporated (🖳 www.catzinc.org.nz).

POLICE

New Zealand has a single national police force, controlled by a commissioner appointed by the Minister of Police, which is divided into six operational regions, each headed by an assistant commissioner. Over 500,000 crimes are reported annually (estimated to be less than half the number actually committed), of which less than half are solved, which is much better than the record of police forces in many other countries. Police officers (known as constables) can be identified by their dark blue (almost black) uniforms and peaked caps with a chequered band.

Police morale is low as a consequence of poor pay and insufficient resources, and the force has undergone something of a manpower crisis in recent years, as Australian state forces have 'poached' New Zealand police officers, who can earn 10 to 20 per cent more in Australia. The fact that policing is similar in both countries and police exams are standardised has contributed to the problem. Police officers are forbidden to strike, although they have taken part in a silent protest marches against poor pay and conditions during their off-duty hours.

New Zealand police officers are generally approachable, although some people consider them tyrannical and their popularity has decreased in recent years. They don't usually carry guns, although they do carry handcuffs, batons and controversial pepper sprays. When guns are necessary (usually only when confronting armed criminals), members of the Armed Offenders Squad (AOS) are called in to deal with incidents. AOS members serve only part-time and many have more mundane duties between armed call-outs. The police force doesn't routinely deal with motorists in New Zealand, which is the responsibility of the Traffic Safety Service that patrols highways, sets speed traps (their favourite pastime) and deals with motoring offences.

POPULATION

New Zealand is a sparsely populated country, with only some 15 inhabitants per square kilometre or around 32 per square mile (there are actually more New Zealanders per square mile in London or Sydney!). Around three-quarters of the population lives in the North Island (some 3.25m), with just over 1m in the whole of the South Island, and 85 per cent in urban areas (half in cities). The estimated populations of New Zealand's major cities in 2011 was: Auckland 1.38m, Wellington 393,000, Christchurch 381,000, Hamilton 206,000, Napier-Hastings 125,000, Tauranga, 122,000, Dunedin 118,000 and Palmerston North 82,000.

The population of New Zealand in March 2012 was 4.43m (see 🖥 www.stats.govt.nz/tools_and_services/tools/population_clock.aspx) and is forecast to reach 5m by around 2025.

New Zealand is less ethnically diverse than most other developed nations, including Australia. Some 68 per cent of New Zealanders are of European (mainly British) descent and are known as *Pākehā* by Maori (meaning 'white man' and not a derogatory term). The majority of the remaining inhabitants are Maori and other Polynesian Islanders; at the 2006 census (the 2011 census was postponed until 2013 due to the Christchurch earthquakes) there were around 14.6 per cent Maori, 9.2 per cent Asian and 6.55 per cent Pacific Islanders. New Zealand is also home to some 150,000 people of Chinese extraction and over 100,000 of Indian origin.

In recent years the population balance has been slowly changing in favour of non-Europeans. Two factors are responsible for this: Firstly the Maori and Polynesian population has an increasing birth rate and a decreasing death rate compared with those of European descent (which have remained static), as standards of health and welfare in these communities have improved; and secondly, the proportion of new immigrants of European descent is falling in favour of immigrants from other regions, particularly Asia.

RELIGION

New Zealand has a tradition of religious tolerance, and residents have total freedom of religion without hindrance by the state or community. It's a secular society with no official state religion, although the majority of people are Christians, the main denominations being Anglican (24 per cent), Presbyterian (18 per cent) and Roman Catholic (15 per cent). Methodist and other Protestant denominations are also represented and there are also considerable numbers of Jews, Hindus, and Confucians. Most Maori are members of the Ratana and Ringatu Christian sects. However, only some 10 per cent of New Zealanders regularly attend religious services and the

number is declining, even among those who claim to be followers of a particular religion.

SOCIAL CUSTOMS

All countries have their own particular social customs and New Zealand is no exception. As a country substantially populated by people of British ancestry, it's inevitable that many social customs are modelled on those of Britain with local influences, which have become more pronounced over the years. In general, New Zealanders tend to think that the British are prudish and snobbish, and that Australians and Americans are crass, although they share their pioneering spirit.

Most New Zealanders try to strike a balance between these two extremes, while also doing things differently, just to prove that they really are different from their neighbours and ancestors. It's also important to bear in mind that although New Zealand's Maori community is a minority in terms of numbers, its cultural influence extends across racial barriers. The following are a few of the most common New Zealand social customs;

♦ New Zealanders tend to prefer first name terms except when it clearly isn't appropriate (for example, when addressing your prospective boss during an interview). When in doubt, take your cue from your host or colleagues. It's usual for people at work to call each other by their first names, even when they're much higher or lower in the pecking order, and those who work together often also socialise together. It's common for friends to shorten names or use nicknames.

♦ It's considered socially acceptable to drop in on friends and acquaintances uninvited, and they will almost certainly do the same to you. You can also expect your neighbours to drop in uninvited, which is usually out of genuine friendliness rather than nosiness (or a desire to pass judgement on your interior decor). Indeed, if your new neighbours don't pop round, it's considered polite to call on them and introduce yourself.

♦ Direct questions about, for example, your likes and dislikes or your family shouldn't be considered as rudeness, as they usually indicate genuine interest and friendship (Kiwis generally prefer not to 'beat about the bush').

♦ Don't be surprised to receive invitations to social gatherings, such as parties or barbecues, from people you hardly know. This is particularly common when moving into a new area or starting a new job. It's done out of genuine warmth rather than any sense of duty, and should be accepted in the spirit in which it's intended. Indeed, it would be considered rude to turn down such an invitation out of hand. It's usual to 'bring a bottle' if you're invited to a party or to a BYO (Bring Your Own) restaurant, i.e. a restaurant that doesn't have a licence to sell alcohol.

♦ Casual dress is normal in most situations, e.g. shorts are often worn to work in the summer and jeans are acceptable in most restaurants and night-clubs. New Zealanders rarely wear formal dress such as evening dresses and dinner jackets. If you're invited to an event where formal attire is required, it will be clearly stated on the invitation.

♦ New Zealanders generally respect other cultures, customs, orientations, tastes and traditions, whether political, sexual or social. In fact, they usually have a particular regard for independent thinkers and those who dare to be different. This dates back to the pioneering days, and tolerance towards other ideas and cultures, provided they don't involve physical or emotional harm, is enshrined in New Zealand law. Nevertheless, if you have any bizarre tastes or habits, it's wise to keep them under wraps until you've ascertained whether or not your colleagues or acquaintances share them. Some New Zealanders, particularly older people, can be prudish.

TIME DIFFERENCE

New Zealand lies within a single time zone. Summer daylight saving time – an advance of one hour – is observed between the first Sunday in October and the third Sunday in March. New Zealand hasn't taken to the 24-hour clock system, and times in most timetables are shown according to the 12-hour clock system, where times are marked either 'am' or 'pm', or are printed in light type to indicate before noon and heavy type to indicate after noon. If in doubt, it's better to ask than to arrive 12 hours late (or early) for your flight or bus!

Bear in mind that there's a substantial time difference between New Zealand and Europe (and to a lesser extent the USA) and you should check the local time abroad before making international telephone calls. For example, when calling Western Europe, you need to phone either first thing in the morning or last thing at night (the difference between New Zealand and the UK is GMT +12 hours – see 🖳 www.timeanddate.com/worldclock). The time difference between Wellington at noon in January and some major international cities is shown below:

TIME DIFFERENCES						
WELL'TON	SYDNEY	LONDON	CAPE TOWN	TOKYO	L.A.	N.YORK
noon	10am	midnight	2am	9am	4pm	7pm
						(the previous day)

TIPPING

Tipping isn't a general custom in New Zealand (Americans please note!), although you may wish to leave a tip when you've had exceptional service or have received good value. New Zealanders almost never tip and, in fact, some people regard it as patronising or even insulting. Neither is it customary to round up amounts (e.g. taxi fares) to the nearest dollar or so, although most people won't complain if you do. Service charges aren't added to bills in hotels and restaurants and you won't be expected to add a tip.

TOILETS

Public toilets in New Zealand are generally clean and are commonly found in bus and railway stations, council and tourist offices, department stores, parks and shopping centres. The most sanitary toilets are found in airports, car parks, galleries, hotels, large stores, museums, petrol stations, popular beaches, public and private offices, and restaurants. Hotel (i.e. pub) and bar toilets vary from no-go areas to spotless. New Zealanders don't use euphemisms such as bathroom, powder room or restroom as Americans do, and the toilet is more likely to be referred to as the 'loo', which is considered quite a polite term, or the 'dunny'. Public toilets are usually free and don't normally have an attendant.

Some toilets have nappy (diaper) changing facilities and facilities for nursing mothers, and an increasing number also have special facilities for the disabled. Toilets are usually marked with the familiar international male and female symbols (so you won't need to distinguish between male and female kiwis), whereas disabled toilets are generally used by both sexes and indicated by the international wheelchair sign. Toilets for the disabled may be locked to keep out 'unauthorised' users, in which case there will be a notice nearby telling you where to obtain the key.

19.
THE KIWIS

Who are the New Zealanders? What are they like? Let's take a candid (and totally prejudiced) look at the Kiwis, tongue firmly in cheek, and hope they forgive my flippancy or that they don't read this bit (which is why it's hidden away at the back of the book). The typical Kiwi is friendly, generous, outspoken, hard working, honest, inquisitive, patriotic, adventurous, chauvinistic, modest, down-to-earth, optimistic, laid-back, parochial, a compulsive gambler, self-reliant, practical, sartorially challenged, a conservationist, hospitable, polite, decent, a beer drinker, open, brave, conservative, prudish, a sports fan, a suicidal driver, a DIY expert, old-fashioned, open, casual, understated, cosmopolitan, a foodie, good-humoured, a conformist, classless, self-deprecating, generous, educated, sincere, naïve, a carnivore, a philistine, competitive, proud, a habitual traveller, informal, sociable, idealistic, a foreigner and a fanatical rugby fan.

You may have noticed that the above list contains 'a few' contradictions (as does life in New Zealand), which is hardly surprising, as there's no such thing as a typical Kiwi and few people conform to the popular stereotype. People from the North and the South Islands are also supposed to have different characters, although foreigners will hardly notice the difference. New Zealand is a multicultural country (although not as much as Australia) and a nation of foreigners – even the Polynesians, the country's oldest inhabitants, came from somewhere else – many of whom have little in common. However, the country isn't a universal melting pot, and different ethnic groups such as Maori, Chinese, British and assorted other Europeans often live separate lives with their own clubs, customs, neighbourhoods, newspapers, restaurants, shops and sports.

New Zealanders pride themselves on their lack of class-consciousness, and don't have the same class distinctions and pretensions common in the 'mother' country (the UK), and consider the British to be snobbish (although descended from the British, the Kiwis have been trying to live it down for years). However, New Zealand isn't exactly a classless society and status is as important there as it is anywhere else, although it's usually based on education or money rather than birthright. New Zealand generally has no class or 'old school tie' barriers to success and almost anyone, however humble his origins, can fight his way to the top of the heap, although colour 'barriers' aren't always so easy to overcome. Kiwis don't particularly like Asians or any 'exotic' foreigners, although you'll generally be accepted provided you can blend into the background (and play rugby). Economic necessity has led to closer ties with Asian and Pacific rim countries and increased immigration from Asia.

Ties between New Zealand and the UK remain strong, although they've loosened somewhat in the last few decades and there has even been serious talk of changing the flag (a silver fern on a black background has been suggested – which would certainly be different) and becoming a republic, although there isn't a strong republican movement, unlike, for example, in Australia. Despite that fact that most Kiwis are of British stock, few still have close connections with the UK and many have no attachment to the Union Jack (which is incorporated in their flag).

However, there remain many similarities between Kiwis and the British, and New Zealand still copies many of the old country's habits (and new ideas) – in some ways Kiwis are considered to be more British than the British. The country even shares the UK's obsession with the weather, which is a popular topic of conversation. Not surprisingly, all New Zealand's bad weather, which usually consists of torrential rain in the South Island and howling gales in the North Island, comes from Australia.

Most enmity is reserved for the Aussies, who spend much of their time making jokes about Kiwis. New Zealanders feel culturally threatened by 'loud-mouthed' Aussies and the country is often referred to disparagingly as the eighth state of Australia (hundreds of thousands of New Zealanders live in Australia, and Sydney has a larger population of Kiwis than most New Zealand cities). Kiwis have much in common with their closest neighbours (who thankfully aren't *too* close) and they've even been known to marry them. Although they

don't much like comparisons being made, Kiwis are actually quite similar to (but much quieter than) Aussies, with whom they share their colourful language (with local idioms and Maori words thrown in for good measure), drinking habits, 'tucker' (food), sports, sheep, alleged lack of 'culture' and isolation from the rest of the world.

The Kiwis (and immigrants) usually get on well with their Polynesian cousins (they officially stopped fighting each other in the 19th century), who sensibly mostly live in the warmer North Island (only one in 16 lives in the South Island). The main cause of (mild) friction is the competition for top dog between the inhabitants of the country's two major cities, Auckland – New Zealand's largest city and the world's largest Polynesian city – and Wellington, the nation's capital. The Maori are believed to have arrived in 'the land of the long white cloud' (*Aotearoa*) by canoe around 925 AD from other Pacific islands (they're superb sailors and have been called the 'Vikings of the South Seas'). The white man (*Pākehā*) didn't arrive in any great numbers until the 19th century, although it didn't take him long to assert his 'authority' and rob the Maori of their land, which was done 'legally' under the Treaty of Waitangi (which cleverly has never been ratified – otherwise the Maori would own a lot more land than they do at present).

In recent years there has been an upsurge in Maori cultural awareness, and *Maoritanga* (the Maori way of life) is now taught in schools along with the Maori language. This has inevitably resulted in the question of land ownership and fishing rights being raised by Maori activists (influenced by the Aborigines' example in Australia), and has led to a number of clashes in recent decades. Although many Maori are second-class citizens, their plight is much better than that of Australia's Aborigines. Despite their differences of opinion, intermarriage between Maori and whites is common and there are fewer and fewer full-bloodied Maori left (it's estimated that 1 in 12 New Zealanders are half Maori and many more are part Maori). This may have something to do with the traditional Maori greeting (*hongi*), which consists of pressing noses together with the eyes closed and making a low 'mm-mm' sound.

Kiwis are passionate about sport and, when not debating the price of lamb, are discussing the latest rugby or cricket results. The All Blacks rugby team is widely acclaimed as the best in the world and star players are feted in the same way as soccer stars are in many other countries. They perform their famous *haka* 'war' dance before matches to intimidate their opponents, which worked well in the 2011 World Cup when the All Blacks became world champions on home soil after beating France in the final.

New Zealand's second-most popular sport is cricket and, although they haven't had much success since Sir Richard Hadlee retired in the '80s, they would *never* resort to such underhand tactics as bowling underarm to win a test match (unlike their neighbours, Australia). The Aussies are the old sporting enemy, with whom the Kiwis compete passionately at all sports (the Kiwis also enjoy beating the Poms).

> Apart from rugby, cricket and a few other sports, most New Zealand 'sports' involve trying to commit suicide by hurling yourself off bridges, out of planes or into boiling rapids – you certainly cannot accuse Kiwis of being timid!

New Zealanders aren't noted for their cuisine, which largely consists of numerous ways of serving lamb, fish and chips, meat pies and the obligatory tomato sauce (which goes with everything), ice cream, kiwi fruit and pavlova. Kiwis are voracious carnivores and among the world's largest meat-eaters – in fact things haven't changed a lot since the first Polynesian settlers ate each other. Kiwis generally have an unhealthy diet of biscuits, cakes, fast food and takeaways, despite the country's abundance of fresh fruit and vegetables (in New Zealand, a meat pie is *haute cuisine*). To compensate for their lack of culinary skills, New Zealanders have been making some passable wines in recent years, although most are beer drinkers. One of the secrets of enjoying a meal in New Zealand is to drink a lot – when you're drunk, most food tastes okay (although, admittedly, the food has improved immeasurably in the last decade or so).

The Kiwis are famous for their relaxed pace of life (except when motoring), particularly in rural areas, where the rush hour consists of a brisk walk to the nearest pub. Outside Auckland and Wellington, night-life usually consists of watching TV or getting drunk (or both), and many Kiwis are tucked up in bed by 9pm (so would you be if you got up at 5am to milk the ewes). Kiwis go to extraordinary lengths to 'amuse' themselves, which is why they partake in all those death-defying sports; a popular pastime in a pub in Napier (called 'bar-fly hopping') involves bouncing on a trampoline and trying to attach yourself to a wall with Velcro! New Zealand is notorious as a cultural backwater (even Australians make fun of it), although it isn't as (all) black as it's painted (at least in the major cities) and the Maori have a thousand years of culture and history in New Zealand.

The Kiwis are slow to make changes, both individually and as a nation, and the country is often reckoned to be around 20 years behind the rest of the world (which isn't surprising, as it used to take that long to get there from Europe or North America – assuming you could find it at all!). A few decades ago ago Kiwis were still wearing '60s fashions and driving around in British Morris Minors and Ford Anglias. However, it isn't true that they don't have electricity, although it may sometimes appear that way when visiting Auckland (they had a blackout that lasted a few weeks some years ago).

The country is so far from anywhere that it was one of the last places on earth to be inhabited by man and although most people have heard of New Zealand, few actually know where it is. Sometimes you don't just feel as if you're in the most isolated country in the world, but on a different planet altogether (the end of the world will probably be a few weeks late reaching New Zealand). Not surprisingly, New Zealand can appear a little detached from the rest of the world, and some newspapers and news bulletins rarely mention anything that happens overseas unless it's something particularly dramatic (such as the All Blacks losing a tour match or the price of lamb going through the floor).

New Zealand politics are deadly boring, even to Kiwis, although things have livened up in recent years with the introduction of proportional representation. Nowadays, you never know which politicians will jump into bed with whom (metaphorically speaking) and how long they will remain bedfellows, which makes for a lively parliament. New Zealand has (surprisingly) always been at the forefront of social change and is something of an social laboratory. It was the first self-governing country to give women the vote (in 1893 – 25 years before the UK) and New Zealand's women are rated fourth in the world by the United Nations for their 'achievements or opportunities' of gaining access to power.

New Zealand was also one of the first countries (in 1938) to establish a system of social security (including a national health service), the first to introduce an old-age pension and the first to institute an eight-hour working day. Both sexes have equal rights and opportunities in law, and it's one of the few countries in the world to have had a woman Prime Minister (in fact, it has had two). However, as in most democracies, Kiwis have a healthy disrespect (contempt) for their politicians, whatever their gender.

Immigration has undeniably made New Zealand a culturally richer, more diverse and interesting country, although it's now closed to many of the sort of people who made it what it is today. However, if you're rejected, try to look on the bright side; the New Zealand Dream isn't always the paradise it's cracked up to be. Despite its isolation from the real world, the country isn't completely detached from the problems that beset other countries. These include a spiralling cost of living, a high crime rate (particularly youth crime and delinquency), relatively high unemployment, homelessness, a worsening drug problem, welfare dependency, a high road toll (aided by widespread drunken driving), a plethora of single-parent families, racial tensions, and an economy that's too dependent on Asian markets (and lamb). However, these problems are by no means unique to New Zealand in today's turbulent world, and are shared by many other Western countries.

Now for the good news! New Zealand is one of the most liberal, open, stable and tolerant societies in the world. It has a strong economy, political stability, an excellent education system, a skilled workforce, universal healthcare, a high standard of living, some of the most desirable cities to be found anywhere and one of the cleanest environments in the world (the country declared itself the world's first nuclear-free zone in 1985). It's also renowned for its wealth of natural beauty, outdoor lifestyle, wholesome food, friendly people, sports prowess, personal freedom and excellent local government.

In many ways New Zealand is a blessed country with an abundance of riches, which include extensive water resources; a plethora of high-quality food and wine; well managed fisheries; vast energy reserves (coal, oil, gas, wind, water, steam and sunlight); a clean, largely unspoilt environment; vast open spaces and a small population; a safe environment (it's one of the most peaceful countries in the world and a long way from any hotspots); and a clean and green image (although it has a surprisingly large ecological footprint).

Although immigrants may occasionally criticise some aspects of life, relatively few consider leaving and most are happy and proud to call themselves Kiwis. In fact, immigrants from a vast range of backgrounds firmly believe that New Zealand (God's Own Country or 'Godzone') is one of the best countries in the world. Put simply, New Zealand is a great place in which to live, work and raise a family.

A final word of caution for newcomers – whatever you do don't make jokes about Kiwis and sheep, which are in bad taste and to be avoided at all costs. (Have you heard the one about two Kiwis in a pub with a black sheep . . .).

Up the All Blacks! Long live New Zealand!

20.
MOVING HOUSE OR LEAVING NEW ZEALAND

When moving house or leaving New Zealand there are many things to be considered and a 'million' people to be informed. The checklists contained in this chapter are designed to make the task easier and, with luck, help prevent an ulcer or a nervous breakdown – provided of course, you don't leave everything to the last minute (only divorce or a bereavement causes more stress than moving house). See also Moving House on page 98 and Relocation Consultants on page 81.

MOVING HOUSE

When moving house within New Zealand the following items should be considered:

♦ If you live in rented accommodation, you must give your landlord notice (the period will depend on your contract). If you don't give sufficient notice, you'll be required to pay the rent until the end of your contract or for the full notice period. This will also apply if you have a separate contract for a garage or other rented property, e.g. a holiday home.

♦ Inform the following:

 – your employer;

 – your present and new council if you're a homeowner and are moving to a new area. When moving to a new area, you may be entitled to a refund of a portion of your property taxes (rates).

 – your electricity, gas and water companies;

 – your telephone, internet and TV company (or companies);

 – your banks, credit and charge card companies, hire purchase companies,

insurance companies (for example car, health and home), local businesses where you have accounts, post office, solicitor and accountant, and stockbroker and other financial institutions;

 – your family GP, dentist and other health practitioners. Health records should be transferred to your new doctor and dentist, if applicable.

 – your children's schools. If applicable, arrange for schooling in your new area. You should try to give a term's notice and obtain a copy of any relevant school reports or records from current schools.

 – all friends and relatives, regular correspondents, subscriptions, social and sports clubs, and professional and trade journals. Give them your new address and telephone number. Arrange to have your mail redirected by NZ Post.

 – your local consulate or embassy, if you're registered with them.

♦ If you have a New Zealand driving licence or a New Zealand registered car, give the authorities your new address as soon as possible after moving.

♦ Return library books and anything else borrowed.

♦ Arrange removal of your furniture and belongings by booking a removal company well in advance. If you have only a few items of furniture to move, you may prefer to do your own move, in which case you may need to hire a van.

♦ If you're renting, make sure that you get your bond returned.

♦ Arrange for a cleaning and/or decorating company for rented accommodation, if necessary.

♦ Cancel milk and newspaper deliveries.

♦ **Ask yourself (again): 'Is it really worth all this trouble?'**

LEAVING NEW ZEALAND

Before leaving New Zealand permanently or for an indefinite period, the following items should be considered *in addition* to those listed above under **Moving House**:

♦ Give notice to your employer(s), if applicable.

♦ Check that your family's passports haven't expired and have at least six-months' validity.

♦ Check whether any special requirements (e.g. inoculations or visas) are necessary for entry into your country of destination by contacting the local embassy or consulate in New Zealand (if applicable). An exit permit or visa isn't required to leave New Zealand.

♦ Book a shipping company well in advance. International shipping companies usually provide a wealth of information and may also be able to advise you on various matters concerning your relocation. Find out the exact procedure for shipping your belongings to your country of destination from the embassy in New Zealand of the country to which you're moving (don't rely entirely on your shipping company). Special forms may need to be completed before arrival. If you've been living in New Zealand for less than a year, you're required to export personal effects, including furniture and vehicles, that were imported tax and duty-free. Arrange to sell anything that you won't be taking with you, e.g. car and furniture.

♦ Sell your house, apartment or other property, or arrange to let it through a friend or a letting agency (see **Chapter 5**).

♦ You may qualify for a rebate on your tax payments. If you're leaving New Zealand permanently and have been a member of a company superannuation scheme, you may be entitled to a refund or may be able to have your fund transferred to a new employer's fund. Contact your company personnel office or superannuation company for information.

♦ If you have a New Zealand-registered car which you're permanently exporting, you should ask the New Zealand authorities to de-register the vehicle and register it in your new country of residence on arrival.

♦ Depending on your destination, your pets may require immunisation or may need to go into quarantine for a period (contact the embassy of your destination country for information).

♦ Contact your telephone and other utility companies well in advance, particularly if you need to have deposits refunded.

♦ Arrange health, travel and other insurance as necessary (see **Chapter 13**).

♦ Depending on your destination, arrange health and dental check-ups for your family before leaving New Zealand. Obtain a copy of your health and dental records, and a statement from your health insurance company stating your present level of cover.

♦ Terminate any outstanding loan, lease or hire purchase contracts and pay any outstanding bills (allow plenty of time, as some companies may be slow to respond).

♦ Check whether you're entitled to a rebate on your car and other insurance. Obtain a letter from your New Zealand car insurance company stating your number of years no-claims' discount.

♦ Check whether you need an international driving permit or a translation of your New Zealand or foreign driving licence for your country of destination.

♦ Give friends and business associates in New Zealand a temporary address, telephone number and email address where you can be contacted overseas.

♦ If you're travelling by air, allow plenty of time to get to the airport, register your luggage, and clear security and immigration.

Have a safe journey!

Bay of Plenty coastline, Coromandel Peninsula, North Island

Lake Hayes, Queenstown, South Island

APPENDICES

APPENDIX A: USEFUL ADDRESSES

Embassies & Consulates

Most foreign embassies in New Zealand are located in the capital Wellington (a selection of which are listed below), although some countries have their missions in Auckland. A full list of embassies and consulates in New Zealand is available from the Ministry of Foreign Affairs and Trade website (💻 www.mfat.govt.nz/embassies/2-foreign-representatives-to-nz/diplomatic-and-consular-list.php).

> ☑ SURVIVAL TIP
>
> The business hours of embassies vary and they close on their own country's national holidays as well as on New Zealand public holidays. Always telephone to confirm opening hours before visiting.

Argentina: Level 14, 142 Lambton Quay, Wellington 6011 (☎ 04-472 8330, 💻 www.arg.org.nz).

Australia: 72-76 Hobson Street, Thorndon, Wellington 6011 (☎ 04-473 6411, 💻 www.australia.org.nz, ✉ nzinbox@dfat.gov.au).

Austria: 57 Willis Street, Wellington 6011 (☎ 04-499 6393, ✉ austria@vodafone.co.nz).

Belgium: Old Wool House, Level 1, 139 Featherston Street, Wellington 6011 (☎ 04-499 8933, ✉ rowland.woods@rowlandwoods.co.nz).

Brazil: Level 9, Deloitte House, 10 Brandon Street, Wellington 6011 (☎ 04-473 3516, 💻 www.brazil.org.nz).

Canada: Level 11, 125 The Terrace, Wellington 6011 (☎ 04-473 9577, ✉ wlgtn@international.gc.ca).

Chile: 19 Bolton Street, Wellington 6011 (☎ 04-471 6270, echile@embchile.co.nz).

China: 2-6 Glenmore Street, Kelburn, Wellington 6011 (☎ 04-472 1382, 💻 www.chinaembassy.org.nz/eng).

Denmark: 12 Ravi Street, Khandallah, Wellington 6143 (☎ 04-471 0520, 💻 www.danishconsulatesnz.org.nz).

Finland: HSBC Tower, Level 24, 195 Lambton Quay, Wellington 6011 (☎ 04-924 3416, ✉ michael.scannell@simpsongrierson.com).

France: 34-42 Manners Street, Wellington 6011 (☎ 04-384 2555, amba.france@actrix.gen.nz).

Germany: 90-92 Hobson Street, Thorndon, Wellington 6011 (☎ 04-473 6063, 💻 www.wellington.diplo.de/vertretung/wellington/en).

Greece: Level 11, Petherick Tower, 38-42 Waring Taylor Street, Wellington 6011 (☎ 04-473 7775, gremb.wel@mfa.gr).

Hungary: 37 Abbott Street, Wellington 6035 (☎ 04-973 7507, 💻 http://hungarianconsulate.co.nz).

India: 9th Floor, 180 Molesworth Street, Thorndon, Wellington 6015 (☎ 04-473 6390, www.hicomind.org.nz).

Indonesia: 70 Glen Road, Kelburn, Wellington 6012 (☎ 04-475 8697-9, ✉ kbriwell@ihug.co.nz).

Iran: PO Box 14733, Kilbirnie, Wellington (☎ 04-386 3065, 💻 www.iranembassy.org.nz).

Italy: 34-38 Grant Road, Thorndon, Wellington 6011 (☎ 04-473 5339, ✉ ambasciata.wellington@esteri.it).

Japan: Majestic Centre, Levels 18 & 19, 100 Willis Street, Wellington 6011 (☎ 04-473 1540, 💻 www.nz.emb-japan.go.jp).

Korea (Republic): Level 11, ASB Bank Tower, 2 Hunter Street, Wellington 6011 (☎ 04-473 9073-4, ✉ pa@koreanembassy.org.nz).

Malaysia: 10 Washington Avenue, Brooklyn, Wellington 6021 (☎ 04-385 2439, ✉ mwwelton@xtra.co.nz).

Mexico: Level 2, AMP Chambers, 187 Featherston Street, Wellington 6011 (☎ 04-472 0555, 💻 www.sre.gob.mx/nuevazelandia).

Netherlands: 10th Floor, Investment House, Corner Ballance & Featherston Streets, Wellington 6011 (☎ 04-471 6390, 💻 www.netherlandsembassy.co.nz).

Norway: Deloitte House, Levels 11-16, 10 Brandon Street, Wellington 6011 (☎ 04-471 2503, ✉ norconsulgen@deloitte.co.nz).

Pakistan: 182 Onslow Road, Khandallah, Wellington 6035 (☎ 04-479 0026, ✉ pakhcwellington@xtra.co.nz).

Papua New Guinea: 279 Willis Street, Wellington 6011 (☎ 04-385 2474-6, ✉ pngnz@globe.net.nz).

Peru: Level 8, Cigna House, 40 Mercer Street, Wellington 6011 (☎ 04-499 8087, ✉ embassy.peru@xtra.co.nz).

Philippines: 50 Hobson Street, Thorndon, Wellington 6011 (☎ 04-472 9848, 💻 www.philembassy.org.nz).

Poland: Level 9, City Chambers, 142 Featherston Street, Wellington 6011 (☎ 04-475 9453, 💻 www.wellington.polemb.net/).

Portugal: 1st Floor, 41/47 Dixon Street, Wellington 6011 (☎ 04-382 7655, ✉ consul@cawl.co.nz).

Russia: 57 Messines Road, Karori, Wellington 6012 (☎ 04-476 6113, 💻 www.russianembassy.co.nz).

Singapore: 17 Kabul Street, Khandallah, Wellington 6035 (☎ 04-470 0850, 💻 www.mfa.gov.sg/wellington).

South Africa: Level 16, Vodafone on the Quay, 157 Lambton Quay, Wellington 6011 (☎ 04-462 6866, ✉ administration@sahcwellington.co.nz).

Spain: Level 11, BNZ Trust House Bldg, 50 Manners Street, Wellington 6142 (☎ 04-802 5665, ✉ emb.wellington@maec.es).

Sweden: Level 7, Molesworth House, 101 Molesworth Street, Thorndon, Wellington 6011 (☎ 04-499 9895, sweden@xtra.co.nz).

Switzerland: Level 12, Maritime Tower, 10 Customhouse Quay, Wellington 6140 (☎ 04-472 1593, 🖥 www.eda.admin.ch/wellington).

Thailand: 2 Cook Street, Karori, Wellington 6012 (☎ 04-476 8616, 🖥 www.mfa.go.th).

Turkey: Level 8, 15-17 Murphy Street, Thorndon, Wellington 6011 (☎ 04-472 1292, ✉ turkem@ xtra.co.nz).

United Kingdom: 44 Hill Street, Wellington 6011 (☎ 04-924 2888, http://ukinnewzealand.fco. gov.uk).

USA: 29 Fitzherbert Terrace, Wellington 6011 (☎ 04-462 6000, www.philembassy.org.nz).

Government Departments

Births, Deaths & Marriages, Level 3, Boulcott House 47 Boulcott Street, Wellington 6011 (☎ 04-463 9362, 🖥 www.bdm.govt.nz).

Citizenship Office, Level 3, Boulcott House, 47 Boulcott Street, Wellington 6011 (☎ 0800-225 151, 🖥 www.dia.govt.nz).

Department of Building & Housing, Level 6/86 Customhouse Quay, Wellington 6011 (☎ 04-494 0260, 🖥 www.dbh.govt.nz).

Department of Child, Youth and Family Services, Level 8, Grand Central Building, 76-86 Manners Street, Wellington 6011 (☎ 04-917 1100, 🖥 www.cyf.govt.nz).

Department of Conservation, Level 1, 181 Thorndon Quay, Pipitea, Wellington 6011 (☎ 04-472 5821, 🖥 www.doc.govt.nz).

Department of Corrections, Level 3, 117 Lambton Quay, Wellington 6011 (☎ 04-915 8862, 🖥 www.corrections.govt.nz).

Department of Internal Affairs, 46 Waring Taylor Street, Wellington 6011 (☎ 04-495 7200, 🖥 www.dia.govt.nz).

Department of Labour, Level 4, Unisys House, 56 The Terrace, Wellington 6011 (☎ 04-915 4000, 🖥 www.dol.govt.nz).

Department of the Prime Minister & Cabinet, Parliament Building, Molesworth Street, Thorndon, Wellington 6011 (☎ 04-817 9700, 🖥 www.dpmc.govt.nz).

Immigration New Zealand, PO Box 27-149, Wellington (☎ 04-917 6640, in NZ – 0508-558 855, 🖥 www.immigration.govt.nz).

Land Information New Zealand, Level 7, Radio New Zealand House, 155 The Terrace, Wellington 6145 (☎ 04-460 0110, 🖥 www.linz.govt.nz).

Ministry for the Environment, Environment House, 23 Kate Sheppard Place, Pipitea, Wellington 6011 (☎ 04-439 7400, 🖥 www.mfe.govt.nz).

Ministry of Agriculture & Forestry, 25 The Terrace, Wellington 6011 (☎ 04-819 0100, 🖥 www.maf.govt.nz).

Ministry of Civil Defence, Level 9, 22 The Terrace, Wellington 6011 (☎ 04-473 7363, 🖳 www.civildefence.govt.nz).

Ministry of Consumer Affairs, 33 Bowen Street, Wellington 6011 (☎ 04-474 2750, 🖳 www.consumeraffairs.govt.nz).

Ministry for Culture and Heritage, Level 5, Radio NZ House, 155 The Terrace, Wellington 6011 (☎ 04-499 4229, 🖳 www.mch.govt.nz).

Ministry of Defence, Level 4 Defence House, 2-12 Aitken Street, Wellington 6011 (☎ 04-496 0999, 🖳 www.defence.govt.nz).

Ministry of Education, Level 3, 45-47 Pipitea Street, Thorndon, Wellington 6140 (☎ 04-463 8000, 🖳 www.minedu.govt.nz).

Ministry of Foreign Affairs & Trade, 195 Lambton Quay, Wellington 6011 (☎ 04-439 8000, 🖳 www.mfat.govt.nz).

Ministry of Health, 133 Molesworth Street, Thorndon, Wellington 6011 (☎ 04-381 5300, 🖳 www.moh.govt.nz).

Ministry of Justice, The Vogel Centre, 19 Aitken St, Wellington 6011 (☎ 04-918 8000, 🖳 www.justice.govt.nz).

Ministry of Maori Development (*Te Puni Kokiri*), Te Puni Kōkiri House, 143 Lambton Quay, Wellington 6011 (☎ 04-819 6000, 🖳 www.tpk.govt.nz).

Ministry of Pacific Island Affairs, Level 2, ASB House, 101 The Terrace, Wellington 6011 (☎ 04-473 4493, 🖳 www.minpac.govt.nz).

Ministry of Research, Science & Technology, 2 The Terrace, Wellington 6011 (☎ 04-917 2900, 🖳 www.morst.govt.nz).

Ministry of Social Development, 38 Bowen Street, Pipitea, Wellington 6011 (☎ 04-916 3300, 🖳 www.msd.govt.nz).

Ministry of Transport, Level 6, 89 The Terrace, Wellington 6011 (☎ 04-439 9000, 🖳 www.transport.govt.nz).

Ministry of Women's Affairs, Level 2, Revera Building, 48 Mulgrave Street, Thorndon, Wellington 6011 (☎ 04-915 7112, 🖳 www.mwa.govt.nz).

Ministry of Youth Development, Level 7, Bowen State Building, Bowen Street, Wellington 6011 (☎ 04-916 3300, 🖳 www.myd.govt.nz).

New Zealand Customs, 17 Whitmore Street, Wellington 6011 (☎ 04-473 6099, 🖳 www.customs.govt.nz).

The Treasury, Level 5, 1 The Terrace, Wellington 6011 (☎ 04-472 2733, 🖳 www.treasury.govt.nz).

Magazines & Newspapers

Australia & New Zealand magazine, Unit 3, The Old Estate Yard, North Stoke Lane, Upton Cheyney, Bristol BS30 6ND (☎ 0117-930 3586, 🖳 www.getmedownunder.com).

Avenues magazine (🖳 www.avenues.net.nz). Bi-monthly Christchurch lifestyle magazine.

Business New Zealand magazine (🖳 www.nzbusiness.co.nz). Monthly.

Cuisine magazine (🖳 www.cuisine.co.nz). Monthly foodie magazine.

The Dominion Post (🖳 www.stuff.co.nz/dominion-post). Wellington's major daily newspaper.

Franchise NZ magazine (🖥 www.franchise.co.nz). Monthly.

Home New Zealand magazine (🖥 www.acpmedia.co.nz/acpmagazines/homenewzealand/tabid/128/default.aspx). Monthly.

Inspire magazine (🖥 www.inspiremagazine.co.nz). Quarterly award-winning travel magazine.

Latitude magazine (🖥 www.latitudemagazine.co.nz). Quarterly Canterbury lifestyle magazine

Mana magazine (🖥 www.manaonline.co.nz). Maori lifestyle magazine.

Metro magazine (🖥 www.acpmedia.co.nz/acpmagazines/metro/tabid/124/default.aspx). Monthly Auckland lifestyle and local issues magazine.

New Zealand Herald (🖥 www.nzherald.co.nz). New Zealand's leading newspaper.

New Zealand News Online Ltd., Suite 5, Eden House, 59 Fulham High Street, London SW6 3JJ (☎ 020-7736 0980, 🖥 www.nznewsuk.co.uk). Online magazine for emigrants.

North & South magazine (🖥 www.acpmedia.co.nz/acpmagazines/northsouth/tabid/127/default.aspx). Monthly topical issues and lifestyle magazine.

NZ Today magazine (🖥 www.nztoday.co.nz). Monthly lifestyle magazine.

The Press (🖥 www.stuff.co.nz/the-press). Christchurch's major daily newspaper.

TNT magazine (🖥 www.tntdownunder.com). Australia & New Zealand travel magazine.

Unlimited magazine (🖥 www.unlimited.co.nz). Monthly business magazine.

Miscellaneous

Archives New Zealand, 10 Mulgrave Street, Pipitea, Wellington 6011 (☎ 04-499 5595, 🖥 www.archives.govt.nz).

Citizens' Advice Bureau (☎ 0800-367 222, 🖥 www.cab.org.nz).

Consumer Institute of New Zealand, Level 1, Defence Careers House, 204 Thorndon Quay, Pipitea, Wellington (☎ 04-384 7963, 🖥 www.consumer.org.nz).

National Library of New Zealand, 77 Thorndon Quay, Pipitea, Wellington 6011 (☎ 04-474 3000, 🖥 www.natlib.govt.nz).

Statistics New Zealand, Statistics House, The Boulevard, Harbour Quays, Boulevard, Wellington 6011 (☎ 04-931 4600, 🖥 www.stats.govt.nz).

TeachNZ, 45 Pipitea Street, Thorndon, Wellington 6011 (☎ 0800-165 225, 🖥 www.teachnz.govt.nz).

APPENDIX B: FURTHER READING

There are many useful reference books for those seeking general information about New Zealand, including the *New Zealand Official Year Book* published annually by Statistics New Zealand (⌨ www.stats.govt.nz). A selection of books about New Zealand is listed below (the publication title is followed by the name of the author and the publisher's name in brackets). Some of the books listed are out of print, but you may still be able to find a copy in a book shop or library.

Culture

Cultural Atlas of Australia, New Zealand and the South Pacific, Gordon Johnson (Facts on File)

Cultural Questions: New Zealand Identity in a Transitional Age, Ruth Brown (Kapako)

Culture Wise New Zealand, David Hampshire & John Irvine (Survival Books)

A Destiny Apart: New Zealand's Search for a National Identity, Kenneth Sinclair (Allen & Unwin)

Fiction

All the Nice Girls, Barbara Anderson (Vintage)

The Bone People, Keri Hulme (Picador)

The Collected Stories of Katherine Mansfield, Katherine Mansfield (Penguin)

Dogside Story, Patricia Grace (Talanoa)

Fifty Ways of Saying Fabulous, Graeme Aitken (Headline)

The God Boy, Ian Cross (Penguin)

The Miserables, Damien Wilkins (Faber)

Once Were Warriors, Alan Duff (Virago/Random House)

Potiki, Patricia Grace (Penguin)

The Stories of Frank Sargeson, Frank Sargeson (Penguin)

Strangers and Journeys, Maurice Shadbolt (Hodder/Atheneum)

Food & Wine

Celebrating New Zealand Wine, Joelle Thomson & Andrew Charles Coffey (New Holland)

Edmonds Illustrated Cookbook, Edmonds (Hachette Livre NZ)

First Catch Your Weka: A Story of New Zealand Cooking, David Veart (AUP)

Fleurs Place, Graham Warman & Paul Sorrell (Penguin)

Harvest: Naturally Good New Zealand Food, Penny Oliver & Ian Batchelor (New Holland)

The Mad Keen Wine Buff's Road Trip, Phil Parker (Random House)

New Taste New Zealand, Lauraine Jacobs & Stephen Robinson (Ten Speed Press)

Pocket Guide to the Wines of New Zealand, Michael Cooper (Mitchell Beazley)

Rough Guide to Auckland Restaurants, Mark Graham (Rough Guides)

Simply New Zealand: A Culinary Journey, Ian Baker (New Holland)

Wine Atlas of New Zealand, Michael Cooper (Hodder Moa)

History

The New Zealand Wars, James Belich (Penguin)

History of New Zealand, George William Rusden (Elibron Classics)

A History of New Zealand, Keith Sinclair (Pelican)

New Zealand and the Second World War: The People, the Battles and the Legacy, Ian McGibbon (Hodder Moa Beckett)

New Zealand's Top 100 History-makers, Joseph Romanos (Trio Books)

Oxford Illustrated History of New Zealand, Keith Sinclair (Oxford University Press)

The Penguin History of New Zealand, Michael King (Penguin)

Language

A Concise Dictionary of New Zealand Sign Language, Graeme Kennedy (Bridget Williams)

A Dictionary of Maori Words in New Zealand English, John Macalister (Oxford University Press)

Dictionary of New Zealand English, H. W. Oarsman (Oxford University Press)

The Godzone Dictionary, Max Cryer (Exisle)

Languages of New Zealand, Alan Bell et al (Victoria University Press)

New Zealand English: Its Origins and Evolution (Cambridge University Press)

New Zealand Ways of Speaking English, Allan Bell & Janet Holmes (Multilingual Matters)

A Personal Kiwi-Yankee Dictionary, Louis S. Leland Jr

The Reed Dictionary of New Zealand Slang, D. McGill (Reed NZ)

Sign Language Interpreting: Theory and Practice in Australia and New Zealand, Jemina Napier (Federation Press)

Maori New Zealand

1,000 Years of Maori History (*Nga Iwi O Te Motu*), M King (Reed)

Being Pākehā: An Encounter with New Zealand and the Maori Renaissance, Michael King (Hodder & Stoughton)

Exploring Maori Values, John Patterson (Dunmore Press)

Maori Art and Culture, ed. D. C. Starzecka (British Museum Press)

Maori Legends, Alistair Campbell (Viking Sevenseas)

Maori Myths and Tribal legends, Antony Alpers (Longman)

The Rough Guide to Maori New Zealand (Rough Guides)

Te Marae: a Guide to Customs and Protocol, Hiwi Tauroa (Reed Books)

Miscellaneous

100 Best Plants for New Zealand Gardens, Fiona Eadie (Random House)

AA Road Atlas New Zealand (Automobile Association)

Back Country New Zealand (Hodder)

Beach Houses of Australia and New Zealand 2, Stephen Crafti (Images Publishing)

Buying a Home in New Zealand, Graeme Chesters (Survival Books)

Cars and Kiwis: The Golden Age of Motoring, John McCrystal (Penguin)

Excellent Short Walks in the North Island, Peter Janssen (New Holland)

Facts New Zealand, Nicky Chapman (David Bateman)

Great New Zealand Railway Journeys, Graham Hutchins (Exisle)

Landscapes of New Zealand, Warren Jacobs & Jill Worrall (New Holland)

Life on the Edge: New Zealand's Natural Hazards and Disasters, Philip Temple (Penguin)

Motorhome Magic: Paradise Found in New Zealand, Jane Dunn (Vanguard Press)

New Zealand: A Natural History, Tui De Roy & Mark Jones (Firefly)

New Zealand Chic, Nicky Adams et al (Thames & Hudson)

New Zealand's Wilderness Heritage, Les Molloy (Craig Potton)

The Penguin Natural World of New Zealand, Gerald Hutching (Penguin)

Politics in New Zealand, Richard Mulgan (Auckland UP)

Reed New Zealand Atlas, Terralink (Reed Publishing)

Sanctuary: New Zealand's Spectacular Nature Reserves, Eric Dorfman (Penguin Putnam)

Tramping in New Zealand, Jim DuFresne (Lonely Planet)

The Truth About New Zealand, A. N. Field (Veritas)

Whale Watching in Australian and New Zealand Waters, Peter Gill & Cecilia Burke (New Holland)

Yates Garden Guide, Yates (HarperCollins)

People

The Governors: New Zealand's Governors and Governors-General, Gavin Mclean (Otago University Press)

Ian Brodie's New Zealand: One Man's Love Affair With His Country, Ian Brodie (HarperCollins)

A Land of Two Halves: An Accidental Tour of New Zealand, Joe Bennett (Scribner)

A Man's Country? The Image of the Pākehā Male, Jock Phillips (Penguin)

My Home Now: Migrants and Refugees to New Zealand Tell Their Stories, Gail Thomas et al (Cape Catley)

Visitor Guides

25 Ultimate Experiences New Zealand, Mark Ellingham (Rough Guides)

Australia and New Zealand on a Shoestring (Lonely Planet)

Blue Guide New Zealand (A & C Black)

DK Eyewitness Travel Guide New Zealand (Dorling Kindersley)

Explore New Zealand: Over 60 Scenic Driving Tours, John Cobb (New Holland)

Fodor's New Zealand (Fodor's)

Frommer's New Zealand, Adrienne Rewi (Frommers)

New Zealand Insight Guide, Donna Blaber (APA Publications)

Kiwi Tracks: New Zealand Journey, Andrew Stevenson (Lonely Planet)

Let's Go New Zealand (Macmillan)

Maverick Guide to New Zealand, Robert W. Bone (Pelican)

National Geographic Traveller, Peter Turner & Colin Monteath (NG)

New Zealand, Charles Rawlings-Way (Lonely Planet)

The Rough Guide to New Zealand, Oaul Whitfield et al (The Rough Guides)

Straying from the Flock: Travels in New Zealand, Dr. Alexander Elder (Wiley)

Touring the Natural Wonders of New Zealand, Peter Janssen & Andrew Fear (New Holland)

APPENDIX C: USEFUL WEBSITES

This appendix contains a selection of useful websites for anyone wishing to learn more about New Zealand and New Zealanders.

Government

Arts Council of New Zealand (🖥 www.creativenz.govt.nz). Provides information about the world of the arts, arts funding and the work of the Arts Council.

Business Government NZ (www.business.govt.nz). Brings together free business resources, tools and information to help people start, manage and grow their business.

Customs (🖥 www.customs.govt.nz). New Zealand customs service.

Immigration New Zealand (🖥 www.immigration.govt.nz). Information about New Zealand's culture, history and lifestyle, plus extensive information about permit/visa requirements and the skills sought.

Inland Revenue Department (🖥 www.ird.govt.nz). Everything you need to know about taxation in New Zealand, whether you're a resident, non-resident or visitor.

Local Government New Zealand (🖥 www.lgnz.co.nz). The national voice of local government.

New Zealand Elections (🖥 www.elections.org.nz). The New Zealand electoral system explained in detail.

New Zealand Government (🖥 http://newzealand.govt.nz). Comprehensive information about government organisations and services, plus useful information and news about various aspects of visiting and living in New Zealand.

New Zealand Trade and Enterprise (🖥 www.nzte.govt.nz). Advice and information for those contemplating doing business in or with New Zealand.

Parliament (🖥 www.parliament.nz). Website of the New Zealand parliament.

Statistics New Zealand (🖥 www.stats.govt.nz). Facts and figures about many aspects of life in New Zealand.

Te Ara (🖥 www.teara.govt.nz) The encyclopaedia of New Zealand (*Te Ara* is 'the pathway' in Maori).

Work and Income (🖥 www.workandincome.govt.nz). Government employment services and financial assistance.

Maori

Maaori.com (🖥 www.maaori.com). Maori culture.

Maori (🖥 www.maori.org.nz). The 'main Maori site on the net', with information and features about Maori customs, genealogy, language, performing arts and more.

Maori gen (www.maori.gen.nz). List of Maori websites and links to the main Maori web portals.

Maori News (🖥 http://maorinews.com). Maori news (*Te Karere Ipurangi*), views, commentary and writings.

Maori Television (🖥 www.maoritelevision.com). The website of the television channel devoted to Maori culture and life.

Maori UK (🖥 www.maori.org.uk). Providers of Maori language & culture courses in London, UK.

Media

The Dominion Post (🖥 www.stuff.co.nz/dominion-post). Wellington's major daily newspaper.

The New Zealand Herald (🖥 www.nzherald.co.nz). New Zealand's major newspaper. As well as coverage of business, news and sport, there are articles about culture, employment, entertainment, lifestyle, motoring, property, technology and travel.

National Business Review (🖥 www.nbr.co.nz).

NZ City (🖥 http://home.nzcity.co.nz). News portal.

NZ On Air (🖥 www.nzonair.govt.nz). Promotes and fosters the development of New Zealand's culture on the airwaves by funding locally-made television programmes, public radio networks and access radio.

Online Newspapers (🖥 www.onlinenewspapers.com/nz.htm). Links to the websites of all New Zealand's major newspapers (listed A-Z by town/city).

Otago Daily Times (🖥 www.odt.co.nz). A good summary of regional, national and international news and sport.

The Press (🖥 www.stuff.co.nz/the-press). Christchurch's major daily newspaper.

Stuff (🖥 www.stuff.co.nz). News and comment from national and regional NZ newspapers owned by Fairfax Media.

The Radio Bureau (🖥 www.trb.co.nz). Self-styled 'Champions of Radio' in New Zealand.

Radio New Zealand (www.radionz.co.nz). The national public radio network.

Scoop (🖥 www.scoop.co.nz). New Zealand's leading news resource for news-makers and the people that influence the news.

Television New Zealand (🖥 http://tvnz.co.nz). The public TV service that operates TV One and TV2.

Migrants

Auckland Regional Migrant Services (🖥 www.arms-mrc.org.nz). A non-profit organisation which helps migrants and refugees to settle in the Auckland region.

Emigrate NZ (🖥 www.emigratenz.org). New Zealand immigration guide.

The Emigration Group (🖥 www.emigrationgroup.co.uk). The UK's leading consultants for New Zealand migration.

Global Footprints (🖥 www.globalfootprints.co.nz). Resources for migrants.

Human Resource Institute of New Zealand (www.hrinz.org.nz). Information about all aspects of human resources and employment in New Zealand.

Kiwi Ora (⌨ www.kiwi-ora.com). Information to help new immigrants settle in New Zealand.

Migrant News (⌨ www.migrantnews.co.nz). Self-styled 'Voice of New Kiwis'. Probably the best 'uncensored' website for migrants – warts 'n all!

Move 2 New Zealand (⌨ http://move2nz.com). Information for prospective migrants.

Newcomers Network (⌨ www.newcomers.co.nz). Offers friendship and support to new arrivals.

New Zealand News Online (⌨ www.nznewsuk.co.uk). Useful online magazine for migrants.

New Zealand Now (⌨ www.newzealandnow.govt.nz). Government website for migrants.

Seek (⌨ www.seek.co.nz). Claims to be New Zealand's #1 job site.

Miscellaneous

The All Blacks (⌨ www.allblacks.com). Website of the iconic national rugby team.

Citizens Advice Bureau (⌨ www.cab.org.nz).

Consumer Institute of New Zealand (⌨ www.consumer.org.nz). NZ consumers' champion.

Enzed (⌨ www.enzed.com). Information from websites in New Zealand and the rest of the world.

Film New Zealand (⌨ www.filmnz.com). A website that covers all aspects of New Zealand's burgeoning film industry, including information for film makers such as film crews, locations, permits, tax and transport.

Financial Services (⌨ www.interest.co.nz and www.sorted.org.nz). Comprehensive financial information.

Geography New Zealand (⌨ www.nzgeography.com). New Zealand's online geographical resource.

Met Service (⌨ www.metservice.co.nz). New Zealand's National Meteorological Service.

NZ English to US English Dictionary (⌨ http://nz.com/NZ/Culture/NZDic.html). A useful resource for Americans bewildered by Kiwis' sometimes unusual way with the English language.

New Zealand in History (⌨ http://history-nz.org). A 'brief overview of prehistoric, colonial and modern periods.'

New Zealand Museums Online (⌨ www.nzmuseums.co.nz). Take a tour of New Zealand's museums, by area, collection or name.

New Zealand Post (⌨ www.nzpost.co.nz). Everything you need to know about the country's postal services.

New Zealand Rugby World (⌨ www.nzrugbyworld.com). Everything you could ever want to know about the latest happenings in the world of New Zealand rugby, the central plank of many a Kiwi life.

New Zealand Search (⌨ www.nzs.com). New Zealand search engine.

New Zealand Wine and Grape Industry (💻 www.nzwine.com). Information about the country's wine exports, events, production statistics, regions and styles.

NZ History (💻 www.nzhistory.net.nz). New Zealand's history online.

Price Me (💻 www.priceme.co.nz) and **Shopbot** (💻 www.shopbot.co.nz). Price comparison websites.

Sport and Recreation New Zealand (💻 www.sparc.org.nz). Information about all aspects of sport in New Zealand and becoming active and healthy.

Trade & Exchange (💻 www.te.co.nz). Free classified ads.

Trade Me (💻 www.trademe.co.nz). Online auction site – New Zealand's answer to Ebay.

Wikipedia New Zealand (💻 http://en.wikipedia.org/wiki/New_Zealand). Comprehensive information about all aspects of New Zealand.

Property

Harcourts (💻 www.harcourts.co.nz). New Zealand's largest real estate group.

Home Sell (💻 www.homesell.co.nz). The country's largest private property sales website.

I Want a Home (💻 www.iwantahome.co.nz). Comprehensive information about buying, selling and owning a home in NZ.

Mortgages by Design (💻 www.mortgagesbydesign.co.nz). Mortgage broker.

Nailed (💻 www.nailed.co.nz). Home improvement advice and information.

Property Talk (💻 www.propertytalk.com). Property newsletter and forum.

Real Estate (💻 www.realestate.co.nz). The official website of the New Zealand real estate industry.

Real Estate Institute of New Zealand (💻 www.reinz.org.nz).

Sue Tierney Mortgages (💻 www.stml.co.nz). New Zealand mortgage broker.

Trade me (💻 www.trademe.co.nz/trade-me-property). Ads for property sales and rentals.

Travel & Tourism

Air New Zealand (💻 www.airnewzealand.co.nz). New Zealand's national flag carrier.

Backpacker Board (www.backpackerboard.co.nz). Travel guide for backpackers in New Zealand.

Destination New Zealand (💻 www.destination-nz.com). Information about accommodation, activities, facts and figures, tours and transport, plus commercial information, maps and a newsletter.

Flight Centre (💻 www.flightcentre.co.nz). New Zealand's leading flight and travel agent.

Interislander (💻 www.interislander.co.nz). The ferry service operator between the North and South Islands.

The New Zealand Guide Book (💻 www.nz.com). Information about places in New Zealand, facts and figures, food, history, language and natural history.

The New Zealand Site (⌨ http://thenewzealandsite.com). Site for travellers.

New Zealand Tourism (⌨ www.tourism.net.nz). A wealth of information about accommodation, attractions, culture, history, key facts, travel, weather and more.

Tourism (⌨ www.tourism.net.nz). Comprehensive guide for tourists and travellers.

Tourism New Zealand (⌨ www.newzealand.com). The official New Zealand tourist website; as well as the usual tourist information there are interesting feature articles about various aspects of New Zealand's culture, history and lifestyle.

Tranz Scenic (⌨ www.tranzscenic.co.nz). New Zealand's passenger railway company.

Maori art

APPENDIX D: WEIGHTS & MEASURES

New Zealand uses the metric system of measurement. Measurements generally used for clothes are indicated below. Those who are more familiar with the imperial system will find the tables on the following pages useful. Some comparisons shown are only approximate, but are close enough for most everyday uses.

In addition to the variety of measurement systems used, clothes sizes often vary considerably with the manufacturer – as we all know only too well! Try all clothes on before buying and don't be afraid to return something if, when you try it on at home, you decide it doesn't fit (most shops will exchange goods or give a refund).

Women's Clothes										
Continental	34	36	38	40	42	44	46	48	50	52
UK		8	10	12	14	16	18	20	22	24	26
US		6	8	10	12	14	16	18	20	22	24

Pullover's												
	Women's						Men's					
Continental	40	42	44	46	48	50	44	46	48	50	52	54
UK		34	36	38	40	42	44	34	36	38	40	42	44
US		34	36	38	40	42	44	sm	med	lar	xl

Men's Shirts										
Continental	36	37	38	39	40	41	42	43	44	46
UK/US	14	14	15	15	16	16	17	17	18	-

Men's Underwear						
Continental	5	6	7	8	9	10
UK		34	36	38	40	42	44
US		sm	med	lar	xl

sm = small, med = medium, lar = large, xl = extra large

Children's Clothes						
Continental	92	104	116	128	140	152
UK	16/18	20/22	24/26	28/30	32/34	36/38
US	2	4	6	8	10	12

Children's Shoes	
Continental	18 19 20 21 22 23 24 25 26 27 28 29 30 31 32
UK/US	2 3 4 4 5 6 7 7 8 9 10 11 11 12 13
Continental	33 34 35 36 37 38
UK/US	1 2 2 3 4 5

Shoes (Women's & Men's)	
Continental	35 36 37 37 38 39 40 41 42 42 43 44 45 46 47
UK	2 3 3 4 4 5 6 7 7 8 9 9 10 11 12
US	4 5 5 6 6 7 8 9 9 10 10 11 11 12 12

Weight			
Imperial	**Metric**	**Metric**	**Imperial**
1oz	28.35g	1g	0.035oz
1lb*	454g	100g	3.5oz
1cwt	50.8kg	250g	9oz
1 ton	1,016kg	500g	18oz
2,205lb	1 tonne	1kg	2.2lb

Area			
British/US	**Metric**	**Metric**	**British/US**
1 sq. in	0.45 sq. cm	1 sq. cm	0.15 sq. in
1 sq. ft	0.09 sq. m	1 sq. m	10.76 sq. ft
1 sq. yd	0.84 sq. m	1 sq. m	1.2 sq. yds
1 acre	0.4 hectares	1 hectare	2.47 acres
1 sq. mile	2.56 sq. km	1 sq. km	0.39 sq. mile

Capacity			
Imperial	**Metric**	**Metric**	**Imperial**
1 UK pint	0.57 litre	1 litre	1.75 UK pints
1 US pint	0.47 litre	1 litre	2.13 US pints
1 UK gallon	4.54 litres	1 litre	0.22 UK gallon
1 US gallon	3.78 litres	1 litre	0.26 US gallon

An American 'cup' = around 250ml or 0.25 litre.

Length			
British/US	**Metric**	**Metric**	**British/US**
1in	2.54cm	1cm	0.39in
1ft	30.48cm	1m	3ft 3.25in
1yd	91.44cm	1km	0.62mi
1mi	1.6km	8km	5mi

Temperature	
°Celsius	**°Fahrenheit**
0	32 (freezing point of water)
5	41
10	50
15	59
20	68
25	77
30	86
35	95
40	104
50	122

Temperature Conversion

- **Celsius to Fahrenheit:** multiply by 9, divide by 5 and add 32. (For a quick and approximate conversion, double the Celsius temperature and add 30.)

- **Fahrenheit to Celsius:** subtract 32, multiply by 5 and divide by 9. (For a quick and approximate conversion, subtract 30 from the Fahrenheit temperature and divide by 2.)

NB: The boiling point of water is 100°C / 212°F. Normal body temperature (if you're alive and well) is 37°C / 98.6°F.

Power			
Kilowatts	Horsepower	Horsepower	Kilowatts
1	1.34	1	0.75

Oven Temperature		
Gas	Electric	
	°F	°C
-	225–250	110–120
1	275	140
2	300	150
3	325	160
4	350	180
5	375	190
6	400	200
7	425	220
8	450	230
9	475	240

Air Pressure	
PSI	Bar
10	0.5
20	1.4
30	2
40	2.8

APPENDIX E: COMMUNICATIONS MAP

The map below shows the main roads, railways and airports in New Zealand.

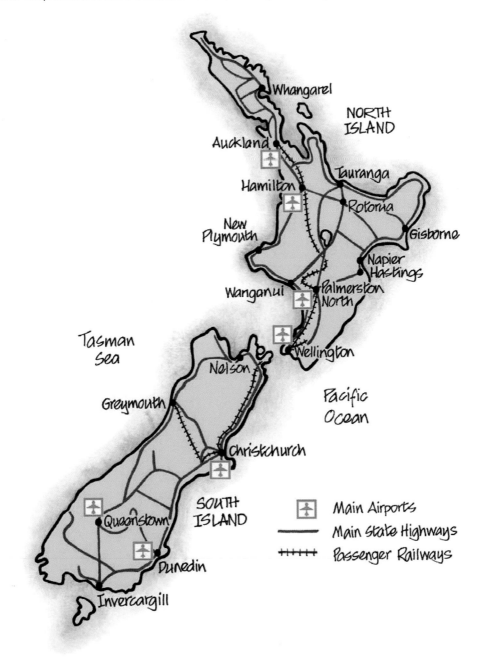

Lake Tekapo, South Island

INDEX

Essential reading for anyone planning to live, work, retire or buy a home abroad

Survival Books was established in 1987 and by the mid-'90s was the leading publisher of books for people planning to live, work, buy property or retire abroad.

From the outset, our philosophy has been to provide the most comprehensive and up-to-date information available. Our titles routinely contain up to twice as much information as other similar books and are updated more frequently. Most of our books are printed in colour and they also contain original cartoons, illustrations and maps.

Survival Books are written by people with first-hand experience of the countries and the people they describe, and therefore provide invaluable insights that cannot be obtained from official publications or websites, and information that is more reliable and objective than that provided by the majority of unofficial sites.

Survival Books are designed to be easy – and interesting – to read. They contain a comprehensive list of contents and index and extensive appendices, including useful addresses, further reading, useful websites and glossaries to help you obtain additional information, as well as metric conversion tables and other useful reference material.

We believe our books are the best available – but don't take our word for it – read what reviewers and readers have said about Survival Books at the front of this book.

Available as Paperbacks, Kindle and eBooks.
Order your copies today by visiting
www.survivalbooks.net

SURVIVAL BOOKS

Buying a home abroad is not only a major financial transaction but also a potentially life-changing experience; it's therefore essential to get it right. Our Buying a Home guides are required reading for anyone planning to purchase property abroad and are packed with vital information to guide you through the property jungle and help you avoid disasters that can turn a dream home into a nightmare.

The purpose of our Buying a Home guides is to enable you to choose the most favourable location and the most appropriate property for your requirements, and to reduce your risk of making an expensive mistake by making informed decisions and calculated judgements rather than uneducated and hopeful guesses. Most importantly, they will help you save money and will repay your investment many times over.

Buying a Home guides are the most comprehensive and up-to-date source of information available about buying property abroad – whether you're seeking a detached house or an apartment, a holiday or a permanent home (or an investment property), these books will prove invaluable.

For a full list of our current titles, visit our website at www.survivalbooks.net

O ur Living and Working guides are essential reading for anyone planning to spend a period abroad – whether it's an extended holiday or permanent migration – and are packed with priceless information designed to help you avoid costly mistakes and save both time and money.

Living and Working guides are the most comprehensive and up-to-date source of practical information available about everyday life abroad. They aren't, however, simply a catalogue of dry facts and figures, but are written in a highly readable style – entertaining, practical and occasionally humorous.

Our aim is to provide you with the comprehensive practical information necessary for a trouble-free life. You may have visited a country as a tourist, but living and working there is a different matter altogether; adjusting to a new environment and culture and making a home in any foreign country can be a traumatic and stressful experience. You need to adapt to new customs and traditions, discover the local way of doing things (such as finding a home, paying bills and obtaining insurance) and learn all over again how to overcome the everyday obstacles of life.

All these subjects and many, many more are covered in depth in our Living and Working guides – don't leave home without them.

The Expats' Best Friend!

LIVING AND WORKING SERIES

Our Culture Wise series of guides is essential reading for anyone who wants to understand how a country really 'works'. Whether you're planning to stay for a few days or a lifetime, these guides will help you quickly find your feet and settle into your new surroundings.

Culture Wise guides:

- Reduce the anxiety factor in adapting to a foreign culture
- Explain how to behave in everyday situations in order to avoid cultural and social gaffes
- Help you get along with your neighbours
- Make friends and establish lasting business relationships
- Enhance your understanding of a country and its people.

People often underestimate the extent of cultural isolation they can face abroad, particularly in a country with a different language. At first glance, many countries seem an 'easy' option, often with millions of visitors from all corners of the globe and well-established expatriate communities. But, sooner or later, newcomers find that most countries are indeed 'foreign' and many come unstuck as a result.

Culture Wise guides will enable you to quickly adapt to the local way of life and feel at home, and – just as importantly – avoid the worst effects of culture shock.

Culture Wise – The Wise Way to Travel

The essential guides to Culture, Customs & Business Etiquette

Sketchbooks series: A series of beautiful sketchbooks with walks, including Cornwall, the Cotswolds, the Lake District and London.

London's Hidden Secrets: A series of three books that are a guide to the city's quirky and unusual sights that most visitors and residents don't get to visit.

London's Secret Walks: A walking book with a difference, taking you off the beaten track to visit London's hidden and 'secret' sights.

Where to Live in London: The only book published to help newcomers choose the best area to live to suit both their lifestyle and pocket.

Weekends to Brag About: The ultimate guide for thrillseekers detailing over 100 adventure sports in Britain's great outdoors.

Retiring in France/Spain: Everything a prospective retiree needs to know about the two most popular international retirement destinations.

Shooting Caterpillars in Spain: The hilarious and compelling story of two innocents abroad in the depths of Andalusia in thelate '80s.

Running Gîtes and B&Bs in France: Essential reading for anyone planning to invest in a gîte or bed & breakfast business.

US Immigration Handbook: Everything you need to know to get a visa and green card to live and work in the US.

For a full list of our current titles, visit our website at www.survivalbooks.net

OTHER SURVIVAL BOOKS

PHOTO

CREDITS

www.dreamstime.com

Pages 16 © Mikenz, 22 © Kurhan, 35 © Rvs, 49 © Devonyu, 51 © Endostock, 59 © Andresr, 73 © Joegough, 84 © Nzgmw2788, 92 © Joegough, 106 © unknown, 114 © Darrenbaker, 126 © Saniphoto, 133 © Martinma, 151 © Chrishowey, 164 © Shootalot, 235 © Onchangwei, 245 © Creativefire, 257 © Martinapplegate, 264 © Sportlibrary, 276 © Lafucina, 279 © Dbajurin, 286 © Antclausen, 291 © Dmitryp, 293 © Grahamp, 301 © Valuesforlife, 307 © Kiwichris, 308 © Nzgmw2788, 312 © Mikenz, 348 © Awcnz62, 348 © Erickn, 349 © Nsilcock, 349 © Elkeflorida.

Survival Books

Pages 86, 90, 103, 106, 152, 156, 171, 182, 187, 226, 239, 298, 300 (© Survival Books).

Others

pages 25, 104, 121, 222 (© Peter Farmer), page 1 (left-hand photo), 70-71, 201 (© Tourism New Zealand), 6, 41, 112 (© Jim Watson), 242 (© seriousfun, www.bigstockphoto.com).

BUYING A HOME
IN NEW ZEALAND

A Survival Handbook by Graeme Chesters

- ★ Major Considerations
- ★ Finding the Best Place to Live
- ★ Funding Your Dream Home
- ★ Money Matters
- ★ The Purchase Procedure
- ★ Moving House
- ★ Taxation
- ★ Insurance
- ★ Letting
- ★ Useful Websites and Maps

Buying a Home in
New Zealand
Graeme Chesters

2nd Edition

Now in full colour

The best-selling book about buying property in New Zealand
with up to twice as much information as similar titles

2.
THE BEST PLACE TO LIVE

6.
MOVING HOUSE

PRINTED IN COLOUR!

Buying a Home in New Zealand is essential reading for anyone planning to buy property in New Zealand, and is designed to guide you through the property maze, and save you time trouble and money! Most importantly, it is packed with vital information to help you avoid disasters that can turn a dream home into a nightmare!

Survival Books - The Homebuyer's Best Friend

CULTURE WISE
NEW ZEALAND

The Essential Guide to Culture, Customs & Business Etiquette

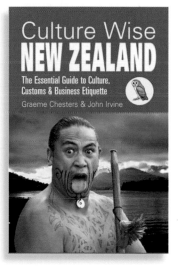

★ How to overcome culture shock

★ Historical and political background to modern New Zealand

★ New Zealand attitudes and values – at home & at work

★ do's, don'ts and taboos

★ how to enjoy yourself in Kiwi style

★ business and professional etiquette

★ New Zealand's spoken and body language

★ getting around New Zealand safely

★ shopping the Kiwi way

PRINTED IN COLOUR!

Culture Wise New Zealand will help you adapt to the New Zealand way of life and enable you to quickly feel at home.

Order your copy today!

Culture Wise - The Wise Way to Travel

LIVING AND WORKING
IN AUSTRALIA

A Survival Handbook by David Hampshire

✓ Fully updated and revised seventh edition. Printed in colour.

✓ The most comprehensive and best-selling book about living in Australia since it was first published in 1988, containing up to twice as much information as some similar books.

✓ Essential reading for anyone planning to emigrate or buy property in Australia, packed with vital information to help readers save time, trouble and money.

✓ Interest in living and working in Australia and buying property there has never been higher, and it's one of the most popular countries for migrants.

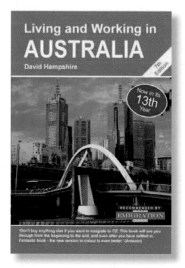

PRINTED IN COLOUR!

Living and Working in Australia is essential reading for anyone planning to live and work in Australia. This book is guaranteed to hasten your introduction to the Australian way of life, irrespective of whether you're planning to stay for a few months or indefinitely.

Survival Books - The Expatriates' Best Friend

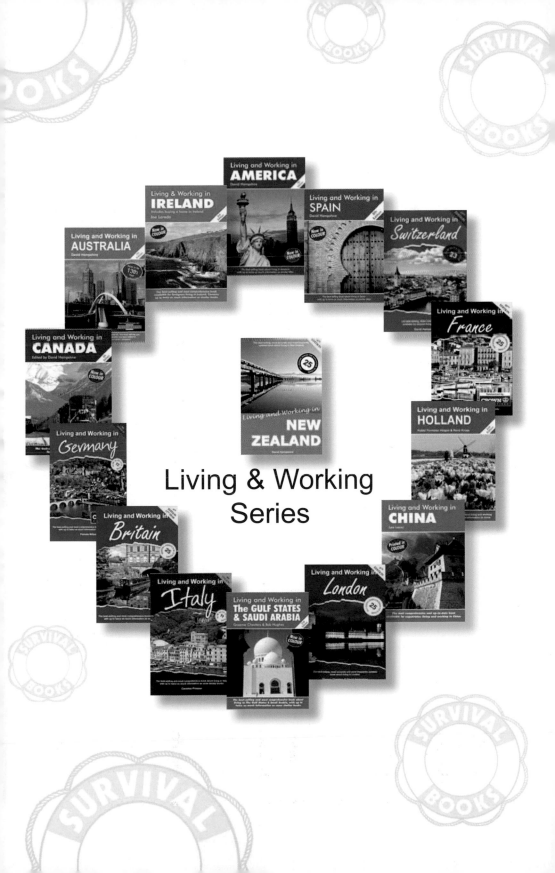

Living & Working
Series

THE EMIGRATION GROUP

Visa & Migration Experts since 1992.

Testimonials

"Having visited New Zealand, I bought a book called Live & Work in New Zealand in which I read testimonials from people who had taken the plunge and followed their dream of a new life elsewhere and had sought the help of The Emigration Group. This inspired me to follow my dream and I could not have done it without your help. You professionally and promptly found me employment to aid my residency application. Thank you, The Emigration Group for guiding me through the minefield of seeking employment abroad and emigration."

Lynn Bell, (Pharmacist)

"Excellent service. Helpful and knowledgable staff, not only regarding the local job market, but other personal matters as well. The Emigration Group secured me a job within 3 days! They were helpful, knowledgeable and pleasant to deal with. Very highly recommended service."

Philip H., (Machinery Mechanic)

"Blimey Jill, at the end of a somewhat draining day (yes it happens in Banking occasionally) that is just the best news possible. So we're in - lock stock and quite a few barrels!!!

I know I keep saying this but could not be more pleased with the help from you Jill - you are an easy recommendation to anyone I meet who shows an interest in coming over!"

Bernie H. (Bank Manager)

"Following 12 months of independent, unsuccessful job applications, I chose The Emigration Group to complete this daunting task for me. Using a professional company proved to be the answer to the problem I had been experiencing. Prospective employers now took my application seriously and a job was very quickly secured. The Emigration Group was brilliant!"

Deborah S., (Facilities Manager)

"We are all fine and we have been approved for the second part of the LTBV. Nice! Life here is fantastic, words cannot describe how happy we are. I will never go back to the UK after living here. The fee we paid you was worth every penny! Kind regards."

Derek L. and family (Long Term Business Visa)

"The Emigration Group secured a job for me within ten days, which eased the process of emigration for us. We decided to emigrate in May 2007, job secured by July, I started work August, family joined me in October, full Residency achieved in December (& bought a house). Thanks for your help. Fully recommend service." *Philip S., (Bricklayer)*

"Imagine this... you are going to move to the other side of the world, you have 3 children aged 9, 8 and 2 and you don't know what to expect ... When I was told about The Emigration Group, I felt a big sigh of relief and knew it was the sensible thing to do. Why struggle with all the big things and important little things, you've got enough on your plate as it is? On arrival, the house found for us was immaculate with all the mod cons...a real home from home. After a few days of relaxing a representative helped with all the little things like bank accounts, car insurance, money transfer advice, etc. Also introducing us to other families that have migrated helped us never feel alone. I can honestly say I do not know what would of happened if I didn't use The Emigration Group service. It took all the stress and worry out of the move and the service was much more than I ever expected."

Nathaly & Shaun B., (Maintenance Engineer)